HARDPRESS.NET
HOME OF HARD-TO-FIND BOOKS

Rob of the Bowl
by John Pendleton Kennedy

ROB OF THE BOWL.

John P. Kennedy

ROB OF THE BOWL.

A LEGEND OF ST. INIGOE'S.

BY
JOHN P. KENNEDY,

AUTHOR OF "SWALLOW BARN," "HORSE-SHOE ROBINSON," ETC.

> *Daniel.* Quot homines tot sententiæ.
> *Martin.* And what is that?
> *Daniel.* 'T is Greek, and argues difference of opinion.
> JOHN WOODVIL.

REVISED EDITION.

NEW YORK:
PUBLISHED BY HURD AND HOUGHTON.
1866.

CAMBRIDGE: PRINTED BY H. O. HOUGHTON AND COMPANY.

PREFACE.

THE tale related in the following pages refers to a period in the history of Maryland, which has heretofore been involved in great obscurity,—many of the most important records connected with it having been lost to public inspection in forgotten repositories, where they have crumbled away under the touch of time. To the persevering research of the accomplished Librarian of the State—a gentleman whose dauntless antiquarian zeal and liberal scholarship are only surpassed by the enlightened judgment with which he discharges the functions of his office—we are indebted for the rescue of the remnant of these memorials of by-gone days, from the oblivion to which the carelessness of former generations had consigned them. Many were irrecoverable; and it was the fate of the gentleman referred to, to see them fall into dust at the moment that the long estranged light first glanced upon them.

To some of those which have been saved from this wreck, the author is indebted for no small portion of the materials of his story. In his endeavor to illustrate these passages in the annals of the state, it is proper for him to

say that he has aimed to perform his task with historical
fidelity. If he has set in harsher lights than may be
deemed charitable some of the actors in these scenes, or
portrayed in lineaments of disparagement or extenuation,
beyond their deserts, the partisans on either side in that
war of intolerance which disfigured the epoch of this tale,
it was apart from his purpose. As a native of the state,
he feels a prompt sensibility to the fame of her Catholic
founders, and, though differing from them in his faith,
cherishes the remembrance of their noble endeavors to
establish religious freedom, with the affection due to what
he believes the most wisely planned and honestly executed scheme of society which at that era, at least, was to
be found in the annals of mankind. In the temper
inspired by this sentiment, these volumes have been
given to the public, and are now respectfully inscribed to
THE STATE OF MARYLAND, by one who takes the deepest
interest in whatever concerns her present happiness or
ancient renown.

THE AUTHOR.

BALTIMORE, *Dec.* 1, 1838.

CHAPTER I.

No more thy glassy brook reflects the day,
But choked with sedges, works its weedy way;
Along thy glades a solitary guest,
The hollow-sounding bittern guards its nest;
Amidst thy desert walks the lapwing flies,
And tires their echoes with unvaried cries.
Sunk are thy bowers in shapeless ruin all,
And the long grass o'ertops the mould'ring wall.
THE DESERTED VILLAGE.

It is now more than one hundred and forty-four years since the ancient capital of Maryland was shorn of its honors, by the removal of the public offices, and, along with them, the public functionaries, to Annapolis. The date of this removal, I think, is recorded as of the year of grace sixteen hundred and ninety-four. The port of St. Mary's, up to that epoch, from the first settlement of the province, comprehending rather more than three score years, had been the seat of the Lord Proprietary's government. This little city had grown up in hard-favored times, which had their due effect in leaving upon it the visible tokens of a stunted vegetation: it waxed gnarled and crooked, as it perked itself upward through the thorny troubles of its existence, and might be likened to the black jack, which yet retains a foothold in this region,—a scrubby, tough and hardy mignon of the forest, whose elder day of crabbed luxuriance affords a sour comment upon the nurture of its youth.

Geographers are aware that the city of St. Mary's stood on

the left bank of the river which now bears the same name (though of old it was called St. George's) and which flows into the Potomac at the southern extremity of the state of Maryland, on the western side of the Chesapeake Bay, at a short distance westward from Point Lookout : but the very spot where the old city stood is known only to a few,—for the traces of the early residence of the Proprietary government have nearly faded away from the knowledge of this generation. An astute antiquarian eye, however, may define the site of the town by the few scattered bricks which the ploughshare has mingled with the ordinary tillage of the fields. It may be determined, still more visibly, by the mouldering and shapeless ruin of the ancient State House, whose venerable remains—I relate it with a blush—have been pillaged, to furnish building materials for an unsightly church, which now obtrusively presents its mottled, mortar-stained and shabby front to the view of the visitor, immediately beside the wreck of this early monument of the founders of Maryland. Over these ruins a storm-shaken and magnificent mulberry, aboriginal, and cotemporary with the settlement of the province, yet rears its shattered and topless trunk, and daily distils upon the sacred relics at its foot, the dews of heaven,—an august and brave old mourner to the departed companions of its prime. There is yet another memorial in the family tomb of the Proprietary, whose long-respected and holy repose, beneath the scant shade of the mulberry, has, within twenty years past, been desecrated by a worse than Vandal outrage, and whose lineaments may now with difficulty be followed amidst the rubbish produced by this violation.

These faded memorials tell their story like honest chronicles. And a brave story it is of hardy adventure, and manly love of freedom ! The scattered bricks, all mouldered in the mother-land, remind us of the launching of the bark, the struggle with the unfamiliar wave, the array of the wonder-stricken savage, and the rude fellowship of the first meeting. They recall the hearths whose early fires gleamed upon the visage of the bold cavalier, while the deep, unconquerable faith of religion, and the impassioned instincts of the Anglo-Saxon devotion to liberty, were breathed by household groups, in customary household terms. They speak of sudden alarms, and quick arming for battle ;—of stout resolve, and still stouter achievement. They tell of the victory won, and quiet gradually confirmed,—and of the increasing rapture as, day by day, the settler's hopes were converted into realities, when he saw the wilderness put forth the blossoms of security and comfort.

The river penetrates from the Potomac some twelve miles inland, where it terminates in little forked bays which wash the base of the woody hills. St. George's Island stretches half across its mouth, forming a screen by which the course of the Potomac is partly concealed from view. From this island, looking northward, up St. Mary's river, the eye rests upon a glittering sheet of water about a league in breadth, bounded on either shore by low meadow-grounds and cultivated fields girt with borders of forest ; whilst in the distance, some two leagues upward, interlocking promontories, with highlands in their rear, and cedar-crowned cliffs and abrupt acclivities which shut in the channel, give to the river the features of a lake. St. Inigoe's creek, flowing into the river upon the right hand, along the base of these cliffs, forms by its southern shore a flat, narrow and grass-clad point, upon which the ancient Jesuit House of the patron saint whose name distinguishes the creek, throws up, in sharp relief, its chateau-like profile, together with its windmill, its old trees, barns and cottages, —the whole suggesting a resemblance to a strip of pasteboard scenery on a prolonged and slender base line of green.

When the voyager from the island has trimmed his sail and

1*

reached the promontories which formed his first perspective, the river, now reduced to a gun-shot in width, again opens to his view a succession of little bays, intercepted by more frequent headlands and branching off into sinuous creeks that lose themselves in the hills.   Here and there, amongst these creeks, a slender beach of white sand separates from its parent flood a pool, which reposes like a mirror in the deep forest ; and all around, high hills sweep down upon these placid lakes, and disclose half-embowered cottages, whose hoary roofs and antique forms turn the musings of the spectator to the palmy days of the Lord Proprietary.

A more enchanting landscape than St. Mary's river,—a lovelier assemblage of grassy bank and hoary grove, upland slope, cliff, cot and strand, of tangled brake and narrow bay, broad, seaward roadstead and air-suspended cape, may not be found beneath the yearly travel of the sun !

The ancient city was situated nearly two miles beyond the confluence of St. Inigoe's creek, upon a spacious level plain which maintained an elevation of some fifty feet above the river.   The low-browed, double-roofed and cumbrous habitations of the townspeople were scattered at random over this plain, forming snug and pleasant groups for a painter's eye, and deriving an air of competence and comfort from the gardens and bowers in which they were sheltered.   The State House stood at the upper extremity of the town, upon a cedar-clad headland which, by an abrupt descent, terminated in a long, flat, sandy point, that reached almost half across the river.   In regard to this building, tradition—which I find to be somewhat inclined to brag of its glory—affirms it to have been constructed in the shape of a cross, looking towards the river, with walls thick enough to resist cannon, and perilous steep roofs, from the top of the chief of which shot up a spire, whereon was impaled a dolphin with a crooked, bifurcated tail. A wooden quay and warehouse on the point showed this to be the seat of trade, and a crescent-shaped bay or indentation between this and a similar headland at the lower extremity of the town, constituted the anchorage or harbor for the scant shipping of the port.

The State House looked rearward over the town common,—a large space of open ground, at the farther end of which, upon the border of a marshy inlet, covered with bulrushes and cat-tails, stood a squat, sturdy and tight little jail, supported—to use the military phrase—on one flank by a pillory and stocks, and on the other by an implement of government which has gone out of fashion in our day, but which found favor with our ancestors as an approved antidote to the prevalent distemper of an unnecessary or too clamorous loquacity in their dames—a ducking stool, that hung suspended over a pool of sufficient depth for the most obstinate case that might occur.

Without wearying my reader with too much description, I shall content myself with referring to but two or three additional particulars as necessary to my future purpose : a Catholic chapel devoted to St. Ignatius, the patron of the province, in humble and unostentatious guise, occupied, with its appurtenances, a few acres in the centre of the plain, a short distance from that confine of the city which lay nearest to St. Inigoe's ; and in the opposite quarter, not far from the State House, a building of much more pretension, though by no means so neat, had been erected for the service of the Church of England, which was then fast growing into the ascendant. On one of the streets leading to the beach was the market-house, surrounded by its ordinaries and ale-houses : and lastly, in the year 1681, to which this description refers, a little hostelry of famous report, known by the sign of " The Crow and Archer," and kept by Master Garret Weasel, stood on the water's edge, at the foot of the bank below the State House, on a piece of level ground looking out upon the harbor, where the traveller may still find a luxuriant wilderness of pear trees, the scions of a notable ancestor which, tradition says, the aforesaid Garret planted with his own hand.

The country around St. Mary's bore, at the period I have designated, the same broad traces of settlement and cultivation which belong to it at the present day. For many miles the scene was one of varied field and forest, studded over with dwellings and farm-yards. The settlement had extended across the neck of land to the Chesapeake, and along both shores of St. Mary's river to the Potomac. This open country was diversified by woodland, and enlivened everywhere by the expanse of navigable water which reflected sun and sky, grove and field and lowly cottage in a thousand beautiful lights. Indeed, all the maritime border of the province, comprehending Calvert, St. Mary's and Charles, as well as the counties on the opposite shore of the Chesapeake, might be said, at this date, to be in a condition of secure and prosperous habitation. The great ocean forest had receded some hundred miles westward from St. Mary's. The region of country comprising the present county of Anne Arundel, as well as Cecil and the Isle of Kent, was a frontier already settled with numerous tenants of the Lord Proprietary. All westward from this was the birthright of the stern Sasquesahannoch, the fierce Shenandoah, and their kindred men of the woods.

They are gone! Like shadows have these men of might sunk on the earth. They, their game, their wigwams, their monuments, their primeval forests,—yea, even their graves, have flitted away in this spectral flight. Saxon and Norman, bluff Briton and heavy Suabian inherit the land. And in its turn, well-a-day! our pragmatical little city hath departed. Not all its infant glory, nor its manhood's bustle, its walls, gardens and bowers,—its warm housekeeping, its gossiping burghers, its

politics and its factions,—not even its prolific dames and
gamesome urchins could keep it in the upper air until this our
day. Alas, for the vaulting pride of the village, the vain glory
of the city, and the metropolitan boast ! St. Mary's hath sunk
to the level of Tyre and Sidon, Balbec and Palmyra ! She hath
become trackless, tokenless.

I have wandered over the blank field where she sank down
to rest. It was a book whose characters I could scarce decipher.
I asked for relics of the departed. The winter evening tale
told by father to son, and the written legend, more durable than
monument of marble, have survived to answer my question, when
brick and tile, hearth and tomb have all vanished from the quest
of the traveller.

What I have gathered from these researches will occupy my
reader through the following pages.

CHAPTER II.

A train-band captain eke was he.
JOHN GILPIN.

AT the extremity of the cape or headland which formed the lower or more seaward point of the crescent-shaped harbor, was erected the Fort of St. Mary's, where it threatened equal defiance to such as might meditate disturbance by sea or by land. A few hundred paces in the rear of the fort, stood the ample dwelling-house of the Lord Proprietary with its gables, roofs, chimneys and spires, sharply defined against the eastern sky. A massive building of dark brick, two stories in height, and penetrated by narrow windows, looking forth, beyond the fort, upon the river, constituted the chief member or main body of the mansion. This was capped by a wooden, balustraded parapet, terminating, at each extremity, in a scroll, and, in the middle, sustaining an entablature that rose to a summit on which was mounted a weathercock. From this central structure, right and left, a series of arcades and corridors served to bring into line a range of subordinate buildings of grotesque shapes, of which several were bonneted like haycocks—the array terminating, on one flank, in a private chapel surmounted by a cross, and, on the other, in a building of similar size but of different figure, which was designed and sometimes used for a banqueting room. The impression produced on the observer, by this orderly though not uniform mass of building, with its various offices for household comfort, was not displeasing to his sense of rural beauty, nor, from its ample range and capacious accommodation, did it fail to enhance his opinion of the stateliness and feudal importance, as well as of the hospitality of the Lord Proprietary. The armorial bearings of the Baltimore family, emblazoned on a shield of free-stone, were built into the pediment of an arched brick porch which shaded the great hall door. In the rear of the buildings, a circular sweep of wall and paling reached as far as a group of stables, kennels and sheds. Vanward the same kind of enclosures, more ornate in their fashion, shut in a grassy court, to which admission was gained through a heavy iron gate swung between square, stuccoed pillars, each of which was surmounted by a couchant lion carved in stone. Ancient trees shaded the whole mass of dwelling-house, court and stable, and gave to the place both a lordly and comfortable aspect. It was a pleasant group of roof and bower, of spire and tree to look upon from the city, towards sunset, when every window-pane flung back the lustre of a conflagration ; and magnificently did it strike upon the eye of the liegemen as they sat at their doors, at that hour, gazing upon the glorious river and its tranquil banks. Nor less pleasant was it to the inmates of the baronial mansion to look back upon the fair village-city, studding the level plain with its scattered dwellings which seemed to sleep upon the grassy and shaded sward.

A garden occupied the space between the proprietary residence and the fort, and through it a pathway led to a dry moat which formed one of the defences of the stronghold, into which admission was obtained from this quarter by a narrow bridge and postern gate. A palisade of sharp pickets fringed the outer and inner slopes of the ditch,—or, to speak more technically, guarded the scarp and counterscarp. The fort itself sat like a square bonnet on the brow of the headland. Its ramparts of earth were

faced outwardly by heavy framework of hewn logs, which, on
the side looking askant towards the town, were penetrated by an
arched gateway and secured by heavy doors studded thick with
nails.   This portal opened upon a road which lay along the
beach beneath the cliff, all the way to the upper extremity of the
town.   Several low buildings within, appropriated to barracks
and magazines, just peered above the ramparts.   A few pieces
of brass cannon showed like watch-dogs against the horizon, and,
high above all, fluttered the provincial banner bearing the cross
of England, and holding the relation of a feather to the squat
bonnet which the outline of the work might suggest to one
curious to trace resemblances.

The province, it may be surmised, was belligerent at this day.
For although the Lords Barons of Baltimore, absolute Pro-
prietaries of Maryland and Avalon, would fain have encouraged
a pacific temper, and desired ever to treat with the Indians upon
terms of friendly bargain and sale, and in all points of policy
manifested an equitable disposition towards the native men of
the forest, the province, nevertheless, had its full share of hard
blows.   There was seldom a period, in this early time, when some
Indian quarrel was not coming to a head ; and, young as the
province was, it had already tasted of rebellion at the hands of
Clayborne, and Ingle,—to say nothing of that Fendall who was
fain to play Cromwell in the plantation, by turning the burgesses
out of their hall, and whose sedition hath still something to do
with my story.——However peaceable, therefore, the Lord Proprietary might incline to be, he could not but choose stand by
his weapons.

In the view of these and kindred troubles, the freemen of the
province had no light service in their obligations of military duty.
One of the forms in which this service was exacted, in addition
to the occasional requisition, on emergency, of the whole popula-

tion fit to bear arms, and in addition also to a force of mounted rangers who were constantly engaged in scouring the frontier was in the maintenance of a regularly paid and trained body of musketeers who supplied the necessary garrisons for the principal forts. That of St. Mary's, which was the oldest and most redoubtable stronghold in the province, was furnished with a company of forty men of this class who were, at the date of this tale, under the command of a personage of some note, Captain Jasper Dauntrees, to whom I propose to introduce my reader with something more than the slight commendation of a casual acquaintance.

This worthy had been bred up to the science of arms from early youth, and had seen many varieties of service,—first, in the civil wars in which he took the field with the royal army, a staunch cavalier,—and afterwards, with a more doubtful complexion of loyalty, when he enlisted with Monk in Scotland, and followed his banner to London in the notable exploit of the Restoration. Yielding to the bent of that humor which the times engendered, and in imitation of many a hungry and peace-despising gallant of his day, he repaired to the continent, where, after various fortunes, he found himself in the train of Turenne and hard at loggerheads with the Prince of Orange, in which passage of his life he enjoyed the soldierly gratification of lending a hand to the famous ravage of the Palatinate.

Some few years before I have presented him in these pages he had come over to Maryland, with a party of Flemings, to gather for his old age that harvest of wealth and ease which the common report promised to all who set foot upon the golden shores of the Indies—Maryland, in vulgar belief, being a part of this land of wonders. The captain neither stumbled upon a gold mine, nor picked up an Indian princess with a dowry of diamonds ; but he fared scarce worse, in his own estimation, when he found himself, in a pleasant sunny clime, invested with the rank of captain of musketeers, with a snug shelter in the fort, a reasonably fair and punctually disbursed allowance of pay—much better, than had been his lot under former masters,—and a frank welcome at all times into the mansion of the Lord Proprietary. Add to these, the delights more congenial to the training of his past life, a few wet companions, namely, to help him through an evening potation, and no despicable choice of wines and other comforts at the Crow and Archer, where the Captain became a domesticated and privileged guest, and it may still better be comprehended how little he was likely to repine at his fortune.

His figure had, in youth, been evidently remarked for strength and symmetry—but age and varied service, combined with habits of irregular indulgence, had communicated to it a bluff and corpulent dimension. His port nevertheless was erect, and his step as firm as in his days of lustihood. His eye still sparkled with rays but little quenched by time, although unseasonable vigils sometimes rendered it bloodshotten. A thick neck and rosy complexion betokened a hale constitution ; and the ripple of a deep and constantly welling humor, that played upon his strongly marked features, expressed in characters that could not be misread, that love of companionship which had been, perhaps, the most frequent shoal upon which his hopes in life had been stranded. His crown was bald and encircled by a fair supply of crisp, curly, and silvery hair, whilst a thick gray moustache gave a martial and veteran air to his visnomy.

His dress served to set off his figure to the best advantage. It consisted of the doublet and ruff, short cloak and trunk hose, the party-colored stocking and capacious boot proper to the old English costume which, about the period of the Restoration, began to give way to the cumbrous foppery of the last century. This costume was still retained by many in the province, and belonged to the military equipment of the garrison of St. Mary's, where it was fashioned of light green cloth garnished with yellow lace.

Arrayed in this guise, Captain Dauntrees had some excuse for a small share of vanity on the score of having worn well up to a green old age; and it was manifest that he sought to improve this impression by the debonair freedom with which he wore a drab beaver, with its broad flap looped up on one side, leaving his ample brow bared to wind and weather.

This combination of the martinet and free companion exhibited in the dress of the Captain, was a pretty intelligible index to his character, which disclosed a compound, not unfrequent in the civil wars of that period, of the precisian and ruffler—the cavalier and economist. In the affairs of life—a phrase which, in regard to him, meant such matters principally and before all others, as related to his own comfort—he was worldly-wise, sagaciously provident, as an old soldier, of whatever advantages his condition might casually supply; in words, he was, indifferently, according to the occasion, a moralist or hot-brained reveller—sometimes affecting the courtier along with the martialist, and mixing up the saws of peaceful thrift with the patter of the campaigns.

As the occasions of my story may enable me to illustrate some of these points in the character of the worthy Captain, I will not forestall the opinion of my readers, regarding him, by further remark, preferring that he should speak for himself, rather than leave his merits to be certified by so unpractised an adept, as I confess myself to be, in unriddling the secret properties of a person so deserving to be known.

CHAPTER III.

" In every creed,
'Tis on all hands agreed,
And plainly confest,
When the weather is hot,
That we stick to the pot
And drink of the best."
                                OLD SONG.

" OF all seasons of the year, autumn is the most voluptuous, and October the loveliest of months. Then may a man sit at his door—in the sun if he choose, for he will not find it too hot—or in the shade, if it liketh him, for neither will he find this too cool, and there hold converse with his own meditations : or he may ride or walk, dance or sing, for in this October time a man hath heart for any pastime, so rich is the air, and such pleasant imaginations doth it engender. And if he be poetical, therein will he be greatly favored ; for surely never Nature puts on such gaudy attire, on earth or sky, as she wears in our October. The morning haze, which the hoar-frost flings up to meet the sun, hangs across the landscape as if made on purpose to enchant the painter ; and the evening sunset lights up the heavens with a glory that shall put that painter—even Claude or Salvator— to shame at the inadequacy of his art. And then the woods ! what pallet hath colors for the forest ? Of all the months of the year, commend me to October !"

Some such rhapsody as this was running through the thoughts, and breaking forth in slight mutterings from the lips of the

Captain of Musketeers, on an afternoon in this much lauded month of October, in the year I have alluded to in a former chapter, as he sat in front of his quarters in the fort. A small table was displayed on the pavement, supplied with a flagon, pipes, and drinking cups. The Captain's solid bulk was deposited in a broad arm-chair, close by the table. His sword and cloak lay upon a bench at the door, and a light breeze flickered amongst his short and hoary locks, where they escaped from the cover of a cloth bonnet which he had now substituted for his beaver. A sentinel stood on post at the gate, towards which the Captain, as he slowly quaffed a cup, ever and anon turned an expectant eye. Once or twice he rose from his seat and strode backward and forward across the parade, then visited the rampart, which afforded him a view of the road leading from the town, and finally resumed his seat and renewed his solitary and slow potation.

When the sun had sunk halfway down the flag-staff, the Captain's wishes were crowned by the arrival of a brace of visitors.

The first of these was Garret Weasel, the publican, a thin, small man, in a suit of gray; of a timid carriage and slender voice. He might have been observed for a restless, undefinable eye, which seemed to possess the habitual circumspection of a tapster to see the need of a customer; and this expression was sustained by a rabbit-like celerity of motion which raised the opinion of his timidity. There was an air of assentation and reverence in his demeanor, which, perhaps, grew out of the domestic discipline of his spouse, a buxom dame with the heart of a lioness. She had trained Master Garret to her hand, where he might have worn out his days in implicit obedience, had it not luckily fallen out for him that Captain Dauntrees had settled himself down in this corner of the New World. The Captain

being a regular trafficker in the commodities of the Crow and
Archer, and no whit over-awed by the supremacy of mine hostess,
soon set himself about seducing her worse-half from his allegiance,
so far as was necessary, at least, to satisfy his own cravings for
company at the fort. He therefore freely made himself the
scapegoat of Garret's delinquencies, confiding in the wheedling
power of his tongue to pacify the dame. With all the tapster's
humility and meekness, he still followed the Captain through his
irregularities with the adhesiveness and submission of a dog—
carousing on occasion like a man of stouter mould, and imitating
the reveller-tone of his companion with an ambitious though not
always successful zeal. He did not naturally lack merriment;
but it was not of the boisterous stamp : there was, at his worst
outbreak, a glimmering of deference and respect, rising up to a
rickety laugh, and a song sometimes, yet without violent clamor;
and the salt tears were often wrung from his eyes by the pent-up
laughter which his vocation and his subordinate temper had
taught him it was unseemly to discharge in a volley.

His companion was a tall, sinewy, and grave person, habited
in the guise of a forester—a cap, namely, of undressed deer skin,
a buff jerkin, guarded by a broad belt and buckle at the waist,
and leggings of brown leather. This was a Fleming, named
Arnold de la Grange, who belonged to the corps of wood rangers
in the service of the Lord Proprietary. He had arrived in the
province in the time of Lord Cecilius, many years before, and had
shared much of the toil of the early settlement. His weather-
beaten and gaunt form, tawny cheek, and grizzled hair, bespoke
a man inured to the hard service of a frontier life, whilst his
erect port and firm step evinced that natural gracefulness which
belongs to men trained to the self-dependence necessary to breast
the ever-surrounding perils of such a service. He was a man of
few words, and these were delivered in a Low Dutch accent,

which his long intercourse with the English had failed to correct.
When his service on his range was intermitted, Arnold found
quarters amongst the retainers of the Proprietary mansion, and
the Proprietary himself manifested towards the forester that
degree of trust, and even affection, which resulted from a high
sense of his fidelity and conduct, and which gave him a position
of more privilege than was enjoyed by the other dependents of
the establishment. Being, at these intervals, an idler, he was
looked upon with favor by the Captain of the fort, who was not
slow to profit by the society of such a veteran in the long watches
of a dull afternoon. By a customary consequence, Arnold was
no less esteemed by the publican.

A bluff greeting and short ceremony placed the visitors at
the table, and each, upon a mute signal from the host, appropriated his cup and pipe.

"You are never a true man, Garret Weasel," said the Captain, "to dally so long behind your appointment ; and such
an appointment, too ! The round dozen which you lost to me on
Dame Dorothy's head gear—a blessing on it!—you did yourself
so order it, was to be broached at three o'clock ; and now it
is something past four. There is culpable laches in it. Idleness
is the canker of the spirit, but occupation is the lard of the body,
as I may affirm in my own person. Mistress Dorothy, I suspect, has this tardy coming to answer for. I doubt the brow
of our brave dame has been cloudy this afternoon. How is it,
Arnold ? bachelor, and Dutchman to boot, you will speak without fear."

"The woman," replied Arnold, in a broken English accent,
which I do not attempt to convey in syllables, "had her suspicions."

"Hold, Captain Dauntrees," eagerly interrupted the innkeeper, drawing up his chair to the table—for he had seated himself.

a full arm's-length off, in awkward deference to his host; "and Master Arnold! my wife rules not me, as some evil-minded jesters report; no, in faith! We were much beset to-day. I could not come sooner. Customers, you know, Captain, better than most men, customers must be answered, and will be answered, when we poor servants go athirst. We were thronged to-day; was it not so, Arnold?"

"That is true," replied the forester; "the wife had her hands full as well as Garret himself. There were traders in the port, to-day, from the Bay Shore and the Isle of Kent, and some from the country back, to hear whether the brigantine had arrived. They had got some story that Cocklescraft should be here."

"I see it," said Dauntrees; "that fellow, Cocklescraft, has a trick of warning his friends. He never comes into port but there be strange rumors of him ahead; it seems to be told by the pricking of thumbs. St. Mary's is not the first harbor where he drops his anchor, nor Anthony Warden the first to docket his cargo. You understand me."

"You have a bold mind, Captain," said the publican; "you men of the wars speak your thoughts."

"You are none the losers by Master Cocklescraft," interposed Arnold, drily.

"My wife pays honestly for the liquors," said Weasel, as his eye glanced timorously from one to the other of his comrades; "I take no heed of the accounts."

"But the head gear, Garret," rejoined Dauntrees, laughing; "you pay for that, though the mercer saw my coin for it. Twelve bottles of Canary were a good return on that venture. The bauble sits lightly on the head of the dame, and- it is but fair that the winnings should rise as lightly into ours. But for Cocklescraft, we should lack these means to be merry. The customs are at a discount on a dark night. Well, be it so. What point of duty calls on us to baulk the skipper in his trade? We are of the land, not of the water; consumers, on the disbursing side of the account, not of the gathering in. The revenue has its own friends, and we should neither meddle nor make. Worthy Garret Weasel has good report in the province for the reasonableness of his wines—and long may he deserve that commendation!"

"I thank heaven that I strive to merit the good will of the freemen," interrupted the innkeeper.

"And he is something given to brag of his wines. Faith, and with reason! Spain and Portugal, the Garonne and the Rhine, are his tributaries. Garret, we know the meridian of your El Dorado."

"Nay, nay, Master Captain—your worship is merry; I beseech you—"

"Never mind your beseeching, my modest friend. You scarce do yourself justice. You have his Lordship's license paid for in good round ducatoons—and that's the fee of a clear conscience. So let the trade thrive! The exchequer is not a baby to be in swaddling bands, unable to feed itself. No, it has the eagle's claw, and wants no help from thee, thou forlorn tapster! Make thine honest penny, Garret; all thirsty fellows will stand by you."

"I would be thought orderly, Master Dauntrees."

"You are so computed—to a fault. You would have been so reckoned in Lord Cecil's time; and matters are less straitened now-a-days. Lord Charles gives more play to good living than his father allowed of. You remember his Lordship's father set his face against wines and strong waters."

"He did, gentlemen," said Weasel, squaring himself in his seat with animation. "Heaven forbid I should speak but as becomes me of the honorable Lord Cecil's memory, or of his

2

honorable son! but to my cost, I know that his Lordship's father was no friend to evil courses, or sottish behavior, or drinking, unless it was in moderation, mark you. But, with humility, I protest the law is something hard on us poor ordinary keepers : for you shall understand, Arnold Grange, that at a sale by outcry, if there should lack wherewithal to pay the debts of the debtor, the publican and vintner are shut out, seeing that the score for wines and strong waters is the last to be paid."

"And good law it is, let me tell you, Garret Weasel! Good and wholesome : wisely laid down by the burgesses, and wisely maintained by his Lordship. You rail without cause. Sober habits must be engendered :—your health, comrades! Then it behooves you publicans to be nice in your custom. We will none of your lurdans that cannot pay scot and lot—your runagates that fall under the statute of outcry. Let them drink of the clear brook! There is wisdom and virtue in the law. Is it not so, Arnold ?"

"It preaches well," replied the forester, as he sent forth a volume of smoke from his lips.

"Another flask, and we will drink to his Lordship," said Dauntrees, who now left the table and returned with the fourth bottle. "Fill up, friends ; the evening wears apace. Here's to his Lordship, and his Lordship's ancestors of ever noble and happy memory!"

As Dauntrees smacked his lips upon emptying his cup, he flung himself back in his chair, and in a thoughtful tone ejaculated : "The good Lord Charles has had a heavy time of it since his return from England ; these church brawlers would lay gunpowder under our hearth-stones. And then the death of young Lord Cecil, whilst his father was abroad, too ; it was a heavy blow. My lady has never held up her head since."

A pause succeeded to this grave reflection, during which the trio smoked their pipes in silence, which was at length broken by an attenuated sigh from the publican, as he exclaimed, "Well-a-day! the great have their troubles as well as the rest of us. It is my opinion that Heaven will have its will, Captain; that's my poor judgment." And having thus disburdened himself of this weighty sentiment—the weight of it increased, perhaps, by the pressure of his previous potations—he drained the heel tap, which stood in his glass, and half whispered, when he had done, "That's as good a drop of Canary as ever grew within the horizon of the Peak of Teneriffe."

"Through the good will of friend Cocklescraft," interrupted Dauntrees, suddenly resuming his former gaiety.

"Pray you, Captain Dauntrees," said the publican, with a hurried concern, "think what hurt your jest may bring upon me. Arnold knows not your merry humor, and may believe from your speech that I am not reputable."

"Pish, man; bridle your foolish tongue! Did I not see the very cask on't at Trencher Rob's? Did I not mark how your sallow cheek took on an ashen complexion, when his Lordship's secretary, a fortnight since, suddenly showed himself amongst the cedars upon the bank that overlooks your door, when your ill luck would have you to be rolling the cask in open day into the cellar. The secretary was in a bookish mood, and did not see you—or, peradventure, was kind, and would not heed."

To this direct testimony, Weasel could only reply by a faint-hearted and involuntary smile which surrendered the point, and left him in a state of silly confusion.

"Never droop in courage, worthy Weasel," exclaimed the Captain; "you are as honest as your betters; and, to my mind, the wine has a better smack from its overland journey from St. Jerome's when there was no sun to heat it."

"The secretary," said the innkeeper, anxious to give the conversation another direction, "is a worshipful youth, and a modest, and grows in favor with the townspeople."

"Ay, and is much beloved by his Lordship," added the Captain.

"And comes, I warrant, of gentle kind, though I have not heard aught of his country or friends. Dorothy, my wife, says that the women almost swear by him, for his quiet behavior and pretty words—and they have eyes, Captain Dauntrees, for excellence which we have not."

"There is a cloud upon his birth," said Dauntrees, "and a sorrowful tale touching his nurture. I had it from Burton, the master of the ship who brought him with my Lord to the province."

"Indeed, Captain Dauntrees! you were ever quick to pick up knowledge. You have a full ear and a good memory."

"Drink, drink, comrades!" said the Captain. "We should not go dry because the secretary has had mishaps. If it please you, I will tell the story, though I will not vouch for the truth of what I have only at second hand."

After the listeners had adjusted themselves in their chairs, Dauntrees proceeded.

"There was, in Yorkshire, a Major William Weatherby, who fought against the Parliament—I did not know him, for I was but a stripling at the time—who, when King Charles was beheaded, went over and took service with the States General, and at Arnheim married a lady of the name of Verheyden. Getting tired of the wars, he came back to England with his wife, where they lived together five or six years without children. The story goes that he was a man of fierce and crooked temper ; choleric, and unreasonable in his quarrel ; and for jealousy, no devil ever equalled him in that amiable virtue. It was said, too, that his living was riotous and unthrifty, which is, in part, the customary sin of soldiership.—I am frank with you, masters."

"You are a good judge, Captain ; you have had experience," said the publican.

"There was a man of some mark in the country where this Weatherby lived, a Sir George Alwin, who, taking pity on the unhappy lady, did her sundry acts of kindness—harmless acts, people say ; such as you or I, neighbors, would be moved to do for a distressed female ; but the lady was of rare beauty, and the husband full of foul fancies.

"About this time, it was unlucky that nature wrought a change, and the lady grew lusty for the first time in six years' marriage. To make the story short, Weatherby was free with his dagger, and in the street, at Doncaster, in the midst of a public show, he stabbed Alwin to the heart."

The wood ranger silently shook his head, and the publican opened his watery eyes in astonishment.

"By the aid of a fleet horse and private enemies of the murdered man, Weatherby escaped out of the kingdom, and was never afterwards heard of."

"And died like a dog, I s'pose," said Arnold de la Grange.

"Likely enough," replied Dauntrees.

"The poor lady was struck down with the horror of the deed, and had nearly gone to her grave. But Heaven was kind and she survived it, and was relieved of her burden in the birth of a son. For some years afterwards, by the bounty of friends, but with many a struggle—for her means were scanty—she made shift to dwell in England. At last she returned to Holland, where she found a resting-place in her native earth, having lived long enough to see her son, a well grown lad, safely taken in charge by her brother, a merchant of Antwerp. The parents were both attached to our Church of Rome, and the son was sent by his uncle to the Jesuit school of his own city. Misfortune overtook the merchant, and he died before the nephew had reached his fourteenth year.

But the good priests of Antwerp tended the lad with the care of parents, and would have reared him as a servant of the altar. When our Lord Baltimore was in the Netherlands, three years ago, he found Albert Verheyden (the youth has ever borne his mother's name) in the Seminary. His Lordship took a liking to him and brought him into his own service. Master Albert was then but eighteen. There is the whole story. It is as dry as a muscat raisin. It sticks in the throat, masters,—so moisten, moisten !"

"It is a marvellous touching story," said the innkeeper, as he swallowed at a draught a full goblet.

"The hot hand and the cold steel," said Arnold, thoughtfully, "hold too much acquaintance in these times. Master Albert is an honest youth, and a good youth, and a brave follower too, of hawk or hound, Captain Dauntrees."

"Then there is good reason for a cup to the secretary," said the Captain filling again. "The world hath many arguments for a thirsty man. The blight of the year fall upon this sadness ! Let us change our discourse—I would carouse a little, friends : it is salutary to laugh. Thanks to my patron, I am a bachelor ! So drink, Master Arnold, mein sauff bruder, as we used to say on the Rhine."

"Ich trinck, euch zu," was the reply of the forester, as he answered the challenge with a sparkling eye, and a face lit up with smiles ; "a good lad, an excellent lad, though he come of a hot-brained father."

The wine began to show itself upon the revellers ; for by this time they had nearly got through half of the complement of the wager. The effect of this potation upon the Captain was to give him a more flushed brow, and a moister eye, and to administer somewhat to the volubility of his tongue. It had wrought no further harm, for Dauntrees was bottle-proof. Upon the forester it was equally harmless, rather enhancing than dissipating his saturnine steadfastness of demeanor. He was, perchance, somewhat more precise and thoughtful. Garret Weasel, of the three, was the only weak vessel. With every cup of the last half hour he grew more supple.

"Ads heartlikens!" he exclaimed, "but this wine does tingle, Captain Dauntrees! Here is a fig for my wife Dorothy! Come and go as you list—none of your fetch and carry! that's what the world is coming to, amongst us married cattle!"

"Thou art a valorous tapster," said the Captain.

"I am the man to stand by his friend, Captain; and I am your friend, Captain—Papist or Roman though they call you!"

"A man for need, Garret!" said Dauntrees, patting him on the head; "a dozen flasks or so, when a friend wants them, come without the asking."

"And I pay my wagers, I warrant, Captain, like a true comrade."

"Like a prince, Garret, who does not stop to count the score, but makes sure of the total by throwing in a handful over."

"I am no puritan, Master Dauntrees."

"You have the port of a cavalier, good Weasel. You would have done deadly havoc amongst the round-heads, if they but took you in the fact of discharging a wager. But you were scarce in debt after this fashion, at Worcester, my valiant drawer. An evil destiny kept you empty on that day."

"Ha, ha, ha! a shrewd memory for a stale jest, Captain Dauntrees. The world is slanderous, though I care little for it. You said you would be merry; shall we not have a song?"

"I am in that humor, old madcap, and will wag it with you bravely," replied Dauntrees, as he struck up a brisk drinking glee of that day, in which he was followed by the treble voice of the publican, who at the same time rose from his seat and accompa-

nied the music with some unsteady gyrations in the manner of a
dance upon the gravel.

> " From too much keeping an evil decorum,
> From the manifold treason parliamentorum,
> From Oliver Cromwell, dux omnium malorum,
>   Libera nos, Libera nos."

Whilst Dauntrees and his gossips were thus occupied in their
carouse, they were interrupted by the unexpected arrival of two
well known persons, who had approached by the path of the
postern gate.

The elder of the two was a youth just on the verge of manhood. His person was slender, well-proportioned, and rather
over the common height. His face, distinguished by a decided
outline of beauty, wore a thoughtful expression, which was
scarcely overcome by the flash of a black and brilliant eye. A
complexion pale, and even feminine, betokened studious habits.
His dress, remarkable for its neatness, denoted a becoming pride
of appearance in the wearer. It told of the Low Countries. A
well-fitted doublet and hose, of a grave color, were partially concealed by a short camlet cloak of Vandyke brown. A black
cap and feather, a profusion of dark hair hanging in curls towards
the shoulders, and a falling band or collar of lace, left it unquestionable that the individual I have sketched was of gentle nurture, and associated with persons of rank. This was further
manifested in the gay and somewhat gaudy apparel of his companion—a lad of fourteen, who walked beside him in the profusely
decorated costume of a young noble of that ambitious era, when
the thoughtless and merry monarch of England, instead of giving
himself to the cares of government, was busy to invent extrava-
gancies of dress. The lad was handsome, though his features
wore the impress of feeble health. He now bore in his hand a
bow and sheaf of arrows.

The visitors had taken our revellers at unawares, and had advanced within a few feet before they were observed. The back of the publican was turned to them, and he was now in mid career of his dance, throwing up his elbows, tossing his head, and treading daintily upon the earth, as he sang the burden,

"Libera nos, libera nos."

"You give care a holiday, Captain Dauntrees," said the elder youth, with a slightly perceptible foreign accent.

Dauntrees started abruptly from his seat, at this accost, smiled with a reddened brow, and made a low obeisance. The cessation of the song left Garret Weasel what a mariner would term "high and dry," for like a bark floated upon a beach and suddenly bereft of its element, he remained fixed in the attitude at which the music deserted him,—one foot raised, an arm extended, and his face turned inquiringly over his shoulder. His amazement upon discovering the cause of this interruption, brought about a sudden and ludicrous affectation of sobriety; in an instant his port was changed into one of deference, although somewhat awkwardly overcharged with what was intended to represent gravity and decorum.

Arnold de la Grange rose from his chair and stood erect, firm and silent.

"Hail, Master Albert Verheyden, and Master Benedict Leonard : God save you both !" said Dauntrees.

"I say amen to that, and God save his lordship, besides !" ejaculated the publican with a drunken formality of utterance.

"I would not disturb your merriment, friends," said the secretary, "but his lordship bade me summon Captain Dauntrees to the hall. You, Arnold de la Grange, will be pleased to accompany the Captain."

Arnold bowed his head, and the visitors retired by the great

2*

gate of the fort.   In a moment young Benedict Leonard came
running back, and addressed the forester—

"Master Arnold, I would have a new bow-string—this is
worn ; and my bird-bolts want feathering : shall I leave them
with you, good Arnold?"   And without waiting an answer, he
thrust the bow and arrows into the smiling wood-ranger's hand,
and bounded away again through the gate.

Dauntrees flung his sword-belt across his shoulder, put on his
cloak, delayed a moment to secure the remaining flasks of wine,
and then beckoned to the ranger to follow him.

"Stop," cried Weasel, with an officious zeal to make himself
useful ; "your belt is awry : it is not comely to be seen by his
Lordship in this slovenly array."

The belt was set right, and the two directed their steps towards the postern, and thence to the mansion.   The publican
tarried only until his companions were out of sight, when, curious
to know the object of the errand, and careful to avoid the appearance of intrusion, he followed upon the same path, at a respectful distance,—stepping wisely, as a drunken man is wont, and full
of the opinion that his sobriety was above all suspicion.

CHAPTER IV.

Oft as the peasant wight impelled
To these untrodden paths had been,
As oft he, horror struck, beheld
Things of unearthly shape and mien.
GLENGONAR'S WASSAIL.

THE day was drawing near to a close, and the Proprietary thoughtfully paced the hall. The wainscoted walls around him were hung with costly paintings, mingled, not untastefully, with Indian war clubs, shields, bows and arrows, and other trophies won from the savage. There were also the ponderous antlers of the elk and the horns of the buck sustaining draperies of the skins of beasts of prey. Muskets, cutlasses and partisans were bestowed on brackets ready for use in case of sudden invasion from that race of wild men whose stealthy incursions in times past had taught this policy of preparation. The level rays of the setting sun, striking through the broad open door, flung a mellow radiance over the hall, giving a rich picture-like tone to its sylvan furniture.

Lord Baltimore, at the period when I have introduced him, might have been verging upon fifty. He was of a delicate and slender stature, with a grave and dignified countenance. His manners were sedate and graceful, and distinguished by that gen‑tleness which is characteristic of an educated mind when chas‑tened by affliction. He had been schooled to this gentleness both by domestic and public griefs. The loss of a favorite son, about two years before, had thrown a shadow upon his spirit, and a succession of unruly political irritations in the province served to prevent the return of that buoyancy of heart which is indifferently slow to come back at middle age, even when solicited by health, fortune, friends, and all the other incitements which, in younger men, are wont to lift up a wounded spirit out of the depths of a casual sorrow.

Charles Calvert had come to the province in 1662, and from that date, until the death of his father, thirteen years afterwards, administered the government in the capacity of Lieutenant-General. Upon his accession to the proprietary rights, he found himself compelled by the intrigues of a faction to visit London, where he was detained nearly four years,—having left Lady Baltimore, with a young family of children, behind him, under the care of his uncle Philip Calvert, the chancellor of the province. He had now, within little more than a twelvemonth, returned to his domestic roof, to mingle his sorrows with those of his wife for the death of his eldest son, Cecilius, who had sunk into the tomb during his absence.

The public cares of his government left him scant leisure to dwell upon his personal afflictions. The province was surrounded by powerful tribes of Indians who watched the white settlers with an eager hostility, and seized every occasion to molest them by secret inroad, and often by open assault. A perpetual war of petty reprisals prevailed upon the frontier, and even sometimes invaded the heart of the province.

A still more vexatious annoyance existed in the party divisions of the inhabitants—divisions unluckily resting on religious distinctions—the most fierce of all dissensions. Ever since the Restoration, the jealousy of the Protestant subjects of the crown against the adherents of the Church of Rome had been growing into a sentiment that finally broke forth into the most flagrant persecution. In the province, the Protestants during the last twenty years had greatly increased in number, and at the date of this narrative constituted already the larger mass of the population. They murmured against the dominion of the Proprietary as one adverse to the welfare of the English Church ; and intrigues were set on foot to obtain the establishment of that church in the province through the interest of the ministry in England. Letters were written by some of the more ambitious clergy of Maryland to the Archbishop of Canterbury to invoke his aid in the enterprise. The government of Lord Baltimore was traduced in these representations, and every disorder attributed to the ascendancy of the Papists. It was even affirmed that the Proprietary, and his uncle the Chancellor, had instigated the Indians to ravage the plantations of the Protestant settlers, and to murder their families. Chiefly, to counteract these intrigues, Lord Baltimore had visited the court at London. Cecilius Calvert, the founder of the province, with a liberality as wise as it was unprecedented, had erected his government upon a basis of perfect religious freedom. He did this at a time when he might have incorporated his own faith with the political character of the colony, and maintained it, by a course of legislation which would, perhaps, even up to the present day, have rendered Maryland the chosen abode of those who now acknowledge the founder's creed. His views, however, were more expansive. It was his design to furnish in Maryland a refuge not only to the weary and persecuted votaries of his own sect, but an asylum to all who might wish for shelter in a land where opinion should be free and conscience undisturbed. Whilst this plant of toleration was yet young, it grew with a healthful luxuriance ; but the popular leaders, who are not always as truly and consistently attached to enlightened freedom as we might be led to believe from their boasting, and who incessantly aim to obtain power and make it felt, had no sooner acquired strength to battle with the Proprietary than they rooted up the beautiful exotic and gave it to the winds.

Amongst the agitators in this cause was a man of some note in the former history of the province—the famous Josias Fendall, the governor in the time of the protectorate—now in a green old age, whose turbulent temper, and wily propensity to mischief had lost none of their edge with the approach of gray hairs. This individual had stimulated some of the hot spirits of the province into open rebellion against the life of the Proprietary and his uncle. His chief associate was John Coode, a coarse but shrewd leader of a faction, who, with the worst inclinations against the Proprietary, had the wit to avoid the penalties of the law, and to maintain himself in a popular position as a member of the house of Burgesses. Fendall, a few months before this era, had been arrested with several followers, upon strong proofs of conspiracy, and was now a close prisoner in the jail.

Such is a brief but necessary view of the state of affairs on the date, at which I have presented the Lord Proprietary to my reader. The matter now in hand with the captain of the fort had reference to troubles of inferior note to those which I have just recounted.

When Lord Baltimore descried Captain Dauntrees and the ranger approaching the mansion from the direction of the fort, he advanced beyond the threshold to meet them. In a moment they stood unbonneted before him.

"God save you, good friends!" was his salutation—"Captain Dauntrees and worthy Arnold, welcome!—Cover,"—he added in a tone of familiar kindness,—"put on your hats; these evening airs sometimes distil an ague upon a bare head."

A rugged smile played upon the features of the old forester as he resumed his shaggy cap, and said, "Lord Charles is good; but he does not remember that the head of an old ranger gets his

blossoms like the dog-wood,—in the wind and the rain :—the dew
sprinkles upon it the same as upon a stone."

"Old friend," replied the Proprietary,—"that grizzly head
has taken many a sprinkling in the service of my father and myself : it is worthy of a better bonnet, and thou shalt have one, Arnold—the best we can find in the town. Choose for yourself, and
Master Verheyden shall look to the cost of it."

The Fleming modestly bowed, as he replied with that peculiar
foreign gesture and accent, neither of which may be described,—
"Lord Charles is good.—He is the son of his father, Lord Cecil,
—Heaven bless his memory !"

"Master Verheyden bade me attend your lordship," said
Dauntrees ; "and to bring Arnold de la Grange with me."

"I have matter for your vigilance, Captain," replied the Proprietary. "Walk with me in the garden—we will talk over our
business in the open air."

When they had strolled some distance, Lord Baltimore proceeded—"There are strange tales afloat touching certain mysterious doings in a house at St. Jerome's : the old wives will have
it that it is inhabited by goblins and mischievous spirits—and, in
truth, wiser people than old women are foolish enough to hold it in
dread. Father Pierre tells me he can scarcely check this terror."

"Your Lordship means the fisherman's house on the beach at
St. Jerome's," said the Captain. "The country is full of stories
concerning it, and it has long had an ill fame. I know the house:
the gossips call it The Wizard's Chapel. It stands hard by the
hut of The Cripple. Truly, my Lord, he who wanders there at
nightfall has need of a clear shrift."

"You give credence to these idle tales ?"

"No idle tales, an please your Lordship. Some of these
marvels have I witnessed with my own eves. There is a curse of
blood upon that roof."

"I pray you speak on," said the Proprietary, earnestly; "there is more in this than I dreamed of."

"Paul Kelpy, the fisherman," continued Dauntrees,—"it was before my coming into the province—but the story goes——"

"It was in the Lord Cecil's time—I knowed the fisherman," interrupted Arnold.

"He was a man," said the Captain, "who, as your Lordship may have heard, had a name which caused him to be shunned in his time,—and they are alive now who can tell enough of his wickedness to make one's hair rise on end. He dwelt in this house at St. Jerome's in Clayborne's day, and took part with that freebooter;—went with him, as I have heard, to the Island, and was outlawed."

"Ay, and returning, met the death he deserved—I remember the story," said the Proprietary. "He was foiled in his attempt to get out of the province, and barred himself up in his own house."

"And there he fought like a tiger,—or more like a devil as he was," added the ranger. "They were more than two days before they could get into his house."

"When his door was forced at last," continued the Captain, "they found him, his wife and child, lying in their own blood upon the hearth-stone. They were all murdered, people say, by his own hand."

"And that was true!" added Arnold; "I remember how he was buried at the cross road, below the Mattapany Fort, with a stake drove through his body."

"Ever since that time," continued Dauntrees, "they say the house has been without lodgers—of flesh and blood, I mean, my Lord,—for it has become a devil's den, and a busy one."

"What hast thou seen, Captain? You speak as a witness."

"It is not yet six months gone by, my Lord, when I was returning with Clayton, the master of the collector's pinnace, from the Isle of Kent ; we stood in, after night, towards the headland of St. Jerome's bay ;—it was very dark—and the four windows of the Wizard's Chapel, that looked across the beach, were lighted up with such a light as I have never seen from candle or faggot. And there were antic figures passing the blaze that seemed deep in some hellish carouse. We kept our course, until we got almost close aboard,—when suddenly all grew dark. There came, at that moment, a gust of wind such as the master said he never knew to sweep in daylight across the Chesapeake. It struck us in our teeth, and we were glad to get out again upon the broad water. It would seem to infer that the Evil One had service rendered there, which it would be sinful to look upon. In my poor judgment it is matter for the church, rather than for the hand of the law."

"You are not a man, Captain Dauntrees, to be lightly moved by fantasies," said the Proprietary, gravely ; "you have good repute for sense and courage. I would have you weigh well what you report."

"Surely, my Lord, Clayton is as stout a man in heart as any in the province : and yet he could scarcely hold his helm for fear."

"Why was I not told of this ?"

"Your Lordship's favor," replied Dauntrees, shaking his head ; "neither the master, the seamen nor myself would hazard ill will by moving in the matter. There is malice in these spirits, my Lord, which will not brook meddling in their doings : we waited until we might be questioned by those who had right to our answer. The blessed martyrs shield me ! I am pledged to fight your Lordship's bodily foes :—the good priests of our holy patron St. Ignatius were better soldiers for this warfare."

The Proprietary remained for some moments silent; at last, turning to the ranger, he inquired—"What dost thou know of this house, Arnold?"

"Well, Lord Charles," replied the veteran, "I was not born to be much afear'd of goblins or witches. In my rangings I have more than once come in the way of these wicked spirits; and then I have found that a clean breast and a stout heart, with the help of an Ave Mary and a Paternoster was more than a match for all their howlings. But the fisherman's house —oh, my good Lord Charles," he added with a portentous shrug, "has dwellers in it that it is best not to trouble. When Sergeant Travers and myself were ranging across by St. Jerome's, at that time when Tiquassino's men were thought to be a thieving,—last Hallowmass, if I remember,—we shot a doe towards night, and sat down in the woods, waiting to dress our meat for a supper, which kept us late, before we mounted our horses again. But we had some aqua vitæ, and didn't much care for hours. So it was midnight, with no light but the stars to show us our way. It happened that we rode not far from the Wizard's Chapel, which put us to telling stories to each other about Paul Kelpy and the ghosts that people said haunted his house."

"The aqua vitæ made you talkative as well as valiant, Arnold," interrupted the Proprietary.

"I will not say that," replied the ranger; "but something put it into our heads to go down the bank and ride round the chapel. At first all was as quiet as if it had been our church here of St. Mary's—except that our horses snorted and reared with fright at something we could not see. The wind was blowing, and the waves were beating on the shore,— and suddenly we began to grow cold; and then, all at once, there came a rumbling noise inside of the house like the

rolling of a hogshead full of pebbles, and afterwards little
flashes of light through the windows, and the sergeant said
he heard clanking chains and groans :—it isn't worth while
to hide it from your Lordship, but the sergeant ran away
like a coward, and I followed him like another, Lord Charles.
Since that night I have not been near the Black House. We
have an old saying in my country—' een gebrande kat vreest
het koude water'—the scalded cat keeps clear of cold water—
ha, I mind the proverb "

"It is not long ago," said Dauntrees,—" perhaps not above
two years,—when, they say, the old sun-dried timber of the
building turned suddenly black. It was the work of a single
night—your Lordship shall find it so now."

"I can witness the truth of it," said Arnold—" the house
was never black until that night, and now it looks as if
it was scorched with lightning from roof to ground sill. And
yet, lightning could never leave it so black without burning
it to the ground."

"There is some trickery in this," said the Proprietary.
" It may scarce be accounted for on any pretence of witchcraft,
or sorcery, although I know there are malignant influences
at work in the province, which find motive enough to do
all the harm they can. Has Fendall, or any of his confederates,
had commerce with this house, Captain Dauntrees? Can you
suspect such intercourse ?"

"Assuredly not, my Lord," replied the Captain, "for
Marshall, who is the most insolent of that faction, has, to
my personal knowledge, the greatest dread of the chapel of all
other men I have seen. Besides, these terrors have flourished
in the winter-night tales of the neighborhood, ever since the
death of Kelpy, and long before the Fendalls grew so pestilent
in the province."

"It is the blood of the fisherman, my good Lord, and of his wife and children, that stains the floor," said Arnold; "it is that blood which brings the evil spirits together about the old hearth. Twice every day the blood-spots upon the floor freshen and grow strong, as the tide comes to flood;—at the ebb they may be hardly seen."

"You have witnessed this yourself, Arnold?"

"At the ebb, Lord Charles. I did not stay for the change of tide. When I saw the spots it was as much as we could do to make them out. But at the flood every body says they are plain."

"It is a weighty matter, a very weighty matter, an it like your Lordship's honor," muttered forth the slim voice of Garret Weasel, who had insinuated himself, by slow approach, into the rear of the company, near enough to hear a part of this conversation, and who now fancied that his interest in the subject would ensure him an unrebuked access to the Proprietary—"and your Lordship hath a worthy care for the fears of the poor people touching the abominations of the Wizard's Chapel."

"What brought thee here, Garret Weasel?" inquired the Proprietary, as he turned suddenly upon the publican and looked him steadfastly in the face—"What wonder hast thou to tell to excuse thy lurking at our heels?"

"Much and manifold, our most noble Lord, touching the rumors," replied the confused innkeeper, with a thick utterance. "And it is the most notable thing about it that Robert Swale—Rob o' the Trencher, as he is commonly called—your Lordship apprehends I mean the Cripple—that Rob lives so near the Wizard's Chapel. There's matter of consideration in that—if your Lordship will weigh it."

"Fie, Master Garret Weasel! Fie on thee! Thou art in

thy cups. I grieve to see thee making a beast of thyself. You had a name for sobriety. Look that you lose it not again. Captain Dauntrees, if the publican has been your guest this evening, you are scarce free of blame for this."

"He has a shallow head, my Lord, and it is more easily sounded than I guessed. Arnold," said Dauntrees apart, "persuade the innkeeper home."

The ranger took Garret's arm, and expostulating with him as he led him away, dismissed him at the gate with an admonition to bear himself discreetly in the presence of his wife—a hint which seemed to have a salutary effect, as the landlord was seen shaping his course with an improved carriage towards the town.

"Have you reason to believe, Captain Dauntrees," said the Proprietary, after Weasel had departed, "that the Cripple gives credit to these tales. He lives near this troubled house?"

"Not above a gunshot off, my Lord. He cannot but be witness to these marvels. But he is a man of harsh words, and lives to himself. There is matter in his own life, I should guess, which leaves but little will to censure these doings. To a certainty he has no fear of what may dwell in the Black building. I have seldom spoken with him."

"Your report and Arnold's," said the Proprietary, "confirm the common rumor. I have heard to-day, that two nights past some such phantoms as you speak of have been seen, and deemed it at first a mere gossip's wonder;—but what you tell gives a graver complexion of truth to these whisperings. Be there demons or jugglers amongst us—and I have reason to suspect both—this matter must be sifted. I would have the inquiry made by men who are not moved by the vulgar love of marvel. This duty shall be yours, friends. Make suitable preparation, Captain, to discharge it at your earliest leisure. I would have you and Arnold, with such discreet friends as you may select,

visit this spot at night and observe the doings there.   Look that
vou keep your own counsel :—we have enemies of flesh and blood
that may be more dreaded than these phantoms.   So, God
speed you, friends !"

"The man who purges the Black House of the fiend, so
please you, my Lord," said Dauntrees, "should possess more
odor of sanctity than I doubt will be found under our soldier's
jerkins.   I shall nevertheless execute your Lordship's orders to
the letter."

"Hark you, Captain," said the Proprietary, as his visitors
were about to take their leave, "if you have a scruple in this
matter and are so inclined, I would have you confer with Father
Pierre.   Whether this adventure require prayer, or weapon of
steel, you shall judge for yourself."

"I shall take it, my Lord, as a point of soldiership," said
Dauntrees, "to be dealt with in soldierly fashion—that is, with
round blows if occasion serves.   I ask no aid from our good
priest.   He has a trick—if I may be so bold as to speak it
before your Lordship—which does not so well sort with my age
and bodily health—a trick, my Lord, of putting one to a fasting
penance by way of purification.   Our purpose of visiting the
Black House would be unseasonably delayed by such a purgation."

"As you will !" said the Proprietary, laughing ; "Father
Pierre would have but an idle sinecure if he had no other calling
but to bring you to your penitentiary.   Good even, friends—
may the kind saints be with you !"

The Captain and his comrade now turned their steps toward
the fort, and the Proprietary retired into the mansion.   Here
he found the secretary and Benedict Leonard waiting his arrival.
They had just returned from the town, whither they had gone
after doing their errand to the fort.   Albert Verheyden bore a

packet secured with silken strings and sealed, which he delivered
to the Proprietary.

"Dick Pagan, the courier," he said, "has just come in from
James Town in Virginia, whence he set forth but four days ago
—he has had a hard ride of it—and brought this packet to the
sheriff for my Lord. The courier reports that a ship had just
arrived from England, and that Sir Henry Chichely the governor
gave him this for your Lordship to be delivered without delay."

The Proprietary took the packet: "Albert," he said, as he
was about to withdraw, "I have promised the old ranger,
Arnold de la Grange, a new cap. Look to it:—get him the
best that you may find in the town—or, perhaps, it would better
content him to have one made express by Cony the leather-
dresser. Let it be as it may best please the veteran himself,
good Albert." With this considerate remembrance of the
ranger, Lord Baltimore withdrew into his study.

CHAPTER V.

—— deep on his front engraven,
Deliberation sat, and public care.
MILTON.

Lend me thy lantern quotha? Marry I'll see thee hanged first.
SHAKSPEARE.

A SMALL fire blazed on the hearth of the study and mingled its light with that of a silver cresset, which hung from the ceiling above a table furnished with writing materials and strewed over with papers. Here the Proprietary sat intent upon the perusal of the packet. Its contents disquieted him ; and with increasing solicitude he again and again read over the letters.

At length the secretary was summoned into his presence. "Albert," he said, "the council must be called together to-morrow at noon. The messengers should be despatched to-night ; they have a dark road and far to ride. Let them be ready with the least delay."

The secretary bowed, and went forth to execute his order.

The letters brought to the Proprietary a fresh importation of troubles. That which most disturbed him was from the Board of Trade and Plantations, and spoke authoritatively of the growing displeasure of the ministry at the exclusiveness, as it was termed, of the Proprietary's favors, in the administration of his government, to the Catholic inhabitants of the province ; it hinted at the popular and probably well-founded discontent—to use its own phrase—of his Majesty's Protestant subjects against the too liberal indulgence shown to the Papists; repeated stale charges and exploded calumnies against the Proprietary, with an earnestness that showed how sedulously his enemies had taken advantage of the disfavor into which the Church of Rome and its advocates had fallen since the Restoration; and concluded with a peremptory intimation of the royal pleasure that all the offices of the province should be immediately transferred into the hands of the Church of England party.

This was a blow at Lord Baltimore which scarcely took him by surprise. His late visit to England had convinced him that not all the personal partiality of the monarch for his family—and this was rendered conspicuous in more than one act of favor at a time when the Catholic lords were brought under the ban of popular odium—would be able finally to shelter the province from that religious proscription which already was rife in the mother land. He was not, therefore, altogether unprepared to expect this assault. The mandate was especially harsh in reference to the Proprietary, first because it was untrue that he had ever recognized the difference of religious opinion in his appointments, but on the contrary had conferred office indiscriminately in strict and faithful accordance with the fundamental principle of toleration upon which his government was founded; and, secondly, because it would bear with pointed injustice upon some of his nearest and most devoted friends—his uncle the chancellor, the whole of his council, and, above all others in whose welfare he took an interest, upon the collector of the port of St. Mary's, Anthony Warden, an old inhabitant of the province, endeared to the Proprietary—and indeed to all his fellow-burgesses—by long friendship and tried fidelity. What rendered it more grating to the feelings of the Proprietary in this instance, was that the collectorship had already been singled out as a prize to be played

3

for by that faction which had created the late disturbances in the province. It was known that Coode had set his eyes upon this lure, and gloated upon it with the gaze of a serpent. The emoluments of the post were something considerable, and its importance was increased by the influence it was supposed to confer on the incumbent, as a person of weight and consequence in the town.

The first expression of irritation which the perusal of the packet brought to the lips of the Proprietary had a reference to the collector. "They would have me," he said, as he rose and strode through the apartment, "discard from my service the very approved friends with whom in my severest toils, in this wilderness, I have for so many years buffeted side by side, and to whom I am most indebted for support and encouragement amidst the thousand disasters of my enterprise. They would have me turn adrift, without a moment's warning, and even with circumstances of disgrace, that tried pattern of honesty, old Anthony Warden. Virtue, in her best estate, has but a step-daughter's portion in the division of this world's goods, and often goes begging, when varnished knavery carries a high head and proud heart, and lords it like a very king. By the blessed light! old Anthony shall not budge on my motion. Am I to be schooled in my duty by rapacious malcontents, and to be driven to put away my trustiest friends, to make room for such thirsty leeches and coarse rufflers as John Coode? The argument is, that here, in what my father would have made a peaceful, contented land, planted by him and the brothers of his faith,—with the kindest, best and most endeared supporters of that faith by my side—worthy men, earnest and zealous to do their duty—they and their children true to every Christian precept—men who have won a home by valor and patient, wise endurance—they must all be disfranchised, as not trustworthy even for the meanest office, and give their places to brawlers, vaporing bullies and factious stirrers-up of discord—and that, too, in the name of religion ! Oh, this viper of intolerance, how has it crept in and defiled the garden ! One would have thought this world were wide enough to give the baser passions elbow room, without rendering our little secluded nook a theatre for the struggle. Come what may, Anthony Warden shall not lack the collectorship whilst a shred of my prerogative remains untorn !"

In this strain of feeling the Proprietary continued to chafe his spirit, until the necessity of preparing the letters which were to urge the attendance of his council, drew him from his fretful reverie into a calmer tone of mind.

In the servant's hall there was an unusual stir occasioned by the preparations which were in train for the outriding of the messengers whom the secretary had put in requisition for the service of the night. The first of these was Derrick Brown, a man of stout mould though somewhat advanced in years. He held in the establishment what might be termed the double post of master of the mews and keeper of the fox hounds, being principal falconer and huntsman of the household. The second was a short, plump little fellow, bearing the name of John Alward, who was one of the grooms of the stable. These two, now ready booted, belted and spurred, were seated on a bench, discussing a luncheon, with the supplement of a large jack or tankard of brown bastard. Several of the other domestics loitered in the hall, throwing in occasionally a word of advice to the riders, or giving them unsolicited aid in the carnal occupation of bodily reinforcement to which they were devoting themselves with the lusty vigor of practised trenchermen. Leaning against the jamb of the ample fireplace, immediately below a lamp which tipped the prominent points of his grave visage with a sharp light, stood an old Indian, of massive figure and swarthy hue, named Pamesack, or, as he was called in the English translation of the Indian word, The Knife. This personage had been, for some years past, at intervals, a privileged inmate of the Proprietary's family, and was now, though consigned to a portion of the duties of the evening, apparently an unconcerned spectator of the scene around him. He smoked his pipe in silence, or if he spoke, it was seldom more than in the short monosyllable characteristic of the incommunicative habits of his tribe.

"When I saw Dick Pagan, the James Town courier, coming into town this evening with his leather pouch slung across his shoulder," said the elder of the riders, " I guessed as much as that there would be matter for the council. News from that quarter now-a-days is apt to bring business for their worships. I warrant the brother of Master Fendall has been contriving an outcome in Virginia. I heard John Rye, the miller of St. Clements, say last Sunday afternoon, that Samuel Fendall had forty mounted men ready in the forest to do his bidding with broadsword and carbine. And he would have done it too, if my Lord had not laid him by the heels at unawares. He has a savage spite against my Lord and the Chancellor both."

"But knew you ever the like before," said John Alward, " that his Lordship should be in such haste to see their worships, he must needs have us tramping over the country at midnight ? There must be a hot flavor in the news ! It was a post-haste letter."

"Tush, copperface ! What have you to do with the flavor of the news ? You have little to complain of, John Alward, for a midnight tramp. It is but twelve miles from this to Mattapany, and your errand is done. You may be snoozing on a good truss of hay in Master Sewall's stable before midnight, if you make speed. Think of my ride all the way to Notley Hall,—and round about by the head of the river too—for I doubt if I have any chance to get a cast over the ferry to-night. Tom Taylor, the boat keeper, is not often sober at this hour : and if he was, a crustier churl—the devil warm his pillow !—doesn't live 'twixt this and the old world. He gets out of his sleep for no man."

" But it is a dark road mine," replied the groom. " A plague upon it ! I have no stomach for this bush and brier work, when a man can see the limb of a tree no more than a cobweb."

" A dark road !" exclaimed the master of the kennels, laughing. " A dark road, John ! It is a long time since there has been a dark road for your night rides, with that nose shining like a lighted link a half score paces ahead. It was somewhat deadened last September, I allow, when you had the marsh ague, and the doctor fed you for a week on gruel—but it has waxed lately as bright as ever. I wish I could buckle it to my head-strap until to-morrow morning."

A burst of laughter, at this sally, which rang through the hall, testified the effect of the falconer's wit and brought the groom to his feet.

" 'S blood, you grinning fools !" he ejaculated, " haven't you heard Derrick's joke a thousand times before, that you must toss up your scurvy ha-haws at it, as if it was new ! He stole it—as the whole hundred knows—from the fat captain, old Dauntrees in the fort there ; who would have got it back upon hue and cry, if it had been his own ;—but the truth is, the Captain filched it from a play-book, as the surveyor told him in my hearing at Garret Weasel's, where the Captain must needs have it for a laughing matter."

" It is a joke that burns fresh every night," replied Derrick ; " a thing to make light of. So, up with the bottom of the pot, boy, and feed it with mother's milk : it will stand you in stead to-night. Well done, John Alward ! I can commend you for taking a jest as well as another."

"Master Derrick," said the other, "this is not the way to do his Lordship's bidding : if we must go, we should be jogging now. I would I had your ride to take, instead of my own,—short as you think it."

"Ha, say you that ! You shall have it, an it please Master Secretary ! But upon one condition."

"Upon what condition ?"

"That you tell me honestly why you would choose to ride twenty miles to Notley rather than twelve to Mattapany."

"Good Derrick," answered the groom, "it is but as a matter of horsemanship. You have a broader road, and mine is a path much beset with brushwood. I like not the peril of being un-horsed."

"There is a lie in your face, John Alward ; the Mattapany road is the broadest and best of the two—is it not so, Pame-sack !"

"It is the first that was opened by the white man," replied the Indian ; "and more people pass upon it than the other."

"John," said the falconer, "you are a coward. I will not put you to the inventing another lie, but will wager I can tell you at one guess why you would change with me." .

"Out with it, Master Derrick !" exclaimed the bystanders.

"Oh, out with it !" repeated John Alward ; "I heed not your gibes."

"You fear the cross road," said the falconer ; "you will not pass the fisherman's grave."

"In troth, masters, I must needs own," replied the groom, "that I have qualms. I never was ashamed to tell the truth, and confess that I am so much of a sinner as to feel an honest fear of the devil and his doings. I have known a horse to start and a rider to be flung at the cross road before now :—there are times in the night when both horse and rider may see what it turns

one's blood into ice to look at. Nay, I am in earnest, masters ·
—I jest not."

"You have honestly confessed, like a brave man, that you
are a coward, John Alward ; and so it shall be a bargain between
us. I will take your message. I fear not Paul Kelpy—he has
been down with that stake through his body, ever too fast to walk
abroad."

"There's my hand to it," said the groom, "and thanks to
boot. I am no coward, Derrick,—but have an infirmity which
will not endure to look by night, in the lonesome woods, upon a
a spirit which walks with a great shaft through it. Willy of the
Flats saw it, in that fashion, as he went home from the Viewer's
feast on the eve of St. Agnes."

"Willy had seen too much of the Viewer's hollands that
night," said Derrick ; "and they are spirits worth a dozen Paul
Kelpys, even if the whole dozen were trussed upon the same stake,
like herrings hung up to smoke. In spite of the fisherman and
his bolt, I warrant you I pass unchallenged betwixt this and
Mattapany."

The secretary, soon after this, entered the hall and confirmed
the arrangements which had just been made. He accordingly delivered the letters intended for Colonel Talbot and Nicholas Sewall to the falconer, and that for Mr. Notley, the late lieutenant
general of the province, to John Alward. To the Indian was
committed the duty of bearing the missions to such members of
the council as resided either in the town or within a few miles of
it. Holding it matter of indifference whether he despatched this
duty by night or by day, The Knife took it in hand at once, and
set forth, on foot, with a letter for Colonel Digges, who lived
about five miles off, at the same time that the other two couriers
mounted their horses for their lonesome journeys through the
forest.

CHAPTER VI.

If we should wait till you, in solemn council,
With due deliberation, had selected
The smallest out of four and twenty evils,
I' faith we should wait long.
Dash and through with it—that's the better watchword,
Then after, come what may come.

                                        PICCOLOMINI.

On the following day, the council, consisting of some four or five gentlemen, were assembled at the Proprietary Mansion About noon their number was rendered complete, by the arrival of Colonel George Talbot, who, mounted on a spirited, milk-white steed that smoked with the hot vigor of his motion, dashed through the gate and alighted at the door. A pair of pistols across his saddle-bow, and a poniard, partially disclosed under his vest, demonstrated the precautions of the possessor to defend himself against sudden assault, and no less denoted the quarrelsome aspect of the times. His frame was tall, athletic, and graceful ; his eye hawk-like, and his features prominent and handsome, at the same time indicative of quick temper and rash resolve. There was in his dress a manifestation of the consciousness of a good figure—it was the costume of a gallant of the times ; and his bearing was characteristic of a person accustomed to bold action and gay companionship.

Talbot was a near kinsman of the Baltimore family, and besides being a member of the Proprietary's council, he held the post of surveyor general, and commanded, also, the provincial militia on the northern frontier, including the settlements on the Elk River, where he owned a large manor, upon which he usually resided. At the present time he was in the temporary occupation of a favorite seat of the Proprietary, at Mattapany, on the Patuxent, whither the late summons had been despatched to call him to the council.

This gentleman was a zealous Catholic, and an ardent personal friend of his kinsman, the Proprietary, whose cause he advocated with that peremptory and, most usually, impolitic determination which his imperious nature prompted, and which served to draw upon him the peculiar hatred of Fendall and Coode, and their partisans. He was thus, although a sincere, it may be imagined, an indiscreet adviser in state affairs, little qualified to subdue or allay that jealous spirit of proscription which, from the epoch of the Protectorate down to this date, had been growing more intractable in the province.

Such was the individual who now, with the firm stride and dauntless carriage of a belted and booted knight of chivalry, to which his picturesque costume heightened the resemblance, entered the apartment where his seniors were already convened.

"Well met!" he exclaimed, as he flung his hat and gloves upon a table and extended his hand to those who were nearest him. "How fares it, gentlemen? What devil of mutiny is abroad now? Has that pimpled fellow of fustian, that swiller of the leavings of a tap room, the worshipful king of the Burgesses, master Jack Coode, got drunk again and begun to bully in his cups? The falconer who hammered at my door last night as if he would have beaten your Lordship's house about my ears, could tell me nothing of the cause of this sudden convocation, save that Driving Dick had come in hot haste from James Town

3*

with letters that had set the mansion here all agog, from his Lordship's closet down to the scullery."

"With proper abatement for the falconer's love of gossip," said the Proprietary, "he told you true. The letters are there on the table. When you have read them, you will see that with good reason I might make some commotion in my house."

Talbot ran his eye over the papers. "Well, and well—an old story!" he said, as he threw one letter aside and took up another. "Antichrist—the Red Lady of Babylon—the Jesuits —and the devil: we have had it so often that the lecture is somewhat stale. The truculent Papists are the authors of all evil! We had the Geneva band in fashion for a time; but that wore out with old Noll. And then comes another flight of kestrels, and we must have the thirty-nine articles served up for a daily dish. That spider, Master Yeo, has grown to be a crony of his grace the Archbishop of Canterbury, and is busy to knit his web around every poor Catholic fly of the province."

"This must be managed without temper," said Darnall, the oldest member present, except the Chancellor. "Our adversaries will find their advantage in our resolves, if made in the heat of passion."

"You say true," replied Talbot. "I am a fool in my humor; but it moves me to the last extremity of endurance to be ever goaded with this shallow and hypocritical pretence of sanctity. They prate of the wickedness of the province, forsooth! our evil deportment, and loose living, and notorious scandal! All will be cured, in the opinion of these solemn Pharisees, by turning that good man, Lord Charles, and his friends out of his own province, and by setting up parson Yeo in a fat benefice under the wing of an established church."

"Read on," said Lord Baltimore, "and you shall see the sum of all, in the argument that it is not fit Papists should bear rule over the free-born subjects of the English crown; and, as a conclusion to that, a summary order to discharge every friend of our church from my employ."

Talbot read the letter to the end.

"So be it!" he ejaculated, as he threw the letter from him, and flung himself back into his chair. "You will obey this high behest? With all humbleness we will thank these knaves for their many condescensions, and their good favors. Your uncle, the Chancellor here, our old frosted comrade, is the first that your Lordship will give bare-headed to the sky. As for myself, I have been voted an incarnate devil in a half dozen conclaves— and so Fendall shall be the surveyor. I hope your Lordship will remember that I have a military command—a sturdy stronghold in the fort of Christina—and some stout fellows with me on the border. It might be hard to persuade them to part company with me."

"Peace, I pray you, peace!" interrupted the Proprietary; "you are nettled, Talbot, and that is not the mood for counsel."

"These pious cut-throats here," said Talbot, "who talk of our degeneracy, slander us to the whole world : and, faith, I am not of the mind to bear it! I speak plainly what I have thought long since—and would rather do than speak. I would arrest the ringleaders upon a smaller scruple of proof than I would set a vagrant in the stocks. You have Fendall now, my Lord—I would have his fellows before long : and the space between taking and trying should not add much to the length of their beards :—between trying and hanging, still less."

"As to that," said the Proprietary, "every day brings us fresh testimony of the sedition afoot, and we shall not be slow to do justice on the parties. We have good information of the extent of the plot against us, and but wait until an open act shall make their guilt unquestionable. Master Coode is now

upon bail only because we were somewhat too hasty in his arrest.
There are associates of Fendall's at work who little dream of our
acquaintance with their designs."

"When does your provincial court hold its sessions?" inquired the Surveyor.

"In less than a month."

"It should make sure work and speedy," said Talbot.
"Master Fendall should find himself at the end of his tether
at the first sitting."

"Ay, and Coode too," said one of the council : "notwith-
standing that the burgesses have stepped forward to protect him.
The House guessed well of the temper against your Lordship in
England, when they stood up so hardily, last month, in favor of
Captain Coode, after your Lordship had commanded his expul-
sion.   It was an insolent contumacy."

"In truth, we have never had peace in the province," said
another, "since Fendall was allowed to return from his banishment.   That man hath set on hotter, but not subtler spirits
than his own.   He has a quiet craftiness which never sleeps nor
loses sight of his purpose of disturbance."

"Alas!" said the Proprietary, "he has not lacked material
to work with.   The burgesses have been disaffected ever since
my father's death.   I know not in what point of kindness I have
erred towards them.   God knows I would cherish affection, not
ill will.   My aim has ever been to do justice to all men."

"Justice is not their aim, my Lord," exclaimed Talbot.
"Oh, this zeal for church is a pretty weapon! and honest
Captain Coode a dainty champion to handle it!   I would cut
the spurs from that fowl, if I did it with a cleaver!"

"He is but the fool in the hands of his betters," interposed
Darnall.   "This discontent has a broad base.   There are many
in the province who, if they will not take an open part against

us, will be slow to rebuke an outbreak—many who will counsel in secret who dare not show their faces to the sun."

"These men have power to do us much harm," said Lord Baltimore; "and I would entreat you, gentlemen, consider, how, by concession to a moderate point, which may comport with our honor, we may allay these irritations. Leaving that question for your future advisement, I ask your attention to the letters. The King has commanded—for it is scarce less than a royal mandate."

"Your Lordship," said Talbot, sarcastically, "has fallen under his Majesty's disfavor. You have, doubtless, failed somewhat in your courtesies to Nell Gwynn, or the gay Duchess; or have been wanting in some observance of respect to old Tom Killigrew, the King's fool. His Majesty is not wont to look so narrowly into state affairs."

"Hold, Talbot!" interrupted the Proprietary. "I would not hear you speak slightingly of the King. He has been friendly to me, and I will not forget it. Though this mandate come in his name, King Charles, I apprehend, knows but little of the matter. He has an easy conscience for an importunate suitor. Oh, it grieves me to the heart, after all my father's care for the province—and surely mine has been no less—it grieves me to see this wayward fortune coming over our hopes like a chill winter, when we looked for springtide, with its happy and cheerful promises. I am not to be envied for my prerogative. Here, in this new world, I have made my bed, where I had no wish but to lie in it quietly: it has become a bed of thorns, and cannot bring rest to me, until I am mingled with its dust. Well, since rebellion is the order of the times, I must e'en myself turn rebel now against this order."

"Wherein might it be obeyed, my Lord?" asked Darnall. "You have already given all the rights of conscience which the freemen could ask, and the demand now is that you surrender your own. What servant would your Lordship displace ? Look around you : is Anthony Warden so incapable, or so hurtful to your service, that you might find plea to dismiss him ?"

"There. is no better man in the province than Anthony Warden," replied the Proprietary, with warmth ; " a just man ; a good man in whatever duty you scan him ; an upright, faithful servant to his post. My Lords of the Ministry would not and could not, if they knew him, ask me to remove that man. I will write letters back to remonstrate against this injustice."

" And say you will not displace a man, my Lord, come what may !" exclaimed Talbot. " This battle must be fought—and the sooner the better ! Your Lordship will find your justification in the unanimous resolve of your council."

This sentiment was echoed by all present, and by some of the more discreet an admonition was added, advising the Proprietary to handle the subject mildly with the ministry, in a tone of kind expostulation, which, as it accorded with Lord Baltimore's own feeling, met his ready acquiescence.

After despatching some business of less concern, the members of the council dispersed.

CHAPTER VII.

An old worshipful gentleman who had a great estate,
That kept a brave old house at a bountiful rate.
THE OLD AND YOUNG COURTIER.

But who the countless charms can draw
That graced his mistress true ?
Such charms the old world seldom saw,
Nor oft, I ween, the new.
Her raven hair plays round her neck,
Like tendrils of the vine ;
Her cheeks, red, dewy rose-buds deck,
Her eyes like diamonds shine.
BRYAN AND PERENNE.

ANTHONY WARDEN had resided in Maryland for forty years
before the period of this story. During the greater portion of
this time he performed the duties of the Collector of the Proprietary's revenues in the port. By the persuasion of Cecilius
Calvert he had become a settler in the New World, where he
had received from his patron the grant of a large tract of land,
which, in progress of time, under a careful course of husbandry,
rendered him a man of easy fortune. One portion of this tract
lay adjacent to the town, and stretched along the creek of St.
Inigoe's, constituting an excellent farm of several hundred acres.
Upon this land the Collector had dwelt from an early period of
his settlement.

A certain sturdiness of character that matched the perils of
that adventurous colonial life, and a vigorous intellect, gave Mr
Warden great authority over the inhabitants of the province,

which was increased by the predominant honesty of purpose and plain, unpretending directness of his nature. A bountiful purse and jocund temper enabled and prompted him to indulge, almost without stint, that hospitality which furnishes the most natural and appropriate enjoyment of those who dwell remote from the busy marts of the world His companionable habits had left their tokens upon his exterior. His frame was corpulent, his features strongly defined, his eye dark blue, with a mastiff kindness in its glance. The flush of generous living had slightly overmastered the wind-and-weather hue of his complexion, and given it the tints of a ripe pear. Seventy years had beaten upon his poll without other badge of conquest than that of a change of his brown locks to white;—their volume was scarcely diminished, and they still fell in curls upon his shoulders.

Two marriages had brought him a large family of children, of whom the eldest (the only offspring of his first nuptials) was Alice Warden, a maiden lady who now, well advanced in life, occupied the highest post of authority in the household, which had, for several years past, been transferred to her by the demise of the second wife. His sons had all abandoned the paternal roof in the various pursuits of fortune, leaving behind them, besides Mistress Alice, a sister, the youngest of the flock, who, at the epoch at which I am about to present her, was just verging towards womanhood.

The dwelling of the Collector stood upon the high bank formed by the union of St. Inigoe's creek and St. Mary's river. It was, according to the most approved fashion of that day, built of imported brick, with a double roof penetrated by narrow and triangular-capped windows. The rooms were large and embellished with carved wainscots and a profusion of chiseled woodwork, giving them an elaborate and expensive aspect. This main building overlooked, with a magisterial and protecting air, a group of sia-

gle-storied offices and out-houses which were clustered around,
one of which was appropriated by the Collector as his place of
business.   This spacious domicil, with its broad porch, cottage-
like appendages and latticed sheds, was embosomed in the shade
of elms and mulberries, whose brown foliage, fanned by the autumnal breeze, murmured in unison with the plashing tide that
beat against the pebbles immediately below.   A garden in the
rear, with trellised and vine-clad gateways, and walks lined with
box, furnished good store of culinary dainties ; whilst a lawn, in
front, occupying some two or three acres, and bounded by the
cliff which formed the headland on the river, lay open to the sun,
and gave from the water an unobstructed view of the mansion.
The taste displayed in these embellishments, the neatness of the
grounds, the low, flower-spangled hedge of thorn that guarded
the cliff, the clumps of rose trees and other ornamental shrubs,
disposed to gratify the eye in the shifting seasons of their bloom,
the various accessories of rustic seats, bowers and parterres—all
united to present an agreeable and infallible index of that purity
of mind which brought into assemblage such simple and attractive
elements of beauty.

All around the immediate domain of the dwelling-house were
orchards, woodlands and cultivated fields, with the usual barns
and other structures necessary in the process of agriculture ;—the
whole region presenting a level plain, some fifty or sixty feet above
the tide, of singular richness as a landscape, and no less agreeable to be looked upon for its associations with the idea of comfortable independence in the proprietor.   This homestead had
obtained the local designation of the Rose Croft,—a name, in
some degree, descriptive of the predominant embellishment of the
spot.

In his attire, Master Anthony Warden, the worshipful Collector (to give him his usual style of address in the province), exhib-

ited some tendency towards the coxcombry of his day. It was marked by that scrupulous observance of the prerogative of rank and age which characterised the costume of the olden time,—smacking no little of the flavor of the official martinet. Authority, amongst our ancestors, was wont to borrow consequence from show. The broad line which separated gentle from simple was recognized, in those days, not less strongly in the habiliments of the person than in his nurture and manners. The divisions between the classes of society were not more authentically distinguished in any outward sign, than in the embroidered velvet or cloth of the man of wealth, and the plain serge, worsted, or leather of the craftsman. The Collector of St. Mary's, on festive occasions, went forth arrayed much after the manner in which Leslie has represented Sir Roger de Coverly, in his admirable painting of that knight ; and although he was too vain of his natural locks to adopt the periwig of that period, yet he had trained his luxuriant tresses into a studied imitation of this artificial adornment His embroidered coat of drab velvet, with wadded skirts and huge open cuffs, his lace wristbands, his ample vest, and white lamb's wool hose rolled above his knees, his buckled shoe and three-cornered hat—all adjusted with a particularity that would put our modern foppery to shame—gave to the worthy burgess of St. Mary's a substantial ascendancy and an unquestioned regard, that rendered him, next to the Proprietary, the most worshipful personage in the province.

This pedantry of costume and the circumspect carriage which it exacted, were pleasantly contrasted with the flowing vivacity of the wearer, engendering by their concourse an amusing compound, which I might call a fettered and pinioned alacrity of demeanor, the rigid stateliness of exterior seeming rather ineffectually to encase, as a half-bursting chrysalis, the wings of a gay nature.

Mr. Warden was reputed to be stubborn in opinion. The

good people of the town, aware of his pertinacity in this particular, had no mind to make points with him, but, on the contrary,
rather corroborated him in his dogmatism by an amiable assentation ; so that, it is said, he grew daily more peremptory. This
had become so much his prerogative, that the Lord Proprietary
himself gave way to it with as good a grace as the rest of the inhabitants.

It may be imagined that so general a submission to this temper would have the tendency to render him a little passionate.
They say it was a rich sight to see him in one of his flashes, which
always took the bystanders by surprise, like thunder in the midst
of sunshine ; but these explosions were always short-lived, and
rather left a more wholesome and genial clearness in the atmosphere of his affections.

The household at the Rose Croft, I have hinted, was regulated by Mistress Alice, who had, some time before our acquaintance
with her, reached that period of life at which the female ambition
for display is prone to subside into a love of domestic pursuits. It
was now her chief worldly care and delight to promote the comfort of those who congregated around the family hearth. In the
administration of this office, it may be told to her praise, that she
manifested that unpretending good sense which is a much more
rare and estimable quality than many others of better acceptation
with the world. As was natural to her tranquil position and
kindly temper, her feelings had taken a ply towards devotion,
which Father Pierre did not omit to encourage and confirm by
all the persuasions enjoined by the discipline of the Romish church.
The gentle solicitude with which the ministers of that ancient
faith watch and assist the growing zeal of its votaries ; the cap-
tivation of its venerable ceremonies, and the familiar and endear-
ing tone in which it addresses itself to the regard of its children,
sufficiently account for its sway over so large a portion of man-

kind, and especially for its hold upon the affections of the female
breast.

Upon the thoughtful character of Alice Warden this influence
shed a mellow and attractive light, and gave to the performance of her daily duties that orderly and uninterrupted cheerfulness which showed the content of her spirit. She found
an engrossing labor of love in superintending the education of her
sister. Blanche Warden had now arrived within a span of her
eighteenth year. Alice had guarded her path from infancy with
a mother's tenderness, ministering to her enjoyments and instilling
into her mind all that her own attainments, circumscribed, it is
true, within a narrow circle, enabled her to teach. The young
favorite had grown up under this domestic nurture, aided by the
valuable instructions of father Pierre, who had the guidance of
her studies, a warm-hearted girl, accomplished much beyond the
scant acquisitions ordinarily, at that day, within the reach of women, and distinguished for that confiding gentleness of heart and
purity of thought and word which the caresses of friends, the perception of the domestic affections, and seclusion from the busy
world, are likely to engender in an ardent and artless nature.

Of the beauty of the Rose of St. Mary's (for so contempora-
ries were wont to designate her) tradition speaks with a poetical
fervor. I have heard it said that Maryland, far-famed for lovely
women, hath not since had a fairer daughter. The beauty which
lives in expression was eminently hers ; that beauty which is
scarcely to be caught by the painter,—which, changeful as the
surface of the welling fountain where all the fresh images of nature
are for ever shifting and sparkling with the glories of the mirror,
defies the limner's skill. In stature she was neither short nor tall,
but distinguished by a form of admirable symmetry both for grace
and activity. Her features, it is scarce necessary to say, were
regular,—but not absolutely so, for, I know not why, perfect reg-

ularity is a hindrance to expression. Eyes of dark hazel, with long lashes that gave, by turns, a pensive and playful light to her face, serving, at will, to curtain from the world the thoughts which otherwise would have been read by friend and foe ; hair of a rich brown, glossy, and, in some lights, even like the raven's wing,— ample in volume and turning her brow and shoulders almost into marble by the contrast ; a complexion of spotless, healthful white and red ; a light, elastic step, responding to the gaiety of her heart ; a voice melodious and clear, gentle in its tones and various in its modulation, according to the feeling it uttered ;—these constituted no inconsiderable items in the inventory of her perfections. Her spirit was blithe, affectionate and quick in its sympathies ; her ear credulous to believe what was good, and slow to take an evil report. The innocence of her thoughts kindled an habitual light upon her countenance, which was only dimmed when the rough handling by fortune of friend or kinsman was recounted to her, and brought forth the ready tear—for that was ever as ready as her smile.

I might tell more of Blanche Warden, but that my task compels me to hasten to the matter of my story.

CHAPTER VIII.

The silk well could she twist and twine,
And make the fine march-pine,
And with the needle work ;
And she could help the priest to say
His matins on a holiday
And sing a psalm in kirk.

DOWSABEL.

WITH such attractions for old and young it will readily be believed that the Rose Croft was a favorite resort of the inhabitants of St. Mary's. The maidens gathered around Blanche as a May-day queen ; the matrons possessed in Mistress Alice a discreet and kind friend, and the more sedate part of the population found an agreeable host in the worthy official himself.

The family of the Lord Proprietary sustained the most intimate relations with this household. It is true that Lady Baltimore, being feeble in health and stricken with grief at the loss of her son, which yet hung with scarcely abated poignancy upon her mind, was seldom seen beyond her own threshold ; but his Lordship's sister, the Lady Maria—as she was entitled in the province —was a frequent and ever most welcome guest. Whether this good lady had the advantage of the Proprietary in years, would be an impertinent as well as an unprofitable inquiry, since no chronicler within my reach has thought fit to instruct the world on this point ; and, if it were determined, the fact could neither heighten nor diminish the sober lustre of her virtues. Suffice it that she was a stirring, tidy little woman, who moved about with indefatigable zeal in the acquittal of the manifold duties which her large participation in the affairs of the town exacted of her—the Lady Bountiful of the province who visited the sick, fed the hungry, and clothed the naked. In the early morning she tripped through the dew, with scrupulous regularity, to mass ; generally superintended the decorations of the chapel in preparation for the festivals ; gossipped with the neighbors after service, and, in short, kept her hands full of business.

Her interest in the comfort and welfare of the townspeople grew partly out of her temperament, and partly out of a feudal pride that regarded them as the liegemen of her brother the chief —a relation which she considered as creating an obligation to extend to them her countenance upon all proper occasions : and, sooth to say, that countenance was not perhaps the most comely in the province, being somewhat sallow, but it was as full of benevolence as became so exemplary a spirit. She watched peculiarly what might be called the under-growth, and was very successful in worming herself into the schemes and plans of the young people. Her entertainments at the mansion were frequent, and no less acceptable to the gayer portion of the inhabitants than they were to her brother. On these occasions she held a little court, over which she presided with an amiable despotism, and fully maintained the state of the Lord Proprietary. By these means the Lady Maria had attained to an over-shadowing popularity in the town.

Blanche Warden had, from infancy, engaged her deepest solicitude ; and as she took to herself no small share of the merit of that nurture by which her favorite had grown in accomplishment, she felt, in the maiden's praises which everywhere rang through the province, an almost maternal delight. Scarcely a day passed over without some manifestation of this concern. New patterns of embroidery, music brought by the last ship from *home*, some invitation of friendship or letter of counsel, furnished occasions of daily intercourse between the patroness and the maiden of the Rose Croft ; and not unfrequently the venerable spinster herself—attended by a familiar in the shape of a little Indian girl, Natta, the daughter of Pamesack, arrayed in the trinketry of her tribe—alighted from an ambling pony at the Collector's door, with a face full of the importance of business.   Perchance, there might be an occasion of merry-making in contemplation, and then the lady Maria united in consultation with sister Alice concerning the details of the matter, and it was debated, with the deliberation due to so interesting a subject, whether Blanche should wear her black or her crimson velvet bodice, her sarsnet or her satin, and such other weighty matters as have not yet lost their claims to thoughtful consideration on similar emergencies.

In the frequent interchange of the offices of good neighborhood between the families of the Proprietary and of the Collector, it could scarce fall out that the Secretary should not be a large participator.   The shyness of the student and the habitual self-restraint taught him in the seminary of Antwerp, in some degree screened from common observation the ardent character of Albert Verheyden.   The deferential relation which he held to his patron threw into his demeanor a reserve expressive of humility rather than of diffidence ; but under this there breathed a temperament deeply poetical, and a longing for enterprise, that all the discipline of his school and the constraint of his position could scarce suppress.   He was now at that time of life when the imagination is prone to dally with illusions ; when youth, not yet yoked to the harness of the world's business, turns its spirit forth to seek adventure in the domain of fancy. He was thus far a dreamer, and dreamed of gorgeous scenes and bold exploits and rare fortune.   He had the poet's instinct to

perceive the beautiful, and his fancy hung it with richer garlands
and charmed him into a worshipper. A mute worshipper he
was, of the Rose of St. Mary's, from the first moment that
he gazed upon her. That outward form of Blanche Warden,
and the motion and impulses of that spirit, might not often haunt
the Secretary's dream without leaving behind an image that
should live for ever in his heart. To him the thought was
enchantment, that in this remote wild, far away from the world's
knowledge, a flower of such surpassing loveliness should drink the
glorious light in solitude—for so he, schooled in populous cities,
deemed of this sequestered province—and with this thought
came breathings of poetry which wrought a transfiguration of
the young votary and lifted him out of the sphere of this "work-
ing-day world." Day after day, week after week, and month
after month, the Secretary watched the footsteps of the beautiful
girl; but still it was silent, unpresuming adoration. It entered
not into his mind to call it love; it was the very humbleness of
devotion.

Meantime the maiden, unconscious of her own rare perfections, and innocent of all thought of this secret homage,
found Master Albert much the most accomplished and gentle
youth she had ever seen. He had, without her observing how
it became so, grown to be, in some relation or other, part and
parcel of her most familiar meditations. His occasions of business with the Collector brought him so often to the Rose Croft,
that if they happened not every day, they were, at least, incidents of such common occurrence as to be noted by no ceremony
—indeed, rather to be counted on in the domestic routine. The
Collector was apt to grow restless if, by any chance, they were
suspended, as it was through the Secretary's mission he received
the tidings of the time as well as the official commands of the
Proprietary; whilst Albert's unobtrusive manners, his soft step,

4

and pretensionless familiarity with the household put no one out of the way to give him welcome. His early roaming in summer sometimes brought him, at sunrise, beneath the bank of the Rose Croft, where he looked, with the admiration of an artist, upon the calm waters of St. Inigoe's Creek, and upon the forest that flung its shades over its farther shores. Not unfrequently, the fresh and blooming maiden had left her couch as early as himself, and tended her plants before the dew had left the leaves, and thus it chanced that she found him in his vocation ; and, like him, she took pleasure in gazing on that bright scene, when it was the delight of both to tell each other how beautiful it was. And when, in winter, the rain pattered from the eaves and the skies were dark, the Secretary, muffled in his cloak, took his way to the Collector's mansion and helped the maiden to beguile the tedious time. Even "when lay the snow upon a level with the hedge," the two long miles of unbeaten track did not stop his visit, for the Secretary loved the adventure of such a journey ; and Blanche often smiled to see how manfully he endured it, and how light he made of the snow-drift which the wind had sometimes heaped up into billows, behind which the feather of his bonnet might not be discovered while he sat upon his horse.

In this course of schooling Blanche and Albert grew into a near intimacy, and the maiden became dependent upon the Secretary for some share of her happiness, without being aware of it. Master Albert had an exquisite touch of the lute and a rich voice to grace it, and Blanche found many occasions to tax his skill : he had a gallant carriage on horseback, and she needed the service of a cavalier : he was expert in the provincial sport of hawking, and had made such acquaintance with Blanche's merlin that scarce any one else could assist the maiden in casting off Ariel to a flight. In short, Blanche followed the bent of her own ingenuous and truthful nature, and did full justice to the Secretary's various capacity to please her, by putting his talents in requisition with an unchidden freedom, and without once pausing to explore the cause why Master Albert always came so opportunely to her thoughts. Doubtless, if she had had the wit to make this inquiry the charm of her liberty would have been broken, and a sentinel would, ever after, have checked the wandering of her free footstep.

The Collector, in regard to this intercourse, was sound asleep. His wise head was taken up with the concerns of the province, his estate, and the discussion of opinions that had little affinity to the topics likely to interest the meditations of a young maiden. He was not apt to see a love-affair, even if it lay, like a fallen tree, across his path, much less to hunt it out when it lurked like a bird amongst the flowers that grew in the shady coverts by the wayside. The astuteness of the lady Maria, however, was not so much at fault, and she soon discovered, what neither Blanche nor Albert had sufficiently studied to make them aware of their own category. But the Secretary was in favor with the lady Maria, and so she kept her own counsel, as well as a good-natured watch upon the progress of events.

CHAPTER IX.

TOWARDS noon of the day on which the council held their session, a troop of maidens were seen issuing from the chapel. Their number might have been eight or ten. The orderly step with which they departed from the door was exchanged for a playful haste in grouping together when they got beyond the immediate precincts of the place of worship. Their buoyant carriage and lively gesticulations betokened the elasticity of health which was still more unequivocally shown in their ruddy complexions and well rounded forms.

Their path lay across the grassy plain towards the town, and passed immediately within the space embowered by an ancient, spreading poplar, scarce a hundred paces in front of the chapel. When the bevy reached this spot, they made a halt, and gathered round one of their number, who seemed to be the object of a mirthful and rather tumultuary importunity. The individual thus beset was Blanche Warden. Together with a few elderly dames, who were at this moment standing at the door of the chapel in parley with Father Pierre, this troop had constituted the whole congregation who had that morning attended the service of the festival of St Bridget.

"Holy mother, how I am set upon!" exclaimed Blanche, as, half smiling and half earnest, she turned her back against the trunk of the tree. "Have I not said I could not? Why should my birth-day be so remembered that all the town must be talking about it ?"

"You did promise," said one of the party, "or at least, Mistress Alice promised for you, full six months ago, that when you came to eighteen we should have a merry-making at the Rose Croft."

"It would not be seemly—I should be thought bold," replied the maiden, "to be turning my birth-day into a feast. Indeed, I must not and cannot, playmates."

"There is no must not nor cannot in our books, Blanche Warden," exclaimed another, "but simply we will. There is troth plighted for it, and that's enough for us. So we hold to that, good Blanche."

"Yes, good Blanche ! gentle Blanche ! sweetheart, we hold to that !" cried the whole party, in a clamorous onset.

"Truly, Grace Blackiston, you will have Father Pierre checking us for noisy behavior," said the maiden. "You see that he is now looking towards us. It is a pretty matter to make such a coil about ! I marvel, has no one ever been eighteen before !"

"This day se'nnight," replied the arch girl to whom this reprimand was addressed, "will be the first day, Blanche Warden, the Rose of St. Mary's has ever seen eighteen ; and it will be the last I trow : and what comes and goes but once in the wide world should be accounted a rare thing, and rarities should be noticed, sweetheart."

"If I was coming eighteen," said a damsel who scarce reached as high as Blanche's shoulder, "and had as pretty a house for a dance as the Rose Croft, there should be no lack of sport amongst the townspeople."

"It is easy to talk on a two years' venture, little Madge," replied Blanche ; "for that is far enough off to allow space for

boasting.   But gently, dear playmates ! do not clamor so loud
I would do your bidding with good heart if I thought it would
not be called something froward in me to be noising my age
abroad, as if it was my lady herself."

"We will advise with Father Pierre and Lady Maria,"
responded Grace Blackiston ; "they are coming this way."

At this moment the reverend priest, and the ladies with
whom he had been in conversation, approached. The sister of
the Proprietary was distinguished as well by her short stature
and neat attire, as by her little Indian attendant, who followed
bearing the lady's missal. The tall figure of Father Pierre,
arrayed in his black tunic and belt, towered above his female
companions. He bore his square bonnet of black cloth in his
hand, disclosing a small silk cap closely fitted to his crown,
fringed around with the silver locks which, separating on his
brow, gave the grace of age to a countenance full of benignity.

The presence of the churchman subdued the eager gaiety of
the crowd, and two or three of the maidens ran up to him with
an affectionate familiarity to make him acquainted with the
subject of their contention.

"Father," said Grace Blackiston, "we have a complaint to
lodge against Mistress Blanche for a promise-breaker. You
must counsel her, father, to her duty."

"Ah, my child ! pretty Blanche !" exclaimed the priest,
with the alacrity of his native French temper, as he took the
assailed damsel by the hand, "what have they to say against
you ?   I will be your friend as well as your judge."

"The maidens, father," replied Blanche, "have taken leave
of their wits, and have beset me like madcaps to give them a
dance at the Rose Croft on my birth-day. And I have stood on
my refusal, father Pierre, as for a matter that would bring me
into censure for pertness—as I am sure you will say it would—

with worshipful people, that a damsel who should be modest in her behavior, should so thrust herself forward to be observed."

"And we do not heed that, Father Pierre," interrupted Grace Blackiston, who assumed to be the spokeswoman of the party, "holding it a scruple more nice than wise. Blanche has a trick of standing back more than a maiden needs. And, besides, we say that Mistress Alice is bound by pledge of word, and partly Blanche, too—for she stood by and said never a syllable against it—that we should have good cheer and dancing on that day at the Rose Croft. It is the feast of the Blessed Virgin, Terese, and we would fain persuade Blanche that the festival should be kept for the sake of her birth-day saint."

"My children," said the priest, who during this debate stood in the midst of the blooming troop, casting his glances from one to another with the pleased expression of an interested partaker of their mirth, and, at the same time, endeavoring to assume a countenance of mock gravity, "we will consider this matter with impartial justice. And, first, we will hear all that Mistress Blanche has to say. It is a profound subject. Do you admit the promise, my child?"

"I do not deny, Father Pierre, that last Easter, when we met and danced at Grace Blackiston's, my sister Alice did make some promise, and I said nothing against it. But it was an idle speech of sister Alice, which I thought no more of till now; and now should not have remembered it if these wild mates of mine had not sung it in my ear with such clamor as must have made you think we had all gone mad."

"It is honestly confessed," said Father Pierre; "and though I heard the outcry all the way to the church door, yet I did not deem the damsels absolutely mad, as you supposed. I am an old man, my child, and I have been taught, by my experience, in what key seven, eight, or nine young girls will make known their desires when they are together : and, truly, it is their nature to speak all at the same time. They speak more than they listen—ha, ha ! But we shall be mistaken if we conclude they are mad."

"Blanche, love," interposed the Lady Maria, "you have scarce given a good reason for gainsaying the wish of the damsels. Have a care or you may find me a mutineer on this question."

"That's a rare lady—a kind lady !" shouted several. "Now, Blanche, you have no word of denial left."

"I am at mercy," said the maiden, "if my good mistress, the Lady Maria, is not content. Whatever my sister Alice and my father shall approve, and you, dear lady, shall say befits my state, that will I undertake right cheerfully. I would pleasure the whole town in the way of merry-making, if I may do so without seeming to set too much account upon so small a matter as my birth-day. I but feared it would not be well taken in one so young as I am."

"I will answer it to the town," said the Lady Maria. "It shall be done as upon my motion ; and Mistress Alice shall take order in the matter as a thing wherein you had no part. Will that content you, Blanche ?"

"I will be ruled in all things by my dear lady," replied the maiden. "You will speak to my father ?"

"It shall be my special duty to look after it forthwith," responded the lady.

"Luckily," said Father Pierre, laughing, "this great business is settled without the aid of the church. Well, I have lost some of my consequence in the winding up, and the Lady Maria is in the ascendant. I will have my revenge by being as merry as any of you at the feast. So, good day, mes enfans !"

With this sally, the priest left the company and retired to his dwelling hard by the chapel. The Lady Maria and her elderly companions moved towards the town, whilst the troop of damsels with increased volubility pursued their noisy triumph, and with rapid steps hastened to their several homes.

4*

CHAPTER X.

THE Crow and Archer presented a busy scene on the evening of the day referred to in the last chapter. A report had been lately spread through the country that the brig Olive Branch—an occasional trader between the province and the coasts of Holland and England—had arrived at St. Mary's. In consequence of this report there had been, during the last two days, a considerable accession to the usual guests of the inn, consisting of travellers both by land and water. Several small sloops and other craft had come into the harbor, and a half score inland proprietors had journeyed from their farms on horseback, and taken up their quarters under the snug roof of Garret Weasel. The swarthy and gaunt watermen, arrayed in the close jackets and wide kilt-like breeches and in the party-colored, woollen caps peculiar to their vocation, were seen mingling in the tap-room with the more substantial cultivators of the soil. A few of the burghers of St. Mary's were found in the same groups, drawn thither by the love of company, the occasions, perchance, of business, or the mere attraction of an evening pot and pipe. The greater portion of this assemblage were loitering between the latticed bar of the common room, and the quay in front of the house, which had somewhat of the occupation and bustle of a little exchange. On a bench, in one corner of the tap-room, sat, in a ragged, patched coat resembling a pea-jacket, a saucy, vagrant-looking fiddler, conspicuous for a red face and a playful light blue eye ; he wore a dingy, pliant white hat, fretted at the rim, set daintily on one side of his head, from beneath which his yellow locks depended over either cheek, completely covering his ears : and all the while scraped his begrimed and greasy instrument to a brisk tune, beating time upon the floor with a huge hob-nailed shoe. This personage had a vagabond popularity in the province under the name of Will of the Flats—a designation no less suited to his musical commodity than to the locality of his ostensible habitation, which was seated on the flats of Patuxent, not above fifteen miles from St. Mary's, where he was tenant of a few acres of barren marsh and a lodge or cabin not much larger than a good dog kennel.

Will's cheef compeer and brother in taste and inclination, though of more affluent fortune, was Dick Pagan, or Driving Dick according to his more familiar appellation, the courier who had lately brought the missives from James Town ; a hard-favored, weather-beaten, sturdy, little bow-legged fellow, in russet boots and long spurs, and wrapped in a coarse drab doublet secured by a leathern belt, with an immense brass buckle in front. Old Pamesack, likewise, formed a part of the group, and might have been observed seated on a settle at the door, quietly smoking his pipe, as unmoved by the current of idlers which ebbed and flowed past him, as the old barnacled pier of the quay by the daily flux and reflux of the river.

Such were the guests who now patronized the thriving establishment of Master Weasel. These good people were not only under the care, but also under the command of our hostess the dame Dorothy, who was a woman by no means apt to overlook her prerogative. The dame, having been on a visit to a neighbor, did not show herself in the tap-room until near the close of the day ; in the mean time leaving her customers to the unchidden enjoyment of their entertainment, which was administered

by Matty Scamper,—a broad-chested, red-haired and indefatigable damsel, who, in her capacity of adjutant to the hostess, had
attained to great favor with the patrons of the tavern by her
imperturbable good nature and ready answer to all calls of business. As for Master Weasel, never did pleasure-loving monarch
more cheerfully surrender his kingdom to the rule of his minister
than he to whatever power for the time was uppermost,—
whether the dame herself, or her occasional vicegerent, Matty of
the Saucepan.

Matty's rule, however, was now terminated by the arrival of
Mistress Weasel herself. It is fit I should give my reader some
perception of the exterior of the hostess, as a woman of un-
doubted impression and consideration with the townspeople.
Being now in her best attire, which was evidently put on with a
careful eye to effect, I may take occasion to say that one might
suspect her of a consciousness of some deficiency of height, as
well as of an undue breadth of figure, both which imperfections
she had studied to conceal. She wore a high conical hat of
green silk, garnished with a band of pink ribbon which was set
on by indentation or teethwise, and gathered in front into a
spirited cluster of knots. Her jacket, with long tight sleeves,
was also of green silk, adapted closely to her shape, now brought
into its smallest compass by the aid of stays, and was trimmed in
the same manner as the hat. A full scarlet petticoat reached
within a span of her ankles, and disclosed a buxom, well-formed
leg in brown stocking with flashy clocks of thickly embossed
crimson, and a foot, of which the owner had reason to be proud,
neatly pinched into a green shoe with a tottering high heel. Her
black hair hung in plaits down her back ; and her countenance
—distinguished by a dark waggish eye, a clear complexion, and
a turned-up nose, to which might be added a neck both fat and
fair, half concealed by a loose kerchief—radiated with an ex

pression partly wicked and partly charitable, but in every lineament denoting determination and constancy of purpose. This
air of careless boldness was not a little heightened by the absence
of all defence to her brow from the narrow rim of the hat and
the height at which it was elevated above her features.

The din of the tap-room was hushed into momentary silence
as soon as this notable figure appeared on the threshold.

"Heaven help these thirsty, roystering men !" she exclaimed,
as she paused an instant at the door and surveyed the group
within. "They are still at it as greedily as if they had just
come out of a dry lent ! From sunrise till noon, and from noon
till night, it is all the same—drink, drink, drink. Have ye news
of Master Cocklescraft ?—I would that the Olive Branch were
come and gone, that I might sit under a quiet roof again !—
there is nothing but riot and reeling from the time the skipper
is expected in the port until he leaves it."

"True enough, jolly queen !" said Ralph Haywood, a young
inland planter, taking the hand of the merry landlady as she
struggled by him on her way to the bar—"what, in good
earnest, has become of Cocklescraft ? This is the second day we
waited for him. I half suspect you, mistress, of a trick to
gather good fellows about you, by setting up a false report of
the Olive Branch."

"Thou art a lying varlet, Ralph," quickly responded the
dame : "you yourself came jogging hither with the story that
Cocklescraft was seen two days ago, beating off the Rappahan-
nock.—I play a trick on you, truly ! You must think I have
need of custom, to bring in a troop of swilling bumpkins from
the country who would eat and drink out the character of
any reputable house in the hundred, without so much as one
doit of profit. You have my free leave to tramp it back again
to Providence, Ralph Haywood, whenever you have a mind."

"Nay, now you quarrel with an old friend, Mistress Dorothy."

"Take your hand off my shoulder, Ralph, you coaxing villain!—Ha, ha, I warrant you get naught but vinegar from me, for your treacle.—But come—you are a good child, and shall have of the best in this house:—I would only warn you to call for it mannerly, Master Ralph."

"Our dame is a woman of mettle," said another of the company, as the landlady escaped from the planter and took her station behind the bar.

"What has become of that man Weasel?" she inquired somewhat petulantly. "The man I am sure has been abroad ever since I left the house! He is of no more value than a cracked pot;—he would see me work myself as thin as a broom handle before he would think of turning himself round."

"Garret is now upon the quay," replied one of the customers;— "I saw him but a moment since with Arnold the Ranger."

"With some idle stroller,—you may be sure of that!" interrupted the hostess:—"never at his place, if the whole house should go dry as Cuthbert's spring at midsummer. Call him to me, if you please, Master Shortgrass.—Michael Curtis, that wench Matty Scamper has something to do besides listen to your claverings! Matty, begone to the kitchen; these country cattle will want their suppers presently.—Oh, Willy, Willy o' the Flats!—for the sake of one's ears, in mercy, stop that everlasting twangle of your old fiddle!—It would disgrace the patience of any Christian woman in the world to abide in the midst of all this uproar!—Nay then, come forward, old crony —I would not offend you," she said in a milder tone to the fiddler. "Here is a cup of ale, and Matty will give you your supper to-night. I have danced too often to your music to deny you a comfort ;—so, drink as you will ! but pray you rest your elbow for a while."

"And there is a shilling down on the nail," said Driving Dick, as he and the fiddler came together to the bar at the summons of the landlady : "when that is drunk out, dame, give me a space of warning, that I may resolve whether we shall go another shot."

"Master Shortgrass told me you had need of me," said Garret Weasel, as he now entered the door ;—"what with me, wife Dorothy ?"

"Get you gone !" replied the wife—"you are ever in the way. Your head is always thrust in place when it is not wanted ! If you had been at your duty an hour ago, your service might have been useful."

"I can but return to the quay," said Garret, at the same time beginning to retrace his steps.

"Bide you !" exclaimed the dame in a shrill voice—"I have occasion for you. Go to the cellar and bring up another stoop of hollands ; these salt water fish have no relish for ale—they must deal in the strong :—nothing but hollands or brandy for them."

The obedient husband took the key of the cellar and went on the duty assigned him.

At this moment a door communicating with an adjoining apartment was thrown ajar and the head of Captain Dauntrees protruded into the tap-room.

"Mistress Dorothy," he said—"at your leisure, pray step this way."

The dame tarried no longer than was necessary to complete a measure she was filling for a customer, and then went into the room to which she had been summoned. This was a little parlor, where the Captain of musketeers had been regaling himself for the last hour over a jorum of ale, in solitary rumination. An open window gave to his view the full expanse of the river, now glowing with the rich reflexions of sunset ; and a balmy October breeze played through the apartment and refreshed without chilling the frame of the comfortable Captain. He was seated near the window in a large easy-chair when the hostess entered.

"Welcome, dame," he said, without rising from his seat, at the same time offering his hand, which was readily accepted by the landlady.—"By St. Gregory and St. Michael both, a more buxom and tidy piece of flesh and blood hath never sailed between the two headlands of Potomac, than thou art! You are for a junketing, Mistress Dorothy ; you are tricked out like a queen this evening! I have never seen you in your new suit before. You are as gay as a marygold : and I wear your colors, thou laughing mother of mischief! Green is the livery of your true knight. Has your good man, honest Garret, come home yet, dame ?"

"What would you with my husband, Master Baldpate! There is no good in the wind when you throw yourself into the big chair of this parlor."

"In truth, dame, I only came to make a short night of it with you and your worthy spouse. Do not show your white teeth at me, hussy,—you are too old to bite. Tell Matty to spread supper for me in this parlor. Arnold and Pamesack will partake with me ; and if the veritable and most authentic head of this house—I mean yourself, mistress—have no need of Garret, I would entreat to have him in company. By the hand of thy soldier, Mistress Dorothy! I am glad to see you thrive so in your calling. You will spare me Garret, dame ? Come, I know you have not learnt how to refuse me a boon."

"You are a saucy Jack, Master Captain," replied the dame. "I know you of old : you would have a rouse with that thriftless babe, my husband. You sent him reeling home only last night.

How can you look me in the face, knowing him, as you do, for a most shallow vessel, Captain Dauntrees ?"

"Fie on thee, dame ! You disgrace your own flesh and blood by such a speech. Did you not choose him for his qualities?— ay, and with all circumspection, as a woman of experience. You had two husbands before Garret, and when you took him for a third, it was not in ignorance of the sex. Look thee in the face! I dare,—yea, and at thy whole configuration. Faith, you wear most bravely, Mistress Weasel ! Stand apart, and let me survey : turn your shoulders round," he added, as by a sleight he twirled the dame upon her heel so as to bring her back to his view—"there is a woman of ten thousand ! I envy Garret such store of womanly wealth."

"If Garret were the man I took him for, Master Captain," said the dame with a saucy smile, "you would have borne a broken head long since. But he has his virtues, such as they are,— though they may lie in an egg-shell : and Garret has his frailties too, like other men : alack, there is no denying it !"

"Frailties, forsooth ! Which of us has not, dame ? Garret is an honest man ;—somewhat old—a shade or so : yet it is but a shade. For my sake, pretty hostess, you will allow him to sup with us ? Speak it kindly, sweetheart—good, old Garret's jolly, young wife !"

"Thou wheedling devil !" said the landlady ; " Garret is no older than you are. But, truly, I may say he is of little account in the tap-room ; so, he shall come to you, Captain. But, look you, he is weak, and must not be over-charged."

"He shall not, mistress—you have a soldier's word for that. I could have sworn you would not deny me. Hark you, dame,— bring your ear to my lips ;—a word in secret."

The hostess bent her head down, as the Captain desired, when he said in a half whisper, "Send me a flask of the best,—

you understand? And there's for thy pains!" he added, as he saluted her cheek with a kiss.

"And there's for thy impudence, saucy Captain!" retorted the spirited landlady as she bestowed the palm of her hand on the side of his head and fled out of the apartment.

Dauntrees sprang from his chair and chased the retreating dame into the midst of the crowd of the tap-room, by whose aid she was enabled to make her escape. Here he encountered Garret Weasel, with whom he went forth in quest of Arnold and the Indian, who were to be his guests at supper.

In the course of the next half hour the Captain and his three comrades were assembled in the little parlor around the table, discussing their evening meal. When this was over, Matty was ordered to clear the board and to place a bottle of wine and glasses before the party, and then to leave the room.

"You must know, Garret," said Dauntrees when the serving-maid had retired, "that we go to-night to visit the Wizard's Chapel by his Lordship's order; and as I would have stout fellows with me, I have come down here on purpose to take you along."

"Heaven bless us, Master Jasper Dauntrees!" exclaimed Garret, somewhat confounded with this sudden appeal to his valor, which was not of that prompt complexion to stand so instant a demand, and yet which the publican was never willing to have doubted—"truly there be three of you, and it might mar the matter to have too many on so secret an out-going"——

"Tush, man,—that has been considered. His Lordship especially looks to your going : you cannot choose but go "

"But my wife, Captain Dauntrees"——

"Leave that to me," said the Captain ; "I will manage it as

handsomely as the taking of Troy. Worthy Garret, say naught against it—you must go, and take with you a few bottles of Canary and a good luncheon of provender in the basket. You shall be our commissary. I came on set purpose to procure the assistance of your experience, and store of comfortable sustenance. Get the bottles, Garret,—his Lordship pays the scot to-night."

"I should have my nag," said Garret, "and the dame keeps the key of the stable, and will in no wise consent to let me have it. She would suspect us for a rouse if I but asked the key."

"I will engage for that, good Weasel," said Dauntrees : "I will cozen the dame with some special invention which shall put her to giving the key of her own motion : she shall be coaxed with a device that shall make all sure—only say you will obey his Lordship's earnest desire."

"It is a notable piece of service," said the innkeeper, meditating over the subject, and tickled with the importance which was ascribed to his co-operation—"and will win thanks from the whole province. His Lordship did wisely to give it in charge to valiant men."

"In faith did he," replied the Captain ; "and it will be the finishing stroke of your fortunes. You will be a man of mark for ever after."

"I am a man to be looked to in a strait, Captain," said Weasel, growing valorous with the thought. "I saw by his Lordship's eye yesternight that he was much moved by what I told him. I have had a wrestle with devils before now."

Arnold smiled and cast his eye towards the Indian, who, immediately after supper, had quitted the table and taken a seat in the window.

"There be hot devils and cold devils," said he, "and he that wrestles with them must have a hand that will hold fire as well as ice : that is true, Pamesack ?"

"Pamesack has no dealing with the white man's devil," replied the Indian; "he has enough to do with his own."

"Drink some wine, old blade," said Dauntrees as he presented a cup to Pamesack; "The Knife must be sharp tonight—this will whet his edge. We shall have need of your woodcraft."

The Indian merely sipped the wine, as he replied, "Pamesack knows the broad path and the narrow both. He can lead you to the Black House day or night."

"Brandy is more natural to his throat than this thin drink," said Weasel, who forthwith left the room and returned with a measure of the stronger liquor. When this was presented Pamesack swallowed it at a draught, and with something approaching a laugh, he said, "It is the white man's devil—but the Indian does not fear him."

"Now, Garret," said Dauntrees, "we have no time to lose. Make ready your basket and bottles, and lay them at the foot of the cedar below the bank, near the Town House steps; then hasten back to the parlor. I will put the dame to sending you on an errand which may be done only on horseback;—you will mount with the basket and make speedy way to the Fort. Tell Nicholas Verbrack, the lieutenant, that I shall be there in reasonable time. We must set forth by ten; it may take us three hours to reach St. Jerome's."

"My heart is big enough," said Weasel, once more beginning to waver, "for any venture; but, in truth, I fear the dame. It will be a livelong night carouse, and she is mortal against that. What will she say in the morning?"

"What can she say, when all is come and gone, but, perchance, that you were rash and hot-headed? That will do you no harm: but an hour ago she swore to me that you were getting old—and sighed too, as if she believed her words."

"Old, did she say? Ho, mistress, I will show you my infirmities! A fig for her scruples! the hey-day blood yerks yet, Master Captain. I will go with you, comrades: I will follow you to any goblin's chapel 'twixt St. Mary's and Christina."

"Well said, brave vintner!" exclaimed the Captain; "now, stir! And when you come back to the parlor, Master Weasel, you shall find the dame here. Watch my eye and take my hint, so that you play into my hand when need shall be. I will get the nag out of the stable if he were covered with bells. Away for the provender!"

The publican went about his preparations, and had no sooner left the room than the Captain called the landlady, who at his invitation showed herself at the door.

"Come in, sweetheart. Good Mistress Daffodil," he said, "I called that you may lend us your help to laugh: since your rufflers are dispersed, your smokers obnubilated in their own clouds, your tipplers strewed upon the benches, and nothing more left for you to do in the tap-room, we would have your worshipful and witty company here in the parlor. So, come in, my princess of pleasant thoughts, and make us merry.

"There is nothing but clinking of cans and swaggering speeches where you are, Captain Dauntrees," said the hostess." "An honest woman had best be little seen in your company. It is a wonder you ever got out of the Low Countries, where, what with drinking with boors and quarreling with belted bullies, your three years' service was enough to put an end to a thousand fellows of your humor."

"There's destiny in it, dame. I was born to be the delight of your eyes. It was found in my horoscope, when my nativity was cast, that a certain jolly mistress of a most-especially-to-be-commended inn, situate upon a delectable point of land in the New World, was to be greatly indebted to me, first, for the good fame of her wines amongst worshipful people ; and, secondly, for the sufficient and decent praise of her beauty. So was it read to my mother by the wise astrologer. And then, dame, you slander the virtue of the Low Countries. Look at Arnold there : is there a more temperate, orderly, well-behaved liegeman in the world than the ranger? And did he not bring his sobriety with him from the very bosom of the land you rail against ?"

" If Arnold de la Grange is not all that you say of him," replied the hostess, " it is because he has lost some share of his good quality by consorting with you, Captain. Besides, Arnold has never been hackneyed in the wars."

" A Dutch head," said Arnold, laughing, " is not easily made to spin. In the Old World men can drink more than in the New : a Friesland fog is an excellent shaving horn, mistress !"

" Heaven help the men of the Old World, if they drink more than they do in our province !" exclaimed Mistress Weasel. " Look in the tap-room, and you may see the end of a day's work in at least ten great loons. One half are sound asleep, and the other of so dim sight that neither can see his neighbor."

" The better reason then, Mistress Dorothy," replied Daun-trees, " why you, a reputable woman, should leave such topers, and keep company with sober, waking, discreet friends. That cap becomes you, mistress. I never saw you in so dainty a head-gear. I honor it as a covering altogether worthy of your comeli-ness. Faith, it has been a rich piece of merchandise to me ! Upon an outlay of fourteen shillings which I paid for it, as a Michaelmas present to my excellent hostess, I have got in return, by way of profit, full thirteen bottles of Garret's choicest Canary, on my wager. Garret was obstinate, and would face me out with it that you wore it to church last Sunday, when I knew that you went only in your hood that day :——he has never an eye to look on you, dame, as he ought—so he must needs put it to a wager. Well, as this is the first day you have ever gone abroad in it, here I drink to thee and thy cap, upon my knees—Success to its travels, and joy to the merry eye that sparkles below it! Come, Arnold, drink to that, and get Pamesack another glass of aqua vitæ:—top off to the hostess, comrades!"

The toast was drank, and at this moment Garret Weasel returned to the room. A sign from him informed the Captain that the preparation he had been despatched to make was accomplished.

"How looks the night, Garret?" inquired Dauntrees: "when have we the moon?"

"It is a clear starlight, and calm," replied the publican; "the moon will not show herself till near morning."

"Have you heard the news, mistress?" inquired the Captain, with an expression of some eagerness; "there is pleasant matter current, concerning the mercer's wife at the Blue Triangle. But you must have heard it before this?"

"No, truly, not I," replied the hostess.

"Indeed!" said Dauntrees, "then there's a month's amusement for you. You owe the sly jade a grudge, mistress."

"In faith I do," said the dame, smiling, "and would gladly pay it.

"You may pay it off with usury now," added the Captain, "with no more trouble than telling the story. It is a rare jest, and will not die quickly."

"I pray you to tell it me, good Captain—give me all of it," exclaimed the dame eagerly.

"Peregrine Cadger, the mercer, you know," said the Captain —"but it is a long story, and will take time to rehearse it. Garret, how comes it that you did not tell this matter to your wife, as I charged you to do ?" he inquired with a wink at the publican.

"I resolved to tell it to her," said Weasel, "but, I know not how, it ran out of my mind—the day being a busy one——"

"A busy day to thee!" exclaimed the spouse. "Thou, who hast no more to do than a stray in the pound, what are you fit for, if it be not to do as you are commanded? But go on, Captain ; the story would only be marred by Garret's telling—go on yourself—I am impatient to hear it."

"I pray you, what o'clock is it, mistress ?" asked the Captain.

"It is only near nine. It matters not for the hour—go on."

"Nine!" exclaimed Dauntrees ; "truly, dame, I must leave the story for Master Garret. Nine, said you? By my sword, I have overstaid my time! I have business with the Lord Proprietary before he goes to his bed. There are papers at the fort which should have been delivered to his Lordship before this."

"Nay, Captain," said the hostess, "if it be but the delivery of a packet, it may be done by some other hand. There is Driving Dick in the tap-room : he shall do your bidding in the matter. Do not let so light a business as that take you away."

"To-morrow, dame, and I will tell you the tale."

"To-night, Captain—to-night."

"Truly, I must go ; the papers should be delivered by a trusty hand—I may not leave it to an ordinary messenger. Now if Garret—but I will ask no such service from the good man at this time of night ; it is a long way. No, no, I must do my own errand."

"There is no reason upon earth," said the landlady, "why Garret should not do it : it is but a step to the fort and back."

"I can take my nag and ride there in twenty minutes," said

Garret. "I warrant you his Lordship will think the message wisely entrusted to me."

"Then get you gone, without parley," exclaimed the dame.

" The key of the stable, wife," said Garret.

" If you will go, Master Garret," said Dauntrees—" and it is very obliging of you—do it quickly. Tell Nicholas Verbrack to look in my scrutoire ; he will find the packet addressed to his Lordship. Take it, and see it safely put into his Lordship's hands. Say to Nicholas, moreover, that I will be at the fort before ten to-night. You comprehend ?"

"I comprehend," replied Garret, as his wife gave him the key of the stable, and he departed from the room.

" Now, Captain."

" Well, mistress : you must know that Peregrine Cadger, the mercer, who in the main is a discreet man———"

" Yes."

" A discreet man—I mean, bating some follies which you wot of ; for this trading and trafficking naturally begets foresight. A man has so much to do with the world in that vocation, and the world, Mistress Dorothy, is inclined by temper to be somewhat knavish, so that they who have much to do with it learn cautions which other folks do not. Now, in our calling of soldiership, caution is a sneaking virtue which we soon send to the—no matter where ; and thereby you may see how it is that we are more honest than other people. Caution and honesty do not much consort together."

" But of the mercer's wife, Captain."

" Ay, the mercer's wife—I shall come to her presently. Well, Peregrine, as you have often seen, is a shade or so jealous of that fussock, his wife, who looks, when she is tricked out in her new russet grogram cloak, more like a brown haycock in motion than a living woman."

5

"Yes," interrupted the dame, laughing, "and with a sun burnt top. Her red hair on her shoulders is no better, I trow."

"Her husband, who at best is but a cotquean—one of those fellows who has a dastardly fear of his wife, which, you know, Mistress Dorothy, truly makes both man and wife to be laughed at. A husband should have his own way, and follow his humor, no matter whether the dame rails or not. You agree with me in this, Mistress Weasel?"

"In part, Captain. I am not for stinting a husband in his lawful walks; but the wife should have an eye to his ways: she may counsel him."

"Oh, in reason, I grant; but she should not chide him, I mean, nor look too narrowly into his hours, that's all. Now Peregrine's dame has a free foot, and the mercer himself somewhat of a sulky brow. Well, Halfpenny, the chapman, who is a mad wag for mischief, and who is withal a sure customer of the mercer's in small wares, comes yesternight to Peregrine Cadger's house, bringing with him worshipful Master Lawrence Hay, the viewer."

At this moment the sound of horse's feet from the court-yard showed that Garret Weasel had set forth on his ride.

"Arnold, I am keeping you waiting," said Dauntrees. "Fill up another cup for yourself and Pamesack, and go your ways. Stay not for me, friends; or if it pleases you, wait for me in the tap-room. I will be ready in a brief space."

The ranger and the Indian, after swallowing another glass, withdrew.

"The viewer," continued Dauntrees, "is a handsome man—and a merry man on occasion, too. I had heard it whispered before—but not liking to raise a scandal upon a neighbor, I kept my thoughts to myself—that the mercer's wife had rather a warm side for the viewer. But be that as it may: there was the most laughable prank played on the mercer by Halfpenny and the viewer together, last night, that ever was heard of. It was thus: they had a game at Hoodman-blind, and when it fell to Lawrence to be the seeker, somehow the fat termagant was caught in his arms, and so the hood next came to her. Well, she was blindfolded; and there was an agreement all round that no one should speak a word."

"Ay, I understand—I see it," said the hostess, eagerly drawing her chair nearer to the Captain.

"No, you would never guess," replied Dauntrees, "if you cudgelled your brains from now till Christmas. But I can show you, Mistress Dorothy, better by the acting of the scene. Here, get down on your knees, and let me put your kerchief over your eyes."

"What can that signify?" inquired the dame.

"Do it, mistress—you will laugh at the explosion. Give me the handkerchief. Down, dame, upon your marrow bones :—it is an excellent jest and worth the learning."

The landlady dropped upon her knees, and the Captain secured the bandage round her eyes.

"How many fingers, dame?" he asked, holding his hand before her face.

"Never a finger can I see, Captain."

"It is well. Now stand up—forth and away! That was the word given by the viewer. Turn, Mistress Dorothy, and grope through the room. Oh, you shall laugh at this roundly. Grope, grope, dame."

The obedient and marvelling landlady began to grope through the apartment, and Dauntrees, quietly opening the door, stole off to the tap-room, where being joined by his comrades, they hied with all speed towards the fort, leaving the credulous dame floundering after a jest, at least until they got beyond the hail of her voice.

CHAPTER XI.

Pale lights on Cadez' rocks were seen,
And midnight voices heard to moan,
'Twas even said the blasted oak,
Convulsive, heaved a hollow groan.
And to this day the peasant still,
With cautious fear, avoids the ground,
In each wild branch a spectre sees,
And trembles at each rising ground.
THE SPIRIT'S BLASTED TREE.

DAUNTREES, after his unmannerly escape from the credulous landlady, hastened with his two companions, at a swinging gait, along the beach to the fort, where they found Garret Weasel waiting for them in a state of eager expectation.

"Is the dame likely to be angry, Captain?" were the publican's first words. "Does she suspect us for a frisk to-night? Adsheartlikens, it is a perilous adventure for the morrow! You shall bear the burden of that reckoning, Master Captain."

"I left Mistress Dorothy groping for a secret at Hoodman-blind," replied the Captain, laughing. "She has found it before now, and by my computation is in the prettiest hurricane that ever brought a frown upon a woman's brow. She would bless the four quarters of you, Garret, if you should return home to-night, with a blessing that would leave a scorch-mark on you for the rest of your days. I shouldn't wonder presently to hear her feet pattering on the gravel of the beach in full pursuit of us—dark as it is: I have left her in a mood to tempt any unheard of danger for revenge. So, let us be away upon our errand. You have the eatables safe and the wine sound, worthy Weasel? Nicholas," he said, speaking to the Lieutenant, "are our horses saddled?"

"They are at the post on the other side of the parade," replied the Lieutenant.

"Alack!" exclaimed Weasel—"Alack for these pranks! Here will be a week's repentance. But a fig for conclusions!— in for a penny, in for a pound, masters. I have the basket well stored and in good keeping. It will be discreet to mount quickly —I will not answer against the dame's rapping at the gate to-night: she is a woman of spirit and valiant in her anger."

"Then let us be up and away," said the Captain, who was busily bestowing a pair of pistols in his belt and suspending his sword across his body.

"A cutlass and pistols for me," said the publican, as he selected his weapons from several at hand.

Arnold and Pamesack were each provided with a carbine, when Dauntrees, throwing his cloak across his shoulders, led the way to the horses, where the party having mounted, sallied through the gate of the fort at a gallop.

Their road lay around the head of St. Inigoe's creek, and soon became entangled in dark, woody ravines and steep acclivities, which presented, at this hour, no small interruption to their progress. Pamesack, on a slouching pony, his legs dangling within a foot of the ground, led the way with an almost instinctive knowledge of his intricate path, which might have defied a darker night. The stars, shining through a crisp and cloudless atmosphere, enabled the party to discern the profile of the tree tops, and disclosed to them, at intervals, the track of this solitary road with sufficient distinctness to prevent their entirely losing it.

They had journeyed for more than two hours in the depths of

the forest before they approached the inlet of St. Jerome's. Dauntrees had beguiled the time by tales of former adventures, and
now and then by sallies of humor provoked by the dubious valor
of the innkeeper,—for Weasel, although addicted to the vanity
of exhibiting himself in the light of a swashing, cut-and-thrust
comrade in an emprise of peril, was nevertheless unable, this night,
to suppress the involuntary confession of a lurking faint-hearted-
ness at the result of the present venture. This misgiving showed
itself in his increased garrulity and in the exaggerated tone of his
vauntings of what he had done in sundry emergencies of hazard,
as well as of what he had made up his mind to do on the present
occasion if they should be so fortunate as to encounter any peculiarly severe stress of fortune. Upon such topics the party grew
jovial and Dauntrees laughed at the top of his voice.

"The vintner's old roystering courses would make us lose our
road in downright blindness from laughing," he said, as, checking
himself in one of these outbreaks, he reined up his horse. "Where
are we, Pamesack? I surely hear the stroke of the tide upon the
beach ;—are we so near St. Jerome's, or have we missed the track
and struck the bay shore short of our aim?"

"The she-fox does not run to her den where she has left her
young, by a track more sure than mine to-night," replied the
guide :—"it is the wave striking upon the sand at the head of
the inlet : you may see the stars on the water through yonder
wood."

"Pamesack says true," added Arnold. "He has found his
way better than a hound."

A piece of cleared land, or old field, a few acres in width, lay
between the travellers and the water, which began now to glim-
mer on their sight through a fringe of wood that grew upon the
margin of the creek or inlet, and the fresh breeze showed that the
broad expanse of the Chesapeake was at no great distance

"The Wizard's Chapel," said Dauntrees, "by my reckoning then, should be within a mile of this spot. It were a good point of soldiership to push forward a vanguard. That duty, Garret, will best comport with your madcap humor—there may be pith in it: so, onward, man, until you are challenged by some out-post of the Foul One—we will tarry here for your report. In the mean time, leave us your hamper of provender. Come, man of cold iron, be alert—your stomach is growing restive for a deed of valor."

"You are a man trained to pike and musketoon," replied the publican; "and have the skill to set a company, as men commonly fight with men. But I humbly opine, Captain, that our venture to-night stands in no need of vanguard, patrol or picket. We have unearthly things to wrestle with, and do not strive according to the usages of the wars. I would not be slow to do your bidding, but that I know good may not come of it: in my poor judgment we should creep towards the Chapel together, not parting company. I will stand by thee, Captain, with a sharp eye and ready hand."

"Your teeth will betray us, Master Vintner, even at a score rods from the enemy," said Dauntrees: "they chatter so rudely that your nether jaw is in danger. If you are cold, man, button up your coat."

"Of a verity, it is a cold night, and my coat is none of the thickest," replied Weasel with an increasing shudder.

"I understand you, Garret," responded the Captain with a laugh; "we must drink. So, friends, to the green grass, and fasten your horses to the trees whilst we warm up the liver of our forlorn vintner with a cup. We can all take that physic."

This command was obeyed by the immediate dismounting of the party and their attack upon one of the flasks in the basket.

"It has a rare smack for a frosty night," said Dauntrees as

he quaffed a third and fourth cup. "When I was in Tours I visited the Abbey of Marmoustier, and there drank a veritable potation from the huge tun which the blessed St. Martin himself filled, by squeezing a single cluster of grapes. It has the repute of being the kindliest wine in all Christendom for the invigorating of those who are called to do battle with the devil. The monks of the abbey have ever found it a most deadly weapon against Satan. And truly, Master Weasel, if I did not know that this wine was of the breed of the islands, I should take it to be a dripping from the holy tun I spoke of :—it hath the like virtue of defiance of Beelzebub. So, drink—drink again, worthy purveyor and valiant adjutant !"

"What is that ?" exclaimed Weasel, taking the cup from his lips before he had finished the contents. "There is something far off like the howl of a dog, and yet more devilish I should say—did ye not hear it, masters ? I pray heaven there be no evil warning in this :—I am cold—still cold, Captain Dauntrees."

"Tush, it is the ringing of your own ears, Garret, or it may be, like enough, some devil's cur that scents our footsteps. Make yourself a fire, and whilst you grow warm we will take a range, for a brief space, round the Chapel. You shall guard the forage till we return."

"That is well thought of," replied the innkeeper quickly. "Light and heat will both be useful in our onslaught :—while you three advance towards the shore I will keep a look-out here ; for there is no knowing what devices the enemy may have a-foot to take us by surprise."

Some little time was spent in kindling a fire, which had no sooner begun to blaze than Dauntrees, with the Ranger and the Indian, set forth on their reconnoissance of the Chapel, leaving Weasel assured that he was rendering important service in guarding the provender and comforting himself by the blazing fagots.

They walked briskly across the open ground towards the water, and as they now approached the spot which common rumor had invested with so many terrors, even these bold adventurers themselves were not without some misgivings. The universal belief in supernatural agencies in the concerns of mankind, which distinguished the era of this narrative, was sufficient to infuse a certain share of apprehension into the minds of the stoutest men, and it was hardly reckoned to derogate from the courage of a tried soldier that he should quail in spirit before the dreadful presence of the Powers of Darkness. Dauntrees had an undoubting faith in the malignant influences which were said to hover about the Wizard's Chapel, and nothing but the pride and subordination of his profession could have impelled him to visit this spot at an hour when its mysterious and mischievous inhabitants were supposed to be endued with their fullest power to harm. The Ranger was not less keenly impressed with the same feelings, whilst Pamesack, credulous and superstitious as all of his tribe, was, like them, endowed with that deeply-imprinted fatalism, which taught him to suppress his emotions, and which rendered him seemingly indifferent to whatever issue awaited his enterprise.

" By my troth, Arnold," said Dauntrees, as they strode forward, " although we jest at yonder white-livered vintner, this matter we have in hand might excuse an ague in a stouter man. I care not to confess that the love I bear his Lordship, together with some punctilio of duty, is the only argument that might bring me here to-night. I would rather stand a score pikes in an onset with my single hand, where the business is with flesh and blood, than buffet with a single imp of the Wizard. I have heard of over-bold men being smote by the evil eye of a beldam

5*

bag ; and I once knew a man of unquenchable gaiety suddenly
made mute and melancholy by the weight of a blow dealt by a
hand which was not to be seen : the remainder of his life was
spent in sorrowful penance.   They say these spirits are quick to
punish rashness."

"As Lord Charles commands we must do his bidding," replied the forester.   "When the business in hand must be done, I
never stop to think of the danger of it.   If we should not get
back, Lord Charles has as good men to fill our places.   I have
been scared more than once by these night devils, till my hair
lifted my cap with the fright, but I never lost my wits so far as
not to strike or to run at the good season."

"*Laet lopen die lopen luste*, as we used to say in Holland,"
returned the Captain.   "I am an old rover and have had my
share of goblins, and never flinched to sulphur or brimstone,
whether projected by the breath of a devil or a culverin.   I am
not to be scared now from my duty by any of Paul Kelpy's brood,
though I say again I like not this strife with shadows.   His
Lordship shall not say we failed in our outlook.   I did purpose,
before we set out, to talk with Father Pierre concerning this
matter, but Garret's wine and his wife together put it out of my
head."

"The holy father would only have told you," replied Arnold,
"to keep a Latin prayer in your head and Master Weasel's wine
and wife both out of it."

"So he would, Arnold, and it would have gone more against
the grain than a hair-shirt penance.   I have scarce a tag of a
prayer in my memory, not even a line of the Fac Salve ; and I
have moreover a most special need for a flask of that vintage of
Teneriffe on a chilly night ;—and then, as you yourself was a
witness, I had most pressing occasion to practice a deceit upon
Mistress Dorothy.   The Priest's counsel would have been wasted

words—that's true : so we were fain to do our errand to-night without the aid of the church.—Why do you halt, Pamesack ?"

" I hear the tread of a foot," replied the Indian.

" A deer stalking on the shore of the creek," said Dauntrees.

" More like the foot of a man," returned Pamesack, in a lowered voice ; " we should talk less to make our way safe.— There is the growl of a dog."

Arnold now called the attention of his companions to the outlines of a low hut which was barely discernible through the wood where an open space brought the angle of the roof into relief against the water of the creek, and as they approached near enough to examine the little structure more minutely, they were saluted by the surly bark of a deep throated dog, fiercely redoubled. At the same time the sound of receding footsteps was distinctly audible.

" Who dwells here ?" inquired Dauntrees, striking the door with the hilt of his sword.

There was no answer, and the door gave way to the thrust and flew wide upon. The apartment was tenantless. A few coals of fire gleaming from the embers, and a low bench furnished with a blanket, rendered it obvious that this solitary abode had been but recently deserted by its possessor. A hasty survey of the hut, which was at first fiercely disputed by the dog—a cross-grained and sturdy mastiff—until a sharp blow from a staff which the forester bestowed sent him growling from the premises, satisfied the explorers that so far, at least, they had encountered nothing supernatural ; and without further delay or comment upon this incident they took their course along the margin of St. Jerome's Creek. After a short interval, the beating of the waves upon the beach informed them that they were not far from the beach of the Chesapeake. Here a halt and an attentive examination of the locality made them aware that they stood upon a bank which descended somewhat abruptly to the level of the beach that lay some fifty yards or more beyond them. In the dim starlight they were able to trace the profile of a low but capacious tenement which stood almost on the tide mark.

"It is the Chapel !" said Dauntrees, in an involuntary whisper as he touched the Ranger's arm.

"It is Paul Kelpy's house, all the same as I have known it these twenty years :—a silent and wicked house," whispered Arnold, in reply.

"And a pretty spot for the Devil to lurk in," said Dauntrees, resuming his ordinary tone.

"Hold, Captain," interrupted the Ranger, "no foul words so near the Haunted House. The good saints be above us !" he added, crossing himself and muttering a short prayer.

"Follow me down the bank," said Dauntrees, in a low but resolute voice ; "but first look to your carbines that they be charged and primed. I will break in the door of this ungodly den and ransack its corners before I leave it. Holy St. Michael, the fiend is in the Chapel, and warns us away !" he exclaimed, as suddenly a flash of crimson light illuminated every window of the building. "It is the same warning given to Burton and myself once before. Stand your ground, comrades ; we shall be beset by these ministers of sin !"

As the flashes of this lurid light were thrice repeated, Pamesack was seen on the edge of the bank fixed like a statue, with foot and arm extended, looking with a stern gaze towards this appalling spectacle. Arnold recoiled apace and brought his hand across his eyes, and was revealed in this posture as he exclaimed in his marked Dutch accent, "The fisherman's blood is turned to fire : we had best go no further, masters." Dauntrees had advanced half-way down .the bank, and the glare disclosed him as suddenly arrested in his career ; his sword gleamed above his head whilst his short cloak was drawn by the motion of his left arm under his chin ; and his broad beaver, pistoled belt, and wide boots, now tinged with the preternatural light, gave to his figure that rich effect which painters are pleased to copy.

"I saw Satan's imps within the chamber," exclaimed the Captain. "I saw the very servitors of the Fiend ! They are many and mischievous, and shall be defied though we battle with the Prince of the Air. What ho, bastards of Beelzebub, I defy thee ! in the name of our patron, the holy and blessed St. Ignatius, I defy thee !"

There was a deeper darkness as Dauntrees rushed almost to the door of the house with his sword in his hand. Again the same deep flashes of fire illumed the windows, and two or three strange figures of men, in muffled cloaks, were seen, for the instant, within. Dauntrees retreated a few steps nearer to his companions, and drawing a pistol, held it ready for instant use. It was discharged at the windows with the next flash of the light, and the report was followed by a hoarse and yelling laugh from the tenants of the house.

"Once more I defy thee !" shouted the Captain, with a loud voice : "and in the name of our holy church, and by the order of the Lord Proprietary, I demand what do you here with these hellish rites ?"

The answer was returned in a still louder laugh, and in a shot fired at the challenger, the momentary light of the explosion revealing, as Dauntrees imagined, a cloaked figure presenting a harquebuss through the window.

"Protect yourselves, friends !" he exclaimed, "with such shelter as you may find," at the same time retreating to the cover of an oak which stood upon the bank. "These demons show weapons like our own. I will e'en ply the trade with thee, accursed spirits !" he added, as he discharged a second pistol.

The Ranger and Pamesack had already taken shelter, and
their carbines were also levelled and fired. Some two or three
shots were returned from the house accompanied with the same
rude laugh which attended the first onset, and the scene, for a moment, would have been thought rather to resemble the assault
and defence of mortal foes, than the strife of men with intangible
goblins, but that there were mixed with it other accompaniments
altogether unlike the circumstance of mortal battle; a heavy
sound, as of rolling thunder, echoed from the interior of the
chapel, and in the glimpses of light, antic figures within were
discerned dancing with strange and preposterous motions.

"It avails us not to contend against these fiends," said Dauntrees. "They are enough to maintain their post against us,
even if they fought with human implements. Our task is accomplished by gaining sight of the Chapel and its inmates. We
may certify what we have seen to his Lordship; so, masters,
move warily and quickly rearward. Ay, laugh again, you
juggling minions of the devil!" he said, as a hoarse shout of exultation resounded from the house, when the assailants commenced their retreat. "Come into the field as veritable men and
we may deal with you! Forward, Arnold; if we tarry, our
retreat may be vexed with dangers against which we are not
provided."

"I hope this is the last time we shall visit this devil's den,"
said Arnold, as he obeyed the Captain's injunction, and moved,
as rapidly as his long stride would enable him to walk, from the
scene of their late assault.

Whilst these events were passing, I turn back to the publican,
who was left a full mile in the rear to guard the baggage and
keep up the fire,—a post, as he described it, of no small
danger.

It was with a mistrusting conscience, as to the propriety of his separation from his companions, that Garret, when he had leisure for reflection, set himself to scanning his deportment at this juncture. His chief scruple had reference to the point of view in which Dauntrees and Arnold de la Grange would hereafter represent this incident : would they set it down, as Weasel hoped they might, to the account of a proper and soldier-like disposition of the forces, which required a detachment to defend a weak point? or would they not attribute his hanging back to a want of courage, which his conscience whispered was not altogether so wide of truth? There are many brave men, he reflected, who have a constitutional objection to fighting in the dark, and he was rather inclined to rank himself in that class. "In the dark," said he, as he sat down by the fire, with his hands locked across his knees, which were drawn up before him in grasshopper angles, and looked steadily at the blazing brushwood ; in the dark a man cannot see—that stands to reason. And it makes a great difference, let me tell you, masters, when you can't see your enemy. A brave man, by nature, requires light. And, besides, what sort of an enemy do we fight? Hobgoblins—not mortal man—for I would stand up to any mortal man in Christendom ; ay, and with odds against me. I have done it before now. But these whirring and whizzing ghosts and their cronies, that fly about one's ears like cats, and purr and mew like bats—what am I saying? no, fly like bats and mew like cats—one may cut and carve at them with his blade with no more wound than a boy's wooden truncheon makes upon the wind. Besides, the Captain, who is all in all in his command, hath set me here to watch, which, as it were, was a forbidding of me to go onward. He must be obeyed : a good soldier disputes no order, although it go against his stomach. It was the Captain's wish that I should keep strict watch and ward here on the skirt of the wood ; otherwise I should have followed him—

and with stout heart and step, I warrant you ! But the Captain
hath a soldierly sagacity in his cautions ; holding this spot, as he
wisely hath done, to be an open point of danger, an inlet, as it
were, to circumvent his march, and therefore straightly to be
looked to.   Well, let the world wag, and the upshot be what it
may, here are comforts at hand, and I will not stint to use
them."

Saying this the self-satisfied martialist opened the basket
and solaced his appetite with a slice of pasty and a draught of
wine.

" I will now perform a turn of duty," he continued, after his
refreshment ; and accordingly drawing his hanger, he set forth to
make a short circuit into the open field.   He proceeded with becoming caution on this perilous adventure, looking slyly at every
weed or bush that lay in his route, shuddering with a chilly fear
at the sound of his own footsteps, and especially scanning, with a
disturbed glance, the vibrations of his long and lean shadow which
was sharply cast by the fire across the level ground.   He had
wandered some fifty paces into the field, on this valorous outlook,
when he bethought him that he had ventured far enough, and
might now return, deeming it more safe to be near the fire and
the horses than out upon a lonesome plain, which he believed to
be infested by witches and their kindred broods.   He had scarcely
set his face towards his original post when an apparition came
upon his sight that filled him with horror, and caused his hair to
rise like bristles.   This was the real bodily form and proportions of
such a spectre as might be supposed to prefer such a spot—an
old woman in a loose and ragged robe, who was seen gliding up
to the burning fagots with a billet of pine in her hand, which she
lighted at the fire and then waved above her head as she advanced
into the field towards the innkeeper.   Weasel's tongue clave to
the roof of his mouth, and his teeth chattered audibly against each

other, his knees smote together, and his eyes glanced steadfastly upon the phantom. For a moment he lost the power of utterance or motion, and when these began to return, as the hag drew nearer, his impulse was to fly; but his bewildered reflection came to his aid and suggested greater perils in advance : he therefore stood stock still.

"Heaven have mercy upon me !—the Lord have mercy upon me, a sinner !" he ejaculated ; "I am alone, and the enemy has come upon me."

"Watcher of the night," said a voice, in a shrill note, "draw nigh. What do you seek on the wold ?"

"Tetra grammaton, Ahaseel—in the name of the Holy Evangels, spare me !" muttered the innkeeper, fruitlessly ransacking his memory for some charm against witches, and stammering out an incoherent jargon. "Abracadabra—spare me, excellent and worthy dame ! I seek no hurt to thee. I am old, mother, too old and with too many sins of my own to account for, to wish harm to any one, much less to the good woman of this wold. O Lord, O Lord ! why was I seduced upon this fool's errand ?"

"Come nigh, old man, when I speak to you. Why do you loiter there ?" shouted the witch, as she stood erect some twenty paces in front of the publican and beckoned him with her blazing fagot. "What dost thou mutter ?"

"I but sported with my shadow, mother," replied Weasel, with a tremendous attempt at a laugh, as he approached the questioner, in an ill assumed effort at composure and cheerfulness. "I was fain to divert myself with an antic, till some friends of mine, who left me but a moment since, returned. How goes the night with you, dame ?"

"Merrily," replied the hag, as she set up a shrill laugh which more resembled a scream, "merrily ; I cannot but laugh to find the henpecked vintner of St. Mary's at this time of night within the sound of the tide at the Black Chapel. I know your errand, old chapman of cheap liquors, and why you have brought your cronies. You pretend to be a liegeman of his Lordship, and you travel all night to cheat him of five shillings. You will lie on the morrow with as sad a face as there is in the hundred. I know you."

"You know all things, worthy dame, and I were a fool to keep a secret from you. What new commodity, honest mistress, shall I find with Rob ? The port is alive with a rumor of the Olive Branch ; I would be early with the Cripple. Ha, ha !" he added, with a fearful laugh, "thou seest I am stirring in my trade."

"Garret Weasel," said the beldam, "you may take it for a favor, past your deservings, that Rob will see you alone at his hut even in day time : but it is as much as your life is worth to bring your huffcap brawlers to St. Jerome's at midnight. It is not lawful ground for you, much less for the hot-brained fools who bear you company. Who showed them the path to my cabin, that I must be driven out at this hour ?"

"Worthy mistress, indeed I know not. I am ignorant of what you say ?"

"They will call themselves friends to the Chapel ; but we have no friends to the Chapel amongst living men. The Chapel belongs to the dead and the tormentors of the dead. So follow your cronies and command them back. I warn you to follow, and bring them back, as you would save them from harm. Ha ! look you, it is come already !" she exclaimed, raising her torch in the air, as the flashes from the Haunted House illumined the horizon : "the seekers have aroused our sentries, and there shall be angry buffets to the back of it !" At this moment the first shot was heard. "Friends, forsooth !" she shouted at the top of her voice : "friends, are ye ? there is the token that you are known to be false liars. Wo to the fool that plants his foot before the Chapel! Stand there, Garret Weasel: I must away. Follow me but a step—raise thy head to look after my path, and I will strike thee blind and turn thee into a drivelling idiot for the rest of thy days. Remember—"

In uttering this threat the figure disappeared; Garret knew not how, as he strictly obeyed the parting injunction, and his horrors were greatly increased by the report of the several shots which now reached his ear from the direction of the Black House.

He had hardly recovered himself sufficiently to wander back to the fire, before Dauntrees, Arnold, and Pamesack arrived, evidently flurried by the scene through which they had passed, as well as by the rapidity of their retreat.

"Some wine, Garret! some wine, old master of the tap!" was Dauntrees' salutation; "and whilst we regale as briefly as we may, have our horses loose from the trees; we must mount and away. To the horses, Garret! We will help ourselves."

"I pray you, Master Captain," inquired the publican, having now regained his self-possession, "what speed at the Chapel? Oh, an we have all had a night of it! Sharp encounters all round, masters! I can tell you a tale!"

"Stop not to prate now," interrupted Dauntrees, in a voice choked by the huge mouthful of the pasty he was devouring; "we shall discourse as we ride. That flask, Arnold—I must have another draught e'er we mount, and then, friends, to horse as quickly as you may; we may be followed; we may have ghost, devil, and man of flesh, all three, at our heels."

"I have had store of them, I can tell you—ghosts and devils without number," said Weasel, as he brought the horses forward.

"You shall be tried by an inquest of both, for your life, if

you tarry another instant," interposed the Captain, as he sprang
into his saddle.

"What! are we set upon, comrades?" cried out the vintner,
manfully, as he rose to his horse's back, and pricked forward
until he got between Pamesack and Arnold. "Are we set
upon? Let us halt and give them an accolado; we are enough
for them, I warrant you! Oh, but it had well nigh been a
bloody night!" he continued, as the whole party trotted briskly
from the ground. "We had work to do, masters, and may tell
of it to-morrow. Good Pamesack, take this basket from me, it
impedes my motion in these bushes. Master Arnold, as we
must ride here in single files, let me get before: I would speak
with the Captain. Who should I see, Captain Dauntrees,"
continued the publican, after these arrangements were made,
and he had thrust himself into the middle of the line of march,
and all now proceeded at a slackened pace, "but that most
notorious and abominable hag, the woman of Warrington, Kate,
who lives, as every body knows, on the Cliffs. She must needs
come trundling down before me, astride a broomstick, with a
black cat upon her shoulder, and sail up to the fire which I had
left, for a space, to make a round on my watch—for you may be
sworn a strict watch I made of it, going even out of my way to
explore the more hidden and perilous lurking-places where one
might suspect an enemy to lie. So, whilst I was gone on this
quest, she whips in and seats herself by the fire, with a whole
score of devils at their antics around her. Then up I come,
naturally surprised at this audacity, and question them, partly in
soldier-wise, showing my sword ready to make good my speech,
and partly by adjuration, which soon puts the whole bevy to
flight, leaving Kate of Warrington at mercy: and there I
constrained her to divulge the secrets of the Chapel. She said
there had been devilish work under that roof, and would be

again; when pop, and bang, and slash, and crash, I heard the outbreak, and saw the devil's lights that were flashed. I could hold no longer parley with the hag, but was just moving off at full speed to your relief, determined in this need to desert my post—which, in my impatience to lend you a hand, I could not help—when I heard your footfall coming back, and so I was fain to bide your coming."

"A well conceived sally of soldiership," said Dauntrees, "and spoken with a cavalier spirit, Master Garret. It has truth upon the face of it: I believe every word. It shall serve you a good turn with his Lordship. What does Kate of Warrington in this neighborhood? She travels far on her broomstick—unless, indeed, what seems likely, she has taken her quarters in the cabin we disturbed to-night. These crows will be near their carrion."

By degrees the party, as they pursued their homeward journey, grew drowsy. The publican had lost his garrulity, and nodded upon his horse. Arnold and Pamesack rode in silence, until Dauntrees, as if waking up from a reverie, said—

"Well, friends, we return from no barren mission to-night. His Lordship may have some satisfaction in our story; particularly in the vintner's. We shall be ready to report to his Lordship by noon, and after that we shall hasten to quiet our Dame Dorothy. The night is far spent: I should take it, Arnold, to be past three o'clock, by the rising of the moon. At peep of day we shall be snug upon our pallets, with no loss of relish for a sleep which will have been well earned."

As the Captain continued to urge his journey, which he did with the glee that waits upon a safe deliverance from an exploit of hazard, he turned his face upwards to the bright orb which threw a cheerful light over the scenery of the road-side, and in the distance flung a reflection, as of burnished silver, over the

5*

broad surface of St. Mary's river, as seen from the height which the travellers were now descending. Not more than two miles of their route remained to be achieved, when the Captain broke forth with an old song of that day, in a voice which would not have discredited a professor :

> " The moon, the moon, the jolly moon,
> And a jolly old queen is she !
> She hath stroll'd o' nights this thousand year,
> With ever the best of company.
>   Sing, Hic and hoc sumus nocturno,
>   Huzza for the jolly old moon !"

" Why, Garret, vintner—asleep, man ?" inquired the Captain. " Why do you not join in the burden ?"

"To your hand, Captain," exclaimed Weasel, rousing himself and piping forth a chorus—

> " Hic and hoc sumus nocturno,
> Huzza for the jolly old moon !"

which he did not fail to repeat at the top of his voice at each return.

Dauntrees proceeded :

> " She trails a royal following,
>   And a merry mad court doth keep,
>   With her chirping boys that walk i' the shade,
>   And wake when the bailiff's asleep.
>   Sing, Hic and hoc sumus nocturno
>   Huzza for the jolly old moon !
>
> " Master Owl he is her chancellor,
>   And the bat is his serving-man ;
>   They tell no tales of what they see,
>   But wink when we turn up the can.
>   Sing, Hic and hoc sumus nocturno,
>   Huzza for the jolly old moon !
>
> " Her chorister is Goodman Frog,
>   With a glow-worm for his link ;
>   And all who would make court to her,
>   Are fain, good faith ! to drink.
>   Sing, Hic and hoc sumus nocturno,
>   Huzza for the jolly old moon !"

This ditty was scarcely concluded—for it was spun out with several noisy repetitions of the chorus—before the troop reined up at the gate of the Fort. The drowsy sentinel undid the bolt at the Captain's summons, and, in a very short space, the wearied adventurers were stretched in the enjoyment of that most satisfactory of physical comforts, the deep sleep of tired men.

CHAPTER XII.

There remains
A rugged trunk, dismember'd and unsightly,
Waiting the bursting of the final bolt
To splinter it to shivers.

THE DOOM OF DEVORGOIL.

THE shore of the Chesapeake between Cape St. Michael—as the northern headland at the mouth of the Potomac was denominated by the early settlers—and the Patuxent, is generally flat, and distinguished by a clear pebbly beach or strand. The shore, comprising about twenty miles, is intersected by a single creek, that of St. Jerome, which enters the bay some five or six miles north of the Potomac. The line of beach, which I have referred to, is here and there relieved by small elevations which in any other region would scarce deserve the name, but which are sufficiently prominent in this locality to attract remark. From the general level of the country they rise high enough to afford a clear prospect over the wide waters, and no less to distinguish the landward perspective to the mariner whose eye eagerly seeks the varieties of landscape as he holds his course up the bay. At a few points these small hills terminate immediately upon the tide in the abrupt form of a cliff, and, at others, take the shape of a knoll sinking away by a rapid, but grass-covered, declivity to the strand. This latter feature is observable in the vicinity of St. Jerome's, where the slope falls somewhat abruptly to the level of the tide, leaving something above fifty paces in width of low ground between its base and the ordinary water-mark. It was upon this flat that, in ancient times, stood the dwelling-house of Paul Kelpy the fisherman—a long, low building of deal boards, constructed somewhat in the shape of a warehouse or magazine. Some quarter of a mile farther up the beach, so sheltered under the brow of the slope as scarcely to be seen amongst the natural shrubbery that shaded it, stood a cottage or hut of very humble pretensions. It was so low that a man of ordinary height, while standing at the door, might lay his hand upon the eaves of the roof, and, correspondent to its elevation, it was so scanty in space as to afford but two apartments, of which the largest was not above ten feet square. It was strongly built of hewn logs, and the door, strengthened by nails thickly studded over its surface, was further fortified by a heavy padlock, which rendered it sufficiently impregnable against a sharper assault than might be counted on from such as ordinarily should find motive to molest the proprietor of such a dwelling.

A small enclosure surrounded the hut and furnished ground for some common garden plants which were not neglected in their culture. A few acres, on the higher plain above the bank, exhibited signs of husbandry ; and the small nets and other fishing tackle disposed about the curtilage, together with a skiff drawn up on the sand, gave evidence of the ostensible thrift by which the occupant of the hut obtained a livelihood.

To this spot I propose to introduce my reader, the day preceding that at which my story has been opened. It was about an hour before sunset, and a light drizzling rain, with a steady wind from the north-east, infused a chilly gloom into the air, and heightened the tone of solitude which prevailed over the scene. A thin curl of smoke which rose from the clumsy chimney of the hut gave a sign of habitation to the premises, and this was further confirmed by the presence of a large and cross-visaged

6

mastiff-bitch, whose heavy head might be discerned thrust forth
from beneath the sill of the gable,—a sullen warder of this sullen
place of strength. The waves, now propelled upon a flood tide,
rolled in upon the shore, and broke almost at the door of the
hut, with a hoarse and harsh and ceaseless plash. Far out over
the bay, the white caps of the wind-driven surge floated like
changing snow-drifts upon the surface of the waters. The water
fowl rose in squadrons above this murky waste and struggled to
windward, in a flight so low as frequently to shield them from
the sight in the spray. An old bald eagle perched on the loft-
iest branch of a lightning-riven tree, immediately upon the bank
above the hut, kept anxious watch upon her nest which, built in
the highest fork, rocked to and fro in the breeze, whilst her
screams of warning to her young seemed to answer to the din of
the waters.

In the larger apartment of the hut a few fagots blazed upon
the hearth, supplying heat to a pot that simmered above them,
the care of which, together with other culinary operations, engaged the attention of a brown, haggard and weather-beaten
woman, who plied this household duty with a silent and mechan-
ical thrift. She was not the only tenant of the dwelling. Remote from the hearth, and immediately below a small window,
sat, apparently upon the floor, a figure eminently calculated to
challenge observation. His features were those of a man of
seventy, sharp, shrewd and imprinted with a deep trace of care.
His frame indicated the possession, at an earlier period of his life,
of the highest degree of strength ; it was broad in the shoulders,
ample in chest, and still muscular, although deprived of its round-
ness by age. His dress, of coarse green serge, made into a doublet with skirts that fell both front and rear, secured by a
leathern belt, was so contrived as to conceal, in his present
posture, his lower extremities. A broad ruff received his locks

of iron gray, which fell over his back in crisp wiry curls : a thick grizzly beard, of the same hue, gave an elongation to his countenance which imparted to the observer the unpleasant impression of a head disproportionably large for the body, at least as seen in its present aspect. His eyes, dark and unusually clear, were sunk deep in their sockets, whilst a shaggy and matted brow, overhanging them like a porch, gave sometimes an almost preternatural brilliancy to their quick and changeful glances—like the sparkling of water when agitated in a well. It was observable from the dropping in of the upper jaw that he had lost his teeth, and this had given a tendency of the strong furrowed lines and seams, with which his features were marked, to converge towards the mouth.

His girdle sustained a long knife or dagger, which apparently constituted a part of his ordinary equipment ; and the oblique flash of his eye, and tremulous motion of his thin lip, betrayed a temperament, from which one might infer that this weapon of offence was not worn merely as an ornament of the person.

The individual described in this summary was familiar to report, throughout the province, as The Cripple. His true name was supposed to be Robert Swale,—but this was almost lost in the pervading popular designation of Rob of the Bowl, or Trencher Rob—an appellative which he had borne ever since his arrival in the province, now some fifteen years gone by. Of his history but little was known, and that little was duly mystified, in the public repute, by the common tendency in the vulgar mind to make the most of any circumstance of suspicion. The story went that he had been shipwrecked, on a winter voyage, upon this coast, and, after suffering incredible hardships, had saved his life only at the expense of the loss of both legs by frost. In this maimed condition he had reached the shore of the province, and some time afterwards built the hut in which he now dwelt, near

the mouth of St. Jerome's. Here he had passed many years,
without attracting other notice than such as the stinted charity
of the world affords when it is exercised upon the fate or fortunes
of an obscure recluse.   This observation began to find a broader
scope as soon as it became obvious that the hermit was not
altogether an object for almsgiving ; and the little world of this
part of the province discovering, in process of time, that he was
not absolutely penniless, were fain to take offence at the mystery
of his means of earning his frugal subsistence.   Before many
years, some few of the traders and country people round had
found out that Rob was occasionally possessed of good merchant-
able commodities much in request by the inhabitants of the port,
and dark whispers were sometimes circulated touching the manner in which he came by them.   These surmises were not made
topics of public discussion for two reasons ;—first, because it was
not inconvenient or unprofitable to the traders in the secret to
deal with Rob ;—and secondly, Rob was not a man to allow this
indulgence of idle speculation ; he was of an irascible temper, free
to strike when crossed, and, what was still more to be feared, had
friends who were not unwilling to take up his quarrel.   The loss
of his legs was supplied by a wooden bowl or trencher, of an
elliptical shape, to which his thighs were attached by a strap,
and this rude contrivance was swayed forward, when the owner
chose, by the aid of two short crutches, which enabled him to lift
himself from the ground and assume a progressive motion.   It
was to the exercise which this mode of locomotion imposed upon
his upper limbs, that the unusual breadth and squareness of his
figure about the shoulders, as well as the visible manifestations
of strength of arm for which he was remarkable, were in part,
perhaps, to be attributed.   Use had made him expert in the
management of his bowl, and he could keep pace pretty fairly
with an ordinary walker.   The Cripple was a man of unsocial

habits and ascetic life, although there were times in which his severe temper relaxed into an approach to companionable enjoyment, and then his intercourse with the few who had access to him was marked by a sarcastic humor and keen ridicule of human action which showed some grudge against the world, and, at the same time, denoted conversancy with mankind and by no means a deficiency of education. But, in general, his vein was peevish, and apt to vent itself in indiscriminate petulance or stern reproof.

A small painting of St. Romuald at his devotions, by the hand of Salvator himself, hung over a dressing table in the back room of the hut in which the bed of The Cripple was placed ; and this exquisite gem of art, which the possessor seemed duly to appreciate, was surmounted by a crucifix, indicating the religious faith in which he worshipped. This might be gathered also from a curious, antique pix, of heavy gilded metal, a ponderous missal with silver clasps, a few old volumes of the lives of the saints, and other furniture of the like nature, all of which denoted that the ingredient of a religious devotee formed an element in his singular compound of character.

The superiority of his mind and attainments over those of the mass of the inhabitants of the province had contributed to render The Cripple an object of some interest as well as of distrust amongst them, and this sentiment was heightened into one approaching to vulgar awe, by the reputation of the person who had always been somewhat in his confidence, and now attended him as his servitress and only domestic. This person was the ungainly and repulsive beldam whom I have already noticed as ministering in the household concerns of the hut. She was a woman who had long maintained a most unenviable fame as The Woman of Warrington, in the small hamlet of that name on the Cliffs of Patuxent, from whence she had been recently transplanted to perform the

domestic drudgery in which we have found her.   Her habitation
was a rude hovel some few hundred paces distant from the hut of
The Cripple, on the margin of St. Jerome's creek, and within gun
shot of the rear of the Black Chapel.   To this hovel, after her
daily work was done, she retired to pass the night, leaving her
master or patron to that solitude which he seemed to prefer to any
society.   The surly mastiff-bitch, we have noticed, alternately
kept guard at the hut of the master and domestic,—roving between the two in nightly patrol, with a gruff and unsocial fidelity,
—no unsuitable go-between to so strange a pair.   It will not be
wondered at, that, in a superstitious age, such an association as
this of The Cripple and the crone, in the vicinity of such a spot,
desecrated, as the fisherman's lodge had been, by the acting of
a horrible tragedy, should excite, far and wide amongst the people, a sentiment of terror sufficiently potent to turn the steps of
the wayfarer, as the shades of evening fell around him, aside from
the path that led to St. Jerome's.

The Cripple, at the time when I have chosen to present him
to my reader, was seated, as I have said, immediately beneath the
window.   A pair of spectacles assisted his vision as he perused
a packet of papers, several of which lay scattered around him.
The dim light for a while perplexed his labor, and he had directed
the door to be thrown wide open that he might take advantage
of the last moment before the approaching twilight should arrest
his occupation.   Whilst thus employed, the deadened sound of a
shot boomed across the bay.

" Ha !" he exclaimed as he threw aside the paper in his hand
and directed his eyes towards the water ; " there is a signal !—an
ill bird is flying homeward. Did you not hear that shot, woman?"

" I had my dream of the brigantine two nights ago," replied
the servitress ; " and of the greedy kite that calls himself her master ;—the shot must be his."

"Whose can it be else?" demanded The Cripple sharply, as he swung himself forward to the door-sill and shook his locks from his brow in the act of straining his sight across the dim surface of the bay. "Ay, ay; there it is. Hark—another shot!—that is the true pass word between us :—Dickon, sure enough!—The brigantine is in the offing. Cocklescraft is coming in with the speed of a gull. He comes full freighted—full freighted, as is his wont, with the world's plunder. What dole hath he done this flight?—what more wealthy knave than himself hath he robbed? Mischief, mischief, mischief—good store of it, I'll be sworn :—and a keener knave than himself he hath not found in his wide venture. He will be coming ashore to visit The Cripple, ha!—he shall be welcome—as he ever hath been. We are comrades,—we are cronies, and merry in our divisions—the Skipper and the Cripple—there is concord in it—the Skipper and the Cripple—merry men both!"

These uprisings of the inner thoughts of the man were uttered in various tones—one moment scarce audible, the next with an emphatic enunciation, as if addressed to his companion in the hut, and sometimes with the semblance of a laugh, or rather chuckle, which was wormwood in its accent, and brought the rheum from his eye down his cheek. The beldam, accustomed to this habit of self-communion in The Cripple, apparently heeded not these mutterings, until he, at length, accosted her with a command.— "Mistress Kate, double the contents of your pot ;—the skipper and some of his men will be here presently, as keen and trenchant as their own cutlasses. They will be hungry, woman,—as these salt-water monsters always are for earthy provender."

"Such sharp-set cattle should bring their provender with them," replied the domestic, as she went about increasing her store of provision in compliance with her master's directions.

"Or the good red gold, or the good red gold, old jade," interrupted The Cripple. "The skipper doth not shrink in the girdle from the disease of a lean purse, and is therefore worthy of our worshipful entertainment. So goes the world, and we will be in the fashion? Though. the world's malisons drive him hither as before a tempest, yet, comes he rich in its gear ; he shall have princely reception. I am king of this castle, and ordain it. Is he taking in sail ?—is he seeking an anchorage ? Ha, he understands his craft, and will be with us anon," he continued, as he marked the movements of the approaching vessel.

There might be dimly seen, nearly abreast of St. Jerome's, a close-reefed brig, holding her course before a fair wind directly across the bay towards the hut of The Cripple. She was, at intervals, lost to view behind the thickening haze, and as often reappeared as she bent under the fresh north-east breeze and bounded rapidly with the waves towards the lee shore. It was after the hour of sunset when the tenants of the hut were just able to discern, in the murky gloom of the near nightfall, that she had lowered sail and swung round with her head seaward, at an anchorage some two miles out in the bay.

"Quick, Mistress Kate, and kindle some brushwood on the shore," said the master of the hut. "It grows dark, and the boat's crew will need a signal to steer by."

The woman gathered a handful of fagots, and, kindling them into a blaze, transferred them to the beach in front of the hut, where, notwithstanding the rain, they burned with a steady light. This illumination had not subsided before the stroke of oars rose above the din of the waves ; and the boat with her crew, sheeted with the broad glare of the signal fire, suddenly appeared mounted on the surf, surrounded with foam and spray, and in the same instant was heard grating on the gravel of the beach.

Cocklescraft, with two seamen, entered the hut. The skipper was now in the prime of youthful manhood ; tall, active and strong, with the free step and erect bearing that no less denoted the fearlessness of nis nature than pride in the consciousness of such a quality. His face, tinged with a deep brown hue, was not unhandsome, although an expression of sensuality, to some extent, deprived it of its claim to be admired. A brilliant eye suffered the same disparagement by its over-ready defiance, which told of a temper obtrusively prone to quarrel. The whole physiognomy wanted gentleness, although a fine set of teeth, a regular profile, and a complexion which, with proper allowance for exposure to the weather, was uncommonly good, would unquestionably have won from the majority of observers the repute of a high degree of masculine beauty.

A scarlet jacket fitted close across the breast, wide breeches of ash-colored stuff, hanging in the fashion of a kirtle or kilt to the knees, tight gray hose, accurately displaying the leg in all its fine proportions, and light shoes, furnished a costume well adapted to the lithe and sinewy figure of the wearer. A jet black and glossy moustache, and tuft below the nether lip, gave a martial aspect to his face, which had, nevertheless, the smoothness of skin of a boy. He wore in his embroidered belt, a pair of pistols richly mounted with chased silver and costly jewels, and his person was somewhat gorgeously and, in his present occupation, inappropriately ornamented with gems and chains of gold. His hair, in almost feminine luxuriance, descended in ringlets upon his neck. A large hat made of the palm leaf, broad enough to shade his face and shoulders, but ill assorted with the rest of his apparel, and was still less adapted to the season and the latitude he was in, though it threw into the general expression of his figure that trait of the swaggering companion which was, in fact, somewhat prominent in his character.

"How dost, friend Rob?" was his salutation in crossing the threshold; "how dost, Rob o' the Bowl, or Rob o' the Trencher?—bowl or trencher,—either likes me; I am sworn friend

6*

to both," he continued as he stooped and took The Cripple's hand.

"Ay, thy conscience has never stayed thee," was The Cripple's reply, as he received the skipper's grasp, "when thou wouldst put thy hand in another man's bowl or trencher,—and especially, Dickon, if they were made of gold. Thou hast an appetite for such dishes. How now! where do you come from?"

"That shall be answered variously, friend of the wooden platter. If you speak to me as Meinherr Von Cogglescraft, I am from Antwerp, master of the Olive Branch, with a comfortable cargo of Hollands, and wines French and Rhenish, old graybeard, and some solid articles of Dutch bulk. But if it be to the Caballero Don Ricardo,—le beso las manos!—I am from Tortuga and the Keys, Senor Capitan del Escalfador (there is much virtue in a painted cloth) with a choice assortment of knicknackeries, which shall set every wench in the province agog. I have rare velvets of Genoa, piled and cut in the choicest fashions : I have grograms, and stuffs, and sarsnets, with a whole inventory of woman trumpery—the very pick of a Spanish bark, bound from Naples to the islands, which was so foolish as to read my flag by its seeming, and just to drop into the Chafing-Dish when he thought he was getting a convoy to help him out of the way of the too pressing and inquisitive courtesies of certain lurking friends of ours in the Keys. I have, besides, some trinkets, which are none the worse for having been blessed by the Church. You shall have a choice, Rob, to deck out your chamber with some saintly gems."

"Ha! I guessed thy deviltry, Dickon," said Rob, with a laugh which, as always happened when much moved, brought tears down his cheeks—" I guessed it when I saw you step across the door sill with that large and suspicious sombrero on your head. It never came from Holland—though you would fain persuade the province folks that you trade no where else : it is of the breed of the tropics, and smells of Hispaniola and Santo Domingo."

"It is a tell-tale," replied Cocklescraft, "and should have been thrown overboard before this. Old Kate of Warrington, your hand—and here is a hand for you! How does the world use you? Fairly, I hope, as you deserve? You shall have the sombrero, Kate: you can truss it up into a new fashion for a bonnet, and I have store of ribands to give you to set it off."

"My share of this world's favor," said the crone, in acknowledgment of the skipper's bounty, "has never been more than the cast-off bravery of such as hold a high head over a wicked heart. I have ever served at the mess of the devil's bantlings. But, as the custom is, I must be civil and thankful for these blessings; and so, Master Cocklescraft, I give you thanks," she added with a courtesy, as she placed the hat upon her head and strutted fantastically in the room, "for your dainty head-gear that you are unwilling to wear, and durst not, master, before the port wardens of St. Mary's."

"How, Kate!" exclaimed the skipper, "you have lost no whit of that railing tongue I left with you at my last venture? I marvel that the devil has not shorn it, out of pure envy. But I know, Kate, you can do justice to the good will of a friend, after all: I would have you to know that you have not been unconsidered, good mother of a thousand devilkins: I have brought you stuff for a new gown, rich and ladylike, Kate, and becoming your grave and matronly years, and sundry trickeries for it, by way of garniture; and, reverend dam of night-monsters, I have in store for you some most choice distillations of the West Indies, both plain and spiced. You do not spurn the strong waters, Kate of Warrington,—nor the giver of them?"

"This is a make-peace fashion of yours," said the beldam, relaxing into a smile. "You thought not of the woman of Warrington—no, not so much as a dog's dream of her—until it chanced to come into your head that the foolish crone had a will which it might not be for your good to set against you. I knew your incoming, Richard Cocklescraft, before it was thought of in the province; and I know when your outgoing will be. You come with a surly sky and a gay brow;—you shall trip it hence with a bright heaven above you, and deftly, boy—but with a heavy heart and a new crime upon your soul."

"Peace, woman! I will hear none of your croakings—it is an old trick; the device is too stale," said Cocklescraft, half playfully and half vexed. You are no conjuror, Kate, as you would make the world believe by these owl-hootings: if you had but a needle's-eyeful of the true witch in you, you would have foretold what bounty my luck has brought you.—Rob, we have packages to land to-night. Is the Chapel ready for our service?"

"How should it be other than ready? Doth not the devil keep his quarters there?" said Rob, with a low-toned chuckle that shook his figure for some moments, and almost closed his eyes; hath he not his court in the Chapel? Go ask the whole country side: they will swear to it on their bible oaths. Sundries have seen the hoofs and horns, and heard the howlings,— ay, and smelt the brimstone—ha, ha, ha! They'll swear to it. Is the Chapel ready, in sooth? It is a precious Chapel! Paul Kelpy, thou wert an honest cut-throat, to bedevil so good a house: we turn it to account—ha, ha! It needs but to take the key, Dickon. I warrant you, ne'er a man in the province, burgher or planter, gentle or simple, ventures near enough to molest you."

"The surf runs high," said Cocklescraft, "and may give us trouble in the landing to-night; and as daylight must not find me in this latitude, I shall put what I may ashore before the dawn, and then take a flight to the opposite side of the bay. To-morrow night I shall finish my work ; and you shall soon after hear, at St. Mary's, that the good and peaceful brigantine, the Olive Branch, has arrived from Holland. Meantime, I will leave you a half dozen men to garrison the Chapel, Rob."

"It is so well garrisoned with my merry goblins already," said Rob, " that it requires but a light watch. The fires alone would frighten his Lordship's whole array of rangers. That was a pretty device of mine, Dickon—blue, green, and red—excellent devil-fires all ! Then I have masks—faith, most special masks ! the very noses of them would frighten the short-winded train-bands of the Port into catalepsy. And the Chapel had an ill name when the fisherman shed blood on the floor : but since we blackened it, Richard—oh, that was a subtle thought !—it is past all power of exorcism : there is an ague in the very name of the Black Chapel." And here The Cripple gave way to a burst of laughter, which had been struggling for vent during all this refer-ence to the arts by which he had contrived to maintain the pop-ular dread of the fisherman's lodge.

Whilst this conference was held, the crone had prepared their evening meal, which being now ready, Rob was lifted upon a low platform that brought him to the proper level with the table, where he was able to help himself. Cocklescraft partook with him, and might almost have envied the keen gust and ravenous appetite with which his host despatched the coarse but savory fare of the board—for The Cripple's power of stomach seemed to be no whit impaired by age. He continued to talk, during his meal, in the same strain which we have described, now indulging a peevish self-communion, now bursting forth with some sarcastic objurgation of the world, and again breaking a jest with his vis-itor.

When the seamen, under the ministration of the aged domes-tic, had got their supper, Cocklescraft took his departure.

All night long lights were gleaming in the Chapel ; the rain continued in a steady misty drizzle, and not a star was seen to tempt a wanderer abroad.   The morning, which broke upon an atmosphere purged of its vapors, showed no trace of the brig in the vicinity of St. Jerome's.   Far down the bay, hugging the eastern shore, might have been discerned what a practised mariner would affirm to be a sail ; but whether ship or brig—whether outward or homeward bound, might not be told without the aid of a glass.

CHAPTER XIII.

Up she rose, and forth she goes,—
I'll mote she speed therefor.
ADAM BELL.

Bell, my wife, she loves not strife,
Yet she will lead me if she can ;
And oft, to live a quiet life,
I'm forced to yield, though I'm goodman.
It's not for a man a woman to threape,
Unless he first give o'er his plea;
As we began we now will leave
And I'll take my old cloak about me.
OLD SONG.

IT was nine o'clock of the morning before Dauntrees and his companions, Garret and Arnold, rose from their beds. Pamesack, whose taciturnity was not greater than his indifference to fatigue, had, at an earlier hour, gone his way. A breakfast was provided in the Captain's quarters, and the three heroes of the past night sat down to it with a relish which showed that, however unfit they might be to contend against spiritual foes, their talents for this encounter of material existences were highly respectable.

"You have had a busy time of it in dreams, Master Weasel," said Dauntrees, "since you laid yourself down on your truckle bed this morning. You have been re-acting your exploits at the Chapel. I heard you at daylight crying aloud for sword and dagger."

"Ah, Captain Dauntrees," replied the publican, "my head has been full of fantasies since I laid me down to rest—for I was exceeding weary—and weariness doth set the brain to ramble in sleep. There was good argument, too, in our deeds at St. Jerome's for a world of dreaming."

"Last night has made a man of you, my gallant vintner. You should bless your stars that you fell into such worthy company. You knew not heretofore—even with your experience at Worcester—what elements of valor it pleased Heaven to mix up in the mould whereof you were made. A man never sufficiently values himself until he has had some such passage as this."

"Ay, and look you, Captain Dauntrees," said Garret, his eye flashing with self-gratulation, "you will reflect that I had the brunt of it *alone*, whilst you three were banded together for common defence and support. There I was, by my single self, in the very centre of them. A man needs more comfort and companionship in a matter with witches and devils, than he does against your sword and buckler fellows. Tut! I wouldn't have cared a fig for a foe that could be struck at; but these pestilent things of the dark—hags on besoms, and flying bats as big as a man, great sword-fishes walking on legs, with their screechings, and mopings, and mewings—how it tries the reins of a solitary man! But you had flashing, and firing, and charging, Captain, which is more in the way of what one expects in a fight, and one is prepared for: it has life in it."

"That is most true, doughty Garret. A culverin is but the whiff of an oaten pipe, compared with a hag upon her broomstick. You were ever the man to encounter these women. It needs your mettle to face them. Now there is your wife, Master Weasel—oh, but that is a peril in store for you! You shall go to her and have it over, whilst I make my report to his Lordship;

when that is done I will straight for the Crow and Archer, to help you in the battle, which by that time will doubtless find you sore at need."

"I must go to his Lordship with you," replied Garret, in a lowered key; "I must have my hand in the report; after that we will set out together for the inn."

"Why, man!" exclaimed Dauntrees, with affected astonishment, "would you tarry to do your duty to Mistress Dorothy? Do you not know that she has suffered agony of mind the live-long night in your behalf, and that she is now in the very tempest of her affection waiting for you?"

"I know it, I know it, worthy Captain; but it does not become my respect for Lord Charles's service to defer his business for mine own."

"You shall not budge an inch," said Dauntrees, "on any other path than that which takes you quickly to your loving wife."

"Truly, Captain," replied Weasel, in a dolorous tone, "I would have you go with me; I beseech you heartily, allow me to bear you company to his Lordship. His Lordship will think it strange I did not come: and it will take more than me to pacify the dame."

"Well, friend Weasel, in consideration that you contended single handed last night with a whole score of devils, and bore yourself gallantly; and, moreover, as it is such heavy odds against you in this matter of Dame Dorothy—for, of a verity, I know she is in a devil of a passion at your contumacy, and not less at mine, I'll be sworn—why we will make a muster of it and breathe our defence in solid column. Arnold will go with us. And mark me, vintner, at the fitting time we shall regale."

"On the best in cellar or larder at the Crow and Archer," replied Garret. "You have the word of a man and a soldier for it."

"I wot of a woman and no soldier, whose word would go further to that bargain, Garret, than yours. Make ready, friends, we must move."

Dauntrees now set his beaver jauntily over his brow, and throwing his short cloak across his arm, marched through the postern of the fort, followed by his trusty allies, to the mansion of the Lord Proprietor.

Lord Baltimore received them in his library, and there heard from the Captain a circumstantial narrative of the events of the preceding night.

"It is a strange tale," he said, " and may well perplex the faith of the simple rustics of the province. That evil spirits preside over that blood-stained house, from your testimony, Captain Dauntrees, may no longer be denied. Friends, you all saw these things ?"

"All," said Garret Weasel, with emphatic solemnity, as he straitened his body even beyond the perpendicular line. " Pamesack and Arnold stood by the Captain and can vouch for him. I maintained a post of danger, an please you Lordship, alone ; what I saw neither the Captain, Arnold, nor Pamesack, saw—it was a fearful sight."

"What was it ?" inquired the Proprietary, with some earnestness.

"A woman," replied Garret, "*seemingly* a woman, an your Lordship comprehends ; but in truth a witch, as we all do know : —Kate of Warrington, of whom your Lordship has heard. She it was who came suddenly down upon the wold. How she came," here Garret shook his head, " and what came with her,—it was a sight to look upon !"

"The vintner affirms to sundry fantastic shapes of imps and spectres in company with the woman of Warrington," said Dauntrees. " We saw nothing of the hag, having left Master Weasel some distance in our rear when we visited the Chapel. He was cold, and required comfort. What he recounts, my Lord, you have his own avouch for."

"And what say you, Arnold?" inquired his Lordship, smiling.

"These ghosts and goblins keep a hot house, and the less we have to do with them the better," replied the forester, gravely.

"They fired upon you, Captain?" said the Proprietary; "with what weapons?"

"They had the sharp crack of the musket and pistol," replied Dauntrees, "or what seemed to be such : yet I would not swear that I saw carnal weapons in the strife, though in the flash I thought I noted fire-arms. This may tell better than guess of mine, my Lord," he added, as he held up his cloak and pointed to a rent in one of its folds ; "this hole was made by some missive from the house : whether it be a bullet mark or an elf-shot, I will not say."

"Body o' me !" exclaimed Garret Weasel, as the Captain pointed to the damage he had sustained, "I knew not this before. There was hot work, I warrant."

"There is knavery in alliance with this sorcery," said the Proprietary, as he examined the cloak. "These wicked spirits ever find kindred amongst men. They have profligate companions of flesh to profit by their devilish arts. I thank you, friends, kindly, for this exploit, and will turn it to wholesome account hereafter. Fare you well."

The party left the room, and now shaping their course towards the Crow and Archer, soon descended below the bank and took the road along the beach.

Whilst they trudged through the sand and gravel, midway between the fort and the town, Dauntrees, looking behind, saw a figure descending on horseback from the main gate of the fort down to the road upon which they now travelled. It was that of a woman, whose gestures, at the distance of half a mile, were sufficiently observable to show that she urged her horse forward with impatient earnestness. As soon as she arrived at the level of the beach, her speed was increased nearly to the utmost of the faculty of the animal which bore her, and she now came flying over the sand, with her garments and loose tresses floating in the wind.

"In the devil's name, what have we here?" exclaimed Daun-trees. "As I live, it is our queen of the hostel! Oh, Garret, Garret, here is a volcano! Here is an out-come with a conclusion at hand! Stand, masters, firmly on your legs, and brace up for the onset!"

"Alack, alack!" groaned the publican; "the woman is bereft. She has my nag from the fort."

"Ay, and rides upon your saddle, as if it were made for her," ejaculated the Captain. "Take post behind me, Garret: I will answer her speech."

"It were no more than the luck she deserves," said Garret, pettishly, "if she should fall from the nag and break her little finger, or at the least sprain an ankle joint."

"Hold, runagates! varlets! out upon you for a filthy Captain!" shouted the dame, in a shrill voice, as she came within call of the party, and now galloped up to the spot at which they had halted. "Give me that idiot from your beastly company. Garret Weasel, Garret Weasel! you have been the death of me!"

"Good lack, Mistress Dorothy, wife, why do you bear yourself in such a sort as this?"

"I will bare you to the buff, driveller, for this. Are you not steeped in wickedness and abomination by evil-consorting with this copper Captain, and this most horrid wood ranger? Have you no eye for your family; no regard for good name, that you must be strolling o' nights with every pot-guzzler and foul-breathed

and cankered cast-off of the wars? I am ashamed of you. You
have been in your cups, I warrant, the live-long night."

"Dame, I must speak, now," said Dauntrees.

"Thou, thou!" interrupted the hostess, with her face scarlet
from anger. "Never in a Christian land should such as you be
permitted to lift your head before honest people. His Lordship
would do but justice to the province to chain you up in a dark
stable, as a bull which may not be trusted at large. Did you
not beguile me last night with a base lie? Did you not practise
upon me, you faithless, false-hearted coward?" here tears fell
from the flashing eyes of the voluble landlady. "Did you not
steal that lob, my husband, from me, thief?"

"Appearances, dame," replied the Captain, with a grave composure, "if they might be trusted, were certainly to my disfavor
last night. But, then, I knew that when this matter was all over,
I had a most sufficient and excellent reason, which a considerate,
virtuous, and tender-hearted woman like yourself would fully
approve, when she came to hear it. There was matter in hand
of great import and urgency; no revelling, dame—no riot—but
brave service, enjoined by his Lordship, and which it was his
Lordship's most earnest desire should be committed in part to
your husband. It was an action of pith and bravery he had on
hand; and his Lordship being well aware, dame, that Garret's
wife was a woman of a loving heart, and gentle withal in her
nature, and not fitted to endure the wringing of her affection by
such a trial as the adventure imposed upon Garret, he charged
me to make some light pretext for withdrawing your husband
from your eye, which, by fraud, I confess, I did, and am now—
since Garret hath worthily achieved his most perilous duty—here
to avow my own treachery. There is promotion and great
advantage at hand for this which will set up your head, dame,
the highest amongst them that wear hoods."

"We have barely escaped with our lives, Mistress Dorothy," said Weasel, in a whining accent of deprecation ; "we should be made much of and praised for our duty, not be set upon with taunts and foul rebukes ; and when you know all, wife, you will be sorry for this wounding of our good name."

"This is but another trick," said the landlady.

"Nay, good Mistress," interrupted the Captain, "I will agree to be gibbeted by your own fair hand, if I do not satisfy you that in this adventure we are deserving of all applause. The Lieutenant at the fort, doubtless, told you that we were absent last night on special duty at his Lordship's command?"

"The varlet did feign such a story, when I thought to catch this fool in your company. And he would deny me, too, the nag ; but I brought such coil about his ears that he was glad to give me the beast and set all gates open. Where do you say you have spent the night?"

"At the Black Chapel, mistress," said Weasel, with a most portentous solemnity of speech : "at the Black Chapel, by his Lordship's order ; and, oh, the sights we have seen! and the time we have had of it, wife! it would make your blood freeze to hear it."

"On the honor of a soldier, dame! by the faith of this right hand!" said Dauntrees, as he offered it to the hostess and took hers, "I swear this is true. We have had a night of wonders, which you shall hear in full when the time suits. We are on our way now to the Crow and Archer, for your especial gratification."

"Can this be true, Arnold?" inquired the mollified and bewildered landlady. "I will believe what you say."

"You may trust in every word of it, as I am a Christian man. There be marvellous doings at the Black Chapel. We have seen spirits and devils in company."

"It is graver matter, wife, than you wot of," said Weasel.

"Ride forward, dame," added Dauntrees; "you shall see us soon at the hostel. And I promise you shall have the story, too, of the Mercer's Wife from beginning to end: you shall, dame."

"You are a wheedling, cogging cheat, Captain; thy roguery will have a melancholy end yet," replied the dame, as she now rode forward with a sunshiny smile playing upon features which but a few moments before were dark with storm.

When they reached the Crow and Archer they found a group of traders assembled on the quay, gazing with a busy speculation towards the mouth of the river. By degrees the crowd increased, and the rumor soon spread about that the Olive Branch was in sight. A vessel was, indeed, discernible across the long flat of St. Inigoe's, just entering the river, and those who professed a knowledge of nautical affairs had no scruple in announcing her as the brigantine of Cocklescraft. She was apparently an active craft, belonging to the smaller class of sea-vessels, and manifestly a faster sailer than was ordinarily to be seen at that period. A fair and fresh breeze impelled her steadily towards her haven, and as she bounded over the glittering waters, the good folks of the little city were seen clustering in knots on every prominent cliff along the high bank, and counting the minutes which brought this messenger from the old world nearer to their salutation.

Meantime the Olive Branch began to show the sparkling foam which broke upon her bow: then to give forth voices from her deck, audible to the crowd; presently to lower sail; and at last, being stripped to her bare poles and naked rigging, she glided with lessening speed, slower and slower, until her extended cable showed that her anchor was dropped and her voyage at an end.

It was past noon when the brig came to her mooring, opposite the Town House wharf, and after a brief interval, Cocklescraft, arrayed as we have before seen him, except that he had changed his sombrero for a tasseled cap of cloth, landed on the quay, and soon became the lion of the Crow and Archer.

CHAPTER XIV.

Every white will have its black,
And every sweet its sour.

OLD BALLAD.

THE birth-day festival at the Rose Croft might be said appropriately to belong to the eminent dominion of the Lady Maria. It therefore lacked nothing of her zealous supervision. With the aid of Father Pierre and some female auxiliaries she had persuaded the Collector—a task of no great difficulty—to sanction the proceeding, and she was now intent upon the due ordering and setting out of the preparations. The day was still a week off when, early after breakfast, on a pleasant morning the business-fraught lady was seen in the hall, arrayed in riding hood and mantle, ready to mount a quiet black-and-white pony that, in the charge of a groom, awaited her pleasure at the door. Natta, the little Indian girl, stood by entrusted with the care of a work-bag or wallet apparently well stuffed with the materials for future occupation—the parcel-fragments which thrifty housewives and idleness-hating dames, down to this day, are accustomed to carry with them, for the sake of the appearance, at least, of industry. Just at this moment the Proprietary came into the hall, and seeing that his worthy sister was bound on some enterprise of more than usual earnestness, he added to his customary morning salutation a playful inquiry into the purport of her excursion.

7

"Ah, Charles," she replied, "there are doings in the province which are above the rule of your burgesses and councils. I hold a convocation at the Rose Croft to-day, touching matters more earnest than your state affairs. We have a merry-making in the wind, and I am looked to both for countenance and advice. It is my prerogative, brother, to be mistress of all revels."

"God bless thine age, Maria!" was the affectionate reply of the Proprietary—"it wears a pleasant verdure and betokens a life of innocent thoughts and kind actions. May the saints bear thee gently onward to thy rest! Come, I will serve as your cavalier, and help you to your horse, sister.—See now, my arm has pith in it. Hither, Natta—there is the wench on the pillion —who could serve thee with a better grace than that?"

"Thanks—thanks, good brother!" ejaculated the lady as the Proprietary lifted her to her seat, and then swung the Indian girl upon the pillion behind her. "Your arm is a valiant arm, and is blessed by more than one in this province. It has ever been stretched forth in acts of charity and protection."

"Nay, Maria, you are too old to flatter. Fie! I have no advancement to offer you. In truth you are sovereign here— though you go through your realm with but scant attendance for one so magnified. Why is not Albert in your train? I may well spare him—as he has a liking for such service."

"Brother, I would not tax the Secretary. He has a free foot for his own pleasure; and, methinks, he finds his way to the Rose Croft easily enough without my teaching. It is an ancient caution of mine in such affairs, neither to mar nor make."

"Heaven help thee for a considerate spinster!" said the Proprietary with a benignant smile as he raised his hands and shook them sportively towards his sister. "Go your ways with your whimsies and your scruples;—and a blessing on them! I wish yours were our only cares :—but go your ways, girl!" he added, as the lady set forth on her journey, and he withdrew from the door.

At the Rose Croft, the approaching merry-making had superseded all other family topics, both in parlor and kitchen. The larder was already beginning to exhibit the plentiful accumulations which, in a place of strength, might portend a siege : the stable boys were ever on the alert, with their cavalry, to do rapid errands to the town, and Michael Mossbank, the gardener, was seen in frequent and earnest consultation with John Pouch, a river-side cotter, touching supplies of fish and wild fowl.

Whilst the elder sister Alice despatched the graver duties of the housekeeping, she had consigned to Blanche the not less important care of summoning the guests, and the maiden was now seated at the table with pen in hand registering the names of those who had been, or were to be, invited to the feast,—or, in other words, making a census of pretty nearly the whole titheable population of St. Mary's and its dependencies.

" A plague upon it for a weary labor !" she exclaimed as she threw down the pen and rested her chin upon the palm of her hand. " I know I shall forget somebody I ought not to forget—and shall be well rated for it. And then again I shall be chid for being too free with my fellowship.—What a world of names is here ! I did not think the whole province had so many. There is Winnefred Hay, the viewer's sister,—they have tales about her which, if they be true, it is not fit she should be a crony of mine—and yet I don't believe them, though many do.—Truly the viewer will be in a grand passion if I slight her ! Sister Alice, give me your advice."

" Bid her to the feast, Blanche. We should be slow to believe these rumors to the injury of a neighbor. Winnefred Hay is not over discreet—and gives more semblance to an evil opinion than, in truth, her faults deserve : but the townspeople are scarce

better in this quickness to censure—especially such as look tc
the tobacco viewing. Lawrence Hay's place has something to do
with that scandal."

"I am glad, sister Alice, you give me an argument to indulge
my own secret wish," replied Blanche ; "for I like not to believe
harsh reports against any of our province.   And so, that is at an
end. Alack !—here is another matter for counsel : Grace Blackiston says Helen Clements is too young to be at my gathering :—
she has two years before her yet at school, and has only begun
embroidering.   Oh, but I would as soon do a barefoot penance
for a month as disappoint her !—she is the wildest of all for a
dance, and looks for it, I know,—though she says never a word,
and has her eyes on the ground when we talk about it.—Ha, let
Grace Blackiston prate as she will, Helen shall be here ! Fairly,
my gossip,—I will be mistress in my own house, I promise you !"

"There is room for all your friends, young and old," said
Alice ; "and you should not stint to ask them for the difference
of a span or so in height.   You are not quite a woman yourself,
Blanche,—no, nor Grace neither,—although you perk yourselves
up so daintily."

"Would you have the gauger's wife, sister ?" inquired Blanche,
with a face of renewed perplexity. "I think my dear Lady Maria
would be pleased if I bid the dame—for the gauger is a good
friend of his Lordship—hot-headed, they say, but that does not
make him the worse—and his dame takes it kindly to be noticed."

"Even as you will, Blanche,—it is a mark of gentle nurture
not to be too scrupulous with your questions of quality—a kind
neighbor will never disgrace your courtesy. But one thing, child,
your father will look to :—see that you avoid these Coodes and
Fendalls and even the Chiseldines. There is a feud between them
and the Proprietary,—and my Lord's friends are warm in the
matter,—your father amongst the rest."

"I protest they get no bid from me," said Blanche, as the color mantled her cheek. "I hate them stock and branch—yes, as my good lady hates them."

Blanche had scarcely uttered these words before the good lady herself rode past the window. The maiden bounded forth to receive her, and Alice with less precipitation followed.

"I come with pony and pillion," said the visitor as she was assisted to the ground, and bustled into the parlor. "I could not rest until I saw Blanche to know if all her biddings were abroad. My pretty bird, pray look you to your task—you have no time to lose : there are the families beyond Patuxent—and our friends across the bay,—besides many at home that I know have not heard from you yet. And here, sweet, I have brought you some trinketry which you shall wear at the feast : a part is for Grace Blackiston, and a part for you. You shall have the choice, Blanche :—but whisht ! not a word of it to Grace, because I think she has a conceit to be jealous of your favor."

Whilst the two sisters welcomed the lady and responded to her voluble communications in a tone of affectionate intimacy, the contents of the work-bag were thrown open to view, and successively gave rise to sundry discussions relating not only to the objects presented, but also collaterally to the thousand matters of detail connected with the festival, thus engrossing the first hour of their interview, until the subject was changed by an exclamation from Blanche, as she looked through the window upon the river—

"Oh, but here is a gallant sight !—see yonder hawk following a heron. He will strike presently—the heron cannot get away. Poor bird ! how he doubles and drops in his flight to escape the swift hawk ;—but it is of no avail. I should almost say it was sinful,—if it was not approved and followed by those I love best —I should hold it sinful to frighten and torture a harmless heron

by such pursuit.   There, the hawk has struck, and down comes
hawk and quarry to the water."

"It is his Lordship's hawk," said the Lady Maria, as she
looked out upon the river.   "Derrick the falconer must be
abroad to-day with his birds :—and now whilst I speak, there
he is walking along the beach.   And he is not alone neither :—
by that short mantle and that feather, Blanche, you may know a
friend."

The color rose on the maiden's cheek as she said, "It is
Albert, his Lordship's secretary."

"His eyes are turned this way," said the sister of the Proprietary.   "A wager he comes to the house in the next ten
minutes !—He would fain find some business with the Collector
—I know Master Albert's occasions : nay, do not flurry thyself,
my sweet Blanche."

"I wish the Secretary *would* come," returned the maiden ;
"we have need of him ; he promised to show me how it were
best to arrange my flower vases."

"Then you would do well to despatch a messenger to him,"
interrupted the Lady Maria, playfully ; "do you not think he
might forget ?"

"Oh no, my dear lady," replied Blanche, "Master Albert
never forgets a promise to me."

"Indeed !   Well, I should have thought that having occasion
to make you so many promises—for he is here at the Rose Croft
thrice a week at least—and every visit has its promise, or I mistake—he would forget full one half."

"I deal but scantily in promises with the Secretary," replied
Blanche.   "Master Albert's errands here are for pastime mostly."

"Ah, he does not forget," exclaimed the Lady Maria ; "for
there I see the feather of his bonnet as he climbs up the bank,—
and now we have his head and shoulders ; we shall get the whole

man anon,—and Master Benedict Leonard in the bargain, for I
see *him* trudging in the Secretary's footsteps, as he is wont to do;
his young Lordship has become the Secretary's shadow. And
there is Derrick behind. They are all bound for this haven."

As the lady spoke, the Secretary was seen from the window
with the heir apparent and the falconer on the verge of the bank
which they had just ascended. Benedict Leonard had a hooded
hawk upon his fist; and Derrick, waving a light rod to which a
small streamer or flag was attached, was busy in luring down the
bird that had just flown at the heron. Whilst the falconer continued his occupation the Secretary and his young companion
entered the mansion.

Albert Verheyden's accost to the ladies was characterized by
a familiarity not unmixed with diffidence, and a momentary flush
passed across his cheek as, after saluting Mistress Alice, and turning to Blanche, his eye fell upon the sister of the Proprietary. " I
did not expect to find my honored lady so early at the Rose
Croft," he said with a profound reverence. " It should have
been my duty, madam, to attend you, but I knew not of your
purpose; and the falconer being bent to fly the cast of lanerets
which Colonel Talbot lately sent to my Lord, would have me
witness the trial, and so I came with Master Benedict to see
this sport."

" Nay, Albert," replied the lady, "you should not have been
of my company even if you had sought permission. I come to-
day on no idle errand which might allow your loitering paces and
customary delays to gaze on headlands and meadows, whereby
you are wont to interrupt the course of your journey. The matter of our present meeting has need of stirring feet, which go
direct to their work,—yours are not such. Still, Master Albert,
you shall not be useless to-day :—here is occupation to your
hand ; Blanche is in much want of a penman, and as you are of

the writing craft, she would gladly enlist you in her service—that is, if you have not been already marshalled and sworn under her colors."

"Master Albert, our dear lady does but jest," said Blanche. "She knows I had at first no need of better penman than myself, and now have need of none,—for, in truth, my work was finished ere she came. But your service I may command in a better task. You did promise to bring me some device for my flower stands."

"The joiner will have them here to-day," replied the Secretary. "I have not failed to spur his industry as well as my own invention to do your wish."

"Then all is done but the rendering of thanks," said Blanche, "which yet I am not in the humor to do, having matter of quarrel with you for that following of the poor heron which, but now, we saw the hawk strike down, whilst you were a looker-on, and, as we suspect, an encourager of the act. It was a cruel thing to assail the innocent fowl, which, being native here, has ever found friends in our house ;—yes, and has daily fed upon the flat below the garden. These herons scarce fly when I walk by them on the beach. I wish the falconer had sought his quarry elsewhere than amongst my harmless birds. You should have controlled him."

"I am deeply grieved," replied the Secretary. "Indeed, I knew not of the bird nor whence he came : nor thought of it, in truth. A feather of his wing should not have come to harm had I been aware that he had ever pleased your eye. I am all unskilled in these out-door sports, and have scarce worn out the complexion of my school at Antwerp, where worldly pastimes were a forbidden thought. A poor scholar of the cloister might go free of blame if, in this sunny and gallant world, the transport of a noble game should rob him of his circumspection. I thought of naught but the glorious circling of the hawk and his swift and imperious assault. I crave your pardon for my inconsiderate error."

"You speak more like a practised cavalier than a scholar of the cloister," said the sister of the Proprietary ; "you have a cavalier's love of the sport, Albert."

"It does not beseem me, madam," was the Secretary's reply " to affect a pastime which belongs neither to my rank nor humble means ; but, in truth, dear lady, I do love hawk, and hound, and steed. And when in my sequestered study—where, being as I thought, destined to the service of the altar, I read mostly of holy men and holy things, little dreaming that I should ever see the world—it sometimes chanced, in my stray reading, I fell upon a lay wherein deeds of chivalry were told ; and then I was conscious of a wish, I am now almost ashamed to confess, that fortune might some day bring me better acquainted with that world to which such deeds belonged. Oh ! it has befallen now :——that is,—I mean to say," continued the Secretary, checking himself, as his flashing eye fell to the floor and a blush flitted across his brow—" it has pleased Heaven to give me a kind master in my good Lord, who does not deny me to look on when these sports are afield."

"And if we did strike down the heron, Blanche Warden," said Benedict Leonard, saucily accosting the maiden, and showing the hawk that was bound to his wrist—"what is a heron good for but to be brought down ? Herons were made for hawks— yes, and for the hawks of the Proprietary above all others ; for I have heard say that every heron on the Chesapeake, within my father's boundary, is his own bird : so Derrick has said a hundred times. And there is my uncle Talbot, who flies a hawk better than any other in the province—I don't care if Derrick hears me— and has the best mews,—he says that these fire-arms have broken up hawking in the old country ; and he told me I must not let it

7*

fall through when I come to the province ; for my father, he thinks, doesn't care much for it. I promise you in my time we shall have hawking enough—chide as you like, Mistress Blanche. It was partly for me that my uncle Talbot sent us this cast of birds. Look at that laneret, Blanche,—look at her ! Isn't that a bird ? Talk to me of a goshawk after that !"

"Benedict—nephew," interposed the Lady Maria, "why dost thou fling thy bird so rudely ? She brushes Blanche's cheek with her wing. Pray, not so bold : Blanche will not like thee for it."   ⸮

"Blanche will never quarrel with me for loving my hawk aunt," replied the boy playfully. "Will you, mistress ? A laneret's wing and Blanche Warden's cheek are both accounted beautiful in this province, and will not grow angry with each other upon acquaintance."

"I know not that, Benedict," replied the maiden ; "my cheek may grow jealous of your praise of the wing, and mischief might follow. She is but a savage bird, and has a vicious appetite."

"I will away to the falconer," said the boy. "It is but wasting good things to talk with women about hawks. You will find me, Master Albert, along the bank with Derrick, if you have need of me."

"That boy has more of the Talbot in him than the Calvert," said the Lady Maria, after he had left the room. "His father was ever grave from youth upwards, and cared but little for these exercises. Benedict Leonard lives in the open air, and has a light heart.—You have a book under your mantle, Master Albert," continued the lady. "Is your breviary needful when you go forth to practise a laneret ?"

"It is a volume I have brought for Mistress Blanche," replied the Secretary, as, with some evident confusion, he produced a gilded quarto with clasps, from beneath his dress. "It is a delightful history of a brave cavalier, that I thought would please her."

"Ah!" exclaimed the sister of the Proprietary, taking the book and reading the title-page—"'*La très joyeuse et plaisante Histoire, composée par le Loyal Serviteur, des faits, gestes et prouesses du bon Chevalier sans peur et sans reproche.*' Ay, and a right pleasant history it is, this of the good Knight Bayard, without fear and without reproach. But, Albert, you know Blanche does not read French."

"I designed to render it myself to Mistress Blanche, in her native tongue," replied the Secretary.

"Blanche," said the lady, shaking her head, "this comes of not taking my counsel to learn this language of chivalry long ago. See what peril you will suffer now in journeying through this huge book alone with Master Albert."

"I see no peril," replied the maiden, unconscious of the raillery. "Master Albert will teach me, ere he be done, to read French for myself."

"When you have such a master, and the Secretary such a pupil," said the lady, smiling, "Heaven speed us! I will eat all the French you learn in a month. But, Master Albert, if Blanche can not understand your legend, in the tongue in which it is writ, she can fully comprehend your music—and so can we. It is parcel of your duty at the Rose Croft to do minstrel's service. You have so many songs—and I saw you stealing a glance at yon lute, as if you would greet an old acquaintance."

"If it were not for Master Albert," said Alice, "Blanche's lute would be unstrung. She scarce keeps it, one would think, but for the Secretary's occupation."

"Ah, sister Alice, and my dear lady," said Blanche, "the Secretary has such a touch of the lute, that I but shame my own ears to play upon it, after hearing his ditties. Sing, Master

Albert, I pray you," she added, as she presented him the instrument.

"I will sing to the best of my skill," replied Albert, "which has been magnified beyond my deservings. With your leave, I will try a canzonet I learned in London. It was much liked by the gallants there, and I confess a favor for it because it has a stirring relish. It runs thus:

'Tell me not, sweet, I am unkind,
    That from the nunnery
Of thy chaste breast and quiet mind
    To war and arms I fly.

'True, a new mistress, now I chase,
    The first foe in the field;
And with a stronger faith embrace
    A sword, a horse, a shield.

' Yet this inconstancy is such
    As you too shall adore:
I could not love thee, dear, so much,
    Loved I not honor more.' "

"Well done! Well touched lute—well trolled ditty! Brave song for a bird of thy feather, Master Verheyden!" exclaimed the Collector, who, when the song was finished, entered the room with Cocklescraft. "That's as good a song, Master Cocklescraft——the skipper, ladies—my friend of the Olive Branch, who has been with me this hour past docketing his cargo: I may call him especially your friend—he is no enemy to the vanities of this world. Ha, Master Cocklescraft, you have wherewith to win a world of grace with the petticoats!—you have an eye for the trickery of the sex! Sit down, sir—I pray you, without further reverence, sit down."

The skipper, during this introduction, stood near the door, bowing to the company, and then advanced into the room with a careless and somewhat overbold step, such as denotes a man who, in the endeavor to appear at his ease in society, carries his acting

to the point of familiarity. Still his freedom was not without
grace, and his demeanor, very soon after the slight perturbation
of his first accost, became natural and appropriate to his character.

"Save you, madam," he said, addressing the sister of the
Proprietary, and bowing low, "and you, Mistress Alice, and
you, my young lady of the Rose Croft. It is a twelvemonth since
I left the port, and I am glad to meet the worshipful ladies of
the province once again, and to see that good friends thrive.
The salt water whets a sailor's eye for friendly faces. Mistress
Blanche, I would take upon me to say, without being thought
too free, that you have grown some trifle taller than before I
sailed. I did not then think you could be bettered in figure."

The maiden bowed without answering the skipper's compli-
ment.

"Richard Cocklescraft," said the Collector, "I know not if
you ever saw Albert Verheyden. Had he come hither before
you sailed? His Lordship's secretary."

"I was not so lucky as to fall into his company," replied
Cocklescraft, turning towards the Secretary, and eyeing him from
head to foot. "I think I heard that his Lordship brought new
comers with him. We shall not lack acquaintance. Your hand,
Master Verdun—I think so you said?" he added, as he looked
inquiringly at the Collector.

The Collector again pronounced the name of the Secretary
with more precision.

"Nearly the same thing," continued the skipper. "Master
Verheyden, your hand : mine is something rougher, but it shall
be the hand of a comrade, if you be in the service of worshipful
Master Anthony Warden, the good Collector of St. Mary's. I
know how to value a friend, Master Secretary, and a friend's
friend. You have a rare voice for a ballad—I pretend to have

an opinion in such matters—an excellent voice and a free finger for the lute."

"I am flattered by your liking, sir," returned Albert Verheyden, coldly, as he retired towards a window, somewhat repelled by the too freely proffered acquaintance of the skipper, and the rather loud voice and obtrusive manner with which he addressed those around him.

"Oh, this craft of singing is the touchstone of gentility now-a-days," said Cocklescraft, twirling his velvet bonnet by the gold tassel appended to the crown. "A man is accounted unfurnished who has no skill in that joyous art. Sea-bred as I am, Collector—worshipful Master Warden—you would scarce believe me, but I have touched lute and guitar myself, and passably well. I learned this trick in Milan, whither I have twice gone in my voyages, and dwelt there with these Italians, some good summer months. That is your climate for dark eyes and bright nights—balconies, and damsels behind the lattice, listening to thrummers and singers upon the pavements below. And upon occasion, we wear the short cloak and dagger. I have worn cloak and stiletto in my travels, Master Collector, and trolled a catch in the true tongue of Tuscany, when tuck and rapier rung in the burden. The hot blood there is a commodity which the breeze from the Alps has no virtue to cool, as it does in Switzerland."

"We will try your singing craft ere it be long," replied the Collector. "We will put you to catch and glee, with a jig to the heel of it, Richard Cocklescraft. You must know, Blanche is eighteen on the festival of St. Therese, and we have a junketing forward which has set the whole province astir. You shall take part in the sport with the townspeople, Master Skipper; and I warrant you find no rest of limb until you show us some new antics of the fashion which you have picked up abroad. You shall dance and sing with witnesses—or a good leg and a topping voice shall have no virtue! I pray you, do not forget to make one of our company on the festival of St. Therese. Your gew gaws, Richard, and woman's gear, could not be more in season every wench in the port is like to be your debtor."

"Thanks, Master Collector, I have a foot and voice, ay, and hand, ever at the service of your good company. I will be first to come and last to depart.—I have been mindful of the Rose of St. Mary's in my voyaging," he said, in a respectful and lowered tone, as he approached the maiden. "Mistress Blanche is never so far out of my thoughts that I might come back to the port without some token for her. I would crave your acceptance of a pretty mantle of crimson silk lined with minever. I found it in Dort, and being taken with its beauty, and thinking how well it would become the gay figure of my pretty mistress of the Rose Croft, I brought it away, and now make bold to ask—that is, if it be agreeable to Mistress Blanche, and if I do not venture too far—that I may be allowed to bring it hither."

"You may find a worthier hand for such a favor," said Blanche, with a tone and look that somewhat eagerly repelled the proffered gift, and manifested dislike at the liberty which the skipper had taken—a liberty which was in no degree lessened to her apprehension by the unaccustomed gentleness of his voice, and the humble and faltering manner in which he had asked her consent to the present. "I am unused to such gaudy trappings, and should not be content to wear the cloak;" then perceiving some reproof, as she fancied, in the countenance of her sister Alice and the Lady Maria, she added, in a kindlier voice, "I dare not accept it at your hand, Master Skipper."

"Nay," replied Cocklescraft, presuming upon the mildness of the maiden's last speech, and pressing the matter with that obtrusiveness which marked his character and nurture, "I shall not take it kindly if you do not ;" and as a flush overspread his cheek, he added, " I counted to a certainty that you would do me this courtesy."

"Men sometimes count rashly, Master Cocklescraft," interposed the Lady Maria, "who presume upon a maiden's willingness to incur such debts."

"Save you, madam," replied the skipper ; "I should be sorry Mistress Blanche should deem it to be incurring a debt."

"I have not been trained," said Blanche, with perfect self-possession and firmness of manner, which she intended should put an end to the skipper's importunity, "to receive such favors from the hand of a stranger."

"You will, perchance, think better of it, when you see the mantle," replied the skipper, carelessly ; and then added with a saucy smile, "Women are changeful, Master Collector ; I will bring the gewgaw for Mistress Blanche's inspection—a chapman may have that privilege."

"You may spare yourself the trouble," said the maiden.

"Nay, mistress, think it not a trouble, I beseech you ; I count nothing a trouble which shall allow me to please your fancy." As the skipper uttered this he came still nearer to the chair on which Blanche was seated, and, almost in a whisper, said, "I pray you, mistress, think not so lightly of my wish to serve you. I have set my heart upon your taking the mantle."

"Master Skipper, a word with you," interrupted the Secretary, who had watched the whole scene ; and aware of the annoyance which Cocklescraft's rudeness inflicted upon the maiden, had quietly approached him and now beckoned him to a recess of the window, where they might converse without being heard by the company. "It is not civil to importune the lady in this fashion. You must be satisfied with her answer as she has given it to you. It vexes the daughter of Master Warden to be thus besought. I pray you, sir, no more of it."

Cocklescraft eyed the Secretary for a moment with a glance of scornful resentment, and then replied in a voice inaudible to all but the person to whom it was addressed. " Right ! perhaps you are right, sir ; but when I would be tutored for my behavior, he shall be a man who takes that duty on him, and shall wear a beard and sword both. I needed not thy schooling, master crotchet-monger !" Then leaving the Secretary, he strode towards the maiden, and assuming a laughing face, which but awkwardly concealed his vexation, he said, " Well, mistress Blanche, since you are resolved that you will not take my mantle off my hands, I must give it over as a venture lost, and so an end of it. I were a fool to be vexed because I could not read the riddle of a maiden's fancy : how should such fish of the sea be learned in so gentle a study ? So, viaggio, it shall break no leg of mine ! I will dance none the less merrily for it at the feast : and as for the mantle, why it may find other shoulders in the port, though it shall never find them so fit to wear it withal, as the pretty shoulders of Mistress Blanche. Master Warden, I must take my leave ; my people wait me at the quay. Fair weather for the feast, and a merry time of it, ladies ! A Dios, Master Collector !"

The gaiety of his leave-taking was dashed with a sternness of manner which all the skipper's acting could not conceal, and as he walked towards the door, he paused a moment to touch Albert Verheyden's cloak and whispered in his ear, " We shall be better acquainted, sir ;" then leaving the house he rapidly shaped his course towards the town.

He had scarcely got out of sight before Blanche sprang from her chair and ran towards her father, pouring out upon him a volley of reproof for his unadvised and especially unauthorized invitation of the skipper to the festival. The maiden was joined

in this assault by her auxiliaries, the Proprietary's sister and
Mistress Alice, who concurred in reading the simple-minded and
unconsciously offending old gentleman a lecture upon his improvi-
dent interference in this delicate matter. They insisted that
Cocklescraft's associations in the port gave him no claim to such
a favor, and that, at all events, it was Blanche's prerogative to
be consulted in regard to the admission of the younger and gayer
portions of her company.

"Have you not had your will, my dear father," was the summing up of Blanche's playful attack, "to your full content, in
summoning all the old humdrum folks of the province, even to
the Dominie and his wife, who have never been known to go
a merry-making anywhere, and who are both so deaf that they
have not heard each other speak this many a day? and now you
must needs be bringing the skipper hither."

"Lackaday, wench! what have I done to redden thy brow?"
interrupted Mr. Warden, with a face of perplexed good humor,
unable longer to bear the storm of rebuke, or to parry the arguments which were so eagerly thrust at him; "I have made mischief without knowing how! The skipper is a free blade, of
good metal, and of a figure, too, which, methinks, might please a
damsel in a dance, and spare us all this coil; his leg has not its
fellow in the province. You take me to task roundly, when all
the while I was so foolish as to believe I was doing you regardful
service."

"He has a wicked look, father," was Blanche's reply; "and
a saucy freedom which I like not. He is ever too bold in his
greeting, and lacks gentle breeding. He must come to me, forsooth, with his mantle, as an especial token, and set upon me
with so much constancy to take it! Take a mantle from him!
I have never even seen him but twice before, and then it was in
church, where he claimed to speak to me as if he were an old

acquaintance ! I will none of him nor his mantle, if he were fifty times a properer man than he is !"

"Be it so, my daughter," replied the Collector. "But we must bear this mishap cheerily. I will not offend again. You women," he said, as he walked to and fro through the parlor, with his hands behind his back, and a good-natured smile playing over his features, "you women are more shrewd to read the qualities of men, especially in matters of behavior, than such old pock-puddings as I am. I will be better counselled before I trespass in this sort again. But remember, Blanche, the skipper has his summons, and our hospitality must not suffer reproach ; so we will e'en make the best we can of this blundering misadventure of mine. For our own honor, we must be courteous, Blanche, to the skipper ; and, therefore, do thou take heed that he have no cause to say we slight him. As I get old I shall grow wise."

Blanche threw her arms around her father's neck and imprinting a kiss upon his brow, said in a tone of affectionate playfulness, "For your sake, dear father, I will not chide : the skipper shall not want due observance from me. I did but speak to give you a caution, by which you shall learn that the maidens of this province are so foolish as to stand to it, and I amongst the rest, that they are better able to choose their gallants than their fathers, —though their fathers be amongst his Lordship's most trusty advisers."

"Now a thousand benisons upon thy head, my child !" said the Collector, as he laid his hand upon Blanche's glossy locks, and then left the apartment.

CHAPTER XV.

Friend to the sea, and foeman sworn
To all that on her waves are borne,
When falls a mate in battle broil
His comrade heirs his portioned spoil—
Chalice and plate from churches borne,
And gems from shrieking beauty torn,
Each string of pearl, each silver bar,
And all the wealth of western war.

ROKEBY.

As the skipper strode towards the town, his dogged air and lowering brow evinced the disquiet of his spirit at what had just occurred. He was nettled by the maiden's rejection of his proffered gift, and a still deeper feeling of resentment agitated his mind against the Secretary. Far other man was he than he was deemed by the burghers of St. Mary's. In truth, they knew but little more of him than might be gained from his few occasional visits to the port in a calling which, as it brought him a fair harvest of profit, laid him under a necessity to cultivate, for the nonce, the good opinion of his customers by such address as he was master of.

Cocklescraft belonged to that tribe of desperate men, until near this period in the full career of their bloody successes, known as "The Brethren of the Coast." His first breath was drawn upon the billows of the ocean, and his infancy was nursed in the haunts of the buccaneers, amongst the Keys of the Bahamas. When but a lad, attending upon these wild bands in their expeditions against the commerce of the Gulf, he chanced to attract the notice of the famous Captain Morgan, whilst that most rapacious of all the pirate leaders was preparing, at Jamaica, for his incursion against Maracaibo. The freebooter was charmed with the precocious relish for rapine conspicuous in the character of the boy ; and, with an affectionate interest, took him under his tutelage, assigning to him a post near his person, rather of pageantry than service—that of a page or armor-bearer, according to the yet lingering forms of chivalry. The incredible bravery of the buccaneers in this exploit, and their detestable cruelties, were witnessed by this callow imp of the sea, with a delight and a shrewdness of apprehension which gave to his youthful nature the full benefit of the lesson. He was scarce two years older when, in the due succession of his hopeful experience, he again attended his patron upon that unmatched adventure of plunder and outrage, the leaguer of Panama ; and it was remarked that amidst the perils of the cruise upon the Costa Rica, the toils of the inland march over moor and mountain, and the desperate hazards of the storming of the city, the page, graceful and active as the minion of a lady's bower, and fierce as a young sea-wolf, was seen every where, like an elfish sprite, tracking the footsteps of his ruthless master. The history of human wickedness has not a more appalling chapter than that which records the fate of the wretched inhabitants of Panama in this assault ; and yet, in the midst of its shocking enormities, the gay and tasseled familiar of the ruffian pirate chief tripped daintily through the carnage, with the light step of a reveller, and pursued the flying virgins and affrighted matrons, from house to house, as the flames enveloped their roof trees, with the mockery and prankishness of an actor in a masquerade. This expedition terminated not without adding another item to the experience of the young freebooter—the only one, perhaps, yet wanting to his perfect accomplishment.—The

Welsh Captain, laden with spoils of untold value, played false to his comrades, by stealing off with the lion's share of the booty; thus, by a gainful act of perfidy, inculcating upon the eager susceptibility of the page an imposing moral, of which it may be supposed he would not be slow to profit.

Such was the school in which Cocklescraft received the rudiments of his education. These harsher traits of his character, however, it is but justice to say, were, in some degree, mitigated by a tolerably fair amount of scholastic accomplishment, picked up in the intervals of his busy life amongst the scant teaching afforded by the islands, of which the protection and care of his patron enabled him to profit. To this was added no mean skill in music, dancing, and the use of his weapon; whilst a certain enthusiasm of temperament stimulated his courage and even whetted the fierceness of his nature.

Morgan, having run his career, returned to England, a man of wealth, and was knighted by the monarch, in one of those profligate revels by which Charles disgraced his kingly state; the page was, in consequence, turned adrift upon the world, as it is usual to say of heroes, "with no fortune but his talents, and no friend but his sword." Riot soon exhausted his stock of plunder, and the prodigal licentiousness of "The Brethren of the Coast," forbade the gathering of a future hoard. About this date the European powers began to deal more resolutely with the banditti of the islands, and their trade consequently became more precarious. They were compelled, in pursuit of new fields for robbery, to cross the isthmus and try their fortunes on the coast of the Pacific—whither Cocklescraft followed and reaped his harvest in the ravage of Peru: but in turn, the Brethren found themselves tracked into these remoter seas, and our adventurer was fain, with many of his comrades, to find his way back to the coves and secret harbors of Tortuga and the Keys, whence he contrived to win a subsistence, by an occasional stoop upon such defenceless wanderers of the ocean as chance threw within his grasp. The Olive Branch was a beautiful light vessel, which, in one of his sea-forays, he had wrested from a luckless merchant ; and this acquisition suggested to him the thought that, with such necessary alterations as should disguise her figure and equipment, he might drive a more secure, and, perchance, more profitable trade between the Atlantic colonies and the old countries ; so, with a mongrel crew of trusty cut-throats, carefully selected from the companions of his former fortunes, and a secret armament well bestowed for sudden emergency, he set himself up for an occasional trader between the Chesapeake and the coast of Holland. A lucky acquaintance with the Cripple of St. Jerome's gave him a useful ally in his vocation as a smuggler ; the fisherman's hut, long believed to be the haunt of evil spirits, admirably favored his design, and under the management of Rob, soon became a spot of peculiar desecration in popular report ; and thus, in no long space of time, the gay, swashing cavalier, master of the Olive Branch, began to find good account in his change of character from the flibustier of the Keys into that of smuggler and trader of the Chesapeake. He had now made several voyages from St. Mary's to the various marts of Holland and England, taking out cargoes of tobacco and bringing back such merchandise as was likely to find a ready sale in the colonies. His absence from port was often mysteriously prolonged, and on his return it not unfrequently happened that there were found amongst his cargo commodities such as might scarce be conjectured to have been brought from the ports of Europe,—consisting some times of tropical fruits, ingots of gold and silver, and sundry rich furniture of Indian aspect, better fitted for the cabinet of the virtuoso than the trade of a new province. Then, also, there were occasionally costly stuffs, and tissues of exceeding richness, such as cloth of

gold, velvets of Genoa, arras tapestry, and even pictures which
might have hung in churches.   These commodities were in-
variably landed at St. Jerome's Bay before the Olive Branch
cast her anchor in the harbor of St. Mary's, and were reshipped
on the outward voyage.   The Cripple of St. Jerome's had a few
customers who were privileged at certain periods to traffic with
him in a species of merchandise of which he was seldom without
a supply at his command—chiefly wines and strong waters, and
coarser household goods, which were charily exhibited in small
parcels at the hut, and when the bargain was made, supplied in
greater bulk by unseen hands from secret magazines, concerning
which the customer was not so rash as even to inquire—for Rob
was a man who, the country people most devoutly believed, had
immediate commerce with the Evil One, and who, it was known,
would use his dagger before he gave warning by words.

The open and lawful dealing of the skipper, in the port of St.
Mary's, had brought him into an acquaintance with most of the
inhabitants, and as his arrival was always a subject of agreeable
expectation, he was, by a natural consequence, looked upon with
a friendly regard.   His address, gaiety of demeanor, and fine
figure—which last was studiously set off to great advantage by a
rich and graceful costume—heightened this sentiment of personal
favor, and gave him privileges in the society of the town which,
in that age of scrupulous regard to rank, would have been denied
him if he had been a constant sojourner.   Emboldened by this
reception he had essayed to offer some gallant civilities to the
maiden of the Rose Croft, which were instantly repelled, however,
by the most formal coldness.   The skipper was not so practised
an observer as to perceive in this repugnance the actual aversion
which the maiden felt against his advances to acquaintance ; and
he was content to account it a merely girlish reserve which importunity and assiduous devotion might overcome.   His vanity

suggested the resolve to conquer the damsel's indifference ; and as that thought grew upon his fancy, it, by degrees, ripened into a settled purpose, which in the end completely engrossed his mind. As he brooded over the subject, and permitted his imagination to linger around that form of beauty and loveliness,—cherished, as it was, during the long weeks of his lonely tracking of the sea, and in the solitary musings and silent night-watches of his deck,—a romantic ardor was kindled in his breast, and he hastened back to the port of St. Mary's, strangely wrought upon by new impulses, which seemed to have humanized and mellowed even his rude nature : the shrewder observers were aware of more gentleness in his bearing, though they found him more wayward in his temper ;—he was prouder of heart, yet with humbler speech, and often more stern than before. The awakening of a new passion had over-mastered both the ferocity and the levity of his character. He was, in truth, the undivulged, anxious, and almost worshipping lover of Blanche Warden.

When such a nature as I have described chances to fall into the loving vein, it will be admitted to be a somewhat fearful category both for the lady and the lover's rival. Such men are not apt to mince matters in the course of their wooing.

This was the person who now plied his way towards the port, in solitary rumination over two distinct topics of private grief, each of a nature to rouse the angry devil of his bosom. He could not but see that his first approach towards the favor of his mistress had been promptly repelled. That alone would have filled his mind with bitterness, and given a harsh complexion to his thoughts ;—but this cause of complaint was almost stifled by the more engrossing sentiment of hostility against the Secretary. That he should have been rebuked for his behavior by a man,—and a man, too, who evidently stood well with the lady of his love ; taken to task and chid in the very presence of his mistress,

8

——was an offence that called immediately to his manhood and demanded redress.   Such redress was more to his hand than the
nicer subtleties of weighing the maiden's displeasure, and he turned
to it with a natural alacrity, as to a comfort in his perplexity. It
is the instinct of a rude nature to refer all cases of wounded sensibility to the relief of battle.   A rejected lover, like a child who
has lost a toy, finds consolation in his distress by fighting any one
that he can persuade himself has stood in his way, and he is made
happy when there chances to be some plausible ground for such a
proceeding.   The skipper thought the subject over in every aspect which his offended pride could fancy.   At one moment the
idea of quarrel with the Secretary pleased him, and almost recon-
ciled him to the maiden's coldness ; at the next he doubted
whether, after all, she had in fact designed to repel his friendship.
He vibrated between these considerations for a space in silence :
his pride quelled the expression of his anger.   But by degrees his
quickened pace and sturdier step, and, now and then, that slight
shake of the head by which men sometimes express determination,
made it plain that the fiery element in his bosom was rising in
tumult.   At length, unable to suppress his feeling, the inward
commotion found utterance in words.

" Who and what is this Master Secretary that has set the
maiden of the Rose Croft to look upon me with an evil spirit ? I
would fain know if he think himself a properer man than I. Does
he stand upon his fingering of a lute, and his skill to dance ?—
Why even in this chamber-craft I will put it to a wager he is no
master of mine.   Is he more personable in shape or figure ?—goes
he in better apparel ? or is that broken English of his more natural to the province than my plain speech, that he should claim
the right to chide me for my behavior ?   Is it that he has a place
in the train of his Lordship ?   Have not I served as near to a
belted knight—lord of a thousand stout hearts·and master of a

fleet of thirty sail ?—ay, and in straits where you should as soon expect to meet a hare as that crotchet-monger. A bookish clerk with no manly calling that should soil his ruff in the space of a moon ! By St. Iago, but I will put him to his books to learn how he shall heal the stroke of a choleric hand, when the time shall serve to give him the taste of it !—Mistress Blanche would not be importuned—indeed ! And he must be my tutor to teach me what pleaseth Mistress Blanche. He lied—the maiden did not mislike my question ;—she but hung her head to have it so openly spoken. I know she does not set at naught my favors, but as damsels from custom do a too public tender of a token. Old Anthony Warden counts his friends by their manhood, and he has shown me grace :—his daughter in the end will follow his likings, and as the father's choice approves, so will hers incline. Am I less worthy in old Master Warden's eyes than yonder parchment bearer—that pen-and-ink slave of his Lordship's occasions ?—he that durst not raise his eye above his Lordship's shoe, nor speak out of a whisper when his betters are in presence ? What is he, to put me from the following of my own will when it pleases me to speak to any maiden of this province ?—I am of the sea—the broad, deep sea ! she hath nursed me in her bosom,—and hath given me my birth-right to be as proudly borne as the honors of any lord of the land. I have a brave deck for my foot, a good blade for my belt, the bountiful ocean before me, and a score of merry men at my back. Are these conditions so mean that I must brook the Secretary's displeasure or fashion my speech to suit his liking ?—We shall understand each other better, in good time, or I shall lack opportunity to speak my mind :—I shall, good Master Verheyden,—you have the word of a 'Brother of the Bloody Coast' for that !"

Before the skipper had ceased this petulant and resentful self-communion, he found himself in the neighborhood of the Catholic chapel, nearly in front of the dwelling of Father Pierre, when the good priest, who was at this moment returning from noon-day service, took him at unawares with the salutation,—

"Peace be with you, son !—you reckon up the sum of your ventures with a careful brow, and speak loud enough to make the town acquainted with your gains, if perchance some of the chapmen with whom you have dealing should be in your path.   How fares it with you, Master Skipper ?"

"Ha, Mi Padre !" exclaimed Cocklescraft, instantly throwing aside his graver thoughts and assuming a jocular tone.   "Well met ;—I was on my way 'o visit you : that would I have done yesterday upon my arrival, but that the press of my business would not allow it.   You grow old, Father, so evenly that, although I see you but after long partings, I can count no fresh touch of time upon your head."

"Men of your calling should not flatter," said the priest smiling.   "What news do you bring us from the old world ?"

"Oh, much and merry, Father Pierre.   The old world plies her old trade and thrives by it. Knavery has got somewhat of the upper hand since they have quit crossing swords in this new peace of Nimeguen. The Hogan Morgans are looking a little surly at the Frenchman for cocking his beaver so bravely ; and our jobbernowl English, now that they can find no more reason to throttle each other, have gone back to their old sport of pricking the side of our poor church.   You shall find as many plots in London, made out of hand and ready for use in one month, as would serve all the stage plays of the kingdom for the next hundred years— and every plot shall have a vile Papist at the bottom of it,—if you may believe Oates and Bedloe.   I was there when my Lord Stafford was made a head shorter on Tower Hill.   You heard of this, Father ?"

"Alack ! in sorrow we heard of this violence," replied the

priest ; "and deeply did it grieve my Lord to lose so good a friend. Even as you have found it in England, so is it here. The discontents against the holy church are nursed by many who seek thereby to command the province. We have plotters here who do not scruple to contrive against the life of his Lordship and his Lordship's brother the Chancellor. Besides, the government at home is unfriendly to us."

"You have late news from England?" inquired the skipper.

"We have,—and which, but that you are true in your creed, I might scarce mention to your ear—the royal order has come to my Lord to dismiss his Catholic servants from office—every one. His Lordship scruples to obey. This, Master Skipper, I confide to you in private, as not to be told again."

"To remove all !" said Cocklescraft. "Why it will sweep off his nearest friends—Anthony Warden and all."

"Even so."

"There is fighting matter in that, upon the spot," exclaimed the skipper. "I hope it may come up while I am in port ! The Collector, old as he is, will buckle on his toledo in that quarrel. He has mettle for it ; and I could wish no better play than to stand by his side. Who is this Secretary of my Lord's private chamber ? I met him at the Collector's to-day."

"Master Albert Verheyden," replied the priest.

"I know his name—they told it to me there—but his quality and condition, father ?"

"You may be proud of his fellowship," said Father Pierre ; "he was once a scholar of the Jesuit school at Antwerp, of the class inscribed 'Princeps Diligentiæ,' and brought thence by my Lord. A youth, Master Cocklescraft, of promise and discretion —a model to such as would learn good manners and cherish virtuous inclinations. You may scarcely fail to see him at the

Collector's : the townspeople do say he has an eye somewhat dazzled there."

" Craving pardon for my freedom, I say, Father Pierre, a fig's end for such a model !" exclaimed the skipper, pettishly ; " you may have such by the score, wherever lazy, bookish men eat their bread. I like him not, with his laced band and feather, his book and lute : harquebuss and whinyard are the tools for these days. I hear the Fendalls have been at mischief again. We shall come to bilbo and buff before long. Your Secretary will do marvellous service in these straits, Father."

" Son, you are somewhat sinful in your scorn," said the priest, mildly ; " the Secretary does not deserve this taunt——"

" By the holy hermits, Father, I speak of the Secretary but as I think. He does not awe me with his greatness. I vail no top-sail to him, I give you my word for it."

" The saints preserve us from harm !" said the churchman. " We know not what may befall us from the might of our enemies, when this hot blood shall sunder our friends. In sober counsel, son, and not in rash divisions shall we find our safety. It does not become you, Master Cocklescraft, to let your tetchy humor rouse you against the Secretary. It might warrant my displeasure."

" Mea culpa, holy father—I do confess my fault," said the seaman, in a tone of assumed self-constraint—" I will not again offend ; and for my present atonement will offer a censer of pure silver, which in my travels I picked up, and, in truth, did then design to give to the Chapel of St. Mary's. I will bring it to the chapel, Father Pierre, as soon as my vessel is unladen."

" You should offer up your anger, too, to make this gift acceptable," returned the priest. " Let thy dedication be with a cleansed heart."

"Ha, Father Pierre," said the skipper, jocularly; "my conscience does easily cast off a burden: so it shall be as you command. I did not tell you that whilst my brigantine lay in the Helder, I made a land flight to Louvaine, where a certain Abbot of Andoyne—a pious, somewhat aged, and, thanks to a wholesome refectory! a good jolly priest,—hearing I came from the province, must needs send for me to ask if I knew Father Pierre de la Maise, and upon my answer, that I did right well, he begs me to bring his remembrance back to you."

"I knew Father Gervase," replied the priest with a countenance full of benignity, "some forty years ago, when he was a reader in the Chair of St. Isidore at Rome. He remembers me?—a blessing on his head!—and he wears well, Master Skipper?"

"Quite as well as yourself," replied Cocklescraft. "Father, a cup of your cool water, and I will depart," he said, as he helped himself to the draught. "I will take heed to what you have said touching the royal order—and by St. Iago, I will be a friend in need to the Collector. Master Verheyden shall not be a better one. Now fare you well, Father. Peregrine Cadger shall have order to cut you off a cassock from the best cloth I have brought him, and little Abbot the tailor shall put it in fashion for you."

"You are lavish of your bounties, son," replied the priest, taking Cocklescraft by both hands as he was now about to withdraw. "You have a poor churchman's thanks. It gives me comfort to be so considered, and I prize your kindness more than the cassock. A blessing on thy ways, Master Cocklescraft!"

The skipper once more set forth on his way towards the port; and with a temper somewhat allayed by the acting of the scene I have just described, though with no abatement of the resentment which rankled at the bottom of his heart, even under the smiling face and gay outside which he could assume with the skill of a consummate dissembler, he soon reached the Crow and Archer. From thence he meditated, as soon as his occasions would permit, a visit to the Cripple of St. Jerome's.

CHAPTER XVI.

"Who be these, sir?"
"Fellows to mount a bank. Did your instructor
In the dear tongues never discourse to you
Of the Italian mountebanks?"
"Yes, sir."
"Why here you shall see one."
"They are quacksalvers,
Fellows that live by vending oils and drugs."
VOLPONE.

The council had been summoned to meet on the morning following that of the incidents related in the last chapter, and the members were now accordingly assembling at the Proprietary mansion.
The arrival of one or two gentlemen on horseback with their servants, added somewhat to the bustle of the stable yard, which
was already the scene of that kind of busy idleness and lounging
occupation so agreeable to the menials of a large establishment.
Here, in one quarter, a few noisy grooms were collected around
the watering troughs, administering the discipline of the curry-
comb or the wash-bucket to some half score of horses. In a corner of the yard Dick Pagan the courier and Willy o' the Flats,
with the zeal of amateur vagrants, were striving to cozen each
other out of their coppers at the old game of Cross and Pile;
whilst, in an opposite direction, Derrick was exhibiting to a group
of spectators, amongst whom the young heir apparent was a
prominent personage, a new set of hawk bells just brought by the
Olive Branch from Dort, and lecturing, with a learned gravity,

8*

upon their qualities, to the infinite edification and delight of his youthful pupil.   Fox hounds, mastiffs, and terriers, mingled indiscriminately amongst these groups, as if confident of that favoritism which is the universal privilege of the canine race amongst good tempered persons and contented idlers all the world over. Whilst the inhabitants of the yard were engrossed with these occupations, a trumpet was heard at a distance in the direction of the town.   The blast came so feebly upon the ear as, at first, to pass unregarded, but being repeated at short intervals, and at every repetition growing louder, it soon arrested the general attention, and caused an inquiry from all quarters into the meaning of so unusual an incident.

"I think that there be an alarm of Indians in the town !" exclaimed the falconer, as he spread his hand behind his ear and listened for some moments, with a solemn and portentous visage. "Look to it, lads—there may be harm afoot.   Put up your halfpence, Dick Pagan, and run forward to seek out the cause of this trumpeting.   I will wager it means mischief, masters."

"Indians !" said Willy ; "Derrick's five wits have gone on a fool's errand ever since the murder of that family at the Zachaiah fort by the salvages.   If the Indians were coming you should hear three guns from Master Randolph Brandt's look-out on the Notley road.   It is more likely there may be trouble at the gaol with the townspeople, for there was a whisper afloat yesterday concerning a rescue of the prisoners.   Truth, the fellow has a lusty breath who blows that trumpet !"

"Ay, and the trumpet," said Derrick, "is not made to dance with, masters : there is war and throat-cutting in it, or I am no true man."

During this short exchange of conjectures, Dick Pagan had hastened to the gate which opened towards the town, and mounting the post, for the sake of a more extensive view, soon discerned the object of alarm, when, turning towards his companions, he shouted,

"Wounds,—but here's a sight! Pike and musket, belt and saddle, boys! To it quickly;—you shall have rare work anon. Wake up the ban dogs of the fort and get into your harness. Here comes the Dutch Doctor with his trumpeter as fierce as the Dragon of Wantley. Buckle to and stand your ground!"-

"Ho, ho!" roared the fiddler with an impudent, swaggering laugh. "Here is a pretty upshot to your valors! Much cry and little wool, like the Devil's hog-shearing at Christmas. You dullards, couldn't I have told you it was the Dutch Doctor,—if your fright had left you but a handful of sense to ask a question? Didn't I see both him and his trumpeter last night at the Crow and Archer, with all their jingumbobs in a pair of panniers? Oh, but he is a rare doctor, and makes such cures, I warrant you, as have never been seen, known or heard of since the days of St. Byno, who built up his own serving man again, sound as a pipkin, after the wild beasts had him for supper."

The trumpet now sent forth a blast which terminated in a long flourish, indicating the approach of the party to the verge within which it might not be allowable to continue such a clamor; and in a few moments afterwards the Doctor with his attendant entered the stable yard. He was a little, sharp-featured, portly man, of a brown, dry complexion, in white periwig, cream-colored coat, and scarlet small clothes: of a brisk gait, and consequential air, which was heightened by the pompous gesture with which he swayed a gold-mounted cane full as tall as himself. His attendant, a bluff, burly, red-eyed man, with a singularly stolid countenance, tricked out in a grotesque costume, of which a short cloak, steeple-crowned hat and feather, and enormous nether garments, all of striking colors, were the most notable components, bore a brass trumpet suspended on one side, and a box of no

inconsiderable dimensions in front of his person ; and thus fur
nished, followed close at the heels of the important individual
whose coming had been so authentically announced.

No sooner had the Doctor got fairly within the gate than he
was met by Derrick Brown, who, being the most authoritative
personage in the yard, took upon himself the office of giving the
stranger welcome.

"Frents, how do you do?" was the Doctor's accost in a strong,
Low Dutch method of pronouncing English. "I pelieve dis is
not de gate I should have entered to see his Lordship de Lord
Proprietary," he added, looking about him with some surprise to
find where he was.

"If it was my Lord you came to see," said the falconer,
"you should have turned to your right, and gone by the road
which leads to the front of the house. But the way you have
come is no whit the longer : we can take you through, Master
Doctor, by the back door."

"Vell, vell, dere is noding lost by peing acquainted at once
wid de people of de house," replied the man of medicine ; "dere
is luck to make your first entrance by de pack door, as de old
saying is. I vas summoned dis morning to appear before de
council, py my Lord's order ; and so, I thought I might trive a
little pusiness, at de same time, wid de family."

"I told you all," said Willy, with an air of self-importance at
his own penetration, "that this was a rare doctor. The council
hath sent for him ! my Lord hath made it a state matter to see
him. It isn't every doctor that comes before the worshipful
council, I trow. Give him welcome, boys, doff your beavers."

At this command several of the domestics touched their hats,
with a gesture partly in earnest and partly in sport, as if expecting some diversion to follow.

"No capping to me, my frents !" exclaimed the Doctor, with

a bow, greatly pleased at these tokens of respect; "no capping to me! Pusiness is pusiness, and ven I come to sell you tings dat shall do you goot, I tank you for your custom and your money, widout asking you to touch your cap."

"There is sense in that," said John Alward; "and since you come to trade in the yard, Doctor, you can show us your wares. There is a penny to be picked up here."

"Open your box, Doctor; bring out your pennyworths; show us the inside!" demanded several voices at once.

"Ha, ha!" exclaimed the vender of drugs, "you are wise, goot frents; you know somewhat! You would have a peep at my aurum potabiles in dat little casket—my multum in parvo? Yes, you shall see, and you shall hear what you have never seen pefore, and shall not in your long lives again."

"Have you e'er a good cleansing purge for a moulting hawk?" inquired Derrick Brown, whilst the Doctor was unlocking the box.

"Or a nostrum that shall be sure work on a horse with a farcy?" asked one of the grooms.

"Have you an elixir that shall expel a lumbago?" demanded John Alward: all three speaking at the same instant.

"Tib, the cook," said a fourth, "has been so sore beset with cramps, that only this morning she was saying, in her heart she believed she would not stop to give the paste buckle that Tom Oxcart gave her for a token at Whitsuntide, for a cordial that would touch a cold stomach. I will persuade her into a trade with the Doctor."

"Oh, as for the women," replied a fifth, "there isn't a wench in my Lord's service that hasn't a bad tooth, or a cold stomach, or a tingling in the ears, or some such ailing: it is their nature—they would swallow the Doctor's pack in a week, if they had license."

The man of nostrums was too much employed in opening out

his commodities to heed the volley of questions which were poured upon him all round, but having now put himself in position for action, he addressed himself to his auditors :

"I vill answer all your questions in goot time ; but I must crave your leave, freuts, to pegin in de order of my pusiness. Dobel," he said, turning to his attendant, who stood some paces in the rear, "come forward and pegin."

The adjutant at this command stepped into the middle of the ring, and after making several strange grimaces, of which at first view his countenance would have been deemed altogether incapable, and bowing in three distinct quarters to the company, commenced the following speech :

"Goot beoplish !"—this was accompanied with a comic leer that set the whole yard in a roar—"dish ish de drice renowned und ingomprbl Doctor Closh Tebor"—another grimmace, and another volley of laughter—"what ish de grand pheseeshan of de greate gofernor of New York, Antony Prockolls, und lives in Alpany in de gofernor's own pallash, wid doo tousand guilders allowed him py de gofernor everich yeere, und a goach to rite, und a body cart to go pefore him in de sthreets ven he valks to take de air. All tish to keepe de gofernor und his vrouw de Laty Katerina Prockolls in goot healf—noding else—on mein onor." This was said with great emphasis, the speaker laying his hand on his heart and making a bow, accompanied with a still more ludicrous grimace than any he had yet exhibited, which brought forth a still louder peal from his auditory.

He was about to proceed with his commendatory harangue, when he was interrupted by Benedict Leonard. It seems that upon the first announcement by the Doctor of the purport of his visit, the youth, fearful lest his mother, who was constitutionally subject to alarm, might have been disturbed by the trumpet, ran off to apprise her of what he had just witnessed ; and giving her the full advantage of Willy's exaggerated estimate of the travelling healer of disease, returned, by the lady's command, to conduct this worthy into her presence. He accordingly now delivered his message, and forthwith master and man moved towards the mansion, with the whole troop of the stable yard at their heels.

The itinerant was introduced into Lady Baltimore's presence in a small parlor, where she was attended by two little girls, her only children beside the boy we have noticed, and the sister of the Proprietary. Her pale and emaciated frame and care-worn visage disclosed to the practised glance of the visitor a facile subject for his delusive art,—a ready votary of that credulous experimentalism which has filled the world with victims to medical imposture. In the professor of medicine's reverence to the persons before him there was an overstrained obsequiousness, but, at the same time, an expression of imperturbable confidence fully according with the ostentatious pretension which marked his demeanor amongst the menials of the household. Notwithstanding his broad accent, he spoke with a ready fluency that showed him well skilled in that voluble art by which, at that day, the workers of wonderful cures and the possessors of infallible elixers advertised the astonishing virtues of their compounds—an art which has in our time only changed its manner of utterance, and now announces its ridiculous pretensions in every newspaper of every part of our land, in whole columns of mountebank lies and quack puffery."

"This is the great Doctor," said young Benedict, who was eager to introduce him, "and he has come I can't tell how far, to see who was ailing in our parts. I just whispered to him, dear mother, what a famous good friend you were to all sorts of new cures. And oh, it would do you good to see what a box of crankums he has in the hall! Yes, and a man to carry it, with a trumpet ! Blowing and physicking a plenty now, to them that like it ! How the man bears such a load, I can't guess."

"Dobel has a strong back and a steady mule for his occasions, my pretty poy," said the Doctor, patting the heir apparent on the head, with a fondness of manner that sensibly flattered the mother. "When we would do goot, master, we must not heed de trouble to seek dem dat stand in need of our ministrations over de world."

The lady's feeble countenance lit up with a sickly smile, as she remonstrated with the boy. "Bridle thy tongue, Benedict, nor suffer it to run so nimbly. We have heard, Doctor, something of your fame, and gladly give you welcome."

"Noble lady," replied the pharmacopolist, "I am but a simple and poor doctor, wid such little fame as it has pleased Got to pestow for mine enteavors to miticate de distemperatures and maladies and infirmities which de fall of man, in de days of Adam, de august progenitor of de human races, has prought upon all his children. And de great happiness I have had to make many most wonderful cures in de provinces of America, made me more pold to hope I might pring some assuagement and relief to your ladyship, who, I have peen told, has peen grievously tormented wid perturbations and melancholics ; a very common affection wid honorable ladies."

"Alack, Doctor, my affections come from causes which are beyond the reach of your art," said the lady with a sigh. "Still, it would please me to hear the cures you speak of. You have, doubtless, had great experience ?"

"You shall hear, my lady. I am not one of dat rabble of pretenders what travel apout de world to cry up and magnify dere own praises. De Hemel is mij getuige,—Heaven is my chudge, and your ladyship's far renowned excellent wisdom forbids dat you should be imposed upon by dese cheats and impos ters denominated—and most justly, on my wort !—charlatans and empirical scaramouches. De veritable merit in dis world is humble, my lady. I creep rader in de dust, dan soar in de clouts : it is in my nature. Oders shall speak for me—not myself."

"But you have seen de world, Doctor, and studied, and served in good families ?"

"Your ladyship has great penetration. I have always lived in friendship wid worshipful peoples. De honorable Captain General Anthony Brockholls, de gofernor of de great province of New York,—hah ! dere was nopody could please him but Doctor Debor. Night and day, my lady, for two years, have I peen physicking his excellency and all his family :—de governor is subject to de malady of a pad digestion and crudities which gives him troublesome dreams. I have studied in de school of Leyden —dree courses, until I could find no more to learn ; and den I have travelled in France, Germany, and Italy, where I took a seat in de great University of Padua, for de penefit of de lectures of dat very famous doctor, Veslingius, de prefect, your ladyship shall understand, and professor of botany, a most rare herbalist. And dere also I much increased and enriched my learning under de wing of dat astonishing man, de grave and profound Doctor Athelsteinus Leonenas, de expounder of de great secrets of de veins and nerves. You shall chudge, honorable ladies, what was my merit, when I tell you de University would make me Syndicus Artistarum, only dat I refused so great honor, pecause I would not make de envy of my compeers. Did I not say true when I tell you it is not my nature to soar in de clouts ?"

"Truly the Doctor has greatly slighted his fame," said the Lady Maria apart to her kinswoman. "I would like to know what you have in your pack."

"Worshipful madam, you shall soon see," replied the Doctor, who now ordered Dobel, his man, into the room. "Here," he said, as he pointed to the different parcels, "are balsamums, penaceas, and elixirs. Dis is a most noted alexipharmacum against quartan agues, composed of many roots, herps, and spices ; dis I call de lampas vitæ, an astonishing exhilirator and promoter of de goot humors of de mind, and most valuable for de rare gift of clear sight to de old, wid many oder virtues I will not stop to mention. Dese are confections, electuaries, sirups, conserves, ointments, odoraments, cerates, and gargarisms, for de skin, for de stomach, for de pruises and wounds, for de troat, and every ting pesides. Ah ! here, my lady, is de great lapor of my life, de felicity and royal reward—as I may say—of all my studies : it is de most renowned and admired and never-to-be estimated Medicamentum Promethei, which has done more penefactions dan all de oder simples and compounds in de whole pharmacopeia of medicine. Your ladyship shall take but one half of dis little phial, when you will say more for its praise dan I could speak widout peing accounted a most windy, hyperbolical and monstrous poaster—ha, waarachtig ! I will speak noting. Dat wise and sagacious and sapient man, de great governor and captain, Antony Brockholls, has given me in my hand so much as five ducatoons,—yes, my lady, five ducatoons for dat little glass, two hours after a dinner of cold endives—Ik spreek a waarachtiglik—I speak you truly, my lady : and now I give it away for de goot of de world and mine own glory, at no more dan one rix dollar,—five shillings. I do not soar in de clouts ?"

"Can you describe its virtues, Doctor ?" inquired the lady.

"Mine honored madam, dey are apundant, and I shall not lie if I say countless and widout number. First, it is a great enemy to plack choler, and to all de affections of de spleen, giving sweet sleep to de eyelids dat have peen kept open py de cares and sufferings and anxieties of de world. It will dispel de charms of witchcraft, magic and sorcery, and turn away de stroke of de evil cye. It corroborates de stomach py driving off de sour humors of de pylorus, and cleansing de diaphram from de oppilations which fill up and torpefy de pipes of de nerves. And your ladyship shall observe dat, as Nature has supplied and adapted particular plants and herps to de maladies of de several parts of de animal pody, as,—not to be tedious,—aniseeds and calamint for de head, hysop and liquorice for de lungs, borage for de heart, betony for de spleen, and so on wid de whole pody—dis wonderful medicament contains and possesses in itself someting of all, peing de great remedy, antidote and expeller of all diseases, such as vertigine, falling sickness, cramps, catalepsies, lumbagos, rheums, inspissations, agitations, hypocondrics, and tremorcordics, whedder dey come of de head, de heart, de liver, de vena cava, de mesentery or de pericardium, making no difference if dey be hot or cold, dry or moist, or proceeding from terrestrial or genethliacal influences, evil genitures, or vicious aspects of de stars—it is no matter—dey all vanish pefore de great medicamentum. You must know, my lady, dis precious mixture was de great secret—de arcanum mirificabile—of dat wonderful Arabian physician Hamech, which Paracelsus went mad wid cudgelling his prains to find out ; and Avicenna and Galen and Trismegistus and Moderatus Columella all proke down in deir search to discover de meaning of de learned worts in which Hamech wrote de signification. De great Swammerdam, hoch ! what would he not give Doctor Debor for dat secret ! I got it, my lady, from a learned Egyptian doctor, who took it from an eremite of Arabia Felix. It was not my merit, so much as my goot fortune. I am humble, my lady, and do not poast, but speak op't woord van een eerlyk man."

"He discourses beyond our depth," said Lady Baltimore, greatly puzzled to keep pace with the learned pretensions of the quack ; "and yet I dare say there is virtue in these medicines

What call you your great compound, Doctor? I have forgotten its name."

"De Medicamentum Promethei," replied the owner of this wonderful treasure, pleased with the interest taken in his discourse. "Your ladyship will comprehend from your reading learned pooks, dat Prometheus was a great headen god, what stole de fire from Heaven, whereby he was able to vivicate and reluminate de decayed and worn-out podies of de human families, and in a manner even to give life to de images of clay; which is all, as your good ladyship discerns, a fabulous narration, or pregnant fable, as de scholars insinuate. And, moreover, de poets and philoshphers say dat same headen god was very learned in de knowledge of de virtues of plants and herps, which your ladyship will remark is de very consistence and identification of de noble art of pharmacy. Well, den, dis Prometheus, my lady— ha, ha!—was some little bit of a juggler, and was very fond of playing his legerdemains wid de gods, till one day de great Jupiter, peing angry wid his jocularities and his tricks, caused him to be chained to a rock, wid a hungry vulture always gnawing his liver; and dere he was in dis great misery, till his pody pined away so small dat his chain would not hold him, and den, aha! he showed Jupiter a goot pair of heels, like an honest fellow, and set apout to find de medicines what should renovate and patch up his liver, which you may be sure he did, my lady, in a very little while. Dis again is anoder fable, to signify dat he was troubled wid a great sickness in dat part of his pody. Now, my lady, see how well de name significates de great virtues of my medicament, which, in de first place, is a miraculous restorer of health and vigor and life to de feeble spirits of de pody : dere's de fire. Second, it is composed of more dan one hundred plants, roots, and seeds, most delicately distilled, sublimed and suffumigated in a limbeck of pure virgin silver, and according to de most

subtle projections of alchemy ; and dere your ladyship shall see
de knowledge of de virtues of plants and de most consummate
art of de concoctions. And now for de last significance of de
fable : dis medicament is a specific of de highest exaltation for
de cure, which never fails, of all distemperatures of de liver ; not
to say dat it is less potent to overcome and destroy all de oder
diseases I have mentioned, and many more. Dere you see de
whole Medicamentum Promethei, which I sell to worshipful
peoples for one rix dollar de vial. Is it not well named, my
lady, and superlative cheap ? I give it away : de projection
alone costs me more dan I ask for de compound."

"The name is curiously made out," said the lady, "and
worthily, if the virtue of the compound answer the description.
But your cures, you have not yet touched upon them. I long to
hear what notable feats you have accomplished in that sort."

"My man Dobel shall speak," replied the professor. "De
great Heaven forpid I should pe a poaster to de ears of such
honorable ladies ! Dobel, rehearse de great penefaction of de
medicament upon de excellent and discreet and virtuous vrouw
of Governor Brockholls—Spreek op eene verstaanbare wijze !"

"Hier ben ik," answered Dobel to his summons, stepping at
the same time into the middle of the room and erecting his person
as stiffly as a grenadier on parade : "Goot beoplish ! dish ish
de drice renowned und ingomprbl Doctor Closh Tebor——"

"Stop, stop, hou stil ! halt—volslagen gek !" exclaimed the
Doctor, horrified at the nature of the harangue his stupid servi-
tor had commenced, and which for a moment threatened to continue. in spite of the violent remonstrance of the master, Dobel
persevering like a thing spoken from rather than a thing that
speaks—"Fool, jack-pudding ! you pelieve yourself on a bank,
up on a stage before de rabble rout ? You would disgrace me
before honorable and noble ladies, wid your tavern bowlings, and

your parkings and your pellowings !   Out of de door, pegone !"

The imperturbable and stolid trumpeter, having thus unfortunately incurred his patron's ire, slunk from the parlor, utterly
at a loss to comprehend wherein he had offended.   The Doctor
in the meanwhile, overwhelmed with confusion and mortified
vanity, bustled towards the door and there continued to vent
imprecations upon the unconscious Dobel, which, as they were
uttered in Low Dutch, were altogether incomprehensible to the
company, but at the same time were sufficiently ludicrous to produce a hearty laugh from the Lady Maria, and even to excite a
partial show of merriment in her companion.   Fortunately for
the Doctor, in the midst of his embarrassment, a messenger
arrived to inform him that his presence was required before the
council, in another part of the house, which order, although it
deprived the ladies of the present opportunity of learning the
great efficacy of the Medicamentum Promethei in the case of the
wife of Governor Brockholls, gave the Doctor a chance of recovering his self-possession by a retreat from the apartment.   So,
after an earnest entreaty to be forgiven for the inexpert address
of his man, and a promise to resume his discourse on a future
occasion, he betook himself, under the guidance of the messenger,
to the chamber in which the council were convened.

Here sat the Proprietary, and Philip Calvert, the Chancellor,
who were now, with five or six other gentlemen, engaged in the
transaction of business of grave import.

Some depredations had been recently committed upon the
English by the Indians inhabiting the upper regions of the
Susquehanna,—especially by the Sinniquoes, who, in an incursion
against the Piscattaways, a friendly tribe in the vicinity of St.
Mary's, had advanced into the low country, where they had plun-
dered the dwellings of the settlers and even murdered two or
three families.   The victims of these outrages happened to be

Protestants, and Fendall's party availed themselves of the circumstance, to excite the popular jealousy against Lord Baltimore by circulating the report that these murders were committed by Papists in disguise.

What was therefore but an ordinary though frightful incident of Indian hostility, was thus exaggerated into a crime of deep malignity, peculiarly calculated still more to embitter the party exasperations of the day. This consideration rendered it a subject of eager anxiety, on the part of the council, to procure the fullest evidence of the hostile designs of the Indians, and thus not only to enable the province to adopt the proper measure for its own safety, but also confute the false report which had imputed to the Catholics so absurd and atrocious a design. A traveller, by the name of Launcelot Sakel, happened, but two or three days before the present meeting of the council, to arrive at the port, where he put afloat the story of an intended invasion of the province by certain Indians of New York, belonging to the tribes of the Five Nations, and gave as his authority for this piece of news a Dutch doctor, whom he had fallen in with on the Delaware, where he left him selling nostrums, and who, he affirmed, was in a short space to appear at St. Mary's. This story, with many particulars, was communicated to the Proprietary, which induced the order to summon the doctor to attend the council as soon after his arrival as possible. In obedience to this summons, our worthy was now in the presence of the high powers of the province, not a little elated with the personal consequence attached to his coming, as well as the very favorable reception he had obtained from the ladies of the household. This consequence was even enhanced by the suite of inquisitive domestics, who followed, at a respectful distance, his movements towards the council chamber, and who, even there, though not venturing to enter, were gathered into a group which from the outside of the door commanded a view of the party within : in the midst of these Willy of the Flats was by no means an unconspicuous personage.

Lord Baltimore received the itinerant physician with that bland and benignant accost which was habitual to him, and proceeded with brief ceremony to interrogate him as to the purport of his visit. The answers were given with a solemn self-complacency, not unmixed with that shrewdness which was an essential attribute to the success of the ancient quack-salver. He described himself as Doctor Claus Debor, a native of Holland, a man of travel, enjoying no mean renown in New York, and, for two years past, a resident of Albany. His chief design in his present journey, he represented to be to disseminate the blessings of his great medicament ; whereupon he was about to launch forth into an exuberant tone of panegyric, and had, in fact, already produced a smile at the council board by some high wrought phrases expressive of his incredible labor in the quest of his great secret, when the Proprietary checked his career by a timely admonition.

" Ay, we do not seek to know thy merits as a physician, nor doubt the great virtue of thy drugs, worthy Doctor ; but in regard thereto, give you free permission to make what profit of them you reasonably may in the province. Still, touching this license, I must entreat you, in consideration that my Lady Baltimore has weak nerves, and cannot endure rude noises, to refrain from blowing your trumpet within hearing of this mansion : besides, our people," he added, looking archly towards the group of domestics, some of whom had now edged into the apartment, " are somewhat faint-hearted at such martial sounds."

" By my hand !" said Willy, in a half whisper to his companions in the entry ; " My Lord has put it to him for want of manners !—I thought as much would come from his tantararas.

Listen, you shall hear more anon. Whist!—the Doctor puts on a face—and will have his say, in turn."

"Your very goot and admirable Lordship mistranslates de significance of my visit," said the Doctor, in his ambitious phrase; "for although I most heartily tank your Lordship's bounty for de permission to sell my inestimable medicament, and which—Got geve het—I do hope shall much advantage my lady wid her weak nerfs and her ailments,—still, I come to opey your most honorable Lordship's summons, which I make pold to pelieve is concerned wid state matters pefore de high and noble council."

"Well, and bravely spoken," said Willy; "and with a good face!—the Doctor holds his own, masters."

"We would hear what you can tell touching a rumor brought to us by one Master Launcelot Sakel, whom you saw at Christian Fort," said the Proprietary.

"There is the point of the matter," whispered Willy, "all in an egg shell."

"Dere is weighty news, my Lord," replied the Doctor. "I have goot reason to pelieve dat de Nordern Indians of New York are meditating and concocting mischief against your Lordship's province."

"Have a care to the truth of your report," said Colonel Talbot, rising from his seat: "it may be worse for you if you be found to trifle with us by passing current a counterfeit story, churned into consistence in your own brain, out of the froth of idle, way-side gossipings. We have a statute against the spreaders of false news."

"Heigh, heigh!—listen to that," said Willy, nudging one of the crowd over whose shoulders he was peering into the room. "There's an outcome with a witness!—there's a flanconade that shall make the Doctor flutter!"

"If I am mendacious," replied the Doctor, "dat is, if I am

9

forgetful of mine respect for trute, dese honorable gentlemens shall teal wid me as a lying pusy pody and pragmatical tale-bearer. Your Lordship shall hear. It is put a fortnight ago, when I was making ready for dis journey, in Alpany, I chanced to see in de town so many as two score, perhaps fifty Indians who were dere trading skins for powder and shot. Dey reported demselves to be Sinniquoes, and said dey came to talk wid de tribes furder back, to get their help to fight against de Piscatta-ways."

"Indeed?—there is probability in that report," said the Proprietary: "well, and how had they sped? what was their success?"

"Some of de Five Nations,—I forget de name of de tribe, my Lord—it might pe de Oneidas—dey told us, promised to march early de next season; in dere own worts, when de sap pe-gin to rise."

"In what force, did they say?"

"In large force, my Lord. De Piscattaways, dey said, were frents to my Lord and de English,—and so dey should make clean work wid red and white."

"What more?"

"Dey signified dat dey should have great help from de Dela-wares and Susquehannocks, who, as I could make it out, wanted to go to war wid your Lordship's peoples at once."

"True; and they have done so. The insolencies of these tribes are already as much as we can endure. Did they find it easy to purchase their powder and lead in Albany? I should hope that traffic would not be allowed."

"My Lord, de traders do not much stop, when dey would turn a penny, to reckon who shall get de loss, so dey get de profit. Dese same Indians I saw afterwards in de town of New York, trading in de same way wid Master Grimes, a merchant."

"Mischief will come of this," said the Proprietary, "unless it be speedily taken in hand. What reason was given by the Northern Indians for joining in this scheme?"

"I tink it was said," replied the Doctor, "dat your Lordship had not made your treaties wid dem, nor sent dem presents, dese two years past."

"True," interposed the Chancellor; "we have failed in that—although I have more than once reminded your Lordship of its necessity."

"It shall not be longer delayed," replied the Proprietary. "You are sure, Doctor Debor, these were Sinniquoes you saw?"

"I only know dem by dere own report—I never heard de name pefore. My man Dobel heard dem as well as me; wid your Lordship's permission I shall ask him," said the Doctor, as he went to the door and directed some of the domestics to call the man Dobel.

It happened that Dobel, after his disgrace, had kept apart from the servants of the household, and was now lamenting his misfortune in a voluntary exile on the green at the front door, where Willy of the Flats having hastened to seek him, gave him the order to appear before the council.

"Dobel, you are a made man," he said by way of encouragement; "your master wants you to speak to their honors: and the honorable council want to hear you, Dobel; and so does his Lordship. Hold up your head, Dobel, and speak for your manhood—boldly and out, like a buckler man."

"Ya, ya," replied Dobel, whose acquirements in the English tongue were limited to his professional advertisement of Doctor Debor's fame, and a few slender fragments of phrases in common use. Thus admonished by Willy, he proceeded doggedly to the council chamber, where as soon as he entered, the Proprietary made a motion to him with his hand to approach the table,—

which Dobel interpreting into an order to deliver his sentiments, he forthwith began in a loud voice—

"Goot beoplish ! dish is de drice renowned und ingomprbl Doctor———"

Before he had uttered the name, the Doctor's hand was thrust across Dobel's mouth, and a volley of Dutch oaths rapped into his ears, at a rate which utterly confounded the poor trumpeter, who was forcibly expelled from the room, almost by a general order. When quiet was restored,—for it may be imagined the scene was not barren of laughter,—the Doctor made a thousand apologies for the stupidity of his servant, and in due time received permission to retire, having delivered all that he was able to say touching the matter in agitation before the Proprietary.

The council were for some time after this incident engaged in the consideration of the conspiracy against the Proprietary, of which new evidences were every day coming to light ; and it was now resolved that the matter should be brought unto the notice of the judicial authority at an early day.

The only circumstance which I have further occasion to notice, related to a diversion which was not unusual at that day amongst the inhabitants of the province, and which required the permission of the council.   It was brought into debate by Colonel Talbot.

"Stark Whittle, the swordsman." he said, " has challenged Sergeant Travers to play a prize at such weapons as they may select—and the Sergeant accepts the challenge, provided it meet the pleasure of his Lordship and the council.   I promised to be a patron to the play."

" It shall be as you choose," said the Proprietary.   " This martial sport has won favor with our people.   Let it be so ordered that it shall not tend to the breach of the peace.   We commit it to your hands, Colonel Talbot."   The council assented, and the necessary order was recorded on the journal.

CHAPTER XVII.

Some do call me Jack, sweetheart,
 And some do call me Jille:
But when I come to the king's faire courte,
 They call me Wilfulle Wille.
 THE KNIGHT AND SHEPHERD'S DAUGHTER.

THE skipper's necessary affairs in the port engaged him all the
day succeeding that of his interview with Father Pierre, and
therefore prevented him from making his intended visit to the
Cripple of St. Jerome's. When the next morning broke upon
him, the early bell of St. Mary's Chapel informed him of the
Sabbath,—a day seldom distinguished in his calendar from the
rest of the week. It was, however, not unheeded now, as it
suggested the thought that an opportunity might be afforded
him to gain a sight of Blanche Warden—and even, perchance,
an interview—at the service of the Chapel. In this hope he at
once relinquished his design of going to St. Jerome's, at least
until after the morning offices of the church were performed.
Accordingly, at an hour somewhat in advance of the general
attendance of the congregation, the skipper was seen loitering in
the purlieus of the Chapel, where he marked with an inquisitive
but cautious watchfulness the various groups that were coming
to their devotions. When at length his strained vision was able
to descry a cavalcade approaching from the direction of St.
Inigoe's, and he discerned the figures of Albert Verheyden and

Blanche Warden dallying far in the rear of the Collector and his
daughter Alice, their horses almost at a walk, and themselves
manifestly engrossed in an earnest conference, he turned hastily
towards the church, and with a compressed lip and knitted brow
ascended the stair and threw himself into an obscure corner of
the little gallery which looked upon the altar.   Here he remained
a sullen and concealed observer of the rites of the temple,—his
bosom rankling with uncharitable thoughts, and his countenance
clouded with feelings the most ungenial to the lowly self-
abasement and contrition of heart which breathed in every word
of the solemn ritual that addressed his ear.

The Collector's family entered the place of worship.   The
Secretary still accompanied Blanche, knelt beside her in prayer,
opened her missal to the various services of the day, and tendered
the customary offices of familiar gallantry common to such an
occasion, with an unrebuked freedom : all this in the view of the
skipper, whose eye flashed with a vengeful fire, as he gazed upon
the man to whom he attributed the wrong he deemed himself to
have suffered in his recent interview with the maiden.   The service ended and the throng was retiring, when Cocklescraft planted
himself on the outside of the door.   His purpose was to exchange
even but a word with the daughter of the Collector—at least to
win a recognition of his presence by a smile, a nod, the smallest
courtesy,—so dear to the heart of a lover.   She came at last,
loiteringly with Father Pierre and Albert Verheyden.   Perhaps
she did not see Cocklescraft in the shade of the big elm, even
although her father's weaker sight had recognized him, and the
old man had stepped aside to shake his hand.   She passed on to
her horse without once turning her head towards him.   The
skipper abruptly sprang from the Collector to help her into her
saddle, but Blanche had already Albert's hand, and in a moment
was in her seat.   Cocklescraft's proffered service was acknow-

lodged by a bow and only a casual word. The Secretary in an instant mounted his steed, and, with the maiden, set forth on their ride at a brisk gallop. The Brother of the Coast, forgetful of his usual circumspection, stood with folded arms and moody visage, looking darkly upon them as they disappeared, and muttering half-audible ejaculations of wrath. He was, after an interval, roused from his abstraction by the hand of Father Pierre gently laid upon his shoulder :

"You have forgotten the censer of virgin silver you promised to offer at this shrine," said the priest in a grave voice. "It was to be an offering for the sin of a wayward spirit of anger. Beware, son, that thou dost no wrong to a brother."

"I have not forgotten the censer, holy Father," returned the skipper, with an ineffectual effort to assume his usual equanimity. "I have only deferred the offering—until I may give it," he added in a stern voice, "with an honest conscience. You shall have it anon. I have business now that stands in the way :—good morning to you, Father." And with these words he walked rapidly away.

In the afternoon Cocklescraft was seen plying his way from the quay in a small boat, attended by two seamen who rowed him to a point some five or six miles below the town, where he landed, and set out on foot for St. Jerome's.

On the following morning, whilst the dawn yet cast its gray hue over the face of the land, two men, in shaggy frize dresses, arrived at the hut of The Cripple. They rode on rough, little beach-ponies, each provided with a sack. The mastiff bitch eyed the visitors with a malign aspect from her station beneath the door sill, and by her low mutterings warned them against a too near approach. They accordingly stood at bay.

"Curse on the slut !" said one ; "she has the eye of a very devil ;—it might not be safe to defy her. Not a mouse is stir-

ring ;—the old Trencherman is as still as his bowl. Were it
safe, think you, to wake him ?"

"Why not ?" demanded the other.   "He will be in a passion
and threaten, at first, with his weapon ;—but when he knows we
come to trade with him, I will warrant he butters his wrinkles as
smoothly with a smile as you could desire. Strike your staff,
Nichol, against the door."

"The fiend fetch me, if I venture so near as to strike, with
that bitch at the step. Try it yourself, Perry Cadger."

"Nay, and it comes to that, I will rouse him in another
fashion," said the other.

"Master Swale—Master Robert Swale—Halloo—halloo !"

"Rob, man, awake,—turn out for friends !" exclaimed the
first. The growl of the mastiff bitch was now changed into a
hoarse bark. Some stir was heard from the inside of the hut,
and, in a moment afterwards, the door was unbolted and brought
sufficiently open to allow the uncouth head and half dressed figure
of The Cripple to be seen. A short blunderbuss was levelled
directly in the face of the visitors, whilst an ungracious repulse
was screamed out in a voice husky with rage.

"Begone, you misbegotten thieves !   What makes you here ?
Do you think I am an ale draper to take in every strolling runa-
gate of the night. Begone, or I will baptize you with a sprinkling of lead !"

"I beseech you, Robert Swale," exclaimed the first speaker,
"turn your weapon aslant ! You may do a deed of mischief
upon your friends. We are Nichol Upstake, and Peregrine
Cadger—friends, Rob,—friends, who have come to drive bargains to your profit. Open your eyes, Master—put on your
glasses—we have gold in pocket, man."

"Ha, ha, ha !" chuckled the tenant of the hut ; "thou art
astir, cronies ! Ha, ha ! I took ye for land loupers— sharks.

By the Five Wounds, I knew ye not! Have patience a space and I will open."

When The Cripple had dressed himself he came swinging forth in his bowl, and passing beyond the curtilage of his dwelling went to the beach, whither he was followed by his two visitors, who had now dismounted from their ponies. Here he halted, and taking off his cap, exposed his bare head and loose white tresses to the morning breeze which came somewhat sharply from the water.

"Soh!" he exclaimed, "there is refreshment in that! It is my custom to expel these night-cap vapors with the good salt water breeze: that is a commodity that may reach the province without paying duty to his Lordship! a cheap physic, masters. Now what scent are you upon, Nichol Upstake? Perry Cadger, man of sarsnet and grogram, I guess your errand."

"In truth, Robert Swale," said Upstake——

"No Robert Swale, nor Master Robert Swale," testily interrupted the owner of the cabin; "none of your worshipful phrase for me! You are but a shallow hypocrite to affect this reverence. Rob of the Bowl is the best I get from you when your longings are satisfied; ay, and it is said with a curl of your lip; and you make merry over my unworthiness with your pot-fellows. So, be honest, and give me plain Rob; I seek no flattery."

"You do us wrong, good Master Rob," interposed Peregrine Cadger——

"To your needs," said Rob, sternly: "speak in the way of your trade! You have no voice, nor I ear, for aught else."

"Then, in brief," said Nichol Upstake, "I would know if you could supply me with Antigua to-day, or aqua vitæ, I care not which?"

"If such a thing might be, where would you take it, Nichol?" inquired Rob.

" To Warrington on the Cliffs."

" Ay, to Warrington on the Cliffs ; good !—and warily to be borne ? no hawk's eye upon your path ?"

" It shall be by night, if you like it," said the dealer.

" Well, well !" replied The Cripple ; " I can give you a little of both, master : a flagon or so ; some three or four. My hut is small, and has a scant cellar. But the money in hand, Nichol Upstake ! Good gold—full weight—and a fair price, too, mark you ! I must have a trifle above my last market—ten shillings the gallon on the brandy, and two more for the Antigua. Leave your kegs, and see me again at sunset. The money in hand ! the money in hand ! there is no trust in my commonwealth."

" It shall be so," said Nichol.

" And now, Master Cadger, what wilt ? You have a scheme to cozen dame and wench with gewgaws ; I see it in your eye : and you will swear upon book and cross, if need be, they have stood you a wondrous hard purchase, even at the full three hundred per cent. excess you purpose to exact above the cost ; and all the while it has come out of Rob's warehouse as cheap as beggars' alms : ha, ha, ha ! This world thrives on honesty ! it grows fat on virtue ! knavery only starves. Your rogue in rags, what has he but his deserts ? Let him repent and turn virtuous, like you and me, Perry, and his torn cloak and threadbare doublet shall be fenced and lined to defy all weathers. Hark you, master, I have camblets, satins, and velvets, cambric, and lawn— choice commodities all. You shall see them in the hut."

" How came you by so rich an inventory, Rob ?"

The Cripple turned a fierce eye upon the mercer, and with one glance conveyed his meaning, as he touched the handle of his dagger and said in a low tone,

" Do you forget the covenant between us ? Peregrine Cadger, you know I brook no such question."

The mercer stood for a moment abashed, and then replied: "An idle word, Master Rob, which meant no harm : as you say, honesty will only thrive. You shall find never a knave that is not some part fool. I will into the hut to look at the wares."

"Do so," said The Cripple. "You will find them in the box behind the door. There is need that you leave me, so follow him, Nichol. I have sudden business, masters, which it does not concern you to witness. When you have seen what you desire, depart quickly; leave your sacks and come back at sunset. I charge you, have a care that your eyes do not wander towards my motions. You know me, and know that I have sentinels upon your steps who have power to sear your eye-balls if you but steal one forbidden glance : away !"

The dealers withdrew into the hut, wondering at the abrupt termination of their interview, and implicitly confiding in the power of The Cripple to make good his threat.

"The Lord have mercy upon us !" said the mercer, in a smothered voice, after they had entered the door ; "The Cripple has matters on hand which it were not for our good to pry into. Pray you, Nichol, let us make our survey and do his bidding, by setting forth at once. I am not the man to give him offence."

The cause of this unexpected dismissal of the visitors was the apparition of Cocklescraft, whose figure, in the doubtful light of the morning, was seen by Rob at a distance, on the profile of the bank in the neighborhood of the Wizard's Chapel. He had halted upon observing The Cripple in company with strangers, and had made a signal which was sufficiently intelligible to the person to whom it was addressed, to explain his wish to meet him.

Rob, having thus promptly rid himself of his company, now swung on his short crutches, almost as rapidly as a good walker

8

could have got over the ground, towards the spot where the buccaneer had halted.

"Steer your cockleshell there to the right, old worm!" said the freebooter, as Rob came opposite to the bank on which he stood. "You shall find it easier to come up by the hollow."

"The plague of a foul conscience light on you!" replied The Cripple, desisting from further motion, and wiping the perspiration from his brow. "Is it more seemly I should waste my strength on the fruitless labor to clamber up that rough slope, or you come down to me? You mock me, sirrah!" he added, with an expression of sudden anger; "you know I cannot mount the bank."

"You know I can drag you up, reverend fragment of a sinful man!" returned Cocklescraft, jocularly; "yes, and with all your pack of evil passions at your back, besides. Would you hold our meeting in sight from the window of the hut, where you have just lodged a pair of your busy meddlers—your bumpkin cronies in the way of trade? It was such as these that, but a few nights ago, set his Lordship's hounds upon our tracks. Come up, man, without further parley."

The Cripple's fleeting anger changed, as usual, to that bitter smile and chuckle with which he was wont to return into a tractable mood, as he said,—

"A provident rogue! a shrewd imp! He has his instinct of mischief so keen that his forecast never sleeps. The devil has made him a perfect scholar. There, Dickon, give me your hand," he added, when he came to the steep ascent which his machine of locomotion was utterly inadequate to surmount. "Give me your hand, good cut-throat. Help me to the top."

The muscular seaman, instead of extending his hand to his companion, descended the bank, and taking the bowl and its occupant upon his shoulder, strode upward to the even ground, and

8*

deposited his load with as little apparent effort as if he had been dealing with a truss of hay.

"Bravely!" ejaculated Rob, when he was set down. "I scarce could have done better in my best day. Now what set you to jogging so early, Dickon? Where do you come from?"

"From the Chapel," replied the other. "I came there from the port last night, express to see you; and having no special favor for the bed I slept on, I left it at the first streak of light to go and rouse you from your dreams, and lo! there you are at one of your dog and wolf bargains with the countryside clowns."

"Discreet knaves, Dickon, who have come to ease us of somewhat of our charge of contraband: stout jerkins—stout and well lined; rogues of substance—Nichol Upstake, the ordinary keeper of Warrington, and Perry Cadger, the mercer of St. Mary's. Seeing you here, I dismissed them until sunset. That Peregrine Cadger is somewhat leaky as a gossip, and might tell tales if he were aware that I consorted with you."

"I see them taking the road on their ponies," said Cocklescraft; "we may venture to the hut. I am sharp set for breakfast, and when I have a contented stomach, I will hold discourse with you, Rob, touching matters of some concern to us both."

The Cripple and his guest, upon this hint, repaired to the hut, and in due time the morning meal was supplied and despatched. Cocklescraft then opened the purport of his visit.

"Has it ever come into your wise brain, Master Rob," he asked, "that you are getting somewhat old; and that it might behoove you to make a shrift at the confessional, by way of settling your account? I take it, it will not be a very clean reckoning without a good swashing penance."

"How now, thou malignant kite!" exclaimed The Cripple; "what's in the wind?"

"Simply, Rob, that the time has come when, peradventure,

we must part.   I am tired of this wicked life.   I shall amend ;
and I come to counsel you to the like virtuous resolution.   I will
be married, Robert Swale, Man of the Bowl !"

"Grammercy ! you will be married ! you ! I spit upon you
for a fool.   What crotchet is this ?"

"I will be married, as I say, neither more nor less.   Now to
what wench, ask you ?   Why to the very fairest and primest
flower of this province—the Rose of St. Mary's—the Collector's
own daughter.   I mark that devil's sneer of unbelief of yours,
old buckler man : truer word was never spoke by son of the sea
or land, than I speak now."

"To the Collector's daughter !" ejaculated The Cripple in a
tone of derision.   "Your carriage is bold in the port, but no
measure of audacity will ever bring you to that favor.   Would
you play at your old game, and sack the town, and take the dain-
tiest in it for ransom?   You know no other trick of wooing,
Dickon."

"By my hand, Rob, I am specially besought by the Collector
to make one at a choice merry-making which his daughter has on
foot for next Thursday.   Ay, and I am going, on his set command, to dance a galliard with Mistress Blanche.   Oh, she shall
be the very bird of the sea—the girl of the billow, Rob !   She
shall be empress of the green wave that nursed me, and the blue
sky, and the wide waste.   Her throne shall be on the deck of
my gay bark : and my merry men shall spring at her beck as
deftly as at the boatswain's pipe !"

"You shall sooner meet your deservings," said Rob, "on the
foal of the acorn, with a hempen string, than find grace with the
Collector's child.   Your whole life has been adversary to the good
will of the father."

"I know it," replied Cocklescraft.   "I was born in natural
warfare with the customs and all who gather them ; the more

praise for my exploit ! I shall change my ways and forsake evil company. I shall be a man of worship. We shall shut up the Chapel, Rob ; expel our devils ; pack off our witches to Norway, and establish an honest vocation. Therefore, Rob, go to Father Pierre, repent of your misdeeds, and live upon your past gains. You are rich and may afford to entertain henceforth a reputable conscience."

"Do not palter with me, sirrah ! but tell me what this imports."

"Then truly, Rob, I am much disturbed in my fancies. I love the wench, and mean to have her—fairly if I can—but after the fashion of the Coast if I must. She does not consent as yet —mainly because she has a toy of delight in that silken Secretary of my Lord—a bookish, pale-cheeked, sickly strummer of stringed instruments—one Master Verheyden, I think they call him."

"Ha !" exclaimed The Cripple, as a frown gathered on his brow ; "what is he ? Whence comes he ?"

"His Lordship's chamber secretary," replied Cocklescraft ; "brought hither I know not when, nor whence. A silent-paced, priestly pattern of modesty, who feeds on the favor of his betters, as a lady's dog, that being allowed to lick the hand of his mistress, takes the privilege to snarl on all who approach her. I shall make light work with him by whipping him out of my way. Why are you angry, that you scowl so, Master Rob ?"

"I needs must be angry to see thee make a fool of thyself," replied the master of the hut. "Verheyden—his Lordship's secretary !" he muttered to himself. "No, no ! it would be a folly to think it."

"Mutter as you will, Rob," said Cocklescraft ; "by St. Iago, I will try conclusions with the Secretary—folly or no folly ! He has taught the maiden," he added, with a bitter emphasis, "to affect a scorn for me, and he shall smart for it."

" Ha ! thy spirit is ever for undoing !" exclaimed Rob, suddenly changing his mood, and forcing a harsh laugh of derision. " Mischief is your proper element—your food, your repose, your luxury. Well, if you must take on a new life, and strive to be worshipful, I would counsel you to begin it with some deed of charity, not strife. I had as well make my lecture to a young wolf ! Ha, Dickon, you will be a prospering pupil to the master that teaches you the virtue of charity ! Such rede will be welcome to you as water to your shoes ! I have scanned you in all your humors !"

" I spurn upon your advice, and will not be scorned, old man !" said Cocklescraft, angrily. " The maiden shall be mine, though I pluck her from beneath her father's blazing roof-tree ; and then farewell to the province, and to you ! Mark you that ! I come not to be taunted with your ill-favored speech ! My men shall be withdrawn from the Chapel. I will put them on worthier service than to minister to your greediness."

" Hot-brained, silly idiot—thou drivelling fool !" shouted Rob. " Do you not know that I can put you in the dust and trample on you as a caitiff ? that I can drive you from the province as a vile outlaw ? Are you such a dizzard as to tempt my anger ? If you would thrive even in your villainous wooing, have a care not to provoke my displeasure ! One word from me, and not a man paces your deck : you go abroad unattended, stiverless—a fugitive, with hue and cry at your heels. How dar'st thou reprove me, boy ?"

" Your hand, Rob," said Cocklescraft, relenting. " You say no more than my folly warrants : I am a wanton fool : your pardon—let there be peace between us."

" Art reasonable again ! Bravely confessed, Dickon ! I forgive your rash speech. Now go your ways, and the Foul One speed thee ! I have naught to counsel, either for strife or peace.

since you have neither wit, wisdom, nor patience for sober advice against the current of your will. It will not be long before this maimed trunk shall sink into its natural resting place—and it matters not to me how my remnant of time be spent—whether in hoarding or keeping. The world will find me an heir to squander what little store it hath pleased my fortune to gather. So go your ways."

"I will see you again, friend Rob," said the buccaneer. "I have matter to look after at the Chapel, and then shall get back to the port, to drive my suit to a speedy issue. I came here but in honest dealing with you, to give you friendly notice of my design, and perchance, to get your aid. You have no counsel for me? It is well; my own head and arm shall befriend me; they have stood me instead in straits more doubtful than this: fare-well—farewell!"

As the skipper stepped along the beach, Rob planted himself in the door of the hut and looked after him for some moments, nodding his head significantly towards him, and muttering in a cynical undertone, "Go thy ways, snake of the sea, spawn of a water devil! You married! ha, ha! Your lady gay shall have a sweetened cup in you: and your wooing shall be tender and gentle—yea, as the appetite of the sword-fish. It shall be festi-val wooing—all in the light—in the light—of the bride's own blazing roof: a dainty wolf! a most tractable shark! Oh, I cannot choose but laugh!"

CHAPTER XVIII.

Some with the ladies in their chambers ply
Their bounding elasticity of heel,
Evolving, as they trip it whirlingly,
The merry mazes of the entangled reel.

ANSTER FAIR.

" You wear a sword, sir, and so do I!"
" Well, sir!"
" You know the use, sir, of a sword?"
" I do—to whip a knave, sir."

THE HUNCHBACK.

THE festival of St. Therese, Blanche's birth-day, so anxiously looked for by the younger inhabitants of St. Mary's, and scarcely less heartily welcomed by the elder, at length came round. Towards sunset of an evening, mild in temperature and resplendent with the glorious golden-tipped clouds of the October sky, the air fraught with that joyful freshness which distinguishes this season in Maryland, groups of gay-clad persons were seen passing on the high road that led from the town to the Rose Croft. The greater number, according to the usage of that day, rode on horseback, the women seated on pillions behind their male escort. Some of the younger men trudged on foot, and amongst these was even seen, here and there, a buxom damsel cheerily making her way in this primitive mode of travel, and showing by her merry laugh and elastic step how little she felt the inconvenience of her walk.

It must not be supposed from this account that the luxury of the coach was altogether unknown to the good people of the province. Two of these vehicles were already within the dominions of the Lord Proprietary; one belonging to his Lordship himself, and the other to Master Thomas Notley, of Notley Hall, member of the council, and sometime, during the Proprietary's late visit to London, the Lieutenant-General of the province. They were both of the same fashion, stiff, lumbering, square old machines which had been imported some twenty years past, and were often paraded in the street of St. Mary's with their bedizened postillions and footmen, to the no inconsiderable enhancement, in the eyes of the burghers, of the dignity and state of their possessors. The bountiful foresight and supreme authority, it may be said, of the Lady Maria had procured the aid of both of these accommodations for the service of the evening, and they were, accordingly, now plying backward and forward between the port and the Collector's, for the especial ease and delectation of sundry worshipful matrons whose infirmities rather inclined them to avoid the saddle, and also for the gratification of such favorites of the good lady, amongst the younger members of the population, as she vouchsafed to honor by this token of her regard. By the help of these conveniences a considerable number of guests had been set down, at the scene of festivity, a full hour before sunset—this early convocation being in conformity with the social usages by which our ancestors were accustomed, on occasions of jollity, to take time by the forelock.

The fame of the preparations at the Rose Croft had attracted, in addition to the invited guests, all such mere idlers as the humbler ranks of the townspeople supplied. These were chiefly congregated about the principal gateway, drawn thither by their desire to witness the coming of the visitors and to feast their eyes with the display of holiday finery, which furnishes so large a fund of interest to persons of this class. The crowd was composed of

serving-men and maids, idle apprentices and vagrant strollers, of
both sexes, with a due admixture of ragged, bare-legged boys,
who drove a business of some little gain, by taking charge of the
horses of such as dismounted at the verge of the enclosure that
surrounded the dwelling. Willy of the Flats, ordinarily but a
comrade of these groups, was now elevated into a character of
some importance on a theatre of higher honor, and having become a personage, in their estimation, of no mean mark, did not
fail to let his consequence be seen and felt by his old compeers.
His rough shoes were greased to give them a more comely
exterior, his linen, new-washed, was ambitiously displayed upon
his breast, and his dilapidated garments, put in the best condition
their weather-stricken service would allow, were ostentatiously
freshened up with knots of party-colored ribbons, which, especially
upon his veteran beaver, flared in streamers, and audibly fluttered
in the zephyr that played across his brow. His fiddle, which was
soon to be called into active employment, was as yet suspended
to the kitchen wall in its green bag, and he strutted, in vacant
leisure, across the lawn in the presence of his envying cronies at
the gateway, with a vain-glorious and self-gratulating step, that
showed, at least, how complacently he viewed his own exaltation,
even if he did not win as much worship from the spectators.

"Michael Mossbank," he said with a significant twinkle of
the eye; "we will make dainty work of it to-night—our junketing
shall be spoken of on both sides of the bay this many a long year.
The quality themselves do not often see the like,—and the simple
folks that have had the luck to be let in, will not forget it, or I
am mistaken, till the young down turns into old bristles. It is
like to be a most capersome and I may say melodious merry-
making. You had no light hand, Michael, in the ordering of
it."

"You may make Bible oath to that," replied the gardener;

"and you would never be forsworn. Order it, I did,—the out-door work, the kitchen-work, and the hall-work. Here was the trimming of hedges to make all smooth at the bank side, and the setting out of the lawn—not a straggling leaf shall you see upon it ; then the herbs for the kitchen, and the flowers for the hall ! Faith it was a handful of work for a week past. If it had not been for Michael there would have been but tame sport to-night."

"Oh, but you have a great head, for such monstrous contri-vances, Michael : you are a gardener of gardeners ! Adam was of the trade before you,—but he had no jig-muster to set out in his time :—his noddle could never have compassed it—or his five wits would have buzzed till he grew blind,—and then all his children would have given up the trade forever after. Oh, was it not lucky for us that Father Adam was not put to the order-ing of a jig-muster ?"

"Out, you beet-face," exclaimed the gardener, half angrily ; "Go put your gibes upon them that have an ear for such cracks ! Why do you stand grinning there with your flaunting ribons, when there is work for you elsewhere ? Look to yon gaping beggars at the gate—they will presently so crowd the way that no one may enter. Look to it, until you are wanted in the hall, and you shall earn your penny-fee and broken victual the better for it."

"Out upon *you*, Michael, yourself, for a churl, a cockle-weed ! I eat no broken victual at your hands : he would have small fare who waited on your charity. A fiddler has as much worship as a spade-lifter any day in the year—so, cock your nose at some one below you !"

"A jest for a gibe, Willy," returned the gardener good-humoredly ; "a jest for a gibe ! Play turkey-cock and swell to your heart's content !—and when you have let off your spite go to the gate where you are wanted "

The fiddler, after this short and ruffling encounter, having regained his equanimity, and not displeased at the chance of showing his importance to the loiterers about the gate, went to the post assigned to him ; where, with a self-complacent tone of admonition, he addressed the assemblage, consisting of some dozen auditors, with a discourse upon the behavior expected of them on this interesting occasion both by himself and the master of the feast.

Prominent amongst those upon whom this instruction was bestowed, was one who regarded Willy with singular deference : this was a lean and freckled lad, just on the verge of manhood, whose unmeaning eye, relaxed fibre and ever present smile denoted a stinted intellect, whilst his unoffending inquisitiveness gained him admission to the skirts of all gatherings, whether festive or sad. His restless foot and characteristic thirst for knowledge habitually impelled him to seek the most conspicuous post of observation, and he was now, accordingly, in the foremost rank of Willy's hearers. Wise Watkin, (for by this name he was familiarly greeted by young and old,) notwithstanding the parsimony with which Nature had doled out to him the gift of wit, was remarkable for his acquaintance with all classes of persons, and for a certain share of cunning in picking up the shreds of whatever rumor might chance, for the time, to agitate the gossip of the town : he was still more remarkable for his inordinate admiration of the fiddler.

Willy had just concluded his lecture at the gate, when his attention was arrested by the rumble of wheels heard at a distance, and by a cloud of dust which was seen rising in the neighboring wood through which the road lay from the town.

"Hearken, neighbors,—his Lordship's coach !" he cried out. "We shall have it here presently, stuffed with people of worship. Take ranks on each side of the road—quickly, I beseech you !

Now remember, at my signal, thus,—hands to your caps, lads,—
and wenches, sink :—do it comely and altogether."

"Ranks, ranks !" exclaimed Wise Watkin, who, with officious
alacrity, began to push the crowd into the array indicated by the
fiddler. "Heed Willy, and do as he bids. He knows what will
please the gentle-folks—hands to your caps !"

The motley ranks being formed according to the fiddler's
direction, awaited the arrival of those for whom this formal salutation was designed.

Instead of the Proprietary's coach, a few moments disclosed
a cart with a little thick-set, shaggy pony attached to it, coming
at high gallop upon the road. On the bench above the shafts
was descried the jolly figure of the landlady of the Crow and
Archer, in the suit of green and scarlet in which we have heretofore noticed her, playing the part of charioteer. Beside her sat
the terrified Garret Weasel, who, of too light bulk to maintain a
solid seat, jolted fearfully to and fro at every spring of the
vehicle. The pony had manifestly taken the speed of his journey
into his own discretion, and, with the shank of the bit gripped
between his teeth, and head curved sidewise, set his course doggedly for the gate, in obstinate resistance of the dame, who, with
both arms at stretch, reddened brow and clenched teeth, tugged
at the reins, to turn him into a road that led, by a circuit,
towards the rear of the dwelling, whither she was now conveying
sundry articles of provision which she had undertaken to supply
for the feast.

"Friends, stop the beast !" shouted the treble voice of the
vintner as soon as he perceived Willy's corps—"stop us for the
love of mercy !"

As the crowd gathered to arrest the runaways, a wave of
the hand from the dame suspended their purpose. Her mettle
was roused by the contumacy of the pony ; whereupon, in disdain

of the proffered aid, she gave loose rein to her beast, and, at the
same time plying her whip across his flanks, whilst her forlorn
helpmate, with eyes starting from their sockets, shouted aloud
for help, flew threw the gateway with increased velocity,——a
broad smile playing upon the face of the dame as she cried out
to the lookers on,——"Never heed the babe, a gay ride will mend
his health."

The address of the landlady, in safely passing through the
narrow way, elicited a general burst of applause, which rang in
shouts until she had fairly got the better of the self-will of her
four-footed antagonist, and had halted him, panting, at the back
of the house.

"By my head," exclaimed Willy, "it was no such great
mistake to set down Dame Dorothy's tumbrel for my Lord's
coach !   If it had been a coach and six it could not have made
more dust or better speed."

"By my head, it could not !" shouted Wise Watkin, in a shrill
response to Willy's laugh.——"There's a tickle to the ribs !——that
fiddler Willy should take Dame Dorothy's cart and bow-necked
Bogle for my Lord's coach !"——and with this reflection he joined
in the chorus which echoed the general merriment.

Meantime the company continued to arrive. The coaches
came with new freights, and fresh parties on horseback alighted
at the gate. The Collector, more than usually precise in apparel, stood at the door receiving the frequent comers with that particularity of observance which so strongly marked the manners of
the past century ; and group after group was ushered into the
hall   Here Mistress Alice, in sad-colored, silken attire, plain and
becoming in its fashion, gave welcome to her visitors ; whilst the
Lady Maria, in character of what might be termed the patroness
of the revel, took post by her side. The neat little figure of the
Proprietary's sister received a surprising accession of bulk from

the style of her dress, which was according to a mode yet new in the province. Her hair, laid flat and smooth upon the crown of the head, was tortured into a sea of curls that fell over either ear to the point of the shoulder, and to the same depth upon the back, fringing her brow with light and fleecy flakes—the whole powdered to a pearly, brownish hue, and inlaid with jewelled bands. Her gown, both body and skirt, was of rich, flowered tabby, whose coruscating folds rustled with portentous dignity, as the lady moved slowly from place to place. This derived still greater increment of stateliness from a stomacher and huge farthingale, or hoop, made after a fashion which the queen of Charles the Second, nearly twenty years before, had brought from Portugal and introduced to the wondering eyes of the merry court dames of England. The glory of this array gave a world of condescension to the deep and awfully formal courtesy with which the benevolent spinster made her salutations to the arriving troops ; who, in their turn, did full homage to the claims of the lady as the presiding genius of the ball.

Blanche Warden, with a playfulness that vibrated between the woman and the girl, abandoned the reception of the guests to the elders of the family, and gave herself up to the guidance of her prevailing humor, as she appeared, at one moment, in the hall smiling amidst the congratulations of friends, and at another, skimming across the lawn with a dozen of her school-mates in the random flight of their wild fancies. Her dress was characterized by the simplicity of a maiden as yet unambitious to assume the privileges of womanhood. It consisted of a bodice of scarlet velvet accurately fitted to her shape, and laced across the bosom with silken cords, the tasseled extremities of which depended almost to the ground ; short white sleeves looped to the shoulder by bands of the color of the boddice ; a skirt of white lawn, and a white slipper disclosing a foot and ankle of faultless proportions.

10

Her neck and shoulders, of matchless beauty, were given uncovered to the evening breeze ; and her glossy hair, constrained above her brow by a fillet of ribbon, fell in rich volume down her back.   No jewel or jem contributed its lustre to grace her person ; but a boquet of choice flowers planted on the upper verge of the boddice, and a white-rose nestling amongst the braided tresses on her forehead, better than carcanet or chain of gold, diamond clasp or ear-ring, consorted with the virgin purity and artless character of the wearer.

For a time, until the thickening shades of twilight and the keenness of the evening air began to admonish them of the comfort of the house, many of the guests, attracted by the unusual mildness of the season, loitered about the door or strolled across the grounds.   Near the brink of the cliff which overlooked the river might have been seen Captain Dauntrees amusing a group of idle comrades.   Here and there, a priest from the Jesuit House of St. Inigoe's, in his long cassock, diversified the general aspect of gay costumes, with a contrast grateful to the eye.   The Proprietary, with the buxom old host, Mr. Warden, and the aged Chancellor, essayed to make merry with some venerable matrons, who, with a sagacious presentiment of rheumatic visitations, were effecting a retreat towards the chimney-corner of the parlor. Talbot played the gallant amongst a half-score maidens, who flitted along the margin of the cliff with a clamor that almost amounted to riot, whilst in his wake, Master Benedict Leonard, as gaudy as a jay, strutted swaggeringly along, apparently but to indulge his admiration of his kinsman or to discharge some shot of saucy freedom amongst the maidens.

With the lighting of candles the first notes of Willy's fiddle were heard in a bravura flourish summoning the dancers to the hall ; and here the ball was opened, according to prescriptive custom, with the country-dance, which was led off by no less a personage than the Lady Maria, attended by the worshipful Collector himself as her partner, the couple affording, both in costume and movement, the richest imaginable portraiture of that "ancientry and state" which so pleased the fancy of our progenitors. Other dances of the same character, mingled with jigs and reels, succeeded, and the company soon rose into that tone of enjoyment which the contagious merriment of the dance diffuses over all such assemblages. Cards, at that day, even more than at present, constituted the sober resource of the elder and graver portions of society of both sexes ; and accordingly, by degrees, the Collector had drawn off to the parlor a respectable corps of veterans, who, grouped around the small tables, pursued this ancient pastime with that eagerness which it has always inspired among its votaries, leaving the hall to the unchecked mirth of the dancers.

"We heard it said that Master Cocklescraft, of the Olive Branch, was to be here to-night," said Grace Blackiston, as she encountered Blanche in the dance. "He told Father Pierre that he was coming : and I have heard it whispered too, that he has brought some pretty presents with him from abroad. I do not behold him yet, and here is the evening half gone. Oh, I do long to see him, for they say he dances so well. Is he not coming ?"

"He has been bidden," replied Blanche, "though not much with my will : I care not whether he comes or stays away."

"Ha, Blanche has no eye but for Master Albert," said the merry maiden, as she turned off and addressed herself to a schoolmate who stood near ; "yet a good dancer is not to be scorned now-a-days, even if the Secretary were a better. And if he were a better, he doesn't dance so much that we should content ourselves with him. The Secretary has not been on the floor to-night, but must be tracking and trailing Father Pierre about the room. I do believe he does so for no purpose but to get sights

of Blanche Warden.   I wonder if the dullard can be in love ?
It looks hugely like it."

The Secretary had, in truth, not yet mingled in the dance, but
from the beginning of the evening had loitered in the hall, apparently watching the sports, and, now and then, communing with
Father Pierre, who, though a priestly, was far from being a silent
or grave looker-on.   The benevolent churchman enjoyed a commanding popularity with the younger portions of the society of
the province, and took so much pleasure in the manifestation of
it, that he was seldom absent from such of their gatherings as the
course of his duty would allow him to attend.   For the same
reason he was generally to be found amongst the assemblages of
his children, as he called them, rather than mingling in the graver
coteries of those of his own period of life.   On the present occasion he had scarcely quitted the dancing apartment during the
evening, but stood by, a delighted spectator of the mirth that sparkled in the faces of the happy groups, and heard with glee, almost
equal to their own, the wild laughter that echoed through the hall.

" They will presently begin to think Master Albert Verheyden
intends to set himself up for a philosopher," he said, as the Secretary encountered him on the skirts of the dancers, the eye of the
priest beaming with a good-natured playfulness.   " It is not usual
for a squire of dames to be so contemplative.   My son, have you
given over the company of damsels to consort with an old priest
in so gay a scene as this ?"

" Father, I would dance if there were need ; but there is not
often an empty space upon the floor, nor want of those who seek
to fill it.   It pleases me as well to discourse with you."

" Ah, benedictus ! my son, it is not at your time of life that
you may be believed for such self-denial.   More than one of the
maidens has put the question to me to-night, how this should come
to pass."

"Reverend father, though I will not deny I love the dance, yet my nurture long made me a stranger to it ; and now, since my fortune has brought me into the world, I can scarcely conquer the diffidence I feel to exhibit myself in such exercise."

"It is an innocent pleasure, son Albert, and a graceful. There is healthful virtue in these laughing faces and active limbs. St. Ignatius forbid that I should commend an unseemly sport ! but it has ever been my belief that the young men can find no better instructors in the gentle perfections of charity and good will than in their sport-mates amongst the maidens,—and so I preach in my office : nor truly, may the maidens better learn how to temper their behavior with the grace of pleasing—which has in it a summary of many excellences, Master Albert—than in the fellowship of our sons. Now, away with you ! There is Blanche Warden, who has sent her eye hither a dozen times, since we have been speaking, to ask the question why I detain you from your duty. Ah, blessed Therese ! daughter Blanche does not suspect I am chiding you for that very fault. Go, my son ; it is a shame to see you so little dainty in your company as to prefer the cassock to the petticoat. Go, go !"

The lively gesture of the priest and his laughing face, as he dismissed the Secretary from his side, attracted the notice of Blanche, who, as Albert Verheyden approached her, saluted him with—

"I am glad, Master Albert, that Father Pierre has seen fit to bestow upon you such chiding as I would have given you myself. I looked to you to help me through my ball to-night, and made sure of it that you would lead out some of the maidens to dance ; for there are many here that have not yet had their turn :—there's Mistress Hay, the viewer's sister,—she has sat there all night, unregarded by mortal man. Ah, you are no true friend to desert me in my need."

"Fair Mistress Blanche," replied the Secretary with a down cast look, "I stand under your displeasure, and acknowledge my fault. Indeed, my dull brain did not perceive your straits. I waited for your bidding. You will pardon me that, waiting for your command, I did not now presume to move without it. I will go and lead forth the viewer's sister on the instant."

"Nay, stay now : I have saved you that errand. Captain Dauntrees, upon my request, has proffered his hand, and, you may see, they are now standing on the floor ready to begin. You shall find other duty."

"To dance with you, gentle mistress, if it like you."

"How can it but like me, Master Albert ? Oh, but I love this dancing ! And yet I much better like it as we have danced many a time at the Rose Croft, on a winter's night, with our household friends, and sister Alice to touch the spinnet to a gay tune, and you to teach us these new over-sea dances. These were pleasant hours, and worth a world of these birth-day junketings. Was it not so ?"

"I love not the crowd," returned the Secretary with a lively emotion. "But these fireside pastimes ! you may praise them with your most prodigal speech, and still fall short. We had no holiday finery there to make proud the eye, nor glozing speech to set up perfections which we did not own, nor studied behavior to win opinion by ; but what we were we seemed, and what we felt we said. There is more virtue in these hearthside communings than you may find in a hemisphere of shows."

"Ah, Master Albert, you have seen the gaudy world on the other side of the sea, and can speak of it with assurance. Our little, unfurnished province has but small pleasures for you : it is a make-believe to praise our homely hearths."

"I speak, Mistress Blanche, the very breathings of my secret heart, and tell you, though little I can boast of acquaintance with that gaudy world, nothing have I seen, dreamed or tasted of worldly pleasure, nor ever fancied of human happiness, that might exceed the rich delight of those household scenes you speak of."

"Were they not happy?" exclaimed Blanche, kindling into a rapture excited by the fervor of the Secretary's earnest and eloquent manner. "We owe so much of it to you, Master Albert. Until you came into the province, we sometimes had a weary hour at the Rose Croft : now, my father finds it weary when you are away. I do not,—because I may surely count that it shall never be long until you are here again. Mercy ! did we not stand here to dance ? and see, our turn has past all unheeded. We will to the foot again and take another turn."

It was as the maiden had said. In the engrossment of their conversation they had been passed by in the country-dance. As they now went to the foot to bring themselves into place, Blanche whispered, "I rejoice the skipper is not come to-night : his shrewdness has taught him, notwithstanding my father's good will, that there is but little relish for his company at the Rose Croft."

"You reckon without your host, Mistress Blanche," replied the Secretary. "There is the skipper outside of the window ; and not well pleased with his own ruminations, if I may judge by his folded arms and earnest eye."

Cocklescraft had been in the porch, looking in upon the scene, some moments before he was observed ; a crowd of domestics having so pre-occupied the same station as almost to shield him from the notice of those within. Whilst Blanche and Albert now danced, he had planted himself in the door. His countenance was grave, his attitude statue-like, and his eye sharply followed the motions of the maiden. His dress, somewhat out-landish, but still within the license of that period, was of a

Spanish fashion, profusely decorated with embroidery and set off by jewels of exceeding richness. It was too ambitious of ornament to be compatible with good taste, and manifested that love of finery which is the infallible index of a tawdry and sensual nature. The thoughtfulness of his countenance denoted an abstraction, of which he was obviously not conscious at the moment, for he no sooner caught the glance of Blanche than his whole bearing underwent a sudden change ; his eye sparkled, his lip assumed a smile, and he became at once, in appearance, the gay and careless reveller.

"God save the Rose of St. Mary's, the beautiful flower of our New World !" he said, as he approached the maiden with what she could not fail to note as an over-acted effort to assume the cavalier. "Viva la Padrona ! The damsels of Portugal will teach you the meaning of that speech, pretty mistress. You have a gallant company to-night," he added, as he cast his eyes around ; in doing which he recognized Albert Verheyden with a scarcely perceptible nod of the head, and then turned his back upon him. "By your leave, Mistress Blanche, I would dance with you at your first leisure : the next dance, or the next,—I am your humble servant for as long as you will. Shall it not be the next dance ?"

"I will tell you presently : I know not whether I may dance again to-night, Master Cocklescraft," replied the maiden coldly.

"There spoke the same tongue that refused my mantle ! Your cruelty, mistress, exceeds that beauty which all men so boast of in this province. I wish I could bring you to look upon me with compassion. Not even a dance with the queen of our feast ! A poor, rough-spoken sailor meets but little grace in a lady's favor, when white-handed lute-players and ballad-singing pages stand ready at her call. It is even as you will ! damsels have the privilege of denial all the world over, and I am too much of a gallant to trouble you with an unwelcome suit—"

"I will dance with you, Master Cocklescraft," said Blanche anxiously, as she saw the chafed spirit of the skipper working in his face notwithstanding his effort to disguise it ; whilst, at the same time, she feared that his peevish allusion to the Secretary might have been overheard : "call on me for the next set, and I will dance with you."

"I thought your goodness would relent ! 'Tis not in your nature to be unkind. Gracia ! I am at your feet, Senora—I shall be on the watch. Scotch jig, reel, or country-dance, they all come pat to me. I can dance the bransle, cinquepace, or minuet—the corant, fandango, or galliard. You shall find me at home, mistress, in every clime. Meanwhile, I will seek our host, the worshipful Collector : I have not seen him yet."

This familiarity in the address of the skipper, and the importune and even offensive freedom of his manner, were the result of an endeavor to conceal a discontented temper under the mask of gaiety. He had brooded over the incidents connected with his late visit to the Rose Croft, until he had wrought himself into a tone of feeling that might engender any extravagance of behavior. The coldness of the maiden, we have seen, he imputed to causes altogether independent of her good will or aversion ; and he was, therefore, determined to persevere in his aim to win her favor— an enterprise which, in his harsh and rude estimate of the proprieties of conduct, he did not deem in any respect hopeless. He made sure, in his reckoning, of the friendship of the Collector, from whom he had experienced those manifestations of good-feeling which a hospitable and kind-hearted man flings around him almost at random, but which Cocklescraft's self-flattering temper magnified into indications of special regard.

The agitation of these topics had thrown him into a perplexed

10*

thoughtfulness which alone was the cause of his tardy appearance at the ball ; and now that he had arrived, the same rumination kept him vibrating, in a moody abstraction, between total silence at one period, and an unnatural exhibition of mirth at the next, giving to the latter that gairish flippancy of manner which was so annoying to the maiden.

The cordial and frank civility with which the Collector recognized the skipper amongst the guests, unfortunately contributed to confirm him in the opinion of Master Warden's favor.

"Why, Richard Cocklescraft," said the host, upon looking up from the cards which had been absorbing his attention, and discovering the skipper, "are you here among the gray-beards? Why should you flock to the old fowl when the young are gathered in the hall? There is no gout in your toe. Get thee back, man—we will have no deserters here ! You promised to bring a blithe foot for a jig, Master Cocklescraft ; are you tired of the sport already ?"

"In truth, worshipful Master Warden," replied the skipper, "I have, but within this half hour, arrived at the house ; 'tis not long since I left my brigantine, where matters on board detained me."

"Ha, and you have not danced to-night. Then you owe Blanche a turn of duty. Go quickly back, Richard, and foot it with my girl. I have praised your leg, man, and said enough to put you on your mettle. Back to the hall, Master Cocklescraft, and say to Blanche I sent you for a straight-backed comrade to hold her to the pledge of a reel."

"I am already bound to that pledge, and the time is at hand to make it good. I but stole away for an instant to pay my duty here," replied the skipper ; and taking heart from the familiar greeting of his host, returned to the dancing apartment with lighter step and more cheerful face

Blanche took the earliest moment to perform her engagement, hoping by this alacrity to acquit herself of her obligation in a manner least calculated to occasion remark, and soonest to disembarrass herself of her partner's importunity. The dance, on her part, was a reluctant courtesy, and was accordingly so manifested in her demeanor, in spite of her resolution to the contrary. Cocklescraft, however, was too much elated to perceive how ill he stood in the maiden's grace. Scant encouragement will suffice to feed the hopes of a lover ; still more scant in a lover of such a temperament as that of the heady seaman. His vanity was quick to interpret favorably every word of civility that fell from Blanche's lips ; and the little that escaped her during the dance seemed anew to brighten his hopes and inspire the zeal of his pursuit.

When the engagement was accomplished the maiden quickly escaped from her distasteful suitor, by retiring from the hall and mingling with other companions.

The guests were now summoned to supper. In a wing of the dwelling-house the tables were loaded with dainty cheer, more to be remarked for its capacity to please the palate, than for the enticements which modern epicurism has invented to gratify the eye. An orderly division of matrons, escorted by the Collector and the elders of the province, moved forward at a measured pace to make the first onslaught. These were followed, after an interval, by active bevies of youthful revellers who thronged in noisier array to the scene of assault.

In the housekeeper's apartment which looked into the supper-room, sundry women, intent upon supplying the tables, were seen ministering their office with scarcely less clamor than that which echoed from the consumers of the feast. Here, in a post of usurped control over the domestics, busy in rinsing glasses, cleansing platters, adjusting pasties, and despatching comfits, was the merry landlady of the Crow and Archer, whose saucy laughing, and not unhandsome face, grew lustrous with the delight afforded by her occupation. Full as she was of the appropriate business of her station, she still had time to watch the banquet and make her comments upon the incidents which transpired there.

"Ho, Bridget Coldcale! Bridget, this way look you!" she exclaimed, as, with napkin in hand, and eye glistening with delight, she beckoned to the thin and busy housekeeper. "If you would live and laugh, pray come this way and take a peep at the table. Who should we have here, as pert and proud as if she was the lady of my Lord, but our gossip, Dolly Cadger? Think of it,—the dame herself, in her own true flesh and blood, amongst all these gentlefolk. Marry! Master Anthony Warden was in straits to choose comers when he went to the mercer's shop to find them. What a precious figure the sea-tortoise makes with her yellow camblet, blue sarsnet, and green satin! And that lace pinner stuck upon her head, with great lappets flaunting down like hound's ears! I cannot but laugh my sides into a stitch—it is such a dainty tire for a mercer's wife. It all comes, you may swear, bran new out of the mercer's pack—for the poor man had never the soul to deny her; there will be a twelvemonth's bragging on the top of this. Good lack! yonder is Dauntrees, like an humble bee, beside the viewer's sister! The old pot-guzzler is never a man to flinch from his trencher. Master Ginger, I know the measure of your stomach of old! I have warmed your insides for you!"

"For the blessing of charity and the love of good works Dame Dorothy, some drink!" cried Willy, the fiddler, who had just stolen from his post and elbowed his way into the housekeep er's room. "Some drink, beautiful mistress; my throat is as dry as a midsummer chimney; swallows are building nests in it: my lips are dusty from long drought, and my elbow is not able to wag for want of oil. Quick, good dame, or I shall crisp! Ha, that is smooth and to the purpose," he exclaimed, after tossing off a glass which the dame presented him. " Now, worthy hostess, a bone to gnaw, for I am fearfully empty and like to cave in! speed, dame : the dancers will be calling before I am filled."

" So,—Willy, set you down and comfort your stomach at your leisure ; there will be no haste to leave the supper-table this half hour," replied the landlady, as she laid a plate before the fiddler, furnished with good store of pasty ; " take your time and make a belly full of it, child—you have earned your provender. I warrant, Willy, you never had a merrier pair of legs to 'Hunt the Squirrel,' than our old Captain gave you to-night."

" Haw, haw!" shouted Willy ; " Captain Dauntrees is a king of Captains, dame. He has put a new spring in Master Warden's old floor. I would have given a piece of eight out of my own pocket, Mistress Dorothy—that is if I had so much—to have seen you on the plank to-night footing it to 'Hunt the Squirrel' with the Captain, or to 'Moll Pately,' or some such other merry frisk as I could have made for you : it would have been as good as a month's schooling to some of our gentlefolks."

" Me on the floor, indeed!" ejaculated the dame with an affected laugh. " Faith, I might be there as well as some that crow under a hood, and the ball suffer no shame neither. But Master Warden does not drop his favor so low as a vintner's wife ; he stops short with the mercer. Willy, did you think before, that the publican was of less worship than the peddler ? Has Dame Cadger better reason to hold up her head than Dame Weasel? Speak the truth, man, honestly."

" Master Perry Cadger has done with peddling more than a year past," replied Willy ; "he is now a 'stablished mercer, with freehold in the town and trade in the common. And they do say, Mistress Dorothy, that he makes money over hand ; he will be

worshipful anon ; money makes worship, dame, all the world
over."

"Maybe it does ; but I would like to know, has not Garret
Weasel as goodly a freehold in the town, as old a trade in the
common, and as full a pouch, as Perry Cadger ? better, older, and
fuller, on my word !   Now, where is that same mortal, my husband ?" inquired the dame, looking around her ; "as I live, there
he is at the chimney-cheek, fast asleep in the midst of all this uproar !   The noddipeake is of too dull a spirit for such a place as
this.   Wake him up, Willy !   Garret, man !" she screamed, in a
tone which instantly brought him to his feet ; "if you are weary,
put Bogle in the cart and get you home to bed ; Matty will bring
the cart back and wait for me."

"I sleepy !" returned the husband, in a husky voice, and with
a bewildered drowsy eye which he endeavored to light up with a
laugh ; "good woman, if you wait here until I grow sleepy, you
will be a weary loiterer,—that's all I have to say.   Sleepy, dame!
If a man but wink his eye in the light, you would swear to a snore.
Adsheartlikens ! I have been in many a rouse, wife, as you well
know ; day-dawn is my twelve o'clock ; chanticleer has crowed
himself hoarse many a time before he could get me to bed.   I'll
see you out."

"Oh, chops, chops ! here's an honest night's work for you !"
drawled out Wise Watkin, who had, ever since dark, occupied a
station at a window as a spectator of the dancing, and now had
pryingly thrust his head into the housekeeper's apartment ; "here
are eatables and drinkables, wet and dry, to set any stomach a
laughing !   Why, how now, Willy!" he ejaculated, with a chuckle,
as he discovered the fiddler regaling himself in the room, and advanced towards him with the skulking step of a dog that is doubtful of his reception ; "you know where the fat and the sweet are.
Oh, Master Willy, you are a wise fiddler ! their worships do well

to make much of you. Have you never a crust for poor Watkin ?"

" Out, you dottrel !" shouted Mistress Coldcale, in a key that thrilled through the frame of the simpleton, and turned him precipitately towards the door. " Havn't we idlers enough in our way without you ? Here, take this and begone," she continued, as relenting she gave the witless intruder a plate of provisions. And as for you, Willy, the young folks are gathering again in the hall, there will be a message for you presently."

" I stay for no message," replied the fiddler, as he rose and shook the crumbs from him, and, with jaws still occupied, withdrew from the apartment, followed by the admiring Watkin.

Upon the lawn in front of the house, Albert Verheyden had erected a bower, which sheltered a rustic altar dedicated to St. Therese, over which the name of Blanche had been wrought in large letters, formed by a number of suspended lamps, which threw a softened light for a considerable space around. Hither, after supper, Mr. Warden, with a small party of his guests, had strolled in the interval before the sports of the evening were resumed. Cocklescraft had watched the opportunity, and now, somewhat elated with wine as well as buoyed up with hope, had tracked the Collector's footsteps until he found him separated some little space from his company.

" Well met, Master Warden !" was the skipper's accost, so familiarly whispered in the ear of his host as to produce a slight movement of surprise. " Well met, Caballero ! I have a word for your private ear ; this way if you please. It is somewhat cool, so I will to my purpose roundly, in seaman's fashion."

" Speak, but quickly, Master Cocklescraft, and in plain phrase: I shall like it the better."

" Master Warden, then, without mincing the matter, I would have your leave to woo our beautiful maiden your daughter."

"Who,—what,—how?" interrupted the Collector, in a voice that spoke his astonishment.

"Your daughter, Mistress Blanche : ay, and have your good word to the suit : I love her like a true son of the sea—heartily, and in that sort would woo her."

"What is it you ask!" again spoke the host with increased surprise.

"I have gear enough, Master Warden ; no man may turn his heel on me for lack of gold."

"How now, sirrah!" interrupted the Collector, as in this brief space the storm had gathered to the bursting point : "You would woo my daughter?—woo her?—my Blanche? Richard Cockle-scraft, have you lost your wits—turned fool, idiot ; or is your brain fevered with drink? You make suit to my daughter! You win and wear a damsel of her nurture! Hear me. Your craft is a good craft—I do not deny it ; an honest calling, when lawfully followed! a brave calling! but you sail on a false reckoning when you hope to find favor with my girl Blanche. Your rough sea-jacket, and your sharking license on the salt sea, mates not with daughter of mine :—the rose-leaf and the sea-nettle! You venture too largely on your welcome, sirrah!" he said, as his anger began to show itself in his quickened speech, above his effort to restrain it. "Master Skipper, there is insolence in this. Hark you, sir! if you would not have me disown your acquaintance and forbid you my house, you will never speak again of my daughter."

With this brief rebuke of the skipper's aspirations the host retreated hastily, and much out of humor, into the house, leaving his guest in a state of bewilderment at the sudden and unexpected issue of the interview. For a moment the seaman stood fixed on the spot, his lips compressed, his hands clenched, and his eye directed to the retiring figure of the Collector : at length beginning to find breath and motion, he muttered, "So it has come to this! he has been playing the hypocrite! It was but a holiday welcome, after all! I shall note it for future remembrance. A sea-nettle! By Saint Anthony he shall find me one! And that sharking license he spoke of : he shall taste its flavor. This girl has been trained in her dislikes. Oh, it is his sport to see me foiled! I am brought here express to the ball by his persuasion, —nay, command ; I am caressed with courtesies, and even challenged to romps with the maiden by his own lips. Who so free in his admission here as I ?—Richard Cocklescraft, forsooth! One would have thought we had been fellow thieves in our time ; there was such cronying in his phrase : and then at last, when frankly I tell him my purpose, I am to be huffed and hectored off the ground with bullying speeches! He must bounce me as if I were a cowardly boy. Oh, wind and wave and broad-sea sky! it was not in your nursing I learned the patience to bear this wrong. You are not too old yet, Anthony Warden, to be taught the hazard of rousing a Bloody Brother! And as for you, gay maiden, dream on of your bookish ballad-singer, Master Albert! I have a reckoning to settle with him. It will be a dainty exploit to send him, feet foremost, into the Chapel for a blessing. Luckily, Sir Secretary, you owe me the worth of an unsatisfied grudge! Softly —Master Verheyden himself! we meet at a fortunate hour."

The soliloquy of the skipper was interrupted by the approach of the Secretary, who entered alone into the bower and paused a moment before the little altar. A light tap on the shoulder made Albert aware of the presence of Cocklescraft, and turning round to confront the person who gave it, he was immediately greeted with the accost, "I have a word for your ear, sir ;—if you be a man you will follow me out of this broad light. What I have to say is better told where no one may observe us ; follow me, sir."

"You are somewhat too peremptory," replied the Secretary,

as he stepped after the skipper toward the cliff: "I follow, though I think more courtesy would befit your station. I have once before marked and reproved your rudeness."

"I have no courtesies to waste on you," said Cocklescraft, sharply; "my business is with your manhood. You have the maiden to thank that I did not bring you to instant account for that insolent reproof you speak of. I come to deal with you upon it now. Are you a man? Dare you meet me to-morrow, at noon, at Cornwaleys's Cross?"

"I dare meet you and any or all who have right to claim it of me," replied Albert, promptly, "in the way of honorable quarrel, if such be the meaning of your challenge. And although I am ignorant of your degree, and may question your right to defy me to equal contest, yet honored as you have been under this roof, I shall rest content with that as sufficient pledge of your claim to my attention. You shall find me, sir, punctual to your summons."

"I scorn the shallow claim," returned the skipper, "to such honor as they who inhabit here may confer. The master of the Olive Branch need not vail his top to a clerkish spinner of syllables, even though the minion's writing-stool be found in my Lord's own ante-chamber. I shall see you to-morrow at noon, at the Cross."

"To-morrow at noon," replied the Secretary, "you shall not complain of my absence, sir."

"It is well! So, good night, Master Secretary!" rejoined the skipper, scornfully, as he bowed to his antagonist and set forth to seek his boat which lay in waiting beneath the bank.

The Secretary turned towards the dwelling, somewhat disturbed by the novel situation into which he had been so unexpectedly thrown, but resolved to conceal the disquiet of his mind and preserve the same outward composure which had marked his deportment during the previous portion of the evening.

"Who lurks there?" he demanded in a stern voice, as he perceived the figure of a man stealing off from his path immediately in the vicinity of the spot where the interview with Cocklescraft had terminated. "Who is it," he added, checking himself and speaking in a gentler tone, "that plays hide and seek here on the lawn?"

"Nobody," returned a voice from the shelter of the shrubbery, "nobody but me, honorable Master Verheyden: me, Watkin," continued the half-witted lad, as he came visibly into the presence of the Secretary. "Haven't we had a famous junketing? Oh, what I have eaten and drunk this blessed night! and what dancing, Master Verheyden! was there ever such fiddling? Willy is a treasure to the quality, I warrant you. Where have you such another?"

"You should be looking on at the dancing," said Albert, anxious to ascertain from the lad if he had heard any thing of what had just passed between himself and Cocklescraft. "How comes it, Watkin, that you are away from your post?"

"Oh, bless you, Master Verheyden, I have more on my hands than you would guess in a week's striving. Now, what should Mistress Coldcale say to me when I had gobbled up my supper, but, Watkin, take this trencher and this pot down to the bank side, and there feed the seamen of Master Cocklescraft's boat, which you shall find at the landing below the garden. And so, truly, there I found the hungry tarpaulins: and they did eat, Master Albert, like fishes, and drink like wolves. It is Mistress Blanche's birth-day, says I, so we will have no hungry bellies here, comrades. And they laughed, and I came up the bank as I went, running almost out of breath to see fiddler Willy strike up again. And that's the way I fell pop upon you, Master Secretary."

"It was a lucky speed, Watkin; now get you gone!" said

Albert, as he slowly bent his steps towards the hall and mingled again in the bustle of the scene.

As midnight drew near the elder guests had all retired ; and at last even the most buoyant began to yield to that weariness of limb, by which Nature has set her limit to the endurance of social pleasure, no less peremptorily to those in the prime of youth than to such as wane in their days of decline.

CHAPTER XIX.

These businesses of fighting
Should be dispatched as doctors do prescribe
Physical pills, not to be chewed but swallowed:
Time spent in the considering deads the appetite.
                                        SHIRLEY.

EARLY in the morning after the ball, Willy of the Flats, who had
spent the night amongst the servants at the Rose Croft, strayed
forth from his truckle bed and betook himself to the margin of
St. Inigoe's creek, where he sat down to look abroad over the
waters at the rising sun, and to profit by the breeze as it cooled
his brow, still aching with the effects of the late revel. He had
not been long in this position before Wise Watkin, fresh from a
truss of hay in the barn, espied him, and now hastened to take a
seat at his side.

"Well, lad of the clear head and mother wit, what has brought
you to the water side so early?" was Willy's question, as the
obsequious Watkin came into the presence of his patron.

"As I lay in the barn, Willy," replied Watkin, with a world
of gravity in his looks, "I heard first a hem, and then a cough;
—and says I, that's Willy of the Flats, by the sound of his
throat. And so, I gets up and looks out through the cranny,
and, sure enough, there was you walking, with your hands in
your pockets and your hat set a one side like a gentleman:—and
then, says I, if Willy's stirring now so early, honest folks ought

to be abroad too.   And with that, out I walked, he, he, he !—
and here I am sitting beside you, like another gentleman."

"Then, Wise Watkin, since we are so sociable, tell me what
you think of our ball last night ?"

"Oh, grand !—grand, grand, Master Willy !   Oh, you have
tickled Toby in the ribs, Master Willy !—you have done it as it
was never done before.   People will talk of Willy of the Flats
after this.   Mistress Blanche will talk of you,—Master Albert
will talk of you.   I shouldn't wonder if his Lordship should send
you a purse of gold.   I'm sure it's no more than folks look to see
done."

"And Mistress Coldcale did not stint to give you plenty to
stay your stomach, Watkin ?"

"Plenty, troth, and to spare, Willy !   Mistress Coldcale is
a mother of open hands.   I could live under Mistress Coldcale
all my born days and never grudge what I did for her."

"Mistress Bridget will give us our breakfasts this morning,"
said the fiddler, patting the simpleton on the head ; "and then,
Watkin, we must away.   It will not be well taken if we tarry
too long after the feast."

"There is more sport on hand to-day, Willy.   We must not
go till that be over.· There is to be a set-to at Cornwaleys's
Cross to-day."

"A set-to ?"

"I know all about it, Master Willy.   I heard them appoint it."

"Heard who ?   What do you mean, Wise Watkins ?"

"Listen, Willy ;—it was as I shall tell you.   When I carried
fodder to the boat last night, as Mistress Bridget ordered—I
call a full trencher of meat fodder, Master Willy—I comes back
by the way of the stile over the hedge, when what should I see
but two gentlefolks in a discourse, and what should I hear but
'I'll meet you, and you will meet me to-morrow morning at noon,

at Cornwaleys's Cross.' Oh, it is a made-up business, Willy."

"Who are you speaking of, you slippery-witted fool?" demanded the fiddler, sharply.

"Nay, if you tax me so keenly, Willy,—I will not answer. I could have told you what Master Albert said to me afterwards, when Master Cocklescraft went over the bank and into his boat —but I will not,—for your sharpness."

"Now, Watkin, wise lad, are you not a fool to take in dudgeon the freedom of an old friend? Come, there's a hand —and in token of good will you will tell what all this story comes to."

"As true as I am an honest man, Willy, I heard it. Master Cocklescraft comes first to the hedge and Master Verheyden following. Oh ho, says I, here's a state matter, and so I doused my head under the hedge. Then Master Cocklescraft says to our honorable Secretary, You will meet me if you are a man. And the Secretary says, I am a man, and I will meet you at the Cross —Cornwaleys's Cross.—When? says Cocklescraft.—At noon to-morrow morning, says the Secretary. I'll go and get ready, says Cocklescraft;—and with that off he marches. There will be a pretty wrestling match for you, Master Willy! And I shouldn't wonder if they should get to a pitch of the bar before they part: Master Cocklescraft has a great arm for heaving a bar. You and me, Willy, will be there to see it. Oh—I made up my mind last night that the first thing I did this day was to tell you, that you might see it. I know you love a wrestle, Willy."

"This is a matter to be looked to, Watkin,—I will cast it over in my mind and tell you whether we shall go to it or not."

"Well," continued Watkin, "the Secretary turns himself about to go to the house, and suddenly, out of the back of his head, he spies me; and so takes me to account to say what I lurked there for.—Oh, bless you, Willy,—I didn't tell him!—I am no fool ;—if I had let on about the wrestling I should never have had the luck to get sight of it—these gentlefolks will not be a country gaze—I know them :—the Secretary was not going to tickle Toby in my ribs. All he got out of me was that I had borne a trencher of fodder to the boatmen—and so he went his way, and I went mine."

"You are a wise boy, Watkin, and all that I would have you do now is to keep your counsel. Say not a word of this to living man. We will have it clean to ourselves."

"My lips shall be as fast as a padlock, Master Willy. Mortal man shall not screw it out of me."

The fiddler having extracted from Wise Watkin the particulars detailed in this dialogue, was shrewd enough to interpret them according to the real nature of the incident to which they referred. He knew that the lad was scrupulous in telling the truth, as well as he comprehended it, in all matters that came under his observation, and Willy therefore had no reserve in the assurance that there was on foot a quarrel between the Secretary and the skipper, which was to be adjusted at Cornwaleys's Cross, on that day. The nature of the quarrel he could not conjecture, although he was not ignorant that the individuals concerned in it, both held a relation to the maiden of the Rose Croft which might very naturally breed ill will between them. It was indeed a part of Willy's vocation to note such matters in the range of his wanderings,—and he had not been so idle since the arrival of Cocklescraft in the port, and especially during the festival of the previous night, as to shut his eye or ear to the deportment of the two young men in the presence of the damsel.

Upon revolving over the circumstances of Watkin's disclosure, a.d maturely perpending, after his own manner, the pressure of the case, he came to the wise conclusion that the best thing he could do would be to communicate the whole story to Blanche and leave the matter in her hands. Accordingly, as soon as the maiden had taken her morning repast, he gained access to her in the little bower of St. Therese, and there made her a confidential relation of the particulars, not only as he received them from Wise Watkin, but with such commentary as occurred to him to belong to the probable state of the facts. Blanche received the communication with the deepest emotion. Whilst the fiddler told his story, her cheek grew pale—tears started in her eyes, her lip quivered, her limbs, at last, became rigid, and she fainted away. Before Willy, however, could quit her side to call in others to her relief, she revived, and with a tottering step made her way into the house. A brief pause enabled her to summon up her strength and more composedly to address herself to the emergency in her view. The thought that Albert Verheyden was placed in circumstances of peril gave her as much alarm as if instant danger threatened herself; and now, for the first time in her life, she became conscious, how deep was the stake she had in his welfare. Then, too, she felt no other conviction but that his jeopardy was the direct consequence of his zeal in her service;—that the skipper had brought him into the quarrel on some ground having relation to her. Cocklescraft, besides, in her estimate of him, was a reckless and ruthless man, of fierce passions and violent hand, and she trembled to think that the gentle Master Albert should be confronted with such an adversary. "But Master Albert is brave," she said, "and will not brook that rough skipper's rudeness; he chides his course behavior,—as well such churl deserves to be chidden. Albert does not count the hazard of his quarrel, but leaves that for timid maidens to do. Oh, blessed virgin Therese!" she exclaimed as she cast her eye upon the picture of the saint which was suspended on the wall of her chamber; "take good Master Albert into thy care, and bear him harmless through this peril. His quarrel cannot but be

11

just, and the saints will guard him as they ever guard the right."

Having come to this conclusion and taken heart at the thought, she straightway resolved, as every maiden in similar circumstances would resolve, notwithstanding the guardianship of the saints which she had invoked, to fall upon some scheme, if possible, to prevent the duel. With this view she called sister Alice into a conference, and their joint conclusion was to make known the matter to Mr. Warden. But the Collector had already gone abroad, and time pressed, leaving but a few hours for action. Their next resource was Father Pierre; and instantly upon the thought of him, Alice sat down and wrote the reverend priest a letter, narrating the brief story and imploring his instant intercession by such offices as he might believe most effectual to frustrate the purpose of the belligerents. When the letter was ready, Willy of the Flats was summoned into the presence of the ladies, and was strictly charged to hie him with all haste to Father Pierre's dwelling, and to put the missive into his own hands, as a matter of the utmost importance requiring his immediate attention. To this charge was added a dozen alternatives adapted to every contingency dependent upon Father Pierre's possible absence or inability to act. Thus commissioned, Willy, followed by his shadow, Wise Watkin, set forth for the town, at a rate which kept the good-natured attendant in a half trot.

Whilst these things were going on at the Rose Croft, the Secretary was not idle in his preparation for the issues of the day. Albert Verheyden was, as I have already hinted, of an ardent and impulsive temper, moved by a keen relish for enterprise, and directed by a lofty tone of honor. His bookish and half-clerical character, the result of the discipline of his school and his early destination for the Church, gave him a gentle and almost diffident motion, which strongly contrasted with the warmth of his feelings, and the eagerness of his spirit. It was,

therefore, with a positive sense of pleasure, that he had seized
the opportunity to appear as the champion of Blanche Warden
in the first hostile passage that took place between the skipper
and himself—a pleasure resulting not less from the alacrity with
which he ever rendered service to the maiden, but also from the
instinct of a romantic nature that delighted in the thought of
matching its manhood with a formidable adversary. He had
never, however, as yet contemplated the reality of an appeal to
arms ; and although in his course of accomplishment, as was the
fashion of that day, after he had renounced his purpose of serving the Church, he had practised the use of his weapon, and even
attained to considerable skill in it, yet he had not brought himself
to look upon it as other than a light exercise which, like dancing,
was intended to fit him for the graceful service of the station he
was to fill. His ecclesiastical training was not yet so forgotten
as to leave him at perfect ease with himself in his present straits.
It was not, therefore, with apprehension, so much as with diffidence, that he found himself now engaged in the appointment of
the duel. He awoke at the dawn of day, full of the thoughts
connected with the affair in hand ; and in casting about for a fit
counsellor and friend in this emergency, he fixed his attention
upon Captain Dauntrees, as a man who would not only do him a
friendly turn, but as one well qualified to advise him how to comport himself through the ordeal of the meeting. Having resolved
instantly to see the Captain, he arose, and before the domestics
were stirring about the Proprietary mansion, threw his cloak
over his shoulder, concealing under its folds his rapier, and
betook himself to the Fort. Being admitted by the sentry, he
hastened to the little parlor of the Captain's quarters, where he
arrived whilst that worthy was still snoring in his bed. The
master of the garrison, however, was soon awakened from his
slumber, by a servant with the announcement of his visitor, and

immediately afterwards threw open his chamber door, which communicated with the parlor, and disclosed to the Secretary his burly figure half attired, whilst he was yet busy in throwing on his garments.

"Good morrow, Master Verheyden!" he said with a yawn, scarcely half awake; "I take shame to myself for a laggard to have so honorable a guest my teacher of good habits in early rising. But the Collector's wine was drugged last night, and had a virtue of sleepiness in it which hath touched me in the brain pan. It is not more than once in a man's lifetime, Master Secretary, that so choice a maiden as our Mistress Blanche comes to so rich an age as eighteen. You may search the two hemispheres for another like her, and still make a bootless errand of it. It was an occasion for a cup, and a most reasonable excuse for a late nap in the morning."

"The sun is just peering above the water, Captain," replied the Secretary; "and he who sleeps no later than sunrise, even without the excuse of a night revel, may scarcely be chid for laziness. I have broken in thus early upon you, that I might speak with you on a matter of moment to myself. I want your counsel and friendship in an affair touching mine honor, Captain Dauntrees."

"Ah, is it there the wind sits? Tarry, Master Verheyden, but a moment, whilst I get my serving man to truss my points, I shall be with you anon. An affair of the sword, truly! It is well to be early in the consideration of such matters. Matchcote, hark ye! come hither,—quickly," he shouted from his door to his valet; "come, gather these points and set me abroad. There, there,—now leave us, and busy thyself about breakfast, Matchcote,—we shall have a relish for the best in the larder. Away, good fellow!" As soon as the servant, in obedience to this order, had left the apartment, the Captain inquired—"Who have we opposed to us, Master Verheyden? Do we take him with long

sword, tuck, or rapier ?   Where do we meet ?   But first begin
the story at the beginning."

"That I propose to do, Captain," said the Secretary, smiling
"This Cocklescraft, the master of the Olive Branch, has chosen
to conceive himself offended by a rebuke I found it necessary to
give him for some unseasonable importunity of our maiden of the
Rose Croft.   It is almost a se'nnight past, and he must needs tax
me with it, last night, and challenge me to a trial of manhood.
His challenge grows out of some sudden moodiness engendered by
somewhat that vexed him at the dance.   Now, though I hold the
skipper as scarce privileged to exact of me the redress of his
weapon, being of a base condition so far as he is known in the
province—yet, Captain, I did not choose to be defied by him, and,
therefore, without parley or asking time for deliberation, accepted
his challenge, wherein it was appointed to hold the meeting this
day at noon at Cornwaleys's Cross.   I would entreat your friendship to stand by me in this appointment ; and, as I am unversed
in the usage of the duel, your better experience may instruct me."

"It was well done on your part, Master Albert,—exceeding
well done," replied the Captain.   "I applaud you for a gentleman of prompt spirit, and careful consideration of his honor.   This
same Master Cocklescraft needs such discipline as you may teach
him.   He tosses the feather of his bonnet somewhat more jauntily over his shoulder than he has warrant to do ; and he has a trick
of turning the buckle of his belt behind more frequently than
peaceable, well-disposed persons may choose to bear.   I have
noted him with greater strictness than others in the port, and
have, from the first, written him down a dog of rough breed,
notwithstanding his velvet jerkin and golden tassels.   I have seen
too many whelps of that litter, Master Verheyden, not to know
them when I meet them.   You did well to receive his challenge,
—although one would hardly have thought you had learned as

much in the seminary at Antwerp. At noon is it ? We have some hours before us, Master Secretary, and may employ the time in practice for the encounter. I will give you some cautions that shall stand you in stead to-day."

CHAPTER XX.

—— He that fights a duel,
Like a blind man that falls, but cares to keep
His staff, provides with art to save his honor,
But trusts his soul to chance: 'tis an ill fashion.
SHIRLEY.

WHILST the Secretary was undergoing the Captain's preparatory training in the Fort, the skipper was no less busy in making provision for the meeting. Having secured the services of a second, he betook himself on board of his vessel, which he caused to be loosed from her mooring and then dropped down the river opposite the creek of St. Inigoe's, where he anchored—his purpose being to take a position convenient to the spot chosen for the encounter, and to which he might proceed without suspicion from the townspeople.

Cornwaleys's Cross was situated near the most inland extremity of a deep and narrow inlet, known by the name of St. Luke's creek—a branch of St. Inigoe's—on a piece of meadow, surrounded by woods, immediately at the foot of a range of hills, not more than four miles, by land, from the port of St. Mary's, and about half that distance by water from the anchorage of the Olive Branch. This spot was traditionally notorious to the inhabitants of the town, as the scene of a melancholy event that had happened nearly fifty years anterior to the date of this story, in which a gentleman of repute in the early history of the province, Captain Cornwaleys, had the misfortune, on a hunting excursion, accident-

ally and with fatal effect to lodge the contents of his carbine in
the bosom of his friend.   The bitterness of this unhappy gentleman's grief, unallayed by active and meritorious service in the
early wars of the colony, induced him, in the decline of his life,
to erect a hermitage on the spot, whither he retired, in obedience
to a penitential vow, and dedicated the remnant of his days to
austere self-denial and religious devotion.   A cross of locust, now
swayed from its perpendicular by age, still reared its shattered
frame above the ruins of the ancient hermitage, of which there
yet remained a few mouldering logs, mingled with the fragments
of the crushed roof, and the hearth-stone showing the scorches of
long-quenched fires, in the light of which the soldier-hermit had
undergone his painful vigils of prayer.   A certain superstitious
notoriety was thus conferred upon the place, and by some strange
association peculiar to the habits of those times, in which the
sword and cross still held a mystical relation in the popular
belief, it had grown to be the customary appointed trysting
ground for those personal combats which constituted, at that era,
almost a lawful and approved ordinance of society.

In the vicinity of this spot, about half an hour before noon,
occasional glimpses through the foliage might have been had of
Captain Dauntrees and Albert Verheyden, followed by Matchcote,
the Captain's man,—all mounted,—as they descended the hill in
the rear of St. Luke's, by a winding, gravelly road, partially
overgrown with bay-tree, alder, and laurel.   The murmur of
cheerful conversation, and now and then an outflash of audible
mirth in the voice of the Captain, for some moments before they
arrived at their halting point, would have puzzled a casual hearer
to guess the nature of their errand : and when they reached the
level ground and finally reined up their horses, hard by the old
wind-shaken cross, Dauntrees was still engaged in narrating to the
Secretary some story of pleasant interest, which had evidently,

for the time, drawn off at least the narrator's thoughts from the main purpose of the day.

"By our patron! Master Verheyden," said the commander of the fort, as he carefully clambered down from his saddle and drew forth his watch, "we have here reached our ground before I was aware of it : a cheerful companion has a marvellous faculty in abridging a long road.—The adventures of this Claude de la Chastre would wear out a winter night in the telling, and never a drowsy ear in the company. I purpose, on a fit occasion, Master Albert, to rehearse to you more of that worthy soldier's exploits. He served under six kings, and fought fifteen duels,—the last at three score and ten. I have seen his chapel and tomb with my own eyes at Bourges and his true effigies cut in stone."

"I have been but a listener, Captain," said the Secretary with a smile, "and would willingly hear more of that valiant gentleman, when we have brought our own adventures to an end. Methinks now, we may find other occupation in the matter we have in hand."

"Why as to that, Master Verheyden," replied the Captain, "as we have very diligently perpended all matters relating to this meeting, before we quitted the fort, and have now nothing left to do but to wait for the accolade, the less thought we give it the better. We should go to this pinking and scratching as a mumbling old priest goes to mass,—even as a thing of custom, wherein there is but little premeditation :—and yet, by my gossip, not exactly as a priest goes to mass, for he goes hungry and dry : I would by no means have it so. Here, Matchcote, that flask from thy wallet! I have ever found that when an affair of business or sport be on hand, it is good grace to begin it, first by devoutly drawing your sleeves, like a Dutch toper, across your mouth, and then to take such reasonable and opportune refreshment as shall

11*

give a fillip to the spirit without clouding the brain.   And so, by
way of example, as your senior, Master Verheyden," he added,
taking the bottle from the servant's hand and applying it to his
mouth, "here I drink—Good fortune to our venture !

> ' True eye and steady hand,
>   Home thrust and keen brand,'

as the rhyme has it.   You will drink, master ?"

"I pray you, excuse me, Captain," replied Albert ; "my head
will not stand so early a freedom, and, to say the truth, I have no
relish for food or drink until this affair be done.   I scarce ate
this morning."

"Over-anxiousness, Master Secretary ! too eager for your
first entry upon the field of Mars !—ha, ha !—the token of a
green soldier, a callow martialist ; but it is natural, and will wear
off when you have fought half-a-dozen of these bouts.   I went
through it all myself.   In my 'prenticeship I could neither sleep
nor eat—faith ! I will not say drink—at the contemplation of a
pitched field, but was ever taken up with the thought of making
ready.   There was always some tag in my bandalier to be looked
to—some strap awry—some furbishing of musketoon, pike or
sword to be cared for :—works of supererogation ! as the Church
has it.   But it is pleasant to behold how use in the wars corrects
a qualmish appetite, and contents one with his accommodation :
it teaches the stomach the custom of instant service.   So keep
yourself cool, Master Verheyden,—it is a cardinal point of
discretion.   And, I beseech you, be not fanciful in your conceit
of skill with your weapon ; for though you play well, you have
a swordsman to deal with.   I have seen some whipsters who
were over-fantastic and dainty in their love of the quarrel ; and
it was as much as their tutors could do to bring them to that
modesty of opinion which should put them on the necessary
cautions of fence.   Such hawklings get their lesson in good

time : this world has store of rubbers for a vaulting temper. I pray, you, therefore, Master Secretary, bear yourself humbly, as it were. Remember, this is your first quarrel."

"You shall find me tractable in all things, worthy Captain, to your better experience."

"I have seen," continued Dauntrees, "almost as many of these dudgeon-prickings as the renowned Claude de la Chastre himself ; and have found, in nine chances out of ten, your cool and cheery gentleman to get the odds of your choleric hot-blood. I had a comrade in Flanders who was a master in this sort—and, by the bell and candle ! a priest. A most comical churchman, truly ! His name was Roger O'Brien, an Irish Jesuit, and most notable for many perfections both of the book and the sword. From a liking to his old trade—for he served with Prince Rupert before he took up the cassock—he must needs, for a fancy, put on the red coat again, and buckle his cheese-toaster to his thigh, and, in this disguise, throw himself abroad amongst the lans-kennets and swash-bucklers of Flanders. There I met him, and we journeyed together to Paris. Ha, ha, ha ! I saw him foil the whole Sorbonne on a great prize question ! There was a thesis debated—a quodlibet wrangle concerning some knot in the cobweb of theology—where the whole world was challenged to the dispute. Thereupon, my Irish friend and myself—both in our livery—went swaggering in to see and hear how these Frenchmen chopped their logic. The thesis was debated in Latin ; when presently, to the amazement of all—myself no less than others—up rises my priest to say somewhat to the point. Well, a Spanish cavalier there present, thinking my comrade could be no other than a man of the wars in his cups, rudely pulls him by the skirt to take his seat ; but he nowise heeding this interruption, pressed on in his discourse, and poured out such a flood of choice Latin, most select in phrase and apt in argument, that the amazement of the company was greatly increased, and our priestly martialist won the whole glory of the day. The Sorbonne was mute, and the assembly in an ecstasy of wonder. Whereupon departing, Father O'Brien touches the Spanish cavalier upon the shoulder, and whispers in his ear a challenge to meet him, at sunset, in the churchyard of St. Genevieve, which the Spaniard could not choose avoid. I went with my friend to the rendezvous ; and on the way, amongst other discourse touching the arrangement of the duel, I shall not forget his commendation of this virtue of coolness, by which I have more than once profited : for he was, Master Verheyden, a most expert swordsman, and singularly versed in the practique of these single combats, and showed it too on that day ; for our testy Spaniard, a fellow of pepper and ginger, was whipt through the lungs whilst he was flourishing at a stoccado. Said Father O'Brien to me,—a man who plays at this craft of phlebotomy, should carry a light heart and a merry eye before his adversary, and, like a rake-helly royster who makes free of the commodity of a tavern, should give no thought to the reckoning. It was excellent advice, Master Verheyden, and I commend it to your notice now."

"I shall do my best," replied the Secretary ; "and if I should chance, Master Dauntrees, to fail in some necessary punctilio, you will pardon it, for my unskilfulness. An acolyte of the Seminary of Antwerp has but scant opportunity to make himself master of the observances of the duello."

"By my honor as a man, Master Secretary, I have not seen amongst the most practised cavaliers, a gentleman who comes to his appointment with better grace, than this same acolyte of the Seminary of Antwerp."

"You commend beyond my desert, good Captain, though I have reasonable trust in my sword. Whilst my Lord tarried some three months in Brabant, being at Louvain, I had a master there—an Italian, one Signor Sacchari—who taught me to ride the great horse and manage my weapon, both rapier and long-sword. And, to say sooth,—though it should shame me to confess it,—I do not dislike this quarrel with the skipper. I do not perceive,—and yet I may misjudge the world's opinion,—but I do not perceive how I may be blamed for taking up this quarrel. I tell you truly, Master Dauntrees," added the Secretary, blushing, " and would beg you say so—to her, Master Dauntrees—if adverse fortune should befall me on this ground to-day—that I would gladly encounter for Mistress Blanche, our maiden of the Rose Croft, a sharper war and more perilous hazard than this single combat with a rude and boisterous seaman ; and now, with right good will I seek to do her honor against the body of this unruly skipper. Say so to her, I pray you, good Captain Dauntrees."

"Tush, man, you heed not my preaching ! When you go to dying speeches, it is summing up of the reckoning. A fig's end for the message ! you shall bear it to the maiden yourself.— Blame you, Master Secretary ! Who would blame, I would fain know, a brave man who does battle for so peerless a maiden ? By my manhood ! I think that nothing short of the maiden herself will be fit guerdon for this exploit. He was a wise and a courteous king, as the ballad feigns him, that gave his daughter to the brave knight who overthrew his adversary in combat. Now I will take on me to say that no king of the ballad ever had more need to be rid of a pestilent suitor to his daughter, than our worshipful friend, old Anthony Warden, has to be free of this sea-dog. You shall fairly win a most fair meed : and here, once more, I do you honor in a sup, with this pledge—

> May'st thou richly wear
> The meed thou winn'st so fair !

There's verse for it—halting verse, ha, ha ! Master Verheyden, but of an honest coinage : it comes from thine and the maiden's well-wisher." And with this flash of merriment, the Captain again plied the flask, and spent some moments laughing at his jest, when he suddenly ceased with the remark, " I hear the stroke of oars—this Master Cocklescraft is at hand. He is punctual, for it is just noon. We shall see him anon."

It was as the Captain said : for at that moment Cocklescraft, attended by two followers, was seen coming up from the margin of St. Luke's, across the meadow, to the place appointed for the combat.

Cocklescraft's bearing was stern ; his brow high charged with passion, and a keen resentment flashed from his eye as he advanced into the presence of his adversary. A slight salute passed between the combatants, and for some moments each party drew aside.

In the presence of his antagonist Dauntrees's whole deportment was changed. He had heretofore, as we have seen, assumed a cheerful vein of intercourse with his principal, considerately adapted with a view to amuse his mind and give him the necessary assurance which the successful conduct of the enterprise required —a labor, however, which was in no degree rendered necessary by the circumstances of the case, as it was very apparent that the Secretary, although a novice in the practice of the quarrel, was altogether self-possessed, and even eager for the issue. The Captain, however, was not slow to perceive that there was still in his carriage that hurried motion and too anxious restlessness which betokened the novelty of the situation in which he found himself, and the earnestness of his desire to acquit himself to the satisfaction of his own feelings. Through all this cheerful colloquy of the Captain, Albert's manner was grave, and scarce responded to his companion's merriment ; but now that the

moment of action arrived, he grew apparently more light-heart-
ed ; whilst, on the other hand, Dauntrees became serious, and
addressed himself to the business in hand, like a careful and provident man.

"The skipper is surly," said Dauntrees, as he stood apart
with the Secretary, wiping the sword that was to be used by his
friend. "I am glad to see it : it denotes passion. Receive the
assault from him ; stand on your defence, giving ground slightly
to his advance : then suddenly, when you have whipped him to a
rage, as you will surely do, give back the attack hotly ; follow
it up, as you did this morning in practice with me, and you will
hardly fail to find him at disadvantage ; then thrust home—for
the shorter you make this quarrel the better for your strength."

"I am more at my ease in this play than you think me,"
replied Albert, smiling ; "you shall find it so. Pray let us go
to our business."

The Captain, with two rapiers in his hand, advanced to the
ground occupied by Cocklescraft and his friends.

"I would be acquainted with your second, Master Cocklescraft," he said. "Here are our swords : shall we measure ?"

"Master Roche del Carmine," replied the skipper, as he
presented a swarthy Portuguese seaman, the mate of the Olive
Branch ; "this other companion is but a looker on."

"I would you had matched me," replied Dauntrees, hastily,
and with some show of displeasure, "with an antagonist of better
degree, Master Skipper, than this mate of yours. He was but
a boatswain within the year past. Our quality deserved that
you should sort us with gentlemen, at least."

"Gentlemen !" exclaimed the Portuguese in a passion ; "St
Salvadore ! are we not gentlemen enough for you. We belong
to the Coast—"

"Peace, sirrah !" hastily interrupted Cocklescraft : "prate

not here—leave me to speak !   Master Roche Del Carmine is
my follower, not my second, further than as your bearing, Master
Dauntrees, may render one needful to me.   I came hither to
make my own battle."

"I came to this field," replied Dauntrees, "prepared with
my sword to make good the quarrel of my friend against any
you might match me with.   So, second or follower, bully or
bravo at your heels, Master Cocklescraft, I will fight with this
Master Roche."

"That is but a boy's play, and I will none of it, Captain
Dauntrees," said Cocklescraft, angrily.   "This custom of making
parties brings the quarrel to an end at the first drawing of blood.
I wish no respite upon a scratch ; my demand stops not short of
a mortal strife."

"My sword, sir !" said Albert Verheyden, hastily striding
up to the Captain and seizing his sword.   "This is my quarrel
alone ; Captain Dauntrees, you strike no blow in it.   Upon your
guard, sir !" he added, whilst his eye flashed fire, and his whole
figure was lighted up with the animation of his anger.   "To
your guard ! I will have no parley !"

"Are you bereft ?" exclaimed Dauntrees, interposing with his
sword between the parties, and looking the Secretary steadfastly
in the face.   "Back, Master Verheyden, this quarrel must proceed orderly."

Then conducting his principal some paces off, the other yielding to his guidance, he again cautioned him against losing his
self-command by such bursts of passion.   The Secretary promised obedience, and begged him to proceed.

"Go to it, in cuerpo—strip to your shirt, Master Albert !"
said the Captain.   When the Secretary had, in obedience to
this order, thrown aside his cloak and doublet, and come to the
spot designated by his second as his position in the fight, Daun-

trees once more approached the opposite party, went through the formal ceremony of measuring swords, and then returned and placed the weapon in Albert's hand, at the same time drawing his own and planting himself within a few paces of his friend.

"We are ready, sir!" he said, bowing to the skipper's attendant.

Cocklescraft lost no time in taking his ground; Master Roche del Carmine carefully keeping out of the way of harm from any party.

The onset was made by the skipper with an energy that almost amounted to rage, and it was with a most lively interest, not unmingled with pleasure, that Dauntrees watched the eye of Albert Verheyden, and saw it playing with an expression of confidence and self-command whilst, with admirable dexterity, he parried his antagonist's assault.

"Bravo!" exclaimed Dauntrees, more than once during this anxious moment. "To it, Master Verheyden! passado—hotly, master!" he cried aloud, at the same time flourishing his own blade above his head when he saw Albert return the attack with great animation upon his adversary, who was thus compelled to give ground.

This rapid exchange of thrust and parry was suddenly arrested by the sword of the skipper being struck from his hand. The Secretary had disarmed him, and instead of following up his advantage, generously halted and brought the point of his own sword to the ground.

"The fight is done; we hold you, sir, at mercy!" said Dauntrees, promptly interposing, and placing his foot upon the skipper's rapier. "Master Verheyden has come hither upon your challenge; you will acknowledge that your life is in his hands. You have had your satisfaction, sir."

As the Captain said this he stepped one pace aside, and

Cocklescraft at the same instant picked up the rapier from the ground, and madly called out for a renewal of the fight, as with extended arm he presented himself again upon his guard.

"Instead of the favor that has been shown you in sparing your worthless life, you deserve to be cloven to the chine for this dastardly bravado !" exclaimed Dauntrees, as his spirit suddenly kindled into wrath, notwithstanding the advice he had given the Secretary to keep his temper. "Out upon thee for a disgrace to thy calling !" he added, in a tone of angry reproof, as advancing nearer to the skipper he struck the extended rapier with a dexterous underblow and made it spin in the air above his head ; "I could almost find it in my conscience to spit thee upon my sword."

"By the Virgin, I will not see my captain put upon !" said Roche del Carmine, as he now advanced towards the combatants, though still keeping a respectable space between himself and the Captain, whose skill of fence he had no mind to try.

"Nor I !" exclaimed the other attendant, at the same time drawing his hanger and shouting, "Whoop, Master Cocklescraft ! Perros, a la savanna ! For the Brothers of the Coast !— let them have it in the fashion of the Costa Rica !"

"Caitiffs !" vociferated Dauntrees, as he and Albert Verheyden now sprang forward to engage with the attendants——

"Back to your boat, you knaves ! is it thus you serve me ?" interposed Cocklescraft, thrusting his officious followers aside, and then whispering to the mate, "there is an end of it—begone !"

"By my sword, but here is a crossing of our plot !" exclaimed Dauntrees, on looking towards the range of upland over which the road towards the town lay, and discovering no less a personage than the Proprietary and Father Pierre approaching them on horseback ; "we have been informed on and tracked.

Thanks to our luck! his Lordship may do nothing better than rail against us, as is his wont. He has ever had a quick nose to scent out a duel—ay, and a nimble tongue, Master Verheyden, to reprove one : this is not my first experience of his reprimand. We shall have it without stint presently."

" To the boat, quickly, and put off!" said Cocklescraft, with a sullen angry tone to his companions. " I may find another day to right myself," he muttered, as he gathered up his sword, cloak, and hat, and, with a moody swagger, hurriedly strode towards his boat which lay in a direction opposite to that from which the Proprietary was hastening towards the scene. In a few moments he had embarked, and was seen shooting along the glassy surface of St. Luke's until he was speedily lost to view by rounding one of the turns of the creek. In the mean time Lord Baltimore and the priest arrived on the ground of the combat before the Secretary had yet resumed his doublet.

" Ah, my son, my son !" exclaimed the good Father Pierre, as he pricked his steed forward in advance of the Proprietary, and made haste to alight and throw his arms around Albert's neck, kissing his cheeks, whilst the tears flowed down his own ; " my son Albert, how could you be so unmindful of poor Father Pierre, to give him all this pain ? We saw swords flashing in the sun, and heard the clank of steel. Are you hurt, my son ? You look pale."

" I am not hurt, Father, more than that I am pained to see you here," replied the Secretary, as he affectionately placed his arm across the old man's shoulders ; " our quarrel has ended without the shedding of blood."

" Albert Verheyden," said the Proprietary gravely, reining up beside the young man, " I take it much amiss that one of my household should dare to contemn the laws of this province by coming forth to such appointment as I find you concerned in

here. I had reason to hope for the setting of good example
from him whom I chose for my secretary; but I find you foster-
ing an evil usage which is worthy no better countenance than
such as it hath gained from hot-bloods and rufflers. Fie on
thee, Albert! Is it for thee, who hast but lately changed thy
square cloister-bonnet for the feathery gewgaw of a page—is it
for thee to play at bilbo and buff like a common royster? Have
we no shallow-pated coxcomb with the privilege of wearing a
sword, who, for lack of other quality to be noted by, hath
learned a trick to vapor and strut, and swear filthy oaths, and
break God's commandments and men's peace with his bloody
broils, but that a scholar and gentleman, nursed in all kindly
studies—ay, and who hath been reared, Master Verheyden,
within the pale of the altar—must needs turn buckler-man
with a rude sea-rover, and quarrel and strike as in an ale-house
fray? Oh, it doth grieve me to find you thus!"

"My honored Lord," replied Albert, not venturing to raise
his eyes from the ground, "I do confess my fault, which with
forethought and weighing of all consequence, except my Lord's
displeasure, I did commit. I was called hither by such defiance
as it would not have consisted with my manhood to refuse. I
have sought no companionship with the skipper, nor knew that
such man was, till within a week—and even now was prone to
slight him off, as one not worthy of my resentment; but, my
good Lord, venturing to presume upon my cloistered schooling
and my unskilfulness with my sword, he must taunt with a
question of my courage, and defy me hither."

"And if a fellow who lives upon the element of his own
brawls, must take a conceit to exalt his base condition by having
a contest with his betters, shall he compass it by bragging words
and bullying questions? Does it mend his manners, or exalt
your deservings, to have a pass with him on the green sward?

Would it comfort you to bring away from this field a hand red with his blood ? Captain Dauntrees, how comes it to pass that I see you here ? Your age should have given you the privilege to be a peace-maker, not the fomenter of a quarrel."

"My Lord," said the Captain, folding his arms across his breast and advancing one foot to give a more sturdy fixedness to his attitude, whilst an expression half comic lurked in his eye, " I am an old ban-dog that has been chidden too often for barking to heed reproof in my old age. Your Lordship hath the credit of a persevering spirit to abolish the duello within the province ; I foretell you will even give over before your work is done : it were but lost pains, if I might be so bold as to say so —at least until your Lordship shall find a more mannerly brood of lieges. By the mass ! we shall win sainthood for our patience, if, in these saucy times, we may reach such perfection of humility as to brook the insolences of some of your Lordship's hopeful children of the province. The skipper was rude to our Mistress Blanche,—and the Secretary, like a cavalier, such as becomes your Lordship's household, rebuked him for it ; and thereupon grew a considered challenge, which Master Verheyden accepting, as, in my poor judgment, he could not otherwise do, I came hither with him to see fair play. It is well I did—for, to my thinking, this seaman would not have stopped at any measure of treachery. He has a deep hate against the Secretary, and the lesson Master Verheyden has taught him will not much sweeten his humor."

"Thy profession, Captain Dauntrees, gives thee a license which makes it but lost breath to chide thee," said the Proprietary calmly, nowise offended with the soldier's familiar and rebellious good nature ; " and, to say the truth, there is much rude speech and provoking action to tempt even a more governed man into quarrel ; yet I would not have you believe that I take this transgression so lightly. Albert Verheyden, you will incur my deepest displeasure, if, under any pretext or advice, you farther prosecute this feud.   Captain Dauntrees, I command you to look to it, and charge you to arrest the first who seeks to revive the quarrel."

"On the faith of my love to your Lordship," replied Albert, "I promise that I will not again offend."

"My dear son," interposed the priest, still holding the Secretary's hand, "my experience has long admonished me, that to preach restraint upon the desires of the young is but struggling up the channel of a torrent : it is hard to teach patience under wrong to those whose blood is hot with the fever of passion. Still, mon enfant, though I may not hope to persuade you—for verily I know the censure of the world leaves to a temper such as thine no choice but obedience to the law of custom—still, my dear son, you will sometimes, perhaps, take old Father Pierre's words to heart : he would entreat you to reflect, that although offence may abound, and the fashion of men's opinions may set disgrace upon the refusal to right a contrived wrong ; and though the pride of manhood may take pleasure in strife—yea, even though thy conscience shall tell thee of a just cause, and worthy of vindication by the sword—yet the heroism of suffering hath better acceptation with Heaven than all the heroism of action.   Do not forget neither, my dear Master Albert, that you are linked in this world with others, whose right to you and to your affections you dare not violate but at the hazard of the displeasure of the God who placed you here and gave you to your kind.   How should Father Pierre have borne the bereavement of his son, if your adversary had chanced to be too skilful for your defence ?   There is yet another," said the good priest, drawing nigh to the Secretary's ear and speaking almost in a whisper, "who takes this peril even more to heart than Father Pierre. Ah, Master Albert, you did not think of them that loved you !"

The Secretary blushed at the last allusion of the priest, as he hurriedly replied, "Father, it is over now—let us say no more about it."

"There, the truce is made!" said the old man, exultingly, whilst he grasped Albert by the hand and shook it, a smile playing amongst the tears that stood in his eyes : "we have made a truce—benedicite ! We shall be as happy and as gay as ever ! Allons, mon enfant, put on your cloak, and get you to your horse. My Lord, we shall reserve our scolding for another time."

"Get back to my house, Master Verheyden," said the Proprietary in a quiet tone, not heeding the appeal to him, but with a thoughtful and serious manner, which stood in marked opposition to the light and laughing air of the priest. "Captain Dauntrees, do not tarry on this field, but follow us back to the port. Come on, Father Pierre, the day is wasting."

In a moment the Captain and Secretary were left to themselves.

"Nay, never take on, Master Verheyden, nor fall into dumps," said Dauntrees, observing that his companion felt the silent displeasure of the Proprietary. "It is ever thus with his Lordship, who, from his cradle, I believe, has set his heart to the extirpation of our noble art of self-defence. A conceit of his which does no harm. His face will be sunny again to-morrow—never heed it."

"I cannot see that I have done wrong," replied Albert, with a sigh ; "I would not offend his Lordship."

"Tut, man, if you watched his eye, you would have seen in a corner of it, that he likes you all the better for this day's hazard. Now to horse !"

The combatants mounted and rode at a moderate pace to the town.

CHAPTER XXI.

I read you by your bugle horn,
And by your palfrey good:
I read you for a Ranger sworn
To keep the king's greenwood.
With burnished brand and musketoon
So gallantly you come,
I read you for a bold dragoon
That lists the tuck of drum.

SCOTT.

THE skipper returned to his vessel in no gentle mood, for, in the language of the ballad, "an angry man was he." Springing alertly from the small boat to the deck of the brigantine, he peevishly flung down his weapon and cloak, and paced to and fro, with a hurried step, for some moments in silence. "Give me drink !—some wine !" he exclaimed at length ; and when a boy, in obedience to this order, brought him what he had called for, and he had put the liquid to his lips, he shouted in a tone that made the lad tremble, as he threw the glass upon the deck and shivered it into fragments, "Knave ! why dost thou bring me this weak stuff ? I would have aqua vitæ, fool !" The stronger potation being supplied, he eagerly swallowed a draught, and threw himself upon the seat at the stern of the vessel, where, for a considerable space, he sat with his eyes fixed upon the broad field of water around him. By degrees the fever of his passion subsided into a sullen thoughtfulness, and he began to meditate, with a more self-possessed consistency of view, over the condition of his affairs. He recurred to the slight put upon him by the maiden, the Secretary's reproof, the contemptuous and insulting rejection of his suit by the Collector, and, bitterest of all these topics of exacerbation, his defeat in the duel by an antagonist whose prowess he had persuaded himself to hold in derision. Verheyden's triumph over him, as he was obliged to confess it, struck like an arrow into his heart: that so light and dainty a minion, as he deemed the Secretary, might win such a victory, and then boast of it to the maiden!—this reflection wrought up to fire the ardor of his hatred and brought his meditation to one stern conclusion—that of revenge.

"I renounce them, their tribe and generation!" he said, mutteringly. "From this day forth, I renounce them and all they consort with—Anthony Warden and his associates; yes— his Lordship and the rest. I abjure all fellowship with them, but such fellowship as my sword may maintain. The maiden!— not so fast, master!" he continued with a smile that betrayed the true devil of his nature: "scornful mistress, it would be over charitable to give thee up. Bonny damsel, thou shalt dance a corant yet to my bidding—and on the deck of my merry Escalfador; but it shall be beneath a warmer sun than thy pride has been nursed in: by my hand, you shall, wench, if there be virtue in these honest cut-throats of mine! And Master Collector shall be cared for. I thank thee, Father Pierre, for thy considerateness:—didst thou not let me into a secret touching the royal order? Faith, did you, holy father! and I will make profit of it. Oh, this excellent church quarrel too! I will join Master Chiseldine and Coode, and teach them devilish inventions! Ha! that's a thought worth the nursing—Coode and the Fendalls! We shall have blows struck; we shall have good store of cutlass and hanger-work, pistol-play and dagger! Bravo! there will be feasting for a hungry man! To it, pell-

12

mell, like gentlemen of the Coast—sink, burn, blow up—stab and
hack—ravish and run ! St. Iago, but there is a merry sequence
for you ! Why need the Brotherhood hover over the nestlings
of Peru, when we have such dainty devilries in the temperate
zone ? I will straight about this plot of mischief, whilst my
blood is warm enough to hatch it. Ho ! Roche ! order me two
men into the shallop—I would visit the port."

Whilst the skipper, in this amiable temper, was making his
way towards the town, I may take the opportunity to give my
reader a brief history of certain persons and events with which
our tale is now connected.

Josias Fendall, when Cromwell had seized upon the Proprietary's rights in Maryland, had the address to obtain the appointment of Lieutenant-General of the province, which he held under
this authority, until, by an act of treachery to those who had
procured his preferment, he was able to secure to himself the
same post by the commission of Cecilius, who, in the decline of
Cromwell's power, found the government restored to its rightful
owner. Having, in turn, attempted to betray the Proprietary,
and to usurp an independent control in the Province, he
was expelled from office ; in consequence of which he was engaged in a rebellion which, after a troublesome contest, ended in
his banishment. The clemency of the Proprietary eventually
restored him to his home, where, before the lapse of many months,
he fell into his old practices and again embroiled himself with
the authorities. He was a man of an eager, seditious temper ;
a skilful dissembler in conduct ; bold in action and dissolute in
manners, although sufficiently crafty to conceal his excesses from
public observation. He was now, in his old age, the ringleader
of the present troubles ; and some months anterior to the opening of this narrative, his threats of violence against the Proprietary, as well as certain well-founded suspicions of a design to

overthrow the provincial government by force, had led to his arrest for treason. He was, consequently, as we have hinted in a former chapter, at this moment, a close prisoner in the jail. His brother, Samuel Fendall, upon this event, took upon himself to stir up his friends to the enterprise of a rescue ; but this had produced no better result than to lodge Samuel in the same prison with his kinsman. The Protestant party,—I mean that portion of them who had been active in sustaining the violent measures set on foot by the Fendalls,—headed by John Coode, Kenelm Chiseldine, and some others, hotly resented this persecution, as they deemed the imprisonment of their friends. They had seduced into their association George Godfrey, a weak-minded yet daring man, who held the post of Lieutenant of the Rangers in the service of the Proprietary, and who in this station found many secret opportunities to promote the purposes of the malcontent party. John Coode himself was, at this epoch, smarting under the exasperation of a personal indignity which he had recently received from the Proprietary in an arrest—from which he was released upon bail—for coarse and insulting conduct to the Chancellor. He had hitherto cunningly avoided or successfully concealed all open participation in the plot which was hatching against the present domination of the province, although he had not, as we have heretofore seen, escaped the suspicion of foul designs. He was a member of the House of Burgesses, and, in the session which had just terminated, had rendered himself conspicuous for a keen, vindictive, and (as he was sustained by the popular party) successful war of vituperation against Lord Baltimore and his council.

About four o'clock in the afternoon, this Captain John Coode, according to a custom which he was prone to indulge, was found seated on a bench that stood at the door of the Crow and Archer, recreating his outward man with the solace of a tankard

of ale and a pipe, whilst his inward self was absorbed with a
rumination that spread its bland repose over every lineament
of his ruddy and somewhat pimpled visage. A limner who took
pleasure in the study of the externals of character would have
halted with satisfaction before this notable personage. He might
have been, at this epoch, about forty-five. His figure was sturdy,
broad in the chest, and supported by short and bowed legs. His
face had that jollity of aspect which comes from an unthrifty
commerce with the wine-cup ; and his eye, though somewhat
clouded and sensitive to the light, twinkled with a sharp expression of cunning and malice. His dress was of sober brown, retaining a general resemblance to the fashion of Cromwell's day,
which had not yet fallen into entire disuse. It was composed of
a coat the skirts of which, sparingly decorated with black braid,
depended, both in front and rear, to the knee ; ample breeches
and wide boots ; conical, broad-brimmed hat, and a double-hilted
Andrew Ferrara hanging from a leathern girdle.

At the moment I have introduced him to the view of my
reader, his meditation was interrupted by the arrival of a horseman,—a tall, athletic person, in the prime of manhood, equipped
partly in the manner of a wood ranger, as was indicated by the
hatchet and knife in his belt and the carbine slung across his
shoulder, and partly in that of a dragoon—betokened by his
horseman's sword and the pistols at his saddle-bow.

"Master Coode, your servant," was the greeting of the rider
whilst he dismounted and flung the rein carelessly upon the neck
of his steed, whose head drooped and sides panted with the toil
of his recent journey. "Your ale is like to grow flat from a lack
of thirst :—I can supply that commodity," he said, as he took up
the tankard and deliberately drained it to the bottom.

"By G—, Lieutenant, you had as well help yourself without

my leave !" exclaimed Coode with a laugh. "Where in the d—i are you from now ?"

"From Potapaco and the parts above," replied Godfrey, (for it was no other than the Lieutenant of the Rangers :) "that painted devil Manahoton and his wild cats have been prowling around the upper settlements. There have been throat-cutting and scalping again. Red-haired Tom Galloway was waylaid on his road to Zacaiah Fort, and the savages stole into his plantation and have murdered his wife and children. Nothing but speed and bottom saved me to-day : a party with that son of Tiquassino's—Robin Hood, they call him—at least I suspect *him* for it, from a limp which I saw in the fellow's walk—lay in cover and fired at me, just over at the head of Britton's bay. They must have been in liquor, for they popped their pieces so much at random, as to strike wide both of me and my horse. I gave them a parting volley, as far as pistols and carbines served, and then bade them good-bye."

"I dare be sworn they were stirred up to these attacks," replied Coode. "These bloody Papists have set a mark upon us all, and not only rouse the savages against us, but disguise themselves, and murder and burn with as hot a hand as the worst red devil of them all. Whilst Charles Calvert is allowed to hector it over the good people of the province, we may hope for nothing better. Did you see Will Clements ?"

"I did, and have news from him that the Huttons and Hatfields, with twenty more on the Virginia side, are ready to cross the river at the first signal."

"Have a care, Lieutenant," whispered Coode, as he cast his eye towards the quay ; "here comes a boat with that fellow Cocklescraft, one of his Lordship's lurchers. It would do you no good to be seen in parley with me. We meet to-night, at

Chiseldine's. Let me see you there : and now, away to your own concerns."

"I will not fail to go to Chiseldine's, worthy Master Coode," replied the Lieutenant, whilst he now turned aside to look after his beast.

"What ho! Garret Weasel, send me some one to this horse!" he cried out as he thrust his head into the door of the inn.

Instead of the innkeeper, the summons was answered by Matty Scamper, who, with a courtesy, announced that both Master Garret and the landlady were abroad ; and upon being made acquainted with the Lieutenant's wish, took upon herself the business of hostler and led off the jaded steed to the stable, whilst Godfrey entered the hostel. At the same instant Cockles-craft arrived at the door.

"Perhaps you could tell me, Master Coode," he inquired, "whether Kenelm Chiseldine is likely to be at home?"

"Faith, most unlikely as I should guess," replied the burgess with a leer at the questioner. "Whilst his Lordship allows the savages to shoot down and scalp the honest people of the province, here under his very nose, a wise man will learn who his visitor may be, before he will allow himself to be seen."

"Master Chiseldine has nothing to fear from me," said Cocklescraft. "I would I might see him," he added with an earnestness that forcibly attracted Coode's attention.

"Why what, in the devil's name, have you to do with Kenelm Chiseldine?"

"More than you suspect, sir. I would speak with him on affairs of importance. It perhaps may concern you to hear what I have to say."

"Wounds, man!—speak out, if thou hast aught to say against me or my friends. This shall be a free land for speech,

Master Cocklescraft—free to all men : it is so already, let me tell you, to us who wear our swords—however, his Lordship and his Lordship's brangling church-bullies would fain force it down our throats to be silent, with what you call sedition."

"Your flurry is but spent breath, Master Coode. If you will allow me an instant's private speech with you, I will open myself in somewhat that may be for your interest to hear. The bench of a public tavern does not well become the matter of my speaking."

"Ha, a private conference and on matter of moment !" ejaculated Coode. "Then follow me, Master Cocklescraft, by the Town House path, amongst the cedars on yon bank. Now, sir, you may speak your mind though it were enough to hang a countryside," said Coode, as he strode slowly in advance of the skipper until they found themselves enveloped by the thicket of cedar.

"I have heard it whispered," quoth the skipper, "since my arrival in the port, that you and others have been brewing mischief, and are like to come to scratches with his Lordship's men of the buff."

"And dost thou come to me with this fool's errand, Master Skipper ?" interrupted the burgess. "Are you sent hither, sirrah, to drain me of a secret which you may commend to the notice of the Proprietary for your own advancement in his good favor ? By my hilt, I have a mind to rap thee about the pate with my whinyard !"

"Tush, cool thy courage, valiant Captain, or spend it where it may give thee more profit. I come to thicken thy hell-broth with new spices of my own devising,—not to weaken it. I say again, I have heard it whispered that you have bloody fancies in the wind. I care not to inquire what they are, but knowing you have no good will towards the council and their friends, I have a hand to help in any devil's crotchet your plot may give life to. Besides, the Olive Branch is a more spiteful imp than she looks to be,—and you may, perchance, stand in need, hereafter, of a salt-water helpmate. I can commend her to your liking, Captain Coode."

Coode gazed with a steadfast and incredulous eye, for some moments, in the face of the skipper. At last he asked—"Art thou in earnest, Master Cocklescraft?—By G— if thou comest here to entrap me, I will have thee so bestowed that the kites shall feed upon thy bowels before the breath be out of thy body!"

"And so they may, if I deceive you," replied the skipper, coolly. "Put me to the proof, Captain,—put me to the proof, and if I fail you may fatten all the kites of St. Mary's with my body."

"Are you willing to say this before witnesses?" inquired Coode.

"A legion—if they hate the friends of the council as I hate them."

"Then come to-night to Master Chiseldine's. You shall find me and others there. Until then, it may be wise that we hold no more discourse together. And so now we part."

Cocklescraft promised to keep the appointment, and took his leave of the burgess who walked onward to the Town House. Here, Coode found Willy of the Flats busy in setting up against the trunk of the mulberry a sheet of paper, designed, according to the custom of the town, to advertise some matter of interest to the inhabitants. To the question, "What have you in the wind, Willy?"—the fiddler's reply was an invitation to the Captain to inform himself by a perusal of the paper. He accordingly read as follows:

7

"ORDER OF COUNCIL.

"License given to Stark Whittle and Sergeant Traverse to play a prize at the several weapons belonging to the Noble Science (such as shall be agreed on by them) publickly at such place in or near St. Marie's City, as they shall for this day appoint : provided that no foul play be used, nor any riott or disturbance tending to the breach of his Lordship's peace, be by them or any of their associates thereupon offered. Dated at his Lordship's mansion, in the City of St. Marie's, this 9th day of October, Anno Domini, 1681.

"J. LLEWELLIN, Clerk."

"On the common, behind the Town House in St. Marie's City, by permission of an order of Council, as above recited, a trial of skill shall be performed between Stark Whittle and Sergeant Gilbert Travers, two masters of the Noble Science of' Defence, at four of the clock in the afternoon of Thursday the twenty-third of October instant.

"I, Stark Whittle, of the town of Stratford, England, who have fought thirty-one times at Hockley in the Hole, at Portugal, and in divers parts of the West Indies, and never left a stage to any man, do invite Gilbert Travers to meet and exercise at the several weapons following, viz :

Back Sword,	Sword and Buckler,
Sword and Dagger,	Case of Falchons,

Single Falchon.

"I, Gilbert Travers, sergeant of musketeers, who formerly served in the Walloon Guard of His Highness the Prince of Orange, and hath held the degree of Master of the Noble Science of Defence in forty-seven prizes, besides four that I

12*

fought as a provost before I took said degree, will not, in regard
to the fame of Stark Whittle, fail to meet this brave inviter at
the time and place appointed ; desiring a clear stage and from
him no favor.

" VIVAT REX."

"This promises well, for a fair sport, Willy," said Coode ;
" they are both pretty fellows with the sword. Who has set this
matter a foot ?"

" I heard, an it please your worship," replied the fiddler : "it
is near a fortnight since,—that Stark Whittle and the Sergeant,
being together at an ale-drinking, on an afternoon, at Master
Weasel's ordinary, and having got into a merry pin, must needs
fall into an argument, and thereupon into a debate, as men commonly do now-a-days, upon church matters. Whereupon Stark,
—you know, Master Coode," said Willy, touching the burgess
on the rib with his knuckle and speaking, in a confidential tone,
with a short dry laugh,—" Stark is a born devil on our side of
the question,—whereupon he raises his voice against the mumbling of masses, as he calls it, and the pictures and images and
the rest of the trumpery ;—while the Sergeant sticks up, like a
true soldier, for the army of martyrs and the canons and what
not besides. So, when words got high, and Stark began to be
puzzled by some of Gilbert's quiddities which he learned from the
priests,—he whips off from the church and turns the discourse
upon sword-craft. And thereupon, after some crowing by Gilbert,
Stark takes him short with a challenge to play a prize—which
the Sergeant accepted, out of hand. Then it was left to Colonel
Talbot to bring it to the council, and the next thing I hear of it
is that Colonel Talbot sends me here to set this writing concerning the whole matter, against the mulberry before the Town
House door."

Before Willy had got through this account of the origin of Stark Whittle's challenge, Godfrey had come to the spot.

"We may find an occasion in this prize fight that shall jump with our plot, Lieutenant," said Coode. "What think you Richard Cocklescraft had to tell me?"

"I cannot guess."

"Why, that these shavelings, who meddle so much in the affairs of the province and rule the council, are downright knaves;—that his Lordship is no better than a sneaking dotard; the council themselves but white-livered whelps of the litter of Babylon, and that the whole brood of craw thumpers, taking in master and serving-man all round, are but scurvy thieves who deserve, each and all, to be set in the stocks. Now, there is a wise skipper!—a clear-sighted, conscientious wight, who has seen his errors and confesses them honestly! This Master Cocklescraft has promised me to meet us at Chiseldine's to-night, which I put it to him to do by way of test to his honesty. If he come not there, I shall hold that he has cozened me with a base, juggling, papistical lie. And in that case, George Godfrey, I desire you to set thy mark upon him;—dost hear? So, until we meet again at Master Chiseldine's, good even, Lieutenant."

The residence of Chiseldine stood upon the river, a short distance beyond the upper limits of the town, from which it was separated by the small creek which I have heretofore described as bounding the common. This creek, at its embouchure where it crossed the river beach, was reduced into a narrow strait, scarcely, in the ordinary state of the tides, beyond the compass of an active man's leap. Here a small bridge gave to the townspeople access at all times to the dwelling-house of Master Chiseldine.

When the twilight had subsided, some three or four visitors were found assembled under this roof, and their number in the course of an hour was gradually increased to as many more. Amongst these, Coode and Godfrey were the first to arrive; they were soon followed by a person of no small influence in stimulating the disorders of that time,—the Reverend Master Yeo—an active and subtle churchman of the English Church, whose emaciated figure, meek countenance, and puritanical simplicity of costume, contrasted with a restless and passion-fraught eye, presented an impersonation of a busy, political ecclesiastic. The host, Master Kenelm Chiseldine, though a young man, had already arrived at some authority in the House of Burgesses by his persevering and zealous hostility to the Proprietary, and had, through the popularity which generally follows resistance to the established order of things, obtained such a control over the course of that unhappy dissension which agitated the peace of the province, as entitled him to be considered, in modern phrase, one of the leaders of the movement. He now appeared in this conclave, in that mixed character of burgher and soldier—partially armed, though professing the pursuits of a man of peace—which the disturbances of the period had rendered common amongst the inhabitants. Conspicuous, at least for his estimate of himself, in this assemblage, whither the love of having something to do, and a thirst for a patriot's immortality, had lured him, was little Corporal Abbot the tailor—a wight remarkable for the vast disproportion between the smallness of his person and the greatness of his aspirations, and still more remarkable for an upspringing walk and an ambitious, erect carriage of the head. Stricken with the grandeur of Lieutenant Godfrey's achievements, and emulous of like glory in the field of Mars, he had, by degrees, wormed himself into an intimacy with the Lieutenant, who, one day, in a freak, settled the little hero's destiny, by enlisting him for a special campaign with the Rangers. In the course of this tour of duty, which lasted sixty days, Ned

Abbot had the good fortune to capture three Indian women, whom he took for warriors belonging to the tribe of King Tiquas sino—a chief whose name diffused a common terror through the province. The Rangers conspired to magnify the hazard and glory of this exploit, and his commander exalted him to the honorable and responsible duties of a corporal. Ever since that event, the tailor looked upon himself as a martialist approved in battle and entitled to boast of his prowess. Being thus seduced into the list of fame, he became a devoted adherent of the Lieutenant, and, as is customary amongst the votaries of greater men than even Lieutenant George Godfrey, he suffered himself to be embarked in all the hazards and committed to all the consequences of his leader's political imbroglios. The corporal's time was divided between the needle and the broadsword;—at one season, when work was slack, playing the man of war in bloodless forays, and at another, when fighting was superabundant, stitching doublets and patching decayed jerkins with a commendable tranquillity of spirit.

Such were the principal personages who were now convened to deliberate upon the course of that secret rebellion which, in a few years later than this period, terminated in what is known in the history of Maryland as the Protestant Revolution. Their more immediate purpose was to devise measures for the rescue or liberation of the Fendalls. Towards the accomplishment of this design, the discontented in various parts of the province had associated under private forms of organization, and held themselves in readiness to obey the signal for an outbreak, whenever the leaders amongst the burgesses should determine the fit moment to have arrived. When these persons were once banded together in arms, their plan was to drive matters to an immediate issue with the Proprietary, by seizing the fort, and even by assailing his person. Their general scheme of rebellion was supposed to derive its hopes of success not only from the increasing bitterness which daily grew up between the two religious sects, but from the avowed inclination of the Court at White Hall to give an established Church to the province, and to restrain the exercise of religious toleration towards the Catholic party. Add to this the fact that a preponderating majority of the inhabitants were of the Protestant faith, and it will be seen that the conspirators had no very strong reason to apprehend any fatal miscarriage of their scheme.

It was late before Cocklescraft made his appearance in this assembly. He had gone into the inn, where he remained in solitude until after nightfall ; and when the retiring day had left everything in shade, he sallied forth, and indulged his moody and fevered temper in lonely musing, as he rambled through the town and along the margin of the river. Callous as he was to the ordinary sensibilities of humanity, it cost him a struggle to pursue his vindictive purpose to the extent of making war against that faith, the devotion to which, in his bosom, was superstition —a superstition that clung to his mind through all the iniquities of his life amongst the Brothers of the Coast, and which he now trembled to renounce. His self-communing on this subject had wrought him up to a state of mind that bordered upon insanity, exhibiting itself, at times, in bursts of apparently jocular recklessness, and driving him to the stimulus of strong drink.

His absence from Chiseldine's began to be remarked. Master Yeo had already let fall—when Coode spoke of his interview with the skipper—some expressions of distrust in the sincerity of such a conversion as the tale implied ; and more than one of the company hinted at a trick contrived by the Papists to entrap them. Private mutterings of dissatisfaction and threats of retribution were growled in whispered tones. Corporal Abbot was remarkably fierce and denunciatory. "By my sword, neighbors !" he said, with a scowling eyebrow, "an I find it should turn out that we have been paltered with by that briny ruffler, it shall go hard with him but he shall find that I wear cold iron, —if he learn as much from never a man in the town beside. And as we are all here together, where we may speak our minds," he added in a stage-whisper, with a significant solemnity of manner, "I would have you know I do not put too much faith in the honesty of these absolution and purgatory men : they are fishy —fishy, masters," he said, laying his finger against his nose, and looking portentously mysterious. "To my seeming, this Richard Cocklescraft ever had a hang-dog——"

"Ay, that's true—a hang-dog devil in his looks," said Cocklescraft himself, taking the parole from the speaker, as he strode into the room immediately behind the Corporal, who stood near the door. His brow was flushed, his air hurried and disturbed, and he had entered the outer door without knocking or ceremony of announcement, and thus came into the apartment where the meeting was assembled, at unawares, and at the moment that his name was upon the Corporal's lips. His cap was drawn conceitedly over one side of his forehead, and his scabbarded sword, detached from the belt, was borne in his hand. A constrained smile gave a disagreeable and unusual expression to his features, and there was an air of affected joviality in his carriage when he interrupted the boasting martialist and accosted the company. "Nay, Master Corporal, you need not shrink, for your brave speaking : 'tis a license of a man of the wars to rail at such as leave their colors ; and as I have left mine, I stand under your reproof.—God save you, my masters, for a set of merry contrivers of mischief ! By St. Iago, but you make a snug house of it here together ! Master Chiseldine, Captain Coode would have me come here to-night to speak before witnesses. Presto, change ! is the word. I have done with the cowls and the cassocks, and

with all who bow to the honorable council : I have done with
my Lord's gentlemen of taffeta and buckram ;—yea, and have
a reckoning to make which shall be remembered in Maryland.
Santo Rosario ! but I *will* make it," he added, as he spoke
through his clenched teeth, " when the foremost man amongst
you all shall cry shame for pity !—We shall foreswear water-
drinking, comrades ! I have renounced it to-day ; for an hour
past I have fed upon the milk of Scheidam—most wholesome
usquebaugh, without taint of Papistry in it : I fetched it myself
from Holland to the Crow and Archer. Ha ! it has baptized
me in the faith of our new quarrel. I will swear by it as your
only holy water."

   " Master Cocklescraft, I would you had brought us a cooler
head—though you are not the less welcome," said Chiseldine.
"Think you, sir, you can strike, if there be need for it, at those
you have lately consorted with ?"

   "Strike !" exclaimed Cocklescraft, "ay, by Saint Anthony,
can I strike ! on the broad sea, or green land,—in pell-mell or
orderly fight,—amongst pikes and muskets, or grenades and cul-
verins. I can strike with sword or dagger,—at waking man or
sleeping babe—gray head or green :—strike, Master Chiseldine,
to drum and trumpet, or to the music of shrieking wives and
sobbing maidens. I have been nursed to the craft. What else
should have brought me here to-night ?"

   "A most monstrous and horrid papistical schooling the wolf
has had !" piously ejaculated Master Yeo, in the ear of a neighbor. "This fellow would have been a Guido Fawkes in time."

   "We must use him, nevertheless, reverend Master Yeo,"
said Coode ; "we shall teach him gentleness, when we have got
over the rough work of our plot."

   The parson assented by a nod of the head ; and then approaching the skipper, inquired, "What argument, worthy

Master Cocklescraft, hath persuaded you to renounce your old associates? There may be much edification in the experience of a man so thoroughly converted."

"That concerns no man here," replied the seaman bluntly. "Enough for you, sir, that I have changed my colors. I come to you not alone, neither: I have men to back me, and follow where I lead, and a trim bark which may serve a turn when you are put in straits. If you will have service out of me, I ask no return for it, but that you set quickly about the work. Do you want motive for present quarrel? I can give it to you. I know it for a truth, that the King hath sent orders hither to dislodge every Papist from his office in this province; and I know, further, that the council do, upon deliberation, refuse to obey the King's bidding. There is a handle for rebellion which may serve you for a throat-cutting! But what is a royal order to Charles Calvert if the wind of his humor set contrary against it? A feather.—Who are they that counsel my Lord Baltimore? The men that feed their own idleness on the substance of the honest folk who toil;—the men who flatter his Lordship with crafty courtesies. First amongst them is that old grout-head, Anthony Warden: I would have you note him, masters, for a chief leech; a most toping blood-sucker. To whom should the offices of this province belong? To such as the good pleasure of the burgesses may appoint——"

"Surely," grunted Coode.

"To such as the King would have—"

"Without question," breathed the reverend Parson Yeo.

"Then, there are reasons for rebellion as thick as you could wish, masters," continued Cocklescraft, by way of close to an harangue which showed him qualified to take a rank amongst the demagogues of the time not inferior to that of the most successful masters of the art of agitation at the present day.

" So, fall to, and make yourselves worshipful dignitaries,—men
of consideration amongst your neighbors : I am here to help."

" Bravely spoken !" shouted Coode, as the skipper concluded
this successful essay in political oratory, whilst several voices re-
echoed the commendation ; " that is the true aspect of our plot,
and Master Cocklescraft shows himself a worthy and apt scholar.
The sooner we come to buffets the better.   We have force enough
to match the pikes and muskets of his Lordship, and make ourselves masters of the fort.   By a placard set against the mulberry at the Town House this afternoon, it seems we are to have
a prize play between Stark Whittle and Sergeant Travers, next
Wednesday week.   This will not fail to bring our friends of the
country swarming to the sport, and the occasion will be apt for us
to manage the appointments of a general revolt."

This suggestion receiving the countenance of the conclave,
was adopted, and the execution of the particulars committed to
Coode himself.   For the present, it was thought advisable that
no immediate step be taken in reference to the rescue of the Fendalls, as it was very obvious, from various intelligence which had
been brought to the conspirators, that a crisis was near at hand
which must be decisive of the question of strength between the
two parties.

After this the company gradually dispersed.

CHAPTER XXII.

She sat hie on the tap tower stane,
Nae waiting may was there;
She lows'd the gowd busk frae her breast,
The kaim frae 'mang her hair,
She wiped the tear blobs frae her ee,
An' looked lang and sair.

THE MERMAID OF GALLOWAY.

IT is proper, before we move onward with our tale, to give some account of affairs at the Rose Croft, towards which the interest of our lady readers especially is very naturally directed.

After Willy of the Flats had departed with the missive that was designed to frustrate the duel, there was, for a considerable time, a general restlessness manifested by the household, extending from Alice Warden and Blanche, downward through the entire roll of domestics; for Willy had not omitted to avail himself of the occasion to give Mistress Coldcale a circumstantial history of the whole affair of the quarrel between the skipper and the Secretary, in the presence of Michael Mossbank, as well as of the housemaids, the cook and the scullion, all of whom were opportunely assembled in the kitchen, at work amongst the litter and wreck of the last night's feast, and were, of course, thrown by the recital into a condition of most extraordinary doubt and curiosity as to the upshot of the adventure. The restlessness to which I have referred seemed equally to defy the consolations of philosophy and the power of remaining stationary in any one place, by any one body, for two consecutive minutes. The com-

mon topic of apprehension was that Willy might not reach Father
Pierre in season, or if he did, that Father Pierre might not find
aid at hand to intercept the combatants ; two very reasonable
grounds of distrust, which brought about that nervous agitation
which is not uncommon in female councils.   In the present case,
after much tribulation and perplexity in the two sisters, it was
thought expedient to call Mistress Coldcale to the consultation
regarding what was proper to be done in the emergency ; and
the matter was now entertained in an ambulatory debate, commencing in the parlor, and moving successively into the hall,
thence upstairs to a chamber window, down again to the front
door, and finally to the verge of the cliff, at the extremity of the
lawn overlooking the river.   At this last spot, Mistress Coldcale
cast her eyes over the water, and there discovered the skipper's
brigantine, which, as my reader is aware, had been dropped down
to this anchorage early in the morning.   This phenomenon
straightway suggested a most ingenious expedient, which, from
the vivacity of its enunciation, it was obvious the housekeeper
considered as decisive of the question under deliberation.

   "Good luck the while !" she exclaimed, "if there is not
Master Cocklescraft's own vessel, the Olive Branch, lying fast
and firm, in the very mouth of the creek.   How lucky for us !
The skipper, Mistress Alice, as we are women, is on board, and
intends to go thence to Cornwaleys's Cross ;—now, as he must
come within hail of our landing, we have only to station Michael
Mossbank here with the long Spanish fowling-piece, and cause
him to warn Cocklescraft, in the name of Master Warden, to
forbear coming up the creek on peril of his life.   Your father
did so in Fendalls' first rebellion, when Sawahega and his men
frightened the priests of St. Inigoe's yonder out of their wits, by
sailing into the creek.   Why shouldn't we try it with the skipper?
Michael shall fire upon him if he dare to make light of the

warning ; and lest bloodshed might come of it, the gardener may take his aim somewhat aslant and overhead. I will promise you, no sailor ventures another stroke of an oar forward after that."

" Mercy on us, Mistress Bridget !" ejaculated Alice Warden, " would you involve us in a war with the skipper and his surly comrades ?"

" At least till Master Anthony Warden, your worshipful father, comes home and takes the matter into his own hands, I would make war as we may, against Cocklescraft, or any one else that should come into our waters to harm Master Albert. Troth, would I !"

"I am sure, I do not know what to do," said Blanche, not heeding the belligerent device of the housekeeper, and looking ruefully, through a tear, over the waste of waters—" I am sure I do not know what to do, unless it be to send for our dear Lady Maria.".

As this last seemed to be the most practicable hint which had yet been suggested, it was seized upon and adopted with entire unanimity ; and the consultation was immediately adjourned to carry it into operation. Mistress Alice and the housekeeper hurried to speed measures to that end, and Blanche remained fixed upon the bank in a mute study, apparently watching the people upon the deck of the brigantine.

Luckily, before Michael Mossbank could make ready a horse to do the errand which Mistress Alice had confided to him, the Lady Maria was descried approaching the house, mounted on her ambling pony, and followed by a body-guard in the shape of an old serving-man of the Lord Proprietary. In brief space she alighted at the door.

The good lady had heard nothing of the tidings which had diffused such sadness over the household at the Rose Croft, and, it may be imagined, now received them with a manifestation of concern commensurate not only with her regard for the Secretary, but also with the peculiar solicitude which she was accustomed to extend over all matters relating to the affairs of the young people within her brother's dominion.

"Oh, the bloody-minded skipper! and oh, rash Master Albert!" she exclaimed, after the narrative was concluded. "I foresaw it—I dreamed of it—I almost knew some mischief was hatching, ever since that wicked look which I marked the skipper give to Master Albert, when the Secretary chid him for being too free in his importunity regarding the mantle—as you may remember, Blanche."

"I wish the fingers of the sempstress over sea had been blistered ere they stitched that foul mantle," said Blanche, "and the skipper in the bottom of the Red Sea, who brought it here!"

"I would rather wish that Master Albert should find no skipper at Cornwaleys's Cross to-day," returned the lady, not knowing exactly what to wish; "or that no such place as Cornwaleys's Cross was to be found in the province."

"Find no skipper there!" exclaimed Blanche; "if a poor wish of mine might bring it to pass, Master Albert's sword should deal so sharply with him that he should never again set foot in the Port. It all comes of that foolish birth-day ball which I must needs be persuaded by Grace Blackiston to give. I would I were not eighteen for five years to come!"

"If harm should befall Master Albert," interposed the housekeeper, who felt herself privileged in this time of general tribulation to give her opinion, "it would be for your comfort that you never saw nor would see eighteen. If I were Mistress Blanche, I know I should never find my natural rest again, to lose so sweet a gentleman as the Secretary. But the crosses of this life come not by desert, nor spare the best, as the proverb says. I fear the skipper is an overmatch for Master Albert."

"Surely, Mistress Coldcale," said Blanche, nettled at the housekeeper's freedom, as well as at her undervaluing the Secretary's prowess, "thou hast no warrant for such speech. Master Albert hath a valiant heart and a hand to defend himself, and may match with the skipper in any quarrel. And if he were not his match," she added, with an ill-concealed struggle to appear indifferent to the result, "he is no kinsman of mine, I trow, that I should wish myself dead." And having thus given vent to an emotion suggested by that reserve which a maiden feels who first begins to be conscious of a secret affection for a lover,—a sentiment that until this day had slumbered unacknowledged at her heart,—she covered her face with her hands, and left the room, to weep in private.

At the top of the Collector's dwelling was a small balcony or platform that had been constructed for an observatory, from which vessels approaching the Port might be described with a perspective glass at the most remote seaward point. From this elevation, looking inland, the road leading from the town around the head of St. Inigoe's, might be discerned for some extent along the plain, and at intervals, through the forest, where it became tangled amongst the hills. To this balcony, in the disquietude of her mind, Blanche had gone secretly to look out upon the road and note those who travelled upon it, hoping by this means to satisfy herself on that anxious question whether any persons were abroad to prevent the duel. Long she gazed there, with her brow shaded by her hand ; and when within an hour of noon, she discerned two figures, on horseback, moving upon the hill-side almost at a walk,—it was with an emotion that produced a shudder through her frame that she recognised at that distance the short dark cloak and the low cap and feather of the Secretary.

"Oh, blessed Mother!" she exclaimed involuntarily, "it is Master Albert: our care has been but lost. So leisurely he moves along, his path has not been followed; nor is it like to be, for noon has almost come, and I see no Father Pierre behind, although the road is open townward to my sight full two good miles. And he hath Master Dauntrees with him, as I take that companion to be; and Master Dauntrees would not guide him so much at ease if there were followers.—Jesu Maria! hither comes the skipper's boat, skimming the water with such speed as makes it sure he shall reach the Cross in time," she continued, as she turned her eye from the land to the river, and saw the shallop cleaving the surface of St. Inigoe's creek, abreast the Rose Croft, under the lusty stroke of two oarsmen, and bearing Cocklescraft and his comrades, so near to her that she was able to distinguish, upon the bench of the boat, the swords which were to be used in the combat. "Well-a-day! it is a foredoomed trial, which may not be averted by any caution of mine. The Holy Martyrs guard our good Master Albert, and turn danger from his path! as for his gentleness and bravery he doth deserve."

The maiden muttered these short and almost incoherent aspirations, half in self-communion, half in prayer, during which a melancholy expression of distress rested upon her countenance, and often, like the forsaken lady of the ballad,

"She wip'd the tear blobs frae her ee,
An' looked lang and sair."

Whilst she thus indulged her secret grief, voices were heard below in the court-yard.

"It is the skipper's boat, Michael Mossbank," said the voice of Bridget Coldcale, "and the skipper in it, with his rufflers at his side. The fowling-piece, Michael!—the long Spanish gun you shoot ducks with in the winter!—haste ye, man, and fetch it, or they will be out of thy reach ! Was ever such a lurdan—such a poking old elf !—I have the heart to load and fire with my own hand. These headstrong men !"

"Go to your kitchen-craft, you silly-witted woman !" returned the voice of the gardener, with a hoarse laugh : "thou'rt a fool with thy prating of the fowling-piece ! Take a ladle of hot water and fling it in the wind—it will scald yon sailors, perchance—'tis but a furlong cast : the creek is but a half mile wide."

"It was not so wide, you crusty mole catcher, but that his worship from this bank could turn that savage Sawahega and his canoes back as they came."

"Tush, Dame Bridget, go and peel your onions !—What do you known of Sawahega and his canoes ? Were there not fifty of us with musket and culverin to boot !—Let these women prate and the world will be so thick set with lies that they will darken the light of the sun—a man would lose his way in day-time, unless he bore a lantern."

This last hit of the gardener's seemed to be decisive, for the voice of Mistress Coldcale was immediately afterwards heard in the house, showing that she had evidently retreated.

"Ah !" cried the maiden, who still retained her position in the balcony, as she now unexpectedly discerned the figures of the Proprietary and Father Pierre riding at a pretty brisk gait along the plain from the direction of the town—"a blessing on him ! Father Pierre has got our message and is on his way with his good Lordship. The saints lend them speed !—though I fear they go too late. The skipper's boat has turned into St. Luke's and will be at the Cross ere his Lordship reach the hills,—though when he reaches the hills his journey is but half performed."

It was not long after this that she heard the bell of St. Inigoe's across the creek, pealing its customary announcement of

13

noon, and still the Proprietary and the priest had not yet ceased to be observed on the road descending from the highland. The boat of the skipper had disappeared in the recesses of St. Luke's, and the Secretary with his companion had already abundant time to reach the appointed ground of the combat. Overcome by doubt, suspense, and apprehension, Blanche retreated, with a stealthy step, as if afraid even to hear the noise of her own footfall to her chamber, and there, with a throbbing heart and trembling frame, threw herself upon her bed. In this condition she lay conjuring up the phantoms of her imagination, and giving full scope to that distressing augury of evil, which, in moments when we are compelled passively to contemplate the dangers to which those we love are exposed, impels us by an almost superstitious presentiment to believe and expect the worst. When two hours and more had elapsed, the housekeeper with precipitate haste thrust herself panting into the chamber, and roused the maiden from this unhappy meditation, with an abruptly-communicated piece of news.

"His Lordship has made safe work of it, Mistress Blanche,—most joyful work of it !—bless him for a charitable, careful, painstaking Lord,—and bless you, Mistress Blanche, for your thoughtful wisdom in sending to Father Pierre. Oh, I have happy news for you !"

"Tell it, I pray you, Mistress Bridget !"

"Michael Mossbank, my dear young lady, comes but now, riding in at full speed from the mill of St. Inigoe's, where he went an hour ago to have a chat with Bolt the miller——"

"In mercy, tell me the pith of this story at once," interposed the maiden with an impatience which could not brook the housekeeper's prolixity.

"Well, there, Michael spied, as he was talking to the miller, —he spied, riding along the road from Cornwaleye's Cross

towards the town, who do you think ?—Why, his Lordship and
Father Pierre, both looking as long-faced as the oldest drudge-
horse that takes a meal-bag to mill—and after them, some good
distance behind, riding as silent as if they were going to a
funeral, Master Albert,—our dear Master Albert,—and that
old sinner and evil adviser, Captain Dauntrees of the Fort. And
as this plainly signified that all was over and no harm done,
Michael mounts his nag and comes clinking home here as fast as
four legs can bring him. Isn't it precious news, Mistress ?"

"Art sure of it, Mistress Coldcale ?" demanded Blanche,
with a sudden sunshine bursting out upon her face and chasing
away the clouds of grief which but a moment before lowered
upon it—"Art truly sure of it, sweet Bridget ?"

"As sure of it,—bless you for a happy young lady !—as
that my name was Bridget Skewer till my dear goodman, peace
to his bones ! changed it into Coldcale."

Blanche laughed outright, and went straight into the parlor to
share the pleasure of this piece of intelligence with her sister and
the Lady Maria. These ladies, however, had already been apprised of all that the housekeeper had told to the maiden, and
the pony being in waiting at the door, the sister of the Proprietary hurried off with a speed stimulated by her eagerness to learn
every thing from her brother, leaving Alice and the maiden happy
in finding that at least no serious harm had befallen the Secretary.

Albert Verheyden, although keenly sensitive to the displeasure of the Proprietary, in reviewing his conduct throughout the
quarrel with the skipper, felt a lively satisfaction at the course
he had pursued. The provocation had been so flagrant, and the
bearing of Cocklescraft towards him so evidently exasperated by
the favor he had won from the maiden, that it was with a natural exhultation he looked back upon the recent meeting and its

result.   His sentiment towards his adversary in this retrospect, was somewhat of the nature of that imputed, in the metrical tale, to the Chieftain at his triumph over his unnatural brothers—

> "I trow ye wad hae gi'en me the skaith,
> But I've gi'en you the scorn."

He had foiled his enemy at his boasted weapon, and sent him humbled from the field.   But what was chiefly pleasing to him in the review was, that the strife had arisen in the cause of Blanche Warden, and that he had, like a knight of ancient adventure, rescued her from the importunity of a disagreeable suitor.   The reproof of the Proprietary was almost lost sight of in the gratulation of his own heart upon the successful issue of this his first essay of manhood ; and, besides, he felt a secret consciousness that however his Lordship might openly chide him for this infraction of the law, still he could not undervalue him for his prompt resentment of an offence to which, especially in that age, it would have been a foul dishonor to submit.   Then the bland interposition and affectionate support of Father Pierre, who rebuked as became a churchman the rude appeal to arms, and yet stood by him as a friend to share the pleasure of his triumph, gave him still further confidence that he should lose neither the countenance nor the esteem of the Proprietary by what had happened.   With a disburdened heart, therefore, and a contented spirit of self-approbation, he went to his bed that night, and enjoyed a sleep as refreshing and deep as the slumber of childhood.

The duel was attended by another consequence still more important.   The Secretary had become the champion of the maiden of the Rose Croft, and it was no more than a natural sequence, justified and approved by all experience, that he should claim to think of her as his mistress, and to render the open homage of a lover.   Heretofore his demeanor towards her had been marked by a quiet humility, an almost worshipping deference—reserved and struggling to conceal the passion which glowed in his bosom: but he now became aware of a sudden change in his estimate of himself, and of a consciousness that his manhood entitled him to speak to the mistress of his heart with bolder speech and more unquestionable pretension.

When morning broke upon him it found his spirits enlivened by gay thoughts, and his countenance made cheerful by the impression of pleasant dreams,—dreams that had conducted him into fairy bowers where all the images that enchanted his view bore some reference to the Rose of St. Mary's. He sprang from his couch with the buoyancy of unusual health, and, whilst he made his toilet, his mind ran with an impatient resolve upon an early visit to the Rose Croft.

Accordingly, as soon in the day as he might with propriety visit at the Collector's dwelling—for all at once he grew scrupulous as to these observances which, until now, had never entered into his reckonings—he was mounted on his steed and forth and away, a gallant cavalier seeking the bower of his lady-love.

When he arrived at the Rose Croft, Blanche and her father were just prepared to set out on a morning's walk, and were upon the lawn sauntering around the rustic temple which contained the altar of St. Therese.

"Welcome, Master Verheyden," said the Collector with a brisk and cordial greeting; "heartily welcome! Zounds, man, you had brought us into a fine coil yesterday!—my women here, Alice and Blanche, yea and Mistress Bridget and Meg and Sue, —the whole of them,—were as much astir as if the Sinniquoes had made an inroad upon us. You have been playing the buckler-man since we saw you last;—you must try your hand at edge and point, Master Albert. Marry, after this thou mayst wear thy toledo with an air, cock thy beaver, and draw at a word, like a pretty fellow of the rapier. Give us a hand, good Albert,—I thank thee for the service thou hast done in lowering the plume of that saucy sea-urchin. Why didst not run him through the body?"

The Secretary was not prepared for this bluff questioning, and as he took the Collector's hand, his cheek reddened and he replied with a modest mien, "I sought no quarrel with the skipper, and am thankful that we parted with so little hurt."

Notwithstanding the complacency with which Albert regarded his recent conduct, and the gaiety of heart with which he now visited the Rose Croft, and despite his resolution to assume a bolder carriage in the presence of Blanche, his bearing at this moment was characterized by more than ordinary diffidence and show of respect. It was even with some confusion that he now approached the maiden and offered her his hand ; and, what was equally to be remarked, Blanche Warden, on her part, seemed to have lost that confiding and unguarded tone of intimacy with which she was ever in the habit of receiving the Secretary. Still, joy sparkled in her eye and warmed her features with a genial flush, as she noted Albert's humbleness in her presence, and read in it his more profound sense of the value of her favor.

" Our birth-day feast," he said, after saluting the maiden, " will be well remembered in the province for the general content it has given. All voices are praising Mistress Blanche : and she has won many sincere wishes from the townspeople for long and happy life."

" Alas !" replied the maiden, " whatever others may think, I have wept sorely for that unlucky feast. I did not wish it at first, and, in the end, had better reason to grieve that I had been persuaded to make it."

" Master Verheyden," interposed the Collector, " thou hast

come most seasonably hither : this girl must have me consent to
trail my old limbs after her, like a young gallant, this morning,
in a ramble to enjoy the air, as she calls it—simply because she
has happened to leave her nest with the merry chirp of a spring
lark. You shall take my place as a fitter man for such service.
There, Blanche, is the Secretary for thee—a better squire than
thy old rusty-jointed father ! I have a more profitable calling
on hand to visit my fields. Ha, Master Albert, you wear a love
token on your breast !" added the old gentleman, with a playful
smile, as he took in his hand a small miniature set in gold, which
hung by a chain from the Secretary's neck, and had accidentally
escaped unobserved from beneath his vest in the action of dismounting from his horse ; " some lady of the other side of the
water, eh ? And on the back, here, letters which my eyes are
too old to make out without my glasses—a posy, no doubt :
' Let fools great Cupid's yoke disdain—' thou know'st the song,
Master ; 'tis the way of all living."

" 'Tis my poor mother's likeness," said Albert, gravely, at the
same time restoring the miniature to his bosom. " She put it
round my neck with her own hands whilst she lay upon her death-
bed : and I have worn it ever since. 'Tis the only remembrance
I have of her. I was a child when she died, but not too young
to feel the loss of one who loved me so well."

The tear started into the Secretary's eye as he spoke, and
when Mr. Warden saw it, a tear also came into his, which he
brushed away with his hand, saying, with an assumed vivacity,
" Pardon, good lad ! a thousand times I ask your forgiveness
for my rude speech. I did not think of what I said : and I but
love thee the more for thy kind memory of thy mother. Hang
up care by his wing ! the world is overstocked with it. You
will stay dinner with us, good master ? I go forth to look after
some necessary affairs, and will be back before this girl has led

you her dance.   At dinner I will have much to say to you concerning that tarpaulin bully.   A plague on the wool cap !   I
could have found it in my heart to fight with him myself ;—
my gray hairs against his raven locks !   Do you know, Master
Verheyden, he was so saucy as to ask my leave to woo our girl
here—this Blanche of mine ?   See, how the child hoists her red
ensign on the cheek at the thought of it :—ay, and pressed it on
me so rudely, and with such clap-me-on-the-back familiarity, as
he would have used to cozen Mistress Dorothy of the Crow and
Archer out of a jack of ale.   You should have spitted him on
your sword, for a public benefaction, and had the thanks of the
Mayor and Aldermen for your good works.   I would as lief see
him so trussed as the haunch of a brocket in my own kitchen."

   " Nay, my dear father," interrupted Blanche, as she saw a
storm rising on the Collector's brow, " pray you say no more
about the skipper.   Master Albert does not like to be tasked
with discourse of his quarrel ; and besides, the skipper—"

   " Hath had his belly full, I warrant thou wouldst say, girl.
Well, well, I will order my horse, and away ; so go your own
road.   Farewell, Master Albert, until I see you again at
dinner."

   The Secretary and the maiden now set forth upon their walk,
and directed their steps along the upper margin of the bank
which overhung the river, until they were soon shaded in the
forest that grew thickly upon the steep slope by which the plain
descended to the beach.   Out of this bank, at frequent intervals,
gushed forth pure springs of water, that found their way to the
river through beds of matted grass and leaves.   A light sunny
haze mantled the whole landscape of forest, field, and river, and
threw a warm and rich tint over the perspective.   The grass was
still green as in spring ; and the woods glittered, as the light
breeze shook their bright and many-colored foliage, which

autumn had flung like a harlequin garb over their limbs. The
scene, at all times pre-eminent for its beauty, was now fraught
with its greatest attraction for the eye : and the genial temper
ature of the season—that delightful period when the first frosts
vanish at the touch of the sun—still enhanced the pleasure which
the spectator felt in wandering abroad.

"Heaven hath garnished out no fairer land than this," said
the Secretary, as at length, after pursuing a path that wound
through this wilderness,—sometimes descending to the pebbly
beach and again rising to the level of the plain above,—Blanche
had seated herself upon the trunk of a fallen tree, in a position
from which the whole extent of the river, the fort, and the upper
headland, with the Town House, were visible ; "nor is there a
nook upon this wide globe which I would more contentedly make
my home."

"I trust it will ever be your home, Master Albert," was the
maiden's reply ; "they who come hither from the old world
seldom think of going back. You can find no reason to return."

"My fortunes are guided by our good Lord," returned the
Secretary, "and even now he sometimes speaks of going hence
again to England. With my own free will I should never leave
this sunny land. These woods are richer to my eye than pent-up
cities ; these spreading oaks and stately poplars, than our groined
and shafted cathedrals and our cloistered aisles : yes, and I more
love to think of the free range of this woodland life, these forest-
fed deer, and flight of flocking wild fowl, than all the busy
assembling of careful men which throng the great marts of
trade."

"Surely his Lordship would not take you hence against your
will," said Blanche, thoughtfully. "Indeed we could not,"—she
continued, and then suddenly checking herself, as if upon some
self-reproof for speaking more freely than was proper, added,

13*

" his Lordship will not leave the province again,—or if he does———"

" I am but an humble secretary of his Lordship," interrupted Albert, " and needs must follow as he shall command."

" He *will* not command it, Master Albert. Our dear Lady Maria loves you well, as I have heard her say, and will persuade his Lordship to command you stay."

" I need not his command," replied the Secretary ; " it would be enough for me I was not constrained to go hence ; your wish, Mistress Blanche,—nay, your permission would keep me here, even if my inclination tended back again to the old world."

" My wish, Master Albert ! how could I have other wish but that you stay ?" inquired the maiden, in all singleness of heart. " Do we not sing and play together ; ride, sail, hawk, and hunt together ? Have you not promised to render that history of the good Chevalier into English for me ? Am I not to be skilled in the French tongue, under your teaching ? Oh, how could I wish other than that you stay with us, Master Albert ?"

" Come what hazards may," said the Secretary, with deep emotion, as he took the maiden's hand, " I swear by this good day and by this beauteous world, that I will never leave thee."

" But few words more passed—and these were of such an import as my reader may well conceive, from what has gone before—till Albert Verheyden kneeled at the maiden's feet and vowed unalterable devotion to her happiness, and rose a betrothed lover. With lingering steps and freer speech, Blanche hanging on Albert's arm, the plighted pair slowly returned to the Rose Croft

CHAPTER XXIII.

I guess by all this quaint array
The burghers hold their sports to-day.

                                    SCOTT.

THE day appointed for the prize-play was mild and clear ; and as the anticipation of the sport had created a stir throughout the province, there was reason to expect a large attendance.

Stark Whittle had, within a year past, emigrated to the dominions of the Proprietary, from Jamaica, and by dint of trumpeting his own renown—an act for which the professors of his craft were somewhat distinguished—had obtained the repute of a skilful master of fence. Sergeant Travers had been several years in the province, and had already established his fame, in more than one trial, with such wandering professors of the Noble Science as, at that era, were to be found in every quarter of Christendom. Great expectations were therefore entertained of an encounter of rare interest to the men of the sword—a class which might be said to have comprehended not only the military men of the times, and such gentlemen in civil life as were educated in the use of the weapon, but also that extensive circle of idlers, boasters, tavern-frequenters, and sport-loving gentry which have always passed under the denomination of choice spirits.

Under the direction of Colonel Talbot—the patron of all sports and pastimes in the province—a platform, or stage of deal boards, about twenty feet square and three feet above the ground, had been constructed, near the centre of the common in the rear of the Town House. A few paces from the platform stood a flag-staff, from which floated a forked pennon bearing the device of the provincial arms, ambitiously executed in oil by Master Bister, the artist of the city. On a skirt of the common, some six or eight tents marked the position of the Court of Guard, formed by the garrison of the fort, under the command of Nicholas Verbrack, the Lieutenant. Opposite to this encampment, a range of booths had been erected by the townspeople, where was displayed every variety of refreshment which the housekeeping stores of the proprietors might afford. These booths were distinguished by various devices in the way of signs ; one presenting a banner hung out on a pole with a rude representation of a Cock in jack-boots and sword, with his neck stretched as in the act of crowing, and a label from his bill having written on it,

"STARK WHITTLE FOR EVER !"

whilst another manifested its partizanship for the adverse champion, by the device of a bull in armor, reared on his hind legs, with the inscription,

"SERGEANT TRAVERS.
THE OLD SWORD AGAINST THE NEW BUCKLER."

Others were designated simply by a green bush, the old sign of good wine within. Amongst these temporary sheds was especially to be noted one which was surmounted by a towering staff bearing a flag embellished with the cross of St. Andrew, whose proprietorship was sufficiently indicated by a flaring sign painted on canvass, aiming, though not very perspicuously, to represent a portraiture of the Crow and Archer, from the pallet of Master Bister. Sundry legends, scrawled in charcoal over the front of

the booth, expressed the utmost impartiality between the combatants and their several friends, as might be read in such as
"Honor to the brave," "A fair field and no favors," and others
of similar import equally guarding against the accident of denoting the party of the host. Within the shed the saucy face of
our jolly Dame Dorothy might have been seen, long before the
appointed hour of the combat, as she busied herself in adjusting
matters to meet the expected pressure of the day.

Such was the picture presented on the Town Common about
noon. Already a large number of the inland inhabitants had
arrived, and troops of new comers were every moment seen halting their horses in the vicinity of the common : others were discerned as far off as the inequalities of the country allowed,
journeying down from the distant highlands, or moving forward
in irregular squadrons across the plain by every road which led
to the town. The river presented a scene not less animated.
Boats of various sizes, from a pinnace down to a canoe, were
sprinkled over the whole expanse of water, ferrying across the
inhabitants who resided beyond the St. Mary's river, as well as
many from the opposite shore of the Potomac. The hostel of
Master Weasel was thronged with guests, and every ale-house
and ordinary of inferior note bore testimony to the attraction
which the projected prize-play presented to the country people
both far and near.

Meantime the combatants were not yet accessible to the sight
of the inquisitive crowd. They were each in charge of their respective friends. Stark Whittle had selected Captain Coode as
his patron, and was now lodged in the house of the burgess,
where he was attended by a troop of those professional backers
who are ever at hand on occasions of sport with their advice,—
men who, whether imbued with skill or not, are still prone to take
the credit of being well versed in the mysteries of the game.

These were now busy, or affected to be so, in preparing their champion for his encounter, exhibiting all that show of science in the minutiæ of the craft which belongs to their class.   Under their direction, the swordsman had been, for several days, put under a diet which was alleged to be scrupulously regulated to produce the due quantum of strength without an increase of bulk ; he had been breathed a certain number of hours each day in the exercise of his weapon ; and now that the moment of trial was at hand, great exactness and care were displayed in anointing his limbs with bear's grease, to give them their requisite suppleness. The same precautions, with the same pedantry, were bestowed upon Sergeant Travers, who, still shut up in the fort, was undergoing the discipline of Captain Dauntrees and Arnold de la Grange,—both of these worthies claiming to be adepts in this important matter of training for a prize play.

About an half hour before four o'clock, the common was filled with the groups of spectators, leaving the town almost emptied of its inhabitants.   These thronged around the booths, or strolled across the plain, or took their places at the platform. Nicholas Verbrack, at this moment, wheeled off his company from the Court of Guard, and, marching to the scene of the expected fight, formed them in two ranks, immediately behind the flagstaff, which might be said to represent the head of the lists. From this position he detached sentinels, armed with pikes, who were posted at intervals, in military fashion, around the platform, at the distance of some ten paces from it, beyond which limit the lookers-on were compelled to retire, leaving the intervening space entirely clear.   The crowd which was thus thrust back, consisted indifferently of both sexes,—the women, as is always the case in public shows wherever they may gain admission, forming no inconsiderable portion of the mass, and they were now seen elbowing their way to the front of the throng, and sustaining

their positions there, with as stout resolve as the sturdiest of
their antagonists. Carts, wagons, tumbrels, and sundry nonde-
script conveyances, fabricated for the occasion and laden to their
utmost capacity with females, formed a kind of rear division sur-
rounding the stage. Several gentlemen, among whom was the
Proprietary, accompanied by his uncle, Philip Calvert the Chancellor, nearly all the members of the council, Master Anthony
Warden, and others, were seen grouped together on horseback.
Albert Verheyden with Benedict Leonard had come in the train
of this party, but were now observed in various quarters of the
field, as they rode around to amuse themselves with the spectacle.
Chiseldine, the reverend Master Yeo, and some others conspicuous in the ranks of opposition to the Proprietary and his party,
were seen frequently reining up their horses together in small
squads, and as often dispersing, as if under some occasional suggestion against the propriety of their consorting too much
together in public. Cocklescraft, with Roche del Carmine and
three or four men in sailors' dress,—the skipper and his mate
being both armed rather beyond what was usual,—strolled about
the field, without ostensibly participating in the affairs of either
party.

The scene presented a lively and striking spectacle. The
musketeers in their green livery, drawn up beneath the pennon
that fluttered above the stage ; the motley crowd of persons of
both sexes that surrounded the platform, taxing all the vigilance
of the sentinels to prevent them from pressing beyond their
allotted boundary ; the scarlet hoods and glittering head-gear,
wimples, coifs, caps, and bright-colored petticoats, mingled in the
mass with the russet serge and round hat of the rustic, and with
the gayer holiday-attire of belted burghers and bluff landholders
arrayed in swords, short cloaks and plumed beavers ; the troops
of spectators that moved over the field on horseback, some with

the sober steadiness of age, and others with the prankishness of
young cavaliers anxious to display their horsemanship in the
caracole, the demi-volte, the courbette, and the various other
points of equestrian skill to which the jargon of that day supplied
names ; the bustle of strolling idlers that hovered about the
booths, where the twangling of a fiddle in one quarter and the
rattle of dice in another rose in a confused din upon the ear,
mingled with the oaths of drinkers and the nimble-tongued and
shrill tones of the authoritative dame of the Crow and Archer,
as she chid or promoted the clamor around her :—all these
images, grouped together on the beautiful plain of St. Mary's,
with that transparent blue heaven above, and the matchless
foliage of the Fall giving to the forest the hues of the dying
dolphin, and the mild, invigorating coolness of that incomparable
season which ushers in the gradual march of winter, diffusing
health and buoyancy into every frame,—afforded a picture which
was calculated to inspire a high sense of enjoyment in those who
witnessed it, and which would scarcely fail to produce something
of the same impression if skilfully delineated on the canvass.

At a signal from Colonel Talbot, a trumpeter bearing an
instrument, which, like himself, was decorated with ribbons,
mounted upon the stage and blew forth a sprightly summons.
When this was repeated thrice, two small parties were seen
entering on the common from different quarters. That which
came from the direction of the centre of the town, was immediately descried as Stark Whittle and his party, consisting of
Captain Coode with three or four attendants. The champion
was wrapped in a horseman's cassock that concealed his figure
from observation, whilst beside him walked his second, a squat,
brawny, fierce little man, with a huge red nose, a squint in one
eye, a scar across his brow, and a large broad-flapped beaver
garnished with a black ostrich feather which hung backward a

span below his shoulder. This worthy enjoyed the designation
of Ensign Tick, being a decayed officer of Lord Cecil's time, and
still retaining his title, though reduced to a sharking livelihood
in a civil station. He was, like his principal, shrouded in a
cloak : in one hand he bore a pair of swords, and in the other a
small creel or basket, containing a bottle of usquebaugh and sundry commodities used for the speedy staunching of a wound,—
furniture familiar to the backers of heroes in such circumstances
as those of his principal at the present moment. The other group
came from the quarter of the Town House, by the road that led
up from the Crow and Archer, where they had betaken themselves to await the summons : it was composed of Travers,
attended by Captain Dauntrees, and his second, the sergeant-
major of the musketeers, bearing the name of Master Stocket,—
one or two privates of the same corps, and a cortege of bare-
headed and bare-legged boys, that stepped forth at the full compass of their stride, to keep pace with the rapid movement of the
principals of the party.

As soon as these adverse bands came within the range of the
crowd, lanes were opened for their admission, and the two champions, advancing to an open space before the guard of soldiers,
there threw aside their cloaks and sprang upon the stage. They
were instantly followed by their seconds, whilst a flourish of the
trumpet and a long ruffle from the drums and fifes of the musketeers announced that the ceremonies of the fight were about
to commence.

The champions were both men of fine shape and sinew, nearly
equal in height and bulk, and both came to their engagement
with apparently composed and cheerful countenances. The only
face of wrath and fire correspondent to the valorous prowess
which had impelled this warlike meeting, was that of Ensign
Tick. He alone seemed to be duly impressed with the resent-

ment which a belligerent should indulge in such a strife.   Ser-
geant-Major Stocket retained a practised calmness that was
altogether professional, and performed his duty on the stage with
exemplary gravity.   The champions were dressed in military
costume ; Travers in that of his corps, Whittle in the cumbrous
scarlet coat of the English uniform.   Both wore the heavy wide-
legged boot, which, immediately after mounting the stage, they
exchanged for shoes.   As soon as this was done, they were seve-
rally disrobed of their coats, and thus presented for the combat in
their shirt sleeves.   A fillet of red ribbon was tied around the right
arm of the challenger above the elbow, whilst one of green was
similarly adjusted on the arm of Travers.   During the arranging
of these preliminaries, Dauntrees and Coode had ascended the
platform, that they might, as patrons of the parties, bear testimony to the due observance of the established laws of the play.
When all was done, and the combatants were announced to be
ready for the encounter, Coode retired from the stage and took
a post at the end of the platform most remote from the flag-staff,
whilst Dauntrees marched with military precision to a post in
front of his company, where taking a halberd from a sergeant
who held it ready for him, he planted himself, erect and stately,
immediately at the head of his men.   The seconds now advanced,
each bearing in his hand a pair of back-swords of moderate
length, and each selecting one for his principal, these were measured in public to show—what had indeed been previously adjusted by private regulation—that no advantage was possessed
by either side in the length of weapon, and after this ceremony
they were placed in the hands of those who were to use them.
The seconds then retired to opposite points on the platform,
whilst the champions themselves, with a praiseworthy courtesy
and some expression of good will, shook hands ; after which,
with a flourish of swords and a gay alacrity of manner, they

wheeled round and took the stations allotted to them by their seconds.

All this time the utmost silence pervaded the crowd of spectators. Every one had pressed towards the stage at the summons of the trumpet : the booths were deserted, or left with but a solitary watchman : a sentinel, here and there, in the verge of the little encampment on the skirt of the common, was the only moving thing that was not crowded up to the scene of conflict. The Proprietary and his friends had a post of honor assigned to them in the rear of Dauntrees's soldiers, whence they might minutely observe all that was going on. Chiseldine and his party occupied a post at the opposite end of the stage, relatively the same as that of the Proprietary ; but, as no space was kept clear for their accommodation, they were forced somewhat in the rear of the crowd of spectators on foot, and a close observer might have seen in their thoughtful countenances that other subjects besides the trivial amusements of the hour occupied their minds.

The champions now took their attitudes of attack and defence and forthwith engaged with great vigor. Blows were made and parried with masterly address. A quick onset, the assailant pressing his antagonist across the full length of the stage, was returned with an assault not less prompt, and the weapons were wielded with a dexterity and sleight that almost defied the eye to follow the several strokes and their counter defences. Nothing was heard but the clank of steel and the sullen stamp of the combatants on the boards of the platform, as they gave and received blows ; but, as yet, neither party had gained advantage ; and the seconds, deeming that the first bout was played long enough, interposed to give their principals time to breathe.

Whilst the combatants, in this interval, were refreshing themselves under the care of their seconds, the busy murmur of conversation amongst the crowd announced the interest which the play inspired. Many tokens of active partisanship began to manifest themselves, and it was obvious, from the emphasis with which the commendations were bestowed upon the new champion Whittle, that he was a decided favorite of, at least, one party on the field,—a party composed exclusively of Protestants; whilst those of the Catholic faith were no less energetic in their advocacy of Travers. It had already grown to be a sectarian division of feeling, founded on the well-known religious professions of the two champions; and as the Protestants were the most numerous on the ground, it may be affirmed that Stark Whittle enlisted the larger share of popular admiration. John Coode was not backward to foment the party spirit, which had thus unfortunately begun to be developed, by such artifices as he well knew how to practise.

"Stark battles with the Papist as old Luther battled with the Devil," he said exultingly to a group of inland proprietors who were casually discussing the expected issue of the fight; "we shall see this cub of Papacy disciplined with a wholesome Protestant purgation presently."

The din of voices was suddenly stilled by the notes of the trumpet, announcing the renewal of the fight. The parties again took their posts; and again the clash of swords was heard, falling thickly upon the ear. All was suspense and silence, except that now, as a casual advantage was gained by one or other of the combatants, notes of applause and exhortation rose in half-stifled tones from the friends of either side, or ejaculations of fear from their opponents,—these proceeding most frequently from the females. This passage, however, suddenly terminated by a stroke from Whittle's sword, the point of which just severed the skin upon Travers's brow. The appearance of blood was a signal to drop their points, and thus the combatants were afforded a second breathing spell. The wound of Sergeant Travers was no sooner perceived than the whole party who had taken such interest in his adversary's success, raised a shout of exultation that rent the air. This manifestation of triumph, rousing the partisans of the opposite champion into a tone of feeling that partook of defiance, they returned the acclamation with no less vehemence, taking the word from Talbot as he galloped round the confines of the crowd —"Success to Gilbert Travers, a tried master of the Noble Science!"

In this temper of the bystanders, the third passage was announced. Again the combatants engaged, with more than their former vehemence,—for, taking the hue of their respective adherents, they were wrought up into a state of ardent hostility, which showed itself in the acerbity and vigor of their blows. The spectators were sensibly impelled, as the struggle waxed fiercer, into more intense and angry maintenance of their champions, and all other thoughts seemed now to be absorbed in the desire of victory. Unlike the former passages, this was accompanied with all the clamor of incensed rivalry. At no instant were the voices of partisans lulled into silence. "Bravo, good Stark!—Well played, Gilbert!" "Huzza, excellent! Nobly parried, Sergeant!"—and similar expressions of encouragement, burst forth from the lips of the excited groups, as they involuntarily laid their hands upon their swords, and, breaking through all constraint, passed up to the frame of the platform. In the height of this animating impulse, Travers threw aside a blow which had been directed with great energy at his breast, and the vigor with which he parried it swayed the sword of his adversary so far out of his sphere of defence, as to leave his body open to the return stroke, which was plied with such effect as to make a deep incision midway down Whittle's thigh and thence across the knee, laying open the flesh, through that whole track, to the bone, and covering the wounded man with his blood. It was observed

that Whittle's previous stroke had been thrown with such violence as to cause him to reel from his footing when the force of
the blow was dashed aside into the air, and many were of opinion
that this slip of the foot was an accident which should have saved
him from the return cut that was made with such disabling effect.
It was instantly apparent that this hit decided the fight and gave
the victory to the Sergeant of Musketeers.

"A Roland for an Oliver!" exclaimed Talbot with wild
exultation. "Admirable, Sergeant!—well done!—you have
shorn the spur of that cock for a while, at least."

"Huzza for Travers!" resounded over the field from the
voices of the large party of his friends; whilst, on the other
side, with equal vehemence, was shouted, "Foul play! Shame,
shame! A papistical, cowardly trick!"

"I'll meet thee, for a beggarly foister," cried an incensed
partisan, who sprang upon the platform and shook his sword in
Travers's face—"I'll meet thee, Master Toasting-iron, when you
dare!—I'll give thee a lesson for striking a man below the knee."

"Push it at him now, Master Hardcastle," exclaimed a second, following in the steps of the new challenger; he deserves no
better than to be put on his defence where he stands—for a
filthy Roman as he is. A foul cut below the knee, and at a man
who had lost his footing! That is the upshot of his valor!"

These invaders of the platform were instantly confronted by
two or three of the opposite party who ascended the stage to
drag them off;—and, in turn, some dozens of either complexion
in the quarrel sprang to the aid of their respective friends—thus
presenting on both sides a compact body of excited opponents
fiercely bent on mischief.

Talbot was instantly off his horse, and, sword in hand, rushed
to the scene of broil, calling upon Dauntrees to advance his men
and make a clear stage. Swords were drawn in all quarters,

and the first person with whom Talbot came in conflict was John
Coode, who, with his naked weapon in his hand, was stimulating
his partisans to commence an assault. Talbot seized him by the
front of his coat, and presenting the point of his sword to his
breast, cried out—"Swiller of a tap room! by my hand, if thou
openest thy rotten throat with but a cough, I will thrust my
sword ell deep into thy worthless body. Begone, hound!"

And with this word he pushed the burgess violently over the
edge of the platform on the brink of which he stood. In a moment the musketeers were marched by Dauntrees, in solid mass,
upon the stage, and the threatened rioters were thus expelled
from the seat of contest. Holding this position, the troops had
the command of the field, and by threatening to fire, which
Dauntrees, with the trained coolness of an old soldier, announced,
in a stentorian voice, he would certainly do if further violence
were menaced, Chiseldine, Coode, and their companions, amongst
whom was Parson Yeo, interfered to quiet the tumult and draw
off their adherents. During all this commotion, Corporal Abbot
was seen on the outer skirt of the crowd, brandishing his weapon,
and hurrying to and fro with a look which had wrath enough
in it to annihilate the whole Church of Rome, yet mixed up with
a discretion which would have left a casual spectator at a loss
to determine exactly on what side he was arrayed. "Odso!"
he ejaculated; "let me into that skirmish! I will teach them
orderly behavior,—the varlets! Shall we have brawls put upon
us? Shall we digest cold iron against our will? No, by my
belt—not whilst my name is Abbot! The fight will be this way
presently—and, I warrant you, my hand is in it."

"Put up your sword, you venturesome fool," exclaimed Verbrack, who, in hurrying round the confines of the crowd with a
small party of the musketeers, encountered the man of war in the
height of his ire—"put up your sword—nor stand vaporing here

like a grain thrasher !"—which exhortation the Lieutenant ac
companied with a slight blow across the offender's shoulders,
laid on with the flat of his sword.

"Ha, ha ! venturesome, you may find me, truly, Master
Lieutenant ; but, as you say, it is a good example to put
up our weapons when headstrong men might be led off by
evil examples ;" with which sage reflection the wrath of the
Corporal suddenly surceased, and his weapon was immediately
consigned to its sheath, whence it was not abstracted for full five
seconds after the Lieutenant had disappeared.

Godfrey had, at the first symptom of confusion, retired
from the field, and Cocklescraft, with his seamen, stood by
an unconcerned spectator of the whole scene—nor passed a
word with any one, except that at one moment, when stalking
around the platform, the halberd of Dauntrees accidentally,
and without the observation of the Captain, was protruded
across his path. The skipper disdaining to walk out of the
way of this impediment, drew his sword and struck it down,
saying fiercely as he did it —

" Find other service for your pike, than to stop my wandering."

" By my troth, saucy master," replied Dauntrees, "but I
will speedily find service for my pike that shall teach thee
more civil behavior. But pass on, sir, you have a license
in the port to go free of all notice except such as shall give thee
accommodation in the stocks."

Lord Baltimore, with the graver gentlemen of his suite, rode
around the scene of disorder, manifesting the utmost concern,
and exhorting all whom he might address with any hope of
persuasion, to retire quietly from the field. The old Collector,
however, was not the most docile of his adherents ; for the
veteran's blood had risen to fever heat, and he repeatedly

charged the rioters, cane in hand, with strenuous reproof of
their misconduct, expressed in no very dainty terms. By
degrees the authors of these tumults began to withdraw from
the scene of action and to form themselves into detached bodies
far apart, where their rage was allowed to spend itself in
unchallenged vituperation and rebuke of their antagonists, and
finally to subside, at least, into a manageable degree of
resentment.

14

CHAPTER XXIV

Nor less upon the saddened town
The evening sunk in sorrow down.
The burghers spoke of civil jar,
Of rumored feuds and mountain war.

SCOTT.

In this state of excitement and exasperation, the early twilight found the greater number of the spectators of the recent show, and crowds still lingered in detached and angry parties about the common, even until the new moon began to shed a pale light over the field. The council, whose suspicions of the disaffected had, for some time past, put them on the strictest observation of Coode and his friends, had now seen enough in the conduct of that party to convince them that the spirit of rebellion was sufficiently bold to manifest itself, on the first occasion, in some decided and dangerous attempt upon the peace of the province. They therefore determined to lose no time in the adoption of such proceedings as should enable them to act most effectually against the ringleaders. With this view, Colonel Darnall was directed by the Proprietary to take measures to obtain accurate information of the movements of Coode and his party. He accordingly repaired to the fort to Dauntrees, who, after duly weighing the delicate nature of the commission, determined to take the matter in his own hand, and promised to report to the council before midnight. This being approved by Darnall, the Captain, after he had taken his supper, threw aside his military dress and equipped himself in that of a burgher or private citizen of the port ; and wrapping himself in a cloak, set forward about nine o'clock on his adventures. His first attention was given to John Coode, and he consequently bent his steps towards the dwelling of the burgess. The house stood retired from a street or shaded lane, in a position somewhat remote from immediate neighbors, whilst a thick bower of foliage threw the mass of building at this hour of midnight into deep obscurity. The Captain approached as near to the premises as he might do with safety, and, under the shelter of shrubberry, found himself in a post where he might observe, without much risk of detection, at least such persons as approached or left the house. He had no difficulty very soon to convince himself that the dwelling was crowded with visitors. This was manifest not only from the figures that were seen passing and repassing the few dim lights that flickered from the casements, but from the constant ingress and egress of persons by the outer gate, the path to which lay immediately past the Captain's place of concealment. Many of the passers he could observe to be persons from the inland settlements. After a brief lapse of time came Parson Yeo, moving from the house to the gate, and, at intervals, following him, Kenelm Chiseldine, Godfrey, and several individuals known to be prominent in promoting the late quarrel between the Burgesses and the Proprietary. The few words that dropped from the visitors of the dwelling-house, as they moved within the range of the Captain's hearing, related to the Fendalls, and he more than once heard Lieutenant Godfrey's name connected with them, in a manner that it greatly puzzled him to comprehend ; for, as yet, Godfrey had altogether escaped the suspicion of the Proprietary's friends. When these had gone by, the redoubtable Corporal Abbot was the next that traversed the pathway. He was alone, and coming from within the house, walked with a brisk pace through the gate, after which he turned into the street in a direction opposite to that which the greater number of those who preceded him had taken. The Captain now boldly left his hiding-place, and, with a free step, followed the lonely professor of war and the " gentle craft," and upon overtaking him, was enabled to discern that the troubles of the day had led to some excess in the little martialist's potations, by which his walk was rendered slightly unsteady. The Captain, confiding in his disguise, and the probable bewilderment of the tailor's brain, accosted him boldly as a fellow-conspirator.

" Zounds, neighbor ! you are in haste to get under cover to-night.   I have striven like a goaded horse to come up to you, all the way from the door of Master Coode's.   Wherefore so fast ?"

" It isn't wise to be seen so near Master Coode's.   The Proprietary hath already an evil eye upon him, and notes his associates."

"Truly, then, it is discreet to make speed away from the dwelling—though it be, after all, but a sneaking thing to fear the Proprietary.   We are enough to master his bullies, to my thinking."

" Enough ! troth are we.   There is Lieutenant Godfrey, as you might have heard him say, has sixty men—a score of them to come across the Potomac—ready to ride into the town any night he may wink his eye ; besides the friends we have in swarms as thick as pigeon-flights 'twixt this and Christina. Enough, truly !—enough and to spare, Master——Your pardon, I have forgot your name ?"

" Whitebread," replied Dauntrees

" Oh, surely !   How addled is my pate !   Master Whitebread, we shall do it," said the Corporal, with an utterance that might just be discerned to trip a little on the tongue, for his excesses had not so much disturbed as quickened his speech, and left him more communicative than in his present circumstances was altogether safe. "We shall do it, Master Whitebread, on the night of the fifth of November, as the reverend Master Yeo has appointed."

"Guy Fawkes's night," said Dauntrees. "But the Fendalls—"

"The Lord love you, Master Wheatbread! thou couldst not have rightly apprehended Captain Coode. Lieutenant Godfrey is to bring his troopers—I am one of them, and counted on : I wear his Lordship's colors and take his pay, though I be not of his cause, mark you—Lieutenant Godfrey is to fetch his minutemen on Wednesday come next sennight, and make an onslaught upon the prison. We begin with that."

"Ay, so I take it, valiant Master Corporal. Captain Coode so laid it down."

"Faith did he ; and he looks to see it done to the last scruple, which, I promise you, it shall be, if there be virtue in steel."

"But he did not explain how these friends from Virginia should reach our shore."

"Thou wert asleep, Master Sweetbread : thou wert dull. Did you not know that Cocklescraft has quarrelled with the Proprietary, and brings us his brigantine? Truly, does he ! When knaves fall out, honest men come by their own, ha, ha ! By cock and pye,—but that's a true word !"

"Now, good night, brave Corporal," said Dauntrees, as soon as he came to a convenient point to free himself of the company of the flustered and leaky hatcher of treasons. "Good night, and mayst thou be soon rewarded for thy deserts."

"Good night, Master Sweetbread—and thank you heartily for your kind wishes—I warrant you I get my deserts. But remember," the tailor added, laying his hand upon his lips ; "mute as a mattock—not a breath !" Having given this parting

admonition, he pursued his way with a confident carriage ; and
very soon after they parted, Danntrees heard his voice lifted up
into a song

"Well," said the Captain, when he was left alone ; "for the
sneaking trade of an eaves-dropper, I have a most apt and commendable talent.   In this, my first traffic in so noble and praiseworthy an employment, have I succeeded to a marvel.   Scarce an
hour since my fertile genius struck out this point of war, and here
have I unravelled a whole web of treason, that shall go nigh to
hanging up these curs by the score.   All's fair in war, they say :
—but, by my faith, I had rather have won my knowledge by some
little show of buckler-work, even if it were but a show.   It would
have been more soldierly.   Yet, as bluff Harry's leather gun in
the Tower has it,—' Non marte opus est cui non deficit Mercurius.'
We win by art when steel may not be struck."

The Captain now took a road that led back towards the common, where he carefully reconnoitered the whole ground.   Some
few persons yet loitered in the vicinity of the booths, and two or
three small bands of men, muffled in cloaks, were seen in close
conference amongst the cedars that formed a thicket near the
Town House.   From this point, looking across the narrow bottom of low and marshy ground which lay between the town and
the homestead of Chiseldine, which was in full view wherever an
opening between the trees gave a range to the eye, he could discover that the dwelling-house was more than usually lighted, and
that visitors were, at this late hour, thronging the apartments.

Whilst he was busy with these observations, Lieutenant
Godfrey and Cocklescraft emerged from the cedars, in earnest
discourse, and slowly followed the path which led down the bank
to Master Weasel's inn.   Without giving himself the trouble to
listen, he could not help hearing the short colloquy which passed
between them before they entered the hostel.

"What would you have with a horse at this hour of the night?" inquired the Lieutenant.

"It is but a freak," replied the skipper. "By St. Iago, Lieutenant, I will deal roundly with him. In honor, I will admonish him beforehand. He shall have warning, on my conscience—warning that it shall make him pale to read."

"I will not baulk your devilment, Dick Cocklescraft : So, you shall have the steed. When will you return?"

"By as early a moment after midnight as I may ride the space with all the speed your beast may afford."

"Ha, ha! a sailor o' horseback and the devil rides at his crupper! Ho, Filch, there—ostler Filch! Hither, man : see that an hour hence, when Master Cocklescraft has finished his supper, you saddle my nag and fetch him—where, Master Skipper?"

"To the Town House steps," said his companion.

"To the Town House steps—do you hear?"

Dauntrees having now gathered all the information which his good fortune through his night's adventure had thrown in his way, betook himself to the Proprietary mansion. Here he found Lord Baltimore, Talbot, Darnall, and others, awaiting his arrival. He narrated circumstantially the strange and ample details connected with the plots in concoction and their contrivers, as he had learned them ;. and laid a tissue of facts before the council which left no room for hesitation as to the judgment to be formed of the shape and pressure of the rebellion. Having thus executed the commission confided to him, he retired to his quarters.

On the following morning, soon after the town was emptied of the press of visitors who had crowded in to the prize play, the greater portion of whom had taken their departure at an early hour, it is sufficient for me only to inform my reader that John

Coode, Lieutenant Godfrey, and Corporal Abbot, with a half score of others less distinguished in this history, were snugly ensconced in jail, sharing the apartment of the persecuted patriots Josias and Samuel Fendall. How they came into this stronghold, and what consternation this decisive act of vigorous administration spread through the town ; who advised the measure and who executed it ; I leave to the conjecture of the imaginative friend who has accompanied me through the dry narrative of these pages.

For the present, neither Kenelm Chiseldine nor the reverend Parson Yeo were molested, though it may be conceived that they did not pass free of that close observation of their outgoings and incomings with which, in all countries, suspected persons are wont to be favored by the guardians of the authority of government.

CHAPTER XXV.

The baffled factions in their houses skulk.
                                        JOHN WOODVIL.

WHEN day broke upon the drowsy burghers of St. Mary's, on the morning after the prize play, the Olive Branch was no longer to be seen in the river. Such a sudden departure of so important a portion of the commercial marine of the port, produced no small degree of speculation amongst the waking citizens as, by degrees, after sunrise, they began to rub their eyes and look abroad. This speculation became still more intense when, in a few hours, they saw files of soldiers passing through the town, and heard, immediately afterwards, the rumor of the arrest of Coode and his compatriots. Still more was it excited by a report which was early brought to town from the Rose Croft, that the broad arrow—the mysterious presignification of mischief, a mark by which a suspected person was proscribed, or a devoted one forewarned—had been found deeply scratched, as with the point of a dagger, on the Collector's door. An unusual stir and buzz of murmured wonder prevailed through the little city, and every body was on foot to learn the cause of these phenomena. By some it was said that the skipper had gone on a trading excursion up the bay to Kent Island, as it was his custom to do. Those in the secret of the last night's conspiracy had no difficulty in ascribing his departure to movements con-

14*

nected with the plot; the broad arrow on the Collector's door was easily accounted for by such as were aware of Cocklescraft's midnight ride on Godfrey's horse; and, on all sides, expectation was raised into silent dread of some eruption that was to break forth, in a moment when none might be aware of it, and from a quarter to which few might look.

The council was convened at the Proprietary mansion, and there the emergency was gravely debated and the most energetic measures of precaution and defence adopted. The escape of Cocklescraft, connected with his recent quarrel with the Secretary, and the disclosure made by Abbot of his concurrence in the plot of the conspirators, left no doubt of his treachery. The outbreak was rendered more formidable by its coincidence in point of time with the contemplated incursion of the Northern Indians, as related by the travelling doctor—a circumstance that seemed to infer correspondence between the leaders of the conspiracy and the savages, and to give the plot a consistency well calculated to excite alarm. To these topics of apprehension, on the part of the council, was added a certain undefined and anxious misgiving that the goblin stories of the Wizard's Chapel, as reported by Dauntrees and Arnold de la Grange, and now repeated by the Proprietary with all the testimony he had obtained to support them, might have some connection with this long-hatched rebellion, and that there were secret ramifications of the plot that had never yet been suspected. The participation of Godfrey and Cocklescraft in the designs of Coode, of which none of the Proprietary's friends had entertained a surmise until the previous night, was a fact adapted to confirm their fears of the wide diffusion of disaffection where it had not been looked for. The result of this deliberation was a resolve to pursue matters to a speedy conclusion by a decisive and bold action. The ring-leaders were to be brought instantly to trial; the military force

was to be increased ; their ranks purged of all who were suspected to want heartiness in the cause ; and every precaution
was to be taken to provide against assault from all quarters, by
night or day. Captain Dauntrees was commanded to look to
the safety of the town, and to endeavor to ascertain what had
become of Cocklescraft.

In this state of preparation and suspense, twenty-four hours
past over without tidings of the skipper, or any new developments
of the designs of the conspirators. The vigorous measures taken
by the Proprietary seemed to have struck terror into his adversaries, and at least driven them into the shelter of silence and
concealment. At the end of this period Willy of the Flats,—
who was one of those expert politicians who make it a point to
manifest their patriotism by the most eager zeal in favor of the
side that is uppermost,—having until the overthrow of Coode been
strongly inclined to take part with the agitators, now made his
way, about ten o'clock at night, into the fort, and thence to the
presence of Captain Dauntrees. Approaching the Captain, with
an air of constrained self-importance, he said in a half whisper—

" News, Master Captain—grave news, worshipful sir,—state
matters ! I have come post-haste to tell you, that twenty
minutes ago—no, that I may not lie, I will say twenty-five
minutes ago—just so long as with good speed—a dog trot we
will say—it might suffice for me to come hither from Master
Weasel's tap-room—who think you I saw, and what did he do ?"

" Speak, Willy, without this windy prologue."

" There comes in Master Cocklescraft, and straight orders a
noggin of brandy,—whereof guzzling it down with a most trea-
sonable haste, he wiped his lips, and asked for Lieutenant Godfrey ; and when he heard that the Lieutenant was in prison, he
bit his lip and gave a kind of ha ! or I might say grunt, and
walked very suspiciously away."

" And you had the wit to follow him ?"

" Follow him, Captain, I did, as far as the cedars of the Town House, where—the moon being down—I lost him. He might have been on his way to the jail, but I stayed not to seek that out, for turning round,—now, said I, Willy, make for the fort as fast as you can, and tell the Captain the whole matter."

" Thanks, at least, for that diligence of yours. You shall have your supper and a stoop of liquor for this."

" Blessings on your worship, for thinking of the need of an empty man !" said Willy, as with his hat tucked under his arm he went towards the Captain's kitchen to acquaint Matchcote with his master's hint touching the refreshment.

Dauntrees lost no time in despatching an inferior officer, with two or three files, in quest of the skipper. These returned after midnight with a tale confirming Willy's narrative ; but with the further intelligence that no traces could be obtained of Cockles-craft beyond his appearance at the Crow and Archer.

The next day the Superior of the Jesuit House of St. Ini-goe's visited the Proprietary to inform him that, at the dawn, the servants of his establishment had found their skiff hauled up on the beach, some fifty or a hundred yards remote from the wharf where, on the preceding night, it had been carefully locked by a chain, which, it appeared, had been broken, showing that the boat had been used by some person of whom no knowledge could yet be obtained. He further stated that Fluke, the fisher man, who lived some distance below St. Inigoe's, on the river bank, had that morning reported, that before daylight his dogs had waked him with loud barking, and that he had heard the footsteps of a man upon the beach : that the fisherman had chal-lenged the stranger from his window, but had got no reply, and was fain to let him pass on without molestation, owing to the darkness of the hour.

This intelligence, combined with that brought to the fort by the fiddler, strongly pointed to the visit and retreat of the skipper, and seemed to indicate that he was lurking somewhere near the mouth of the river, and had, in the night, crossed St. Inigoe's creek immediately from the wharf of the Jesuit House to that of the Rose Croft, by which road he had visited the town and returned again before daylight.

Dauntrees, upon receiving this information, lost no time in visiting the House of St. Inigoe's, to inquire into the particulars; after which he went to see the fisherman. The result of this journey was to confirm him in the impression of the secret correspondence of the skipper with the town, and to engage Fluke in the service of watching the future motions of the same visitant.

Simon Fluke lived some two or three miles below St. Inigoe's, near the mouth of the river, where a small cabin gave shelter to his wife and a troop of children—an amphibious brood of urchins who seemed to be at home either on land or water, and whose rude habits of life had inured them to the scant accommodation and precarious protection of the hut into which they were all huddled. This man earned a hard livelihood by supplying his neighbors of St. Inigoe's and the townspeople with fish ; and it was greatly to his content that he now found himself engaged in the service of the Proprietary, with the promise of a handsome reward if his good fortune should enable him to aid effectually in securing the person of the skipper.

It was a few days after his employment in this service, that the sun was seen to set amongst thickly scudding clouds and blasts of wind, such as, with the near approach of November, are apt suddenly to break in upon the serene autumn, giving rude foretastes of winter. The horizon was dark, and the overmastered sun hopelessly struggled to fling a parting beam upon the ruffled waters.

The fisherman had hauled his boat upon the sand, bestowed his nets and other tackle in safety for the night, and taken his seat at his fireside, with a lighted pipe, where he challenged the besmirched, white-haired boy that toddled across the room—the youngest of his troop—to a game of romps, or more demurely chatted of household cares with his meagre and sad-visaged dame. The door of his hut standing wide open and looking southwardly, showed him the Potomac, even across to that remote cape called by the early settlers after St. Gregory, but now known as Smith's Point.

"Look out, wife," said the fisherman, as he cast his eye over this extensive sheet of water, yet illumined with the light of parting day, "and you shall see a strange craft beating up from the Virginia shore ; she is almost too light a skiff for such a sea as that now running in. Have you seen it go down the river ? Where can it belong ?"

"It is a new sight to me," replied the wife ; "I saw nothing like it go down from St. Mary's to-day."

"He does not shape his course, either, up the river, so much as he makes for this shore," added the fisherman. "He comes from some harbor on the other side, short of St. Gregory. His business must drive him hard, to bring him out at this hour, in the teeth of such a wind. I will keep an eye on that fellow, wife ; there is enough in his venturing to raise a suspicion."

The homely supper of the family, soon after this, called off the fisherman from his watch, which indeed the thickening shades of night soon rendered useless, and the only vigilance which the master of the hut could now exercise was shown in an occasional walk to the beach, in the hope that the nearer approach of the boat might inform him with more certainty whether her course lay towards the town. Nothing however was gained by these visits ; no boat came in view, and the gloom forbade further observation. The craft was some seven or eight miles, at least, from shore when she was last seen, and the fisherman, giving up all hope of learning more that night, threw his weary frame upon his tattered couch and sunk shortly into a profound sleep.

During the night a growl of the house-dog, and the tread of a foot upon the gravel, woke the uneasy-slumbering dame, but the sound had died away amidst the plash of waves upon the strand, before she could rouse the heavy and torpid frame of her snoring lord. When at last he woke, it was only to utter a drowsy and bewildered reproof for the annoyance he had suffered, and to fall back again into his former deep unconsciousness. At early dawn, however, he was abroad, breathing the sharp, cold breeze of the clear morning. Below his hut, seaward, he could descry upon the beach, some miles short of Point Look Out, the small craft which, on the previous evening, he had noted standing across the river. It was a suspicious sight to see a boat at such a time in such a place ; and connecting it with the circumstances his wife had remarked in the night, Fluke found reason enough to put himself on the watch for the person who controlled its motions. He accordingly went into his hut, and sticking under his girdle a horseman's pistol which he kept for domestic defence, and taking a stout white-oak staff in his hand, he trudged forth along the margin of the river, resolved to plant himself in some advantageous position, whence he might intercept any one who should approach the boat by land. He had not left his door above half an hour, before his wife observed a traveller, in a seaman's dress partially concealed by a gray cloak, striding on foot along the field contiguous to the beach, in the same direction that her husband had just taken. The mastiff of the household was the first to challenge the stranger, by springing almost to his heel,—a trespass that was instantly re-

sented by a sturdy blow from a walking stick that sent the dog
yelping back to the hut.

"St. Iago ! I will kill the dog !" exclaimed the wayfarer.
"Woman," he added, as soon as he became aware that the dame
had her eye upon him, "why do you not chain up the beast ?
By my hand ! I will make short work with him if he interrupt
me again." And without waiting to hear the dame's half-chiding,
half-encouraging address to the dog—"Get thee in, for a saucy,
old, honest snarler !" or her defence of him : "He will not hurt
you, sir ; his growl is worse than his bite,"—he strode so rapidly
onward as soon to be out of view.

In less than an hour after sunrise, the little chaloupe was seen
laying her course gallantly before the wind, with her tiny sail filled
almost to bursting, as she bore for the opposite side of the Potomac.   The dame busied herself in preparing her morning meal, to
be in readiness for her husband's return, and in checking the
impatient petitions of her urchin brood, who hung around to beg
for a morsel of fish from the pan, or a slice of corn bread, to stay
their fresh appetites, until the coming of the father should be a
signal for a more orderly assault.   Ever and anon, she went to
the door to cast an eye along the river bank, and to watch the
little craft, the subject of so much curiosity, as it measured its
rapid transit towards the Virginia shore.

"Simon Fluke, I believe in the heart of me," she said, after
having gone a dozen times to the door, "thinks no more of his
breakfast than if it were wet sea-weed just out of the river : the
fish, with one turn more, will not be fit for a Christian to eat ;—
and here are these children ready to munch their own fingers for
food.   I wish to the saints, the man could learn some thought of
his meals when they are ready for him !   But I might as well
talk to a flounder as to Simon Fluke."

CHAPTER XXVI.

It creeps, the swarthy funeral train,
The corse is on the bier.

LEONORA.

THE distant bell of St. Inigoe's was heard summoning the priests of the house to the chapel service of the Vigil of All Souls,—the season had now advanced as far as high noon on the last day of October,—when the quay in front of the Crow and Archer was enlivened by the gossipping faces of a group of quidnuncs who had assembled there in the warm sunshine, to discuss a most melancholy piece of intelligence which had just come to town, and which was debated with that characteristic respect for truth and decent spirit of condolence with which horrible accidents and distressing casualties are generally propagated.

"There's proclamation of hue and cry out," said Willy of the Flats, speaking as one who had obtained possession of a state secret—"I heard it myself, but now, at the mansion, from Master Llewellen, who was sent for, on purpose, by his Lordship, to make proclamation by hue and cry as fast as it can be writ down."

"Good reason!" replied Mug the Sexton; "I'll warrant you Tiquassino's men have slipped across the bay, with Jackanapes or Robin Hood at their lead, to whet their knives on Christian flesh; and if they are to be caught, we must do it quick, I can tell you, neighbors. Will the body be brought to town?"

"That shall be as the Coroner shall order," said Garret

Weasel, with the air of a man who felt himself entitled to instruct the company in matters of law. "No one durst touch the body till the coroner has dealt with it. Giles Ferret must have a fancy to summon me on his jury! but I foiled him on privilege, d'ye see, masters,—for the Sheriff hath set me down on the panel for the provincial court next week ;—so no two juries for me, Master Coroner, says I. Lord, Lord! I could no more face Simon Fluke's family,—to say nothing of the dead man himself,—in their distress, than I could look upon my own dame in her winding-sheet."

"Troth! you shall never look at me in that dress," exclaimed the laughing landlady, who stood on the skirt of the crowd, hitherto unseen by her husband. "I have pranked out two as pretty men in woollen as yourself, Garret Weasel, before I had the good luck to clap eyes on you ; and, faith, I mean to put you to bed with the shovel, ere I go myself. What are the townsfolk good for, that they are not up and abroad to find out the villains who murdered the fisherman ?"

"They talk of a following with hot hand," said Derrick Brown, in reply to the question of the hostess, "as soon as the Coroner comes back. The Indians are lurking somewhere upon the border of the settlements ; take my word it will be proved so."

"If we were sure of that," said Garret Weasel, "I should be for boot and spur, harquebuss and hanger, up and away, lads ;—but we must move with caution in the matter till we get lawful ground for an out-riding. Give us the hue and cry before we start."

"Some do say," interposed Master Clink, a mender of kettles, who had left his work so hastily that he had not thrown aside his leather apron, "that the murder was done by Papists in the disguise of Indians."

"I'll warrant you as many lies will be pinned upon the back of this murder as it will hold," said a tall, sallow, spare-built man, who was known as the head constable of the riding of St. George's. "It is the fashion now, when a piece of mischief has been practised, for one side or the other to turn it into a church matter. Every body knows that Simon Fluke was as good a Roman as there was in the riding. Why do you prate about the Papists, Tom Clink? Who told you that monstrous lie?"

"By the faith of my body! I did hear it whispered," replied the tinker; "though, as I am an honest man, I did not believe it."

Whilst this little knot of newsmongers continued upon the quay, discussing the rumors of the day, and now and then enlivening their drooping spirits with a resort to the red lattice of the Crow and Archer, behind which Matty Scamper and Dame Dorothy by turns administered the refreshment of a cup of ale or some stronger potation, two boats were discovered approaching the harbor from a point below St. Inigoe's, and making as much speed as their complement of oars would allow. As they neared the quay, it became apparent that the first contained a coffin attended by the fisherman's family, and two priests; the second was freighted with the jury under the charge of Master Giles Ferret, the Coroner.

Whilst the boats are approaching, we recur to our narrative where we left it at the conclusion of the last chapter; deeming it necessary to say that the anxious wife, after venting some unavailing and affectionate expressions of impatience at her husband's delay in returning to his breakfast, sat down to her meal, unconscious of the cause that detained her mate and ascribing his absence to that carelessness of hours which grew out of the nature of his calling. Noon came, and the frugal board was again spread for dinner, but to it came no father of the wonder-

ing household ;—still the vacant seat was not so unusual a
spectacle as to excite alarm.   But when the sun began to dip
upon the verge of the western horizon, and no trace could be
discerned of the homeward step of the fisherman, fears arose in
the bosom of his wife,—and long and earnestly she paced the
beach and strained her sight to catch his expected form.   At
length, heading her little household troop, she sallied forth, with
hurried steps, along the sands, for more than a mile ; and finding
no vestige of him, returned sorrowfully to her humble roof and
gave up the night to that sharpest of all the trials by which grief
may assail the human breast,—the half-hoping, half-fearing, silent,
doubting watchfulness for the approach of evil tidings, which the
heart, by a strange presentiment, sometimes truly foretells.

At daylight her eldest boy was despatched to the house of
St. Inigoe's for aid, and very soon some four or five persons were
on foot to scour the country in quest of the lost man.   A short
search disclosed the dreadful truth : the body was found in a
thicket of cedar, with the marks of a bullet through the brain ;
the spot within a hundred paces of the shore of a small inlet (at
this day known as Smith's creek) that flowed from the Potomac
a few miles westward of Point Lookout.   There were the foot-
prints of men upon the beach, and marks of the keel of a boat
which had been drawn up on the sand.   The wretched wife could
only tell of her husband's departure in the morning :—all other
recollections, in the depth of her sorrow, were swept from her
mind ; and the persons who were busy in seeking out the facts
of the murder were obliged to leave the spot with nothing better
than vague conjectures as to the agency by which it was per-
petrated.

The tidings were quickly brought to the town, and the
Coroner instantly proceeded with a jury to the spot to perform
the duties required by the law.   His office was soon discharged,

and, as we have seen, he was now, early in the afternoon, on his
return with the body of the deceased, attended by the wailing
family and the jury who had pronounced their verdict of 'inten-
tiona. homicide by persons unknown.'

In the excited state of parties, at this crisis, the Proprietary
did not choose to risk a popular tumult. Already, as was usual
at that day, regardless of any ascertained fact relating to the
murder, common opinion ascribed it to the Indians : whilst the
more violent of the factionists noised it abroad as a contrivance
of the Catholic party to overawe their adversaries,—directly
charging the murder upon the friends of the Proprietary, who, it
was alleged, had accomplished it in the garb of Indians. The
animosity with which this improbable and, in this case, absurd
report (for the deceased was known by many to be of the same
faith with his imputed murderers) was propagated, induced, in
the mind of Lord Baltimore, an apprehension of some disturbance, and he had accordingly directed Captain Dauntrees to
keep his force in readiness to suppress any attempt at disorder
which might arise. The boats, therefore, were no sooner discovered approaching the quay, than the garrison of the fort were
drawn out by their Captain and marched to the foot of the
mulberry at the Town House, where they awaited the funeral
procession, which it was designed they should accompany to the
grave.

Curiosity, that eager impulse to feast on popular horrors, had
brought a considerable crowd of the townspeople to the landing
place ; community of faith with the deceased had brought many,
and the angry and disturbed temper of the times still more. The
whole together formed a mass of persons actuated by various
passions. The idle stare of that vacant portion of the spectators
who came merely to gape at the spectacle, was contrasted with
the serene thoughtfulness of those who made it their duty, from

religious affinity with the deceased, to attend the remains to the tomb ; and still more did it strike the beholder, when it was compared with the stern hatred and ill-concealed scorn of that class of lookers-on who, belonging to the lately baffled party of the disaffected, stood by with scowling brows, whispering contemptuous sneers against their opponents, as these latter busied themselves in ordering the hasty procession which was formed from the quay up the bank towards the Town House.

The two priests who attended the body, clad in their robes, took the lead of the funeral train. The body, borne by four stout men, comrades of the deceased, followed ; and immediately behind it tottered along with uncertain step, the fisherman's wife, in rude and neglected attire, sobbing convulsively—her apron thrown over her head, and her walk guided by a friendly matron whose frequent but abortive efforts at consolation seemed only to produce fresh bursts of sorrow. After these came the unconscious children, dressed in their homely holiday suits, looking around them with faces of constrained seriousness, which scarcely repressed the broad expression of the gratified interest they took in the novel scene around them. Many of the townspeople of both sexes formed in the procession, which was brought up in the rear by the company of musketeers, who wheeled into the line of march, as the last of the marshalled followers of the body passed from beneath the shade of the mulberry. The bell of the Chapel of St. Mary's tolled whilst the train moved, at a measured pace, towards the church door, where, being met by Father Pierre, the corpse was deposited in the aisle ; and the good priest, with such despatch as might comport with the solemnity of his duty, performed the appointed service of the dead, in the presence of the large body of spectators who had pressed into the building.

Whilst the crowd was still engaged as witnesses of this scene, a rumor was whispered around that the proclamation of hue and cry had just been put forth by the council. A messenger came for Captain Dauntrees, who was observed, immediately afterward, silently to steal forth from the church, and to take his way with hasty strides towards the Proprietary mansion. By degrees, one after another, the spectators followed, and were soon discovered in groups scattered about the town ; until, at last, the corpse was left with but few more attendants than were necessary to perform the proper duties of sepulture.

Half an hour had scarcely elapsed before mounted men were seen gallopping through the avenues of the little city. The silence which attended the funeral procession was exchanged for busy and clamorous conversation ; the bell had ceased to toll. and in its place the notes of a trumpet were successively heard at several points, as a horseman paced from place to place, and read the proclamation calling on the burghers to follow with hue and cry the perpetrators of the vile murder of honest Simon Fluke. In process of time, this bustle subsided into a more orderly and quiet gossip ; the trumpeter had spent his last breath in braying forth the official summons to pursue the murderer, and had gladly put away his noisy instrument ; the riders had ceased to throw up the dust of the highways ; the inquisitive dames of the town and its marvelling maidens had no more news to seek in the open air, and had withdrawn beneath the shelter of their respective roofs : —the churchyard was deserted by all but the sexton and his comrade of the spade, who now were smoothing the sides of the new-made grave ; and the tap-room of the Crow and Archer was once more enlivened by the pot-and-pipe companions who were wont to render its evening atmosphere murky and political. In short, the murder of Simon Fluke, had, in the marvellous brief period of a few hours, ceased to be the engrossing wonder of the day, and the city of St. Mary's was partially restored to its usual routine of ale-drinking and news-telling ;—making proper allowance for the fact, that about a dozen men had ridden forth to scour the country in quest of the murderers, who, on their part, had only been allowed a day and a half to make their escape, and that the good people who staid at home were holding themselves in readiness to be as much excited as ever with any tidings that might arrive tending towards the probable ascertainment of the perpetrators of the crime.

CHAPTER XXVII.

WHILST the burial of the fisherman, and the topics to which it gave rise, engrossed the attention of young and old in the town, Albert Verheyden, dressed in a riding suit with a winter surcoat or horseman's cassock loosely thrown around his person, made his appearance on horseback at the Rose Croft. He had engaged to ride towards the Chesapeake with Colonel Talbot and a troop of followers, to explore the country as far down as Point Lookout, where rumor had already affirmed certain Indians of suspicious bearing to have recently landed from the opposite shore of the Chesapeake. Talbot himself had projected this expedition mainly with a view to sift out and expose the calumny which imputed the recent murder to the friends of the Proprietary ; and he was the more whetted in his purpose by a secret expectation that a vigorous endeavor would enable him not only to refute the slander, but to furnish evidence of the agency of the opposite party in the perpretration of the crime. It is one of the base arts of unprincipled politicians, he argued, ever to be among the first in charging upon the innocent the wicked devices by which they accomplish their own designs. He had resolved, therefore, to take the matter in hand himself, and, at the head of a party of the townspeople, ransack the country around the scene of the murder, for every item of proof which might bring to light its authors. There was, in addition to this motive, an undefined and misty connection in his mind, of the murder with the stories told

15

of the goblins of the haunted Chapel,—a conviction of some wicked influence—active, he did not exactly know how, in stimulating the crime.   He was no disbeliever in sorcery and witchcraft, and a vague thought hovered over his meditation that the fisherman's death might be traced to persons holding relations with the spirits of the Chapel.   He set forth, therefore, on his adventure with a presentiment that some startling disclosure would soon be made, which should still more awaken the thoughts of the government to the mischievous character of the beings who infested the region bordering on the bay.

His purpose being made known in the family of the Proprietary, it was with a modest yet eager petition that Albert Verheyden asked leave to accompany him on the expedition,—a request which was granted with even more alacrity than that with which it was made.   The hour appointed for setting out was delayed only until a sufficient party should be collected ; and this was retarded by the ceremony of the funeral and the common anxiety to await the tidings expected by the coroner and his attendants.   In the mean time, the Secretary, feeling more concern in the affairs at the Rose Croft than in the gossip of the town, repaired thither to await the moment of departure, having commissioned the young Benedict Leonard to ride as far as the Collector's and give him warning when the troop should take the road—a service which the heir apparent promised to perform with the greater satisfaction, as it assigned him some show of duty in the general engrossment of the household, and therefore conferred upon him an importance interesting to his vanity.

The Secretary had been seated for some time in the parlor with Blanche, where he related to her the story of the fisherman's murder ; and when he told her of his purposed adventure, it was with a prouder tone than he had ever assumed before ; there was even perceptible in it a trace of self-exaltation altogether unusual in his speech. He was now a bolder and more assured man, and his character began to assume a more confident development. Blanche listened with maidenly reserve, as if she was almost ashamed to confess the interest she took in Master Albert's communication. She was solicitous for his health and comfort in the dreary ride through the woods he was about to undertake, and which might be prolonged until late at night; and she was fain almost to advise him against such an exposure—but she feared to tell him so much, lest it might be thought taking too great a freedom. Thus engrossed, the hours flew by unheeded, and, in truth, forgotten, until the afternoon had reached nearly four o'clock, when suddenly Benedict Leonard, without announcement or even premonitory rap at the door, entered the parlor.

"Goodness, Master Albert!" he exclaimed, "think of me—such a crack-noddle! You will never trust me again, I may make sure of that. Would you believe it, I rode full two miles past the Rose Croft here, with my uncle Talbot and John Alward, and all the people on their way to hunt the murderers, without so much as ever once thinking of you? I said, when we started, I would ride as far as St. Inigoe's mill, and then come back; and I as clear forgot you till I stopped at the mill, as if there was no such person as you or Blanche Warden in the wide world: and I might have thought of Mistress Blanche, too, because my Aunt Maria gave me a message for her—now what is it? Oh, it is gone,—it is gone! a plague on it! that's got out of my head too. No matter, Master Albert, my uncle Talbot told me to say, when we parted, that he would be on the path which leads down to Point Lookout, and that you must follow as fast as you can."

"It is late in the evening for so long a ride, Master Albert," said Blanche, as with a look of alarm she involuntarily laid her hand upon his shoulder ; " you will not venture alone so near nightfall ?"

" I should be accounted a most faithless laggard, if I stayed behind now," replied the Secretary.   " There is a broad road for some four miles, and I will go at speed till I overtake the riders. At the greatest mischance," he added, smiling, whilst he buttcned his overcoat closely across his breast, " 'tis but a night in the woods.   I will keep this vigil of Hallow Mass like a hermit— or rather like a squire of chivalry undergoing the ordinance of knighthood, by watching over his sword.   The saints be with you, mistress ! I must set good store by the day-light and turn it to account : farewell, till we meet again !".

" Farewell !" faintly echoed the maiden ; " Master Albert, let us see you to-morrow."

" If I was Master Albert," said Benedict Leonard to Blanche, when the Secretary left the room, " I would court favor with Mistress Coldcale to get a slice of something from the larder ; oh, this riding gives an appetite, I warrant you, that a man will eat his sleeve for want of better provender ! There, Master Albert is gone," added the youth, as the Secretary was seen to pass the window, " and I must back to the mansion before sun- set ; my mother will be making me a pretty discourse about rheums and catarrhs and all her other ailments, if I be caught abroad after candle light this time o' year—especially, too, as it looks like rain : so, good even, Mistress Blanche !" and with this speech the heir apparent took his leave, abandoning the maiden to her meditations.

When Albert Verheyden turned out upon the high road he put spurs to his horse and raised his speed to a gallop, until he found himself immersed in the hills and ravines which lay about the head of St. Inigoe's.   One or two wayfarers whom he had chanced to meet, had answered his inquiry after his companions, by informing him that a troop of townspeople, consisting of some eight or ten, had passed along the road at a pretty brisk motion, not less than three or four miles ahead of him. The broken country into which he had plunged, (the road winding through narrow dells and surmounting short and steep acclivities,) the thickets that tangled his path, and the occasional swamps of the low grounds, forced him to slacken his pace and proceed with greater caution on his route. The prints of horses' hoofs upon the damp soil, in places, were fresh and showed him that he was not only on the right track, but also that he was at no great distance behind his company. The sky was overcast, and the clouds, as the sun came nearer to the horizon, assumed by degrees still more and more of that misty, dun-colored hue which indicated the approach of rain. A sombre, dark gray tint, unrelieved by light and shade, fell over the whole landscape and gave a cheerless and sullen aspect to the woods. Once or twice the Secretary reined up his horse and directed his eyes towards the heavens, as he meditated an abandonment of his expedition and a return home before nightfall, but as often his pride forbade a retreat whilst his comrades were afield, and he resumed his journey. He was in momentary expectation of overtaking the party in advance, and made sure of doing so when he should reach the fisherman's hut upon the river beach, towards which it was his purpose to direct his way. Occasionally, a farm-house opened upon his view across a distant field ; but he was unwilling to lose the time which a digression from his road to visit it would have required, only for the sake of assuring himself of his road, with which he believed himself to be sufficiently acquainted. At length, night began to fall around him, and his path to become sadly perplexed. At times, he could scarce make out its traces in the obscurity of the wood ; at times, it broke upon his view with fresh distinctness, as it traversed a region of white sand,

and thus served only to lure him forward with more alacrity, in
the hope of soon reaching the margin of the river, from whence,
even in the dark, he knew he could find his way back—at least,
as far as the house of St. Inigoe's, where he could get shelter for
the night.   Now and then, his hopes were dashed by finding himself involved in those thickets of alder and bay which denote the
presence of a marsh, and he was obliged to thread his difficult
track around the head of some inlet from the river.   It grew at
last to be dark night, and, to add to his discomfort, the rain
began to fall.   The Secretary dismounted from his horse and
stood, with suppressed breath, endeavoring to catch the sound of
distant waves, hoping to find himself near enough to the river to
obtain this guide to his footstep; but all was silent, except the
pattering of rain upon the dry leaves of the forest, and the impatient pawing of his horse upon the sod.   He shouted aloud for
his lost companions, but his voice echoed, without a response,
through the lonesome wood.   "I jested with thee," he muttered
to himself, in a jocular tone, referring to the maiden who was
ever uppermost in his thoughts, "I jested with thee, but a few
hours ago, upon my keeping a vigil of Hallow Mass in the woods.
Dear Blanche, I thought nothing farther away than that jest
should be true; but here my evil destiny hath brought me, for a
punishment, to make it real.   Well, I can endure.   Heart of
grace,—I will confront it manfully!   I would I could but raise
a fire.   I can fast upon my vigil and think nothing of it,—if it
were not that my limbs are chilled and my joints growing stiff
with cold."

He now groped around to gather some dry wood, hoping, by
the aid of his pistol, to kindle a blaze by which he might warm
himself and prepare to spend the night in more comfort than on
his horse.   He labored in vain, for every thing he could lay his
hand on was saturated with moisture.   At length, he mounted

again into his saddle, determined to ride onward until he should chance to find some place of shelter. He had now not only lost his path, but also all perception of his course : the darkness con-fused him, and he therefore plodded on at a slow pace, uncon-scious to what quarter of the compass his footsteps tended, and discouraged with the thought that every moment, perhaps, carried him still further from the home he was anxious to seek.

For a while his spirits sustained him without drooping. A man in such a situation sometimes finds motives of cheerfulness in the very desperation of his circumstances. Under some such impulse our wanderer, as he plied his uneasy journey through the dark, broke forth in song, and in succession poured out nearly the full treasures of his musical memory ; but wearying of this at last, his note changed to whispered sighs of self-reproof for the folly of venturing alone into such a wilderness at such an hour. His mind then ran upon the images which the creed of that day sup-plied to the imagination of our progenitors,—the " swart fairy," " blue, meagre hag," the spirit of the wood, the wizard and the spectre ; then came dreams of banditti and outlaws, prowling savages, and thoughts of some accidental coming alone upon the den of the murderers, whose recent doings had occasioned his present ride. With these fancies swaying his mind, he grew apprehensive and distrustful at every step. There are moments when the stoutest heart will quail before the conjurations of the imagination : and it is no disparagement of the bravery of the Secretary to say, that, on this night, he sometimes felt a shudder creeping over him, at the fictions of his own excited fancy. The rustle of leaves, or the short snap of a rotten bough, as the fox prowled along his stealthy path, more than once caused him to put his hand upon his sword and to ride cautiously forward, as if in certain expectation of a foe ; and not until he had thrice challenged the imaginary comer, did he relax his grasp of his weapon.

In this state of mind, for full four hours after dark, did he wander, uncertain of his way, through wood and over plain, mid brush and brier, over fen and field. At length, his ear could plainly distinguish the beat of waves upon a strand, and it was with a joyful change of feeling that he believed himself, after so weary a circuit, approaching the margin of the river, along which he was aware he should have a plainer ride, with the certainty, in the course of a mile or two, of finding some human habitation. As the sound of the waters grew stronger, whilst he advanced to the beach, his eye was, all at once, greeted with the welcome sight of a taper glimmering through the glade, and, by its steady light, assuring him that no Will-o'-the-wisp, as sometimes he feared, had risen to bewilder his journey.

With new courage and reviving strength he shaped his course towards the friendly ray ;—on which pursuit we must now leave him to attend to other personages in our story.

CHAPTER XXVIII.

Have not we
A commonwealth amongst ourselves, ye Tripolites?
A commonwealth? a kingdom! And I am
The prince of Qui-va-las, your sovereign thief,
And you are all my subjects.
                                        THE SISTERS.

WHEN Cocklescraft asked for Godfrey's horse on the night that
succeeded the prize-play, the reader will remember that, as Captain Dauntrees overheard the conversation, it was accompanied
with an avowal of a purpose to *warn* an enemy, whose name was
not disclosed, of some premeditated harm which the speaker
designed to inflict.

The broad arrow scratched on the door of the Collector's
dwelling, when discovered on the ensuing morning, plainly
enough referred to the fearful menace of the seaman, and sufficiently indicated how bitter was his change of feeling against
the peaceful inmates of the Rose Croft. Mr. Warden attached
but little consequence to the implied threat, nor troubled himself with measures to guard against the intended mischief,
believing it to be but an ebullition of that spirit of disaffection
which the prompt measures of the council had already so far
rebuked as to leave but little to apprehend.

Cocklescraft, immediately after returning to the town from
his midnight ride, went on board of his brigantine, and quietly
weighing anchor, set sail down the river and thence across the
15*

Potomac—here some eight miles wide—and finally, before daylight, made his way into a small creek on the Virginia shore, a
few miles above Smith's Point, or Cape St. Gregory.   Here his
vessel lay sheltered from the observation of the few boats which
passed up and down the Potomac—thus affording him probable
security against pursuit ; whilst, at the same time, the inhabitants of this region were reputed generally to be friends to the
cause of the Fendalls, and enemies of long standing to the Proprietary.   He had, therefore, only to make known the colours
under which he had lately taken service, and he might assure
himself of stout partisans in his defence.

On the second night after his arrival at this retreat, up to
which period he had remained ignorant of all that had transpired
in the town in regard to the arrest of his comrades, he threw a
cloak over his shoulders and taking a common sailor-cap got into
his yawl, which was now rigged with a mast and sail, and steered
for a point on the Maryland shore but a short distance below the
hut of the fisherman.   His motive for this caution, in not approaching nearer to the town, arose from an apprehension that
he might be watched by the garrison of the fort, and perhaps
pursued to his lurking place—an apprehension suggested by that
sense of guilt which predominated over every other feeling, since
his desertion of his late friends and—what weighed with heavier
terror upon his mind—his abandonment of his church.   To avoid
this notice he landed near the mouth of St. Mary's river, and
proceeded from that point, on foot, to the town, a distance of
some five or six miles.   In his journey along the beach, he had
passed by the hut of the fisherman, and had crossed the creek of
St. Inigoe's, immediately from the Jesuit House over to the Collector's landing place, being enabled to make this passage in the
manner detailed by the Superior to the Lord Proprietary.   Upon
his arrival at the Crow and Archer after night, he became ac-

quainted, for the first time, with the arrest of the conspirators. This intelligence hastened him away to hold a short interview with Chiseldine, by whom he was admonished to tarry as short a time as possible in the port, as orders were already abroad for his apprehension. The advice thus timely offered enabled him to effect a speedy retreat to his boat, by the same route that he had taken in coming to the town ; and he was thus saved from the fate that would have overtaken him, if he had remained a half hour longer than the moment of the fiddler's visit to Captain Dauntrees.

Tired of lying perdue so long on the Virginia shore, he determined to proceed with his brig, first to St. Jerome's, where he proposed to wait two or three days to observe the course of events, and then either to sail abroad or take his course up the Chesapeake, where, if pursued, he was willing to trust to the speed of his vessel to baffle all endeavors towards his arrest. Upon the deck of the Olive Branch—or, as she has now laid aside her peaceful character, we may call her the Escalfador—he felt himself secure against annoyance from any naval force at the disposal of the Proprietary, and this circumstance, together with a strong confidence in the number of the disaffected with whom he was associated, inspired him with an audacity that almost defied the public authorities even in their own resorts.

With a view to communicate his intended change of position to his confederates, he made his second visit to the town pretty nearly in the same manner that he had accomplished the first. His stay in the port, however, was longer than on the former night, and it was consequently after break of day that he passed the hut of Simon Fluke. On his near approach to the spot where his skiff awaited him, he encountered the fisherman, who was lurking upon his path, and who, at the moment they came within speaking distance, was endeavoring to conceal himself in a

thicket of cedars.   Cocklescraft was not a man to hesitate in the
commission of a crime under any circumstances, and least of all
when it concerned his safety.   On the present occasion he did
not stop to parley with the person who waylaid his footsteps, but
obeying the impulse of his habitual sense of hostility to his kind,
and the ferocity of his nature, he drew a pistol from his girdle
and discharged the contents with such certain effect, that the
fisherman fell dead at his feet without a groan.   He tarried not
to look upon the murdered man, nor to take any concern even
for the disposal of the body,—but leaving it a prey to the wild
birds that hovered near, he stepped into his boat with as little
emotion or remorse as if he had despatched some prowling beast,
not caring to inquire who or what he was that invaded his path.

On the night that followed this adventure the Olive Branch
quitted her temporary harbor, and the next morning found her
secretly ensconced behind a woody headland, in a nook of St.
Jerome's creek,—about two miles above its mouth, where she lay
safe from the view of all who navigated the Chesapeake.

Cocklescraft began already to feel that he had joined his new
associates in an hour not the most auspicious to his fortunes.
The arrest of the leaders and the quiet that seemed to prevail
throughout the land, created a doubt in his mind whether any
thing was likely to be achieved in the way that he desired ; and
more than once he meditated a retreat from the province, yet
resolved, before he did so, to signalize the event by some flagrant
act of vengeance upon his enemies.   This thought seemed to
please him ; and he spent the day in ruminating over schemes
of retribution against those who had of late treated him with
such contumely.   Uppermost in his breathings of hatred was the
name of Albert Verheyden, and a demon smile curled upon his
lip when he muttered it.

Such provision as might hastily be made for a short voyage

now engrossed the attention of his crew. His armament was put in order ; water taken in, and every thing done,—except the stowing on board of such commodities as he designed to take away to other markets,—to prepare him for sailing within the next twenty-four hours, if occasion should require.

When night came on, and the rain fell, and the moon was quenched, and the murky, cheerless atmosphere, so congenial with the unlawful complexion of his designs, admonished him how little likely it was that prying feet or watchful eyes should be abroad, a revel was held in the Wizard's Chapel. Amidst the lumber that lay piled in confusion over the floor of the rude but spacious building, room was found for a rough table, around which empty casks, broken boxes and other appropriate furniture of a smuggler's den, supplied seats sufficient for the accommodation of twelve or fifteen persons. Here were assembled the crew of the Escalfador, with an abundant supply of strong liquors and tobacco. A fire blazed on the ample hearth, furnishing to such as desired it the means of cooking, in a simple fashion, some substantial elements of the evening meal ; an opportunity which was not neglected, as was apparent from the bones and scraps of broken victuals which lay scattered about the fire-place, and from the strong fumes of roasted meat which sent their savor into every corner of the apartment.

The men who constituted this company, numbering without their leader full sixteen, were robust, swarthy seamen,—the greater portion of them distinguished by the dark olive complexions and curling black hair which denoted their origin in Portugal or other parts of the south of Europe. Several wore rings in the ears and on the fingers, and were bedizened with strange and outlandish jewelry. The thick moustache and shaggy brow gave a peculiar ferocity to more than one of the company, whilst the close and braided seaman's jacket, gaudy woollen caps

and white breeches—the common costume of the crew—imparted
a foreign air to the whole group.   Some wore rich girdles with
ornamented pistols and daggers ; and the plainest amongst them
showed a knife secured under a leathern belt.   Their only attendant was Kate of Warrington, who grudgingly answered the
frequent call for fresh potations, as the revellers washed down
their coarse mirth with draughts of brandy and usquebaugh.

Cocklescraft sat, somewhat elevated above the rest, at the
head of the board, where, without carousing as deeply as his
sailors, he stimulated their noisy jollity by clamorous applause.
A witness, rather than a partaker of this uncouth wassail, was
The Cripple, who, having matters of account to settle with
several of the crew before they took their departure, had now
swung himself into a corner where, with a lighted fagot stuck in
a crevice of the wall, he alternately gave his attention to a
pouch containing his papers of business, and to the revelry of the
moment ; chiding the prodigal laughter of the crew, one moment
with querulous reproof, and the next with a satirical merriment.

" Bowse it, lads !" exclaimed Cocklescraft, as he brandished a
cup in his hand ; "drain dry to the Escalfador !—our merry little
frigate shall dance to-morrow on the green wave,—so, do honor
to the last night we spend ashore.   Remember, we have a reckoning to settle before we depart, with the good folks of St.
Mary's.   Are you all ready to follow me in an exploit of rare
devilry ?—Speak, boys !"

" Ay, ready, Master Captain !" was the response in a general
shout.

This outburst roused The Cripple, who, lifting his head from
the paper, which at that moment he was perusing, and looking
from under his spectacles upon the crew, was heard to mutter
when the shout subsided—" As ready as wolves to suck the blood
of lambs.   How can they be else under thy nursing, Dickon ?"

"Ha, old dry bones, art thou awake? By St. Iago! I thought that thy leaden eyelids, Rob, had been sealed before this. Ho, lads, bring Master Robert Swale forward—we shall treat him as becomes a man of worship :—upon the table with him, boys."

The face of The Cripple grew instantly red, as a sudden flash of passion broke across it. He dropped the paper from his hand and drew his dagger ;—then, with a compressed lip and kindling eye, spoke out—"By St. Romuald! the man that dares to lay hand on me to move me where it is not my pleasure to go, shall leave as deep a blood stain on this floor as flowed from the veins of Paul Kelpy. Who are you, Dickon Cocklescraft, that you venture to bait me with your bullies?"

"How now, Master Rob?" exclaimed the skipper, as he rose from his seat and approached The Cripple. "Would'st quarrel with friends? 'Twas but in honest reverence, and not as against your will, that I would have had thee brought to the table. Come, old comrade, we will not be ruffled when we are to part so soon. What would you have, good Rob?"

"These bills shall be first paid by your drinking roysters before they go to sea," replied The Cripple, somewhat appeased by the skipper's manner. "Here are items of sundry comforts supplied—meat and drink and lodging ;—and here are services of Mistress Kate both in making and mending ;—here for trampling down my corn, and for killing——"

"Pshaw—a fig's end for your trampings and killings, and all this rigmarole of washing and mending!" interrupted Cocklescraft. "I would be sworn your conscience has undercharged your commodity :—so, there is enough to content you for the whole, with good usury to the back of it," he said, putting a well-stored purse of gold into Rob's hand. "You have ever been too modest in your dealings, friend Robert of the Trencher :—

when you get older you will know how to increase your gear by lawful gain."

"A hang-dog—a scape-grace—a kill-cow—a devil's babe in swaddling bands of iniquity, thou art, Child Dickon!" said Rob, laughing with that bitter salt laugh that gave to his countenance the expression of extreme old age. "Thou dost not lack, with all thy wickedness, an open hand. I have ever found thee ready with thy gold. It comes over the devil's back—Dickon, ha, ha!—over the devil's back, youngster,—and it goes—you know the proverb. This closes accounts, so now for your humor, lads, I will pledge you in a cup."

"To the table with him, boys," said Cocklescraft, nodding his head to those who sat near him ; and, in a moment, The Cripple was lifted up in his bowl and set, like a huge dish, in the middle of the board,—a ghastly grin of acquiescence playing all the time upon his sallow features.

"Fill me a glass of that wine of Portugal," said Rob, as soon as he found himself in the centre of the company. "Here, boys," he added when the wine was put in his hand, "here is success to your next venture, and a merry meeting to count your gains."

"Amen to that!" shouted Cocklescraft. "Our next venture will be a stoop upon the doves of St. Mary's."

"And a merry meeting will it be when you count your gains," interposed the harsh voice of Kate of Warrington. "Robert Swale will keep the reckoning of it."

"Peace, old woman," said Cocklescraft, sharply ; "your accursed croaking is ever loudest when least welcome."

"Fill for me," cried out Roche del Carmine, in his Portuguese accent. "I will pledge the captain and our company, with 'His Lordship's Secretary,'—we owe him a debt which shall be paid in the coin of the Costa Rica."

"Bravo,—A la savanna, perros !—Huzza, boys,—shout to that !" clamored Cocklescraft, at the top of his voice. "Drink deep to it, in token of a deep vengeance ! I thank you, Master Roche, for this remembrance. Now, comrades, you have but half an hour left before you must depart to bring down the brigantine to the mouth of the creek. A pipe and a glass more—and then away ; so, to it roundly, and make profit of your time !—Tobacco, Mistress Kate,—fill Master Swale's pipe first, and then mine :—make the bottle stir, my merry men all !"

Having thus given a new spur to the revelry of the board, the skipper, unasked, broke forth with a smoking song familiar to the tavern haunters of that era.

> "Tobacco's a musician,
>   And in a pipe delighteth ;
> It descends in a close
> Through the organ of the nose,
>   With a relish that inviteth.
> This makes me sing, So, ho, ho! so, ho, ho, boys.
>   Ho, boys, sound I loudly,
>   Earth never did breed
>   Such a jovial weed
> Whereof to boast so proudly."

"The cackle of a wild goose, the screech of a kingfisher in foul weather, hath more music in it, Dickon Cocklescraft, than this thou call'st singing," said Rob. "I would counsel thee stick to thy vocation—thy vocation, Master Shark, of drinking and throat-cutting, and leave this gentle craft of music-making to such as have no heart to admire thy virtues. Ha, ha !"—he paused a moment to indulge his laugh. "When a galliard of your kidney, dashed with such poisonous juices as went into the milk that fed you, has a conceit to be merry, the fire-crackling of roof trees and the clashing of steel are the fittest melody for his mirth. Dickon, try no more ditties, thou wilt never make a living by the art."

"By St. James ! I have sung at more honorable feasts than it ever féll to your lot to partake of.   Ay, and lady-songs, too, —and been applauded for my voice, old goblin of the Bowl ! Have I not sung at the back of Sir Harry Morgan's chair, in the great hall of the Governor of Chagres, in the Castle St. Lawrence, when we made feast there after the sack of the place ?"

"Truly," replied The Cripple ; "whilst the hall streamed with blood, and the dead corpse of the Governor was flung like rubbish into a corner, to give more zest to your banquet—and the women—"

"You have a license, Rob of the Trencher," interrupted Cocklescraft, "to snarl at those you cannot excel.   So e'en take your own sweep !   When you can better sing a better song, then I will hearken to you."

"On my conscience, can I now, at this very speaking, Dickon Cocklescraft," said The Cripple, "a better song than ever trilled through thy pipes.

> 'All dainty meats, I do defy,
> Which feed men fat as swine,' "—

he sung, by way of proof of his skill, with a tremulous cadence and melancholy whine, as he flourished his pipe in a line with his eyes, and nodded his head to mark the time.

"The man has gone clean mad," ejaculated Kate of Warrington, who had for some time past been quietly seated on a stool near the fire, and who now arose and stepped up to the table to satisfy herself that it was actually The Cripple whose voice had aroused her.   "You had better be telling your beads and repenting of your sins upon your shrivelled hams, than tinkling your cracked and worn-out voice at midnight, to be laughed at by guzzling fools—barked at by sea-dogs !   It is time, Robert Swale, your old bones were stretched on your bed."

"Faith, thou say'st true, Mistress Nightshade," replied Rob; "thou speak'st most truly : I am over easy to be persuaded into unwholesome merriment—it has been the sin of my life. So, put me on the floor—and now my crutches—my sticks, Kate There—thy lantern, Kate."

"Away, lads, to the brigantine," said Cocklescraft, rising from his seat. "When you get her at anchor off the Chapel, come ashore and pipe me up with the boatswain's whistle. We have some boxes here to put on board ; and then, good fellows, we will make a flight into the city, and ruffle the sleep of some of the burghers, by way of a farewell. Rob, I will go with you to your cabin : I shall catch an hour's sleep in my cloak."

"As thou wilt—as thou wilt, Dickon," returned The Cripple as he set forth, with a brisk fling, on his journey, lighted by the lantern of the beldam.

"Leave the lamp burning," said Cocklescraft to the last of the crew, as the man was about to follow his companions who had already left the room ; "it will serve to steer by when the brigantine comes out of the creek."

In the next moment the Wizard's Chapel was deserted by all its late noisy tenants, and the skipper was on his way, in the track of The Cripple, towards the hut.

CHAPTER XXIX.

Cold drove the rain—November's wind
  Sang to the night with dreary din:
A wanderer came, but did not find
  A heart or hand to let him in.

                    GLENGONAR'S WASSAIL.

As Albert Verheyden approached nearer to the light that had broken upon his view and cheered his footstep, he was able to discern the dim outline of a building of ample dimensions, obscurely traced on the eastern horizon, now relieved of that back-ground of forest which had hitherto circumscribed his vision. The rain still continued to fall in a soft and steady drizzle, through which a feeble, diffused light barely sufficed to show that the moon, now entering on her second quarter, struggled to assert her dominion over the night. The wave rolling in upon the sand with a ceaseless and sharp monotony, apprised him of the proximity of a broad expanse of water, and he had accordingly little doubt that he had now reached the shore of the Potomac—somewhere, as he conjectured, in the neighborhood of the cabin of Simon Fluke, whither he supposed his steps had unknowingly tended through the long and perplexed circuit of his bewildered journey.

When within an hundred paces of the light, he found his further progress on horseback embarrassed by a somewhat precipitous bank, which induced him to alight and make the rest of his way on foot, leaving his horse attached to the drooping

limb of the tree under which he had dismounted. With eager
step he advanced to the house, and on reaching the door, knocked
loudly for admission.

"Good people," he exclaimed as he repeated his knocks,
"arouse for the sake of a benighted wanderer who has lost his
way in the wood. Pray you, give me admittance."

There was no answer ; and finding that upon touching the
latch the door yielded to his thrust, he entered without farther
ceremony. The embers of a large fire glowed on the hearth : a
solitary iron lamp, supplied with the fat of some animal, instead
of oil, burned, with a bickering flame, upon the middle of a coarse
table, over which cups and cans, glasses and bottles were strewed
in disorder ; pipes lay scattered around, and the coarse hempen
covers of bales and cordage of broken packages lumbered up the
corners of the room. As the Secretary raked up the glowing
coals and warmed himself before the welcome fire, it was with an
air of wonderment, not unmixed with apprehension, that he cast
his eyes around this strange and uncouth place, and lost himself
in the attempt to conjecture whither his erring fortune had conducted him.

"Here have been dwellers," he said, "and recently ; but
whither have they fled ? Can I have so far lost my way as to
have straggled to the Patuxent, instead of the Potomac ? Faith,
I believe it ; for I have heard my Lord has a store-house there,
where he collects his customs—and this, by what I see around
me, must be some such place. Well, Patuxent or Potomac, I
care not which ;—most heartily is the roof welcome : for, beyond
this I venture not again to-night. I would I might see the
keepers here ! Surely they are not far off, since their flagons are
left behind—and not drained, neither, for here I find good drinking ware, which, to my poor spent frame, is no boon to be des-
pised. I greet you, honest nectar," he said, as he poured out

some wine and drank it off; you come at a good time, and with
a smack that your dainty wine-bibbers wot not of.—Heigho!
was ever man so weary? I shall stretch me down on these
coarse wrappings. And there, good cassock, you have done me
faithful service to-night : before the fire I spread you out to dry,
and in this corner make my bed."

As these muttered ruminations escaped the Secretary's lips,
he collected the remnants of bags and the rough cloths that had
formerly served to envelop items of merchandise, into a heap on
one side of the fire-place near the wall ; and spreading his wet
surcoat in front of the live embers which he had now renovated
with some billets of wood that lay at hand, he flung his exhausted
frame upon his hastily-gathered bed, and in a few moments was
locked in a sleep that might have defied the clamor of a marching host.

Here we leave him, whilst we turn to the hut of The Cripple.
The skipper, intending to meet his men as soon as they should
despatch the business upon which they were sent, and desirous to
snatch a short repose in the interval of their absence, had thrown
himself, immediately after entering Rob's cabin, upon a couch of
the skins of wild animals, which the woman of Warrington had
spread for him ; Rob had withdrawn into his own apartment, and
the crone, having now discharged her household cares, hastened
over the bank to her solitary lodge. For some time The Cripple
remained in an abstracted self-communion, whispering to himself
bitter taunts upon his own folly in consorting with the ruffians
of the Chapel, and occasionally chuckling with his customary
sneer at the profligate arts by which they collected their wealth,
and the dissolute liberality with which it was squandered. After
this, according to a usage which was observed with singular exactness for one of his habits of life, he addressed himself to his
devotions, with the apparent fervor of a sincere penitent, and

scrupulously performed the offices of prayer and meditation appointed by the ordinances of the church to which he belonged. When, at length, he was about to retire to rest, he was not able contentedly to do so, until, with that characteristic solicitude which belonged equally to his temper and the period of his life, he gave a few parting moments to the computation of the gains of the day.

"Dotard!" he exclaimed, as he began to cast up this account, "I have left my wallet in yonder Chapel, with all my papers. Oh these cup-riots—these heady revels, made for hot brained fools and prodigal unthrifts! What fellowship should my white hairs and hollow wrinkles find with them, that I must needs turn herdsman to these bears? Folly goeth armed with a scourge, and layeth on roundly, good faith! How have I been whipped by that most wise fool in my time! Well, for a penance, get thee back, thou curtailed and misshapen sinner! get thee back the weary way to the Chapel. Ha! should these night-birds make prize of my written memorials!—Hasten—hasten thee, Rob!—The lantern—the lantern! and then away."

The lantern was lighted and swung by a small chain across his shoulder, and taking his crutches, he was soon beyond his threshold, making good speed to the Wizard's Chapel.

This sudden motion had so far roused his spirit and altered his mood—which was ever fitful and subject to rapid change—that, as he swung briskly onward, he found himself humming a tune; and when he had reached the door of the Black House, he was engaged in audibly singing the words of the song which had been so unceremoniously suspended by the interposition of Kate of Warrington :

> " He needs no napkin for his hands,
> His finger-ends to wipe,
> That keeps his kitchen in a box
> And roast meat in a pipe."

"Marry, I can troll it with the best of them yet !" he said, evidently proud of his performance, as he pushed the door open and entered the apartment. His first movement was towards the corner where he had been sitting before he was lifted to the table ; here he discovered the leather pouch as he had left it. His eagerness to find what he sought in this spot, rendered him for the moment unobservant of everything else ; but now, on casting his eyes around him, he perceived the coat of the Secretary hanging in front of the fire, and in the next instant, the figure of Albert Verheyden himself prostrate on his rude pallet, breathing the long and audible inspirations of profound sleep. It was apparent to The Cripple, at a glance, that the person who lay stretched before him was not of the crew of the skipper. With an instinctive motion he drew his long knife, or dagger, from its sheath, and swayed himself forward to the very side of the sleeping man. The dagger was uplifted, and about to descend with the impulse of a brawny muscle that would have pinned the victim to the floor, when The Cripple suspended the blow, only to make more sure, by the flash of the light of his lantern across the sleeper's face, that the person he was about to assail was one who had no claim, from acquaintance or confederacy, to the privilege of entering under this forbidden roof. When the secret of the Black House was endangered by the rash curiosity of prying eyes, or even by the involuntary knowledge of the casual wanderer, no scruple of conscience, nor shrinking reluctance to do a deed of murder, might withhold the arm of the ruthless ascetic who ruled unquestioned over this fearful domain. A savage scowl lowered upon his sallow front as he stretched forth his long arm and passed the lantern across the quiet visage of his unconscious victim, whilst his right hand still held the dagger in act to strike. The scowl suddenly changed, as he stooped forward more narrowly to scan the countenance of the sleeping man,—and a strange expression of instant terror took its place. For some seconds his gaze was riveted upon Albert Verheyden's beautiful features, as heaving his head upward, in a casual motion of his slumber, the Secretary threw the whole contour of his face into the full blaze of the light, and disclosed his glossy and almost womanish ringlets, which now straggled over his ear and upon his beardless cheek.

"Blessed St. Romuald, shield me from this sight!" murmured Rob, with a slow utterance and whispered voice, whilst with still fixed eyes and a frame trembling in every fibre, he stared upon the image before him. "It is a spectre conjured hither from the grave, or the juggling cheat of a fiend, that reads to me, in that face, the warning of a life of sin? Oh God!—I cannot strike thee, whatsoe'er thou art! So, in very truth, *she* looked whilst slumbering on her pillow! that same fair forehead—that silken eye-lash, that curling lip. Who art thou, and whence comest? What witchcraft hath thrown thee into this foul abode? Sure, I am awake! I have not closed mine eye to-night. There stand the tokens of this night's debauch;—these cups, these flasks, and this familiar den of villainy, all bear testimony that I do not wander in my sleep. These limbs are flesh and blood," he added, as he raised Albert's yielding hand from his bosom; "and that brow is warm with the heat of healthful action. Holy saints of Heaven! can it be?—What is here?" he suddenly demanded, as his eye caught a glimpse of a jewelled trinket, which, as the sleeper lay, was disclosed in the inner folds of his vest, and which The Cripple drew forth by the chain to which it was attached. "To Louise!" he exclaimed, when his eyes fell upon the simple inscription on the back of the richly mounted miniature—"God of Heaven, by what miracle am I haunted with this sight! Louise—Louise—poor girl! that little portraiture of thyself I gave thee with mine own hand—'tis now two and twenty years

16

age .—it was a stolen effort of the painter's skill, and thou wert then an angel of light that shed a blissful radiance upon my path. And is it then true, that this may be Verheyden, his Lordship's Secretary, upon whose head I have heard ruffian curses heaped and pledged in maddening draughts by devils at their carouse, is thy child, Louise? Mine, I would fain confess, after a long and stubborn life of passionate denial and scornful hate. Oh, Louise !" he groaned aloud, as tears coursed down his withered cheek, whilst he bent over the Secretary and parted the hair from the forehead, upon which he imprinted a kiss ; " hapless was thy fate, but doubly wretched mine. William Weatherby, thou hast been the fool and dupe of that devilish disease of thy blood which hath brought showered curses upon thee and thine ! There, sleep on the bosom of thy child, mother of an unhappy destiny !" he said, as he quietly replaced the miniature. "This is no place for thee, unwary boy ! I must rouse him ere these blood-hounds fall upon his track——"

"A soaking night, by St. Anthony !" ejaculated the boatswain of the Escalfador, who, at this instant, thrust open the door, and, with four or five of the seamen, came clamorously towards the fire. "Push us yon bottle, and let us see if there be any of the stuff left."

"And let us have fire, Master Boatswain ; I am chilled to the marrow. Pipe thy best whistle for the Captain : he told thee to pipe it roundly, as soon as the brigantine was out of the creek."

"I warrant you, I will wake him," replied the boatswain, as he went to the door and blew his shrill note.

"Ho, old boy of the bowl ! what i' the devil makes thee here ?" demanded one of the crew, when his eye fell upon Rob, who had, at the entrance of the men, extinguished his light.

"Knave !" returned The Cripple ; "who gave thee license to huff and swagger under this roof ? Where is Roche ?"

"Aboard the brigantine with five of our messmates. They have her at hand ready to take in the stowage the Captain spoke of."

"We heard as we came across the field," said the boatswain, "the snort of a runaway horse, which this fool Francis must take to be a devil in earnest—and he falls to crossing himself like an old monk in a battle with Beelzebub."

"Whisht! we have a traveller here," said Rob, whose restless eye and anxious motion had evinced the disquiet of his mind, ever since the sailors had burst into the room, and who had now placed himself in such a position as to screen the Secretary from their observation, "a traveller who has doubtless lost his way and wandered into the Chapel."

"Why dost not give him the knife?" interrupted the boatswain, in a whisper; "'tis the old law of the Black House."

"Cut-throat!" ejaculated Rob, "am I to be schooled by thee in the law of the Black House? The stranger hath come at unawares, and is now asleep. He hath seen nothing, heard nothing, and can report against no one. Put a bandage across his eyes before he awakes, and let two of the men bear him, in silence, on their shoulders free of the Chapel, and set him down in the woods. Thou hast stabbing enough, John of Brazil, in thy proper calling, without doing murder in sport."

"Ha, ha! thou preachest, by Saint Longface! Thou'rt growing tender-hearted, Father Robert!" said the boatswain, laughing.

"Caitiff! wolf! kite!—thou shark of the bloody mouth!" exclaimed The Cripple, in a voice suppressed by the fear of waking the sleeper, whilst his face grew crimson with rage; "but that I have no limb to reach thee, that taunt should be thy last. Here, Francis! thou and Pedro, muffle this traveller in his cassock and take him hence; when thou hast borne him a quarter of a mile in the woods, set him down to make his own way."

Before the sailors could obey this order, and whilst they hesitated to perform what seemed to them a useless service of humanity, Cocklescraft entered the apartment. At the same moment, Albert Verheyden, whose slumber had been disturbed by the clamor of conversation, now awoke, and startled by the first impression which the inmates of the place made upon him, sprang to his feet, retreated to the wall and drew his sword.

"Where am I—and who are ye?" he exclaimed, with a confused perception of the persons around him, and of the spot he inhabited. "Your pardon, friends," he added, as gaining more self-possession, he turned the point of his weapon to the ground, and smiled; "I had an evil dream that awoke me. Will your goodness let me know—for I am a benighted traveller—what place this is, and to whom I am indebted for this shelter?"

"Ha, by St. Iago, you are most welcome, Master Verheyden!" said the skipper, as he recognized his enemy in the person who had made this appeal to the good-will of the company. "'Tis my house; make free of it, master! I did not hope for the honor of this courtesy;—thrice welcome! You have been abroad to-day to seek the man who made bold to lodge a bullet in the brain of yon caster of nets, below St. Inigoe's; do I not guess well? You have had most marvellous good luck; for, first, before all the world, you, his Lordship's Secretary, have chanced upon the very murderer. What will you do with him, Master Verheyden?"

"A misadventure has thrown me into the power of banditti," replied the Secretary, with quiet resignation. "I have naught to say. I know you daring to do the purpose of a wicked will, and can hope for no mercy."

"You guess me right," replied Cocklescraft sternly. "I dare do what I *will* to do You and yours, especially I hate—and have sworn against your life. No to-morrow's sun rises on my Lord's dainty and darling minion. By the law of our brother-hood, thou diest this night, Albert Verheyden. John of Brazil, take him forth—and, by the lamplight, discharge a brace of pistols into his heart. His heart—be sure of it! I would strike his heart :—it shall kill more than one," he muttered as he turned fiercely away.

"Dickon Cocklescraft," said Rob, with a gathering anger that was ill concealed under the show of calmness which he now assumed, "have I lost my authority under this roof,—mine own roof, let me tell thee,—that thou venturest to usurp my right to ordain the fate of the rash fool who invades our secret? At peril of your future peace and thriving fortune, John of Brazil, dare to do the bidding of your Captain! Would'st have the evidences of his death rising up in judgment against us, in the blood thou spill'st? Thou art but an apprentice, Dickon, to thy devil's craft, and a halter will yet reward thee for thy folly. I will pronounce the doom of this intruding spy. Drown him! let the wide waters wash away all trace of the deed :—let the ravening shark devour him."

"Ha, ha!" ejaculated Cocklescraft, with a sneer, "you have a conceit in your humanity, Rob! Do it—do it in your own way; but, in the devil's name, be quick about it. I have a merry sport for these lads to-night, and little time to lose :—so, despatch."

"Give me Francis and Pedro," said Rob, "and I will order the matter myself."

"Away then, about it!" said Cocklescraft; "we lose time in prating like women at this baby-play. You have commodities to go aboard to-night—look to it, John. Give a signal to the brigantine to send the yawl ashore—briskly, boys; we must work : so, to it!"

And in this strain of ordinary business occupation, the skipper turned from the horrible fate of his victim with a careless indifference—almost forgetting, in the concern of shipping some contraband merchandise, (the rapine of his last voyage,) the dreadful tragedy which, at his instance, was now in a course of acting.

Albert, calm and silent, like the victim of a Pagan sacrifice, neither gave vent to the agony of his feelings in sighs, or offered resistance to the savage hands that pinioned his arms. Under the direction of The Cripple, the two sailors conducted their captive towards the hut, Rob himself following with the coat of the Secretary thrown over his own shoulder.

The rain still poured steadily down, and the faint light of the moon had disappeared, leaving the scene in almost perfect darkness. Albert Verheyden, his arms bound with cords, moved at the bidding of his ruthless conductors, at a brisk and firm pace, along the beach, until the party arrived opposite the hut of The Cripple. They approached the door, which being thrown open, gave to their view the smouldering fire that still threw forth a glimmering ray from the hearth. A pine fagot soon kindled up a blaze, and cast a broad, lurid light over the apartment. At Rob's command the prisoner was brought in and stripped of his doublet, his boots, and his weapon, all which were taken in charge by the master of the hut. A deadly paleness was spread over the Secretary's face whilst these preparations were making : but his lip did not quiver, nor did his eye lose its lustre.

"Why not take my life at once ? Why mock my spirit with this horrible delay?" he asked, in a tone that partook as much of anger as of grief. "I appeal to stones—to brutes, more senseless than stones ! Holy martyrs, aid me in my extremity !" he added, with a subdued and resigned temper. "God will avenge this wrong."

"Why dost falter, knaves ?" exclaimed Rob, when he saw the

sailors retreat a pace and mutter inaudible whisperings to each other. " Ha, thou must be wrought, by thine accustomed devil, to this work. There, go to it : there are strong waters to aid thy lacking courage—drink your fill ! I will help thee."

Rob now gave to the seamen a bottle, which they put alternately to their lips. " Fear it not, Pedro ! Stint not, Francis ! 'Tis an ugly job at best, and needs the countenance of a man's draught. Drink again !"

" Ay, will I, like a Bloody Brother !" replied Pedro, making good his word by a second application of the bottle. " I have been on the Coast, Master Rob, with Mansvelt, before I ever saw Captain Cocklescraft."

" Ha " said Francis, in a French accent, " and wasn't François Le Grand at the taking of Maracaibo, and in the fight with the three Spanish galleons ? Diavolo ! give me the bottle !"

" Brave lads, both !" shouted Rob, with an attempt to laugh ; " brave lads, and worthy ! We shall be late with our work,— haste thee !"

" The necklace !—I had forgot the necklace !" said Pedro, with a somewhat thick utterance ; and leaving the room for a moment, he returned with a large round stone, which was expertly enveloped in cords and fastened around the Secretary's neck.

" Now to the skiff, lads ! get it ready upon the beach—see that thou hast the oars."

At this command the sailors went forth to make their preparations.

" In God's name, boy !" eagerly demanded The Cripple, the moment the seamen had left the room, " canst swim ? Answer quickly ; I would save thy life."

" I can."

" Thanks for that word ! Thou wilt sit beside me in the

boat—I will cut these cords. When I extinguish my light, spring into the wave ; make to this shore. You will find your weapons and your garments under the door-sill. These drunken knaves I will detain from pursuit. Make your way northward, along the beach. Four miles from here you will reach the dwelling of one Jarvis—you will find him friendly."

" All ready, Master Rob !" shouted one of the seamen, as he thrust his head within the door.

" Take more drink, Pedro—'tis a wet night," said Rob.

Whilst the sailor obeyed this command, The Cripple took up a billet of resinous pine, which he lighted at the fire, and, under the guidance of this flaming torch, Albert was led to the boat.

The two mariners took their places at the oars ; the captive was seated alóngside of The Cripple, who assumed the helm, and all things made ready for their eventful voyage. The surf ran high under the pressure of an easterly wind, which blew in upon this shore ; and nothing was heard but the stunning sound of the surge, whose foam sparkled as it broke on the beach from the dark waste of waters of the bay. The torch streamed aloft in the wind, flinging its light full upon the faces of the sturdy oarsmen, and plainly enough disclosed to Rob the stupefying effect of their late debauch at the Chapel, redoubled as it was in the recent potations which had been supplied at the hut. Albert Verheyden, unable to account for the sudden interest which The Cripple had so hurriedly expressed in his fate, scarcely could persuade himself to believe in its sincerity. But still, like one in a dreadful hazard resolved to avail himself of every chance, he inclined his body towards his companion, anxiously waiting to find himself relieved of the strictures that bound his limbs. From suspense, doubt, and almost despair, he was suddenly elevated to the most exhilarating hope, when he found the knife of The Cripple applied to sever the cord that suspended the weight to his neck, and, in almost the same instant, to set his arms free. The boatmen were struggling to push the boat over the sand in which she was partially imbedded, and having got afloat waited the moment to go out upon the ebbing surf.

"Steady! strike together, and briskly!" said Rob. "You will bring home a lighter load than you take. There—sturdily—as we ride the wave! Ha, the fiend on that white cap! this salt sea is an unruly monster—it has quenched my light. Pull away, —we have shipped a hogshead of brine! A plague on thee for handling an oar! thou hast left me never a dry thread to my back :—mine eyes flash fire with this dripping sea. In the name of the wizard! are we not too light in our craft for such a heavy sea?"

"All free!" said Pedro. "A little salt water will do no harm : we have good space before us. Keep her head to it, Master Rob. You may throw the landlouper over, now. If the tide should wash him ashore, there's a berth to be found for him in the sand."

"Over with him!" said Francis ; "I would not row a cable's length in so dark a night to drown a king."

"Ha! by my body, I believe that wave hath rid us of the spy before we were willing to part with him!" said Rob ; "he is not in the boat—I can feel nothing of him around me. Thou hast better eyes than I, Francis : look under the seat. Seest thou the prisoner?"

"I see nothing here," replied the seaman.

"Nor I," added his comrade ; "these landsmen have never a liking to a long voyage—ha, ha! Well, he sleeps where no one will call to wake him in the morning. Put about, Master Rob!"

"I know not right hand from left—north from south, in this darkness," returned the Man of the Bowl, as he still kept the boat heading on her outward course.

16*

"Down to leeward!" cried Pedro. "Dost not know when the wind is in your teeth?"

"Ay," responded Rob, "thou'rt a wise teacher, master frize-jacket! So, now for the surf again—another drenching! I am a mad-cap fool to be playing the boy, in my old days, with these storm-chickens. But, to your oars, lads! we must back to shore."

Some time was taken up in manœuvring the boat so as to bring her bow towards the shore, and a full half hour elapsed before the voyagers had again reached the hut.

As Rob made haste towards his dwelling, he heard footsteps approaching from the direction of the Chapel, and anxious to relieve his mind, on the instant, from the doubt whether the secretary had been fortunate in his endeavor to reach the shore, he swung himself the more rapidly forward, and before he entered his door, thrust his arm beneath the sill to ascertain if the clothes, to which he had directed Albert's attention, were removed.

"Holy St. Romuald, my blessed patron, I thank thee!" he ejaculated, upon assuring himself that the articles deposited had been taken off; "and here, on this threshold, in the sincerity of a godly vow, I dedicate the remnant of a sinful life to penitence and prayer! Is it you, Master Cocklescraft?" he demanded, confusedly, as the footstep he had heard now arrived at the gate of his enclosure. "A stormy night we have had for this foul play."

"Have you done it,—and well?" eagerly inquired the skipper. "Hast given that saucy jack to the supper of the crabs? By my fellowship, I envy you, Robert Swale!—and would have chosen to do the deed myself, if it were not, that having made a miss in my encounter with him with swords, it might be taken cowardly in me to handle him in this fashion. I was glad, Rob, you took it upon yourself. Didst make a clear plunge of it? Did he pray for his life, ha? Oh, it was a rare chance that gave him to us this night! Tell me how he bore himself."

The sailors coming up at this moment, Rob was obliged to confess that neither he nor the oarsmen had seen the prisoner go overboard; and thereupon he related the extinguishment of his light, the heavy surf, and the subsequent missing of the victim.

"A weight was fastened around him?" sharply inquired the skipper.

"It was."

"And he did not shuffle it off?—Art sure of it? A light there, Pedro! let me see the boat."

The light was brought, and the boat examined, and the stone which had been prepared to sink the body found lying under the stern-seat.

"Ten thousand devils!—he has escaped," roared Cocklescraft. "Fool that I was, to trust this matter to a deformed cripple!—how happened he to be so weakly bound and lightly watched, that in such brief time he could release his arms and cast away this weight?"

Rob listened to the outpouring of the skipper's wrath and impatience, with an unaccustomed calmness. Ordinarily his fretful and rebellious temper would have broken out, at such rebuke, into imprecation and defiance, and he would have spoken in a tone which would have made the leader of the pirate crew quail before him. There was, in the countenance and bearing of the misshapen tenant of the hut, an expression of command and harsh and fiery resolve, which alone might master the rough minds with whom he held his daily commerce; but there was, besides, a personal awe of him, derived from his secluded life and greater intelligence, approaching to the fear inspired by a supernatural being, which was sufficiently potent to disarm the hostility

and secure the obedience of the credulous seamen who followed
the fortunes of Cocklescraft. An answer of defiance and reproof
hesitated on his tongue. His eye glistened like that of a basi-
lisk, his lip quivered, and his nostril began to distend,—but the
instant thought that it became him not at this moment to quarrel with the skipper, and that he might only countervail the
mischievous designs (as he was now resolved to do to the utmost
of his power,) of this vengeful and merciless man, by the coolest
watch upon his motions, changed his mood and prompted him to
assume a milder tone.

" Thou must needs have a revel to-night, in the Chapel, Dickon," he said with a laugh in which he could not entirely disguise his
scorn ; " and these tarred monsters of thine have grown muddy-
brained and thick-sighted ; they have neglected to do their work
of breath-stopping so featly, as thou hast taught them of old."

" Whither has the slave fled ?" exclaimed Cocklescraft, as
they returned to the hut. " Lurks he not in the bush,—may he
not yet be followed and retaken ?"

" Oh, truly !" replied The Cripple ; " it is the nature of an
escaped captive to lurk around his prison : an eaglet that hath
broken his cage will fret against the wires for admittance—the
wolf will dally upon the footstep of the hunter. When thou
canst believe these, Dickon, thou mayst hope to find the prisoner
still prowling in the neighborhood of the Chapel."

" The curse of the Brethren of the Coast upon him ! By St.
Iago—I will have my vengeance yet ! Rob, as the fox hath
scaped from your hand, I may claim a service of you. I shall
set forth instantly for St. Mary's, with a dozen of my picked
men. I have doings on foot, old sinner, that shall delight thee
in the telling. Mischief, mischief, Master Rob of the Trencher !
which I shall keep secret until it be done. I would put such of
my crew as remain behind—barely enough to sail the brigantine

—under your command. You will go aboard and direct her to an anchorage on the outer side of the Heron Islands nearest the mouth of St. George's river. There will I join you soon after daylight. Oh! but his Lordship's city shall ring with wailing at my leave-taking! What say'st thou, Rob? Wilt go aboard?"

"When do you set forth?" inquired Rob.

"Now, on the instant—as soon as I may gather my cut-throats in the yawl."

"And at what hour shall the brigantine sail?"

"By two o' clock, at latest, as much sooner as you choose."

"Ha, ha! Thou wilt make me a limb to help thy devilry. Well, so be it, Dickon!" said The Cripple, after a moment's pondering over the proposal. "I will take on the office of skipper for the nonce, as thou takest on thy more accustomed garb of an incarnate devil."

"'Tis agreed," cried Cocklescraft, turning around to leave the cabin; "behind the first of the Heron Islands, Master Rob —St. George's, I think it is called—remember! And have a caution that, before you cast anchor, you have got a position from which the brigantine may not be observed from the town."

"Ay, truly," returned The Cripple, nodding his head and smiling in derision, as the skipper departed and closed the door after him—"I will take good care that the brigantine be not observed from the town!"

It was now an hour past midnight. Cocklescraft hurried to the Black House where he found his crew awaiting his return. Francis and Pedro were directed to take Rob on board of the brigantine, and with two other seamen, who were appointed to go before them, to await The Cripple's orders. The rest of the crew, amounting to twelve men, were armed with cutlasses, pikes, and pistols, and, under the immediate command of Cocklescraft, took possession of the yawl. In brief space, the Captain himself stepped on board. With the turn of the night the rain began to abate ; the wind was veering round westwardly, and appearances seemed to indicate a change of weather before morning.

The word being given, the boat was shoved off from the strand ; and the regular, sturdy, and rapid stroke of the oar was heard, long after she was lost to view, as she laid her course towards Cape Look Out.

Soon after this, Francis and Pedro knocked at the door of Rob's cabin. " We are ready to put you on board of the Escalfador, Master Swale," said the first, just thrusting his capped head and frize-clad shoulders into the hut.

" I am with you, honest gentlemen," returned The Cripple, as he came forth and followed them to the boat.

" Up with your anchor," cried out Rob, when he found himself on the deck of the brigantine. " Pedro, make what sail thou think'st best, and stand out into the bay."

In less than half an hour the sailor waited on his new captain for orders. " We have a fair berth up and down, master. Whither do we steer ?"

" To the Patuxent," replied Rob.

" Ay, ay—our course is northward." And the brig was soon under easy sail with the wind abeam, as it blew moderately from the west, with here and there a star twinkling through the breaking clouds, as she made her way towards the headlands of the Patuxent.

CHAPTER XXX.

Both child and nurse are fast asleep,
And closed is every flower,
And winking tapers faintly peep
High from my lady's bower.
Bewildered hinds with shortened ken,
Shrink on their murky way:
Up rouse ye then, my merry men,
It is our opening day.

JOANNA BAILLIE.

COCKLESCRAFT had not communicated to his men the exact nature of the expedition in which they had embarked. They were only aware that their leader had conceived a deep and mortal hatred to certain individuals in the port ; that he had fled from it as an outlaw ; and that their services were required in some daring enterprise which was designed to inflict chastisement upon his enemies : they cared to know no more. Bred to rapine and aggression, knowing no law but the law of their own fraternity ; unpitying and unsparing in their violence ; the greater portion of them strangers to the port,—for Cocklescraft had recruited more than half of his band amongst the islands of the Gulf, on his last voyage—these desperate men were ready to do the behests of their chief in any act of outrage to which he might command them.

In an hour they had doubled Cape Look-Out and were making dextrous speed up the Potomac. The refreshing breeze gradually swept away the clouds, and whistled. as it came directly

ahead upon the course of the voyagers ; the moon was just sinking below the horizon, and the stars shone forth through a crisp
and frosty atmosphere ; the waving forest murmured with a rush-
ing sound from the land ; the billows of the wide estuary of the
river, under the impulse of the suddenly-changed wind, came in
conflict, with a sharp concussion that sometimes gave forth a
note resembling the scream of the human voice ; no friendly light
was seen glimmering from the shore nor from wandering craft
upon the river : the marauders were alone upon the water, plying the lusty stroke to give a more fatal speed to their purpose
of crime, and the hour was beguiled with ribald jests and obscene
ballads, with wild and drunken laughter, and the meditation of
horrid outrage.

Cocklescraft himself was moody and silent.   His thoughts
dwelt upon the past scenes of the night, and upon his present
long-revolved purpose, which, during the last twenty-four hours,
scarce left him leisure to think of other matters.   Even the accidental capture of his enemy at the Chapel, and the escape of
that enemy from the fate allotted to him, lost their power to
move him, whilst he gloated upon the cherished design of this
night.

In another hour the boat had weathered the headland at the
mouth of St. Mary's river.   As the skipper entered the river the
first of the Heron islands lay upon his left, and he anxiously surveyed the localities, to regulate the course of his retreat to his
brigantine, which by his order was to be in waiting for him
abreast the outer shore.   "The blessed sun," he muttered to
himself—"shall light me with his first rays to-morrow, on my
seaward track, with my vengeance satisfied to the last scruple.
Ay, by St. Iago," he added, as he shook his clenched hand, and
gnashed his teeth with the energy of his resolve,—"to the last
doit of the debt !"

Another interval of silent labor at the oar, and the dim light in the windows of the Chapel attached to the House of St. Inigoe's, yet far off, upon the narrow strip of land which jutted entirely across the direct line of the boat's course, as she hugged the shore, showed the mariners that some one of the officials of the house was at the service of early matins on the vigil of the Feast of All Souls; and their familiarity with the watches of the night apprized them that the hour approached four of the morning.

And now the creek of St. Inigoe's is opened upon their view; and on the further bank, the house of the Rose Croft, with its embowering trees, is distinctly traced against the clear starlit sky. A solitary taper glimmering through an upper window, denotes a lady's bower, where, under the protection of the friendly ray, Blanche Warden, perchance, reposes in innocent slumber,—her fancy sporting in dreams of him who day and night lives in her thoughts.

This reflection flashed across the brain of Cocklescraft as he directed the head of the boat into the creek.

"Pull, with a long sweep and a quick," he said in a low but stern voice. "These watch-dogs of the fort may catch a glimpse of us." Then having advanced far enough to interpose the bluff bank of the Rose Croft between him and the fort, he commanded the men to cease rowing, whilst they muffled their oars.

"Not a word above your breath," he now added in giving the orders which were to guide his followers through the enterprise for which they had been brought hither. "Listen to me: we land under yonder bank—creep in silence to the dwelling you see above, and pluck from her bed the fairest damsel of this Western world. Mark me, comrades,—you have sacked towns and spoiled many an humble roof; you have torn children from the breasts of their mothers, and wives from the arms of their husbands;

you have dragged maidens from the inmost chambers of their dwelling and laughed at their prayers for safety,—and you have rioted over all, with the free license of the Bloody Brothers—but take it to your souls this night, that if, in the assault of yonder house, one unnecessary blow be struck, a war-cry be raised or deed of violence done, the man who offends dies by my hand. And further, when the maiden is brought into your presence let no rude speech assail her ear. I go to seek a bride, not to plunder ; and I command you all, on the duty you owe your leader, as Brethren of the Coast, that you do her all honor as mistress of the Escalfador. My sweetest revenge,"—he muttered without intending to be heard by the crew—"is to marry the worshipful Collector's daughter without his leave—or her own, by St. Iago ! The rose shall consort with the sea-nettle, Anthony Warden !—though it be not to your liking. Do ye heed me, messmates ? Roche del Carmine, to you I look to see this order enforced !"

"If it be but the taking of a single damsel," murmured Roche, "it was hardly worth leaving the warm fire and the bottle of the Chapel. Ha ! it will be a story to tell in the Keys that our last frolic in St. Mary's was at the Captain's wedding !"

"Dost thou prate, sirrah ?" demanded Cocklescraft. "By my sword, I am in earnest in what I say—I will shoot down the man that disobeys my order."

"I will answer for the crew," said Roche de Carmine ; "the lady shall be handled as gently as a child in the arms of its nurse."

"Ay," responded several of the sailors ; "the Captain shall not complain of us."

The oars were muffled, and the boat was once more in full progress towards her destination. A few minutes sufficed to bring the voyagers to the small wharf beneath the cliff of the Rose Croft, and in a moment all were ashore, except a single mariner who was left to guard the boat.

"Peace!" whispered Cocklescraft; "peace with that rattling of pikes. Form under the bank and remain quiet until I ascend and examine the place."

The leader now crept, with noiseless footstep, up the pathway which terminated upon the plain in front of the dwelling. He walked across the lawn, by the very spot where, scarce a fortnight gone by, he had had his hostile interview with Albert Verheyden. The little rustic temple of St. Therese yet stood, with its faded foliage, upon the grass-plot : the flower-stands were still there, although the plants were removed to their shelter from the frost : nothing met the eye of the foul-purposed rover but the images of content and innocence which marked the abode of a happy family : even the house dog, who at first growled as with show of battle, changed his threat into greeting as the Skipper proffered his hand and claimed acquaintance. The tokens of confiding security were all around him, and as he recalled the last time he had visited this place, and remembered the incidents of the festival of St. Therese—the maiden's coldness, her father's disdain, and the Secretary's favor, he laughed with the thought of the mastery he now held over the fate of the household. He could scarcely withdraw himself from the luxury of his present rumination, but wandered to and fro in front of the dwelling,—then made a circuit around it, and, returning again to the front, stood beneath the window through which the feeble taper shone with that steady but subdued ray which of itself was a symbol of the deep repose of the tenant of the chamber.

"I could wake thee, lady gay," he said, "with as blithe a serenade as ever tuned thy dream to pleasant measures—but

16

that I lack the instrument.   And though I be not the cavalier
of thy fancy, Blanche Warden, pretty rose of St. Mary's,—yet,
by my soul, I love thee well enough to put myself to some
pains to teach thee how thou shalt love me.   We dance together
on the green wave to-morrow, lass !—little as you dream of such
merriment now.   And as I would not have thy blushes seen, I
must e'en lead thee forth before the day."

With this sally, he returned to his comrades, and commanded
them to ascend the bank.   Three men were detached around the
house to keep a look-out, and the other eight, following Cocklescraft himself, approached the hall door.

"What, ho !   Fire, thieves, robbers !" shouted Cocklescraft,
aided, in raising a clamor, by his men, at the same time striking
loudly with the butt of a pike against the door.   "Rouse ye,
rouse ye, or you will have a house about you ears !   Fire,
Master Warden, thieves, rovers, and savages !"

A scream was first heard in the chamber from the window of
which the light had been seen—and Cocklescraft, putting his
hand to his ear, laughed as he recognized the voice of the
maiden.

"By our lady," he said—"our gentle mistress sings well !"

In the next instant a window was thrown open on the
opposite side of the house, and the figure of Anthony Warden,
in his night gown, with a candle in his hand, was partially
thrust out, whilst he exclaimed—

"What is this pother ?   Who comes at this hour to alarm
the family ?   Who are ye, I say, that seek to disturb the rest
of my household with your villainous shoutings ?"

"Answer him, Roche," whispered Cocklescraft ; "I dare
not."

"Open your doors, Collector," said Roche ; "we have business with you."

"Get you hence, drunken knaves!" returned Mr. Warden. "I will call my servants and drive you off the ground."

"By my hand, if you do not open your doors, Master Warden," said Cocklescraft, finding that he could not trust the conduct of the assault to his mate, "we will break them open, and quickly——"

"Who are you that speak so saucily?" demanded the Collector.

"Richard Cocklescraft—an old friend, Master Anthony, who being about to put to sea, would make his last visit to the officer of the port. Throw wide your doors and let us in, old man, or it may be the worse for thy gray hairs."

"Ho, Michael Mossbank, Nicholas, Tomkin!" shouted Mr. Warden, as he withdrew his head from the window; "up, get up —bring me my blunderbuss—we are beset—stir yourselves, my trusty fellows!"

The house was now lighted in various parts, and every one was on foot. Blanche, at the first summons, sprang from her bed, and ran to her sister Alice, screaming in a paroxysm of alarm; but whilst the invaders parleyed with her father, she had sufficiently resumed her self-possession to make a hasty toilet, and then to repair to the protection of Mr. Warden's presence. The old man, not coolly — for he was wrought into excessive rage— but with all necessary discretion and forecast, made his arrangements for the coming struggle. Two or three servants had gathered around him, as he descended the staircase to meet the assailants who were still battering at the door; and it was with difficulty that he could shake off the females, who clung around his step with piteous entreaties that he would not venture into collision with the band, who, it was now evident, must, in a few moments, make good their entrance into the house.

"Leave me, daughters—get back to your chamber," he cried, as he forced his way through their feeble impediment, with a blunderbuss in his hand, and, followed by the servants, took a station midway in the hall, whence he was able to direct his defence to either the front or the rear.

The precautions to which the inhabitants of the province were accustomed to resort for the purpose of guarding their dwellings against the attacks of the Indians, had rendered, in fact, every house almost a castle, and it was no easy matter, without the proper tools, to force an admission against the will of the owner. The stubborn character of the defences of Mr. Warden's dwelling detained the assailants longer than they expected, and gave time to the small garrison within to take all measures for guarding themselves that the condition of the house afforded.

The door at length yielded to the vigor of the attack, and as it flew wide open, the veteran master of the mansion stood with dauntless front, in full view of the eager seamen ;—in the same instant his piece was discharged with such effect that the two foremost men reeled and fell across the threshold.

" Give me thy gun, Michael," he exclaimed, as he turned to the gardener and seized the long Spanish fowling-piece with which my reader has already had some acquaintance ; " I will teach these ruffians good manners ! Back, knaves !—unhand me, villains !—Michael, Nicholas !"

" Stay that blow, coward !" roared Cocklescraft at the height of his voice, in the exertion of his full command over the crew, as they had, immediately on receiving the Collector's fire, rushed forward and overcome the old man by the press of numbers,—the servants having fled at this onset. " Strike him, and you shall fall by my own sword !" he continued, as with his cutlass he turned aside the pike of a seaman who had aimed it at the Collector's breast. " Is it for men to war against gray hairs ?"——

" Save my father—oh God, spare his life !" screamed

Blanche, as she now sprang, wild with terror, half way down the stair. "Men of blood, have mercy on his age !—he is old—too old to do you harm. Oh, save him !"

"By the Blessed Virgin, gentle mistress, I swear not one hair upon his head shall suffer harm,—for thy sake, dainty lady, if for no other !" exclaimed Cocklescraft, as with one bound he placed himself beside the maiden ; and raising her aloft on his arm, he leaped back to the hall and thence out upon the lawn. "Follow me, comrades !" he shouted, as he bore the screaming maiden stoutly on his shoulder down the bank, and laid her senseless upon the seat of the boat. Here he threw his cloak over her person, and summoned his men immediately to their posts,— having taken care to bring away the two wounded seamen.— The boat was about to be shoved off from the wharf, when the figure of a female was descried coming, at a rapid flight, from the direction of the dwelling, and uttering a shrill note of lamentation, as she begged them to stop :

"For the love of God, leave her behind ! Oh, have pity, good men, and do not tear away the Collector's daughter, our young mistress ! Christian men, spare her to us ! She will die of cold—she will perish on the water—her blood will be on your heads !"

"Thou'rt a good nurse, Mistress Coldcale," said the Skipper with a sportive tone which mocked the distress of the sufferers ; "and as our queen will want an attendant, thou shalt even go with us. Put the old woman aboard, comrades !" he added, speaking to some of the men, who, almost before the housekeeper could utter the shriek which now rose from her lips, was lifted over half a dozen heads, and deposited beside her young lady.

"Cheerily, now to your oars !" shouted Cocklescraft, exulting in the success of his inroad. "Lay your sinews to it, lads, until we get clear of the creek, and then up with your sail !—we have

a fair wind and a merry voyage before us.   Speed thee ! I scent
the coming dawn."

Almost in as brief space as we have taken to relate it, the
boat had shot forth into the middle of the creek, and now glided
over the waters like an imp of darkness flying homeward to his
ocean cave freighted with the spoils of some evil errand.

CHAPTER XXXI.

And hurry skurry, forth they go,
  Unheeding wet or dry;
And horse and rider snort and blow,
  And sparkling pebbles fly.
                                    LENORA.

ALBERT VERHEYDEN, at the appointed signal from The Cripple,
had sprung into the surf, at the moment when it broke with its
greatest violence against the bow of the boat, and, almost without an effort, was swept in upon the hard beach. His first
motion, on gaining his breath, was to hasten to the hut, seize
the clothes that had been stripped from him, as well as his
weapons, and to speed, at the full measure of his strength,—now
stimulated by his mysterious and almost miraculous deliverance,
—northwardly along the margin of the bay ; keeping sufficiently
remote from it, however, to screen himself by the thickets, which
grew a short distance from the water's edge, from detection by
those who might, perchance, be on the watch to observe his course.
His limbs were chilled, but by degrees, exercise threw a glow over
his frame, and he soon found himself recovering his suppleness and
power to endure the toilsome walk by which he labored to reach
the friendly shelter indicated by Rob's hurried instruction in the
hut. After what seemed a progress of at least twice the space in
which he was told he should find the dwelling of Jarvis, he was,
at length, greeted with the cheerful sight of an humble home-
17

stead, seated upon the plain, within a hundred paces of the tide-
mark.   He walked at once to the door and rapped loudly, as a
distressed man is apt to feel it his right to do in a Christian land.

"I pray you, good people, open your door to me," he said;
"rise, Master Jarvis, and admit a friend : in the name of charity,
I entreat the shelter of your roof."

In a moment the door was ajar, and a sleepy voice heard
from within challenging the comer—

"Who are you that knocks so late and loud at this door ?"

"A friend, good Master Jarvis."

"Is it shipwreck ?" inquired the master of the house, as he
opened the door and admitted the wanderer.   "Stand a moment
until I get a light.   Are you alone ?"

Before an answer could be given to these queries, the questioner had departed, and in a few moments returned with a
candle, whose ray disclosed to the Secretary a comfortable family
room, furnished according to the primitive fashion of a substantial
tiller of the soil of that era.   It took but little time for Albert to
rehearse the eventful story of the night, and his narrative was
answered with a kindness that gave him assurance of being now
under the protection of a friend.   The good man of the house
detained him no longer than was requisite to enable his dame to
prepare a couch, to which the Secretary, upon the housewife's
summons, eagerly repaired, and soon turned his sufferings to a
happy account, as, in self-felicitation at his escape, and in rendering thanks to God for the mercy that had raised him up a friend
in his extreme need, he sank into sweet oblivion of his troubles.

"At the dawn of day, he rose refreshed and invigorated, and,
being provided with a horse by the hospitable farmer, staid only
to express his gratitude to his host for the favors he had received,
and then, with as much expedition as he could command, pricked
onward to the town.

The rising sun gilded the chimney-tops of the dwelling of the Rose Croft, as the Secretary descended from the distant hill which gave him a glimpse of, what he deemed, that happy homestead, through the embowering trees. The atmosphere was instinct with a keen and bracing healthfulness which imparted a cheerful tone to the aspect of the scene ; and as he stood in his stirrups and looked around him, it was with a gladness he had never known before in his life, that he contemplated his near approach to his home. Thither he resolved to go only to refit his disordered dress, and then to hie with quickest speed to the mistress of his heart, to whom, with an impassioned delight natural to the romance of his mind, he hoped to tell his perilous and startling adventure.

The roofs and bowers of the Rose Croft sank from his view, as he hastened onward ; and he, at length, found himself on the skirts of the little city. There were ominous gatherings of the burghers in the street ; and the speakers shook their heads, and seemed to the Secretary to converse with a mysterious gravity.

"They have heard," he said to himself, " of my mischance in losing my way, and are fancying that I have encountered the Indians. No,—they see me riding here, yet no one comes to greet me :—there are other tidings in the wind."

And with this conclusion, anxious to know what had occasioned this early commotion in the little mart of news, he pressed forward to the Proprietary mansion.

An hour before the arrival of the Secretary, Rob of the Bowl, mounted on a sober-paced horse,—his thighs grasping the saddle with more security than one might expect from his diminished quantity of limb, his trencher hanging by a strap like a huge shield at his back, entered the town. He had run the Escalfador into the little inlet of Mattapany, just inside the Patuxent, where he left her under the guns of the fort which the Proprie-

tary maintained at this post ; and going immediately on shore,
he communicated to the commander of the garrison the circumstances which induced his visit, requesting that the brigantine
should be detained at her present mooring until his Lordship's
pleasure might be known. Then, having procured a horse, he set
forth, long before daylight threw its flush upon the eastern sky,
upon his journey to St. Mary's, not doubting to hear, upon his
arrival there, a story of outrage (though against whom, or how
perpretrated, he could not guess) done by the band of the Wizard's
Chapel. Without stopping to notice the wandering gaze of the
townsfolk at the strange and unfamiliar spectacle he exhibited to
them, he made his way directly to the dwelling of Father Pierre.

By the aid of the good father himself, he was dismounted
from his horse and straightway conducted into the study of the
churchman.

"You have reason to be amazed at this early visit, reverend
father," he said, "but my errand will allow no ceremony."

"You come to tell somewhat of the ruffians," hastily answered
Father Pierre, with a look and tone of sorrow, which informed
The Cripple, at the outset, that some deed of horror had already
been done,—"who last night violated the sanctuary of the
worthy Collector's roof, and stole away his daughter——"

"Hah !" exclaimed Rob, kindling with sudden wonder ;
"was that the drift of Dickon Cocklescraft's raid last night !
He has stolen the damsel ? Viper ! hell-hound ! I heard it not,
holy father : but I guessed some such outrage. I have hastened
hither faster than these crippled limbs are wont to travel, to tell
thee where the robber may be found. I knew his purpose of
mischief, though not against whom it tended—ha, ha, ha ! I
have baulked him ! I have baulked him !"

"Speak, old man, more coherently : we are lost in doubt, and
overcome with grief,—say, where has the ravisher fled ?"

"To the Heron islands, at the mouth of the river. There he hopes to find his brigantine—but I have cheated him, Father Pierre! Lose no time—but set pursuit on foot."

"The town is wild with conjecture," returned the priest; "Master Warden's servants have told the dreadful tale: but whither to search, no one yet has told. Come instantly with me to the Proprietary's. He who can point out the path of rescue will be more than a welcome guest."

The priest lost no time in causing Rob to be again set in his saddle; and walking beside the horse across the plain which separated the dwelling of the Proprietary from the city, Father Pierre soon halted with his companion at the door.

Previous to the arrival of The Cripple, and afterwards, during the conference between him and the Proprietary, in which measures were debated for the pursuit of the pirates, the excitement of the inhabitants of St. Mary's was aroused to the most intense agitation. The tidings brought from the Rose Croft had awakened the town at the dawn of day, and rumor told in every dwelling the sad history of the skipper's onslaught. The fate of Blanche was bewailed by all with bitter lamentation. Old and young grew frantic at the thought of a delicate and defenceless maiden, torn from her parent bower, in the dead of the night, and abandoned to the custody of miscreants, in whose bosoms not one sentiment of pity or remorse mitigated the fury of their brutal passions; and they uttered deep imprecations as they dwelt upon the dreadful fate which had befallen their cherished Rose of St. Mary's. All were astir to do something for her rescue, yet none seemed to know what was proper to be done. The women wrung their hands and wept, running wildly from place to place; the elder burghers conversed in doubting and dilatory consultations; and the young men of the port vented their anger in loud cries for vengeance against the perpetrators of the outrage,—suggesting as many plans of pursuit as there were varying rumors of the retreat of the invaders, and calling loudly to be led into immediate action.

"The Olive Branch did not slip off so quietly on a harmless flight," said Nicholas Verbrack, the lieutenant of the fort, as he stood in the midst of some eight or ten companions, on a bluff bank, which, near the middle of the town, gave a view of the whole extent of the river. "I thought that there was something too saucy both in the craft and in her skipper, to have either of them accounted honest dealers in the port."

"Honest dealers!" exclaimed Master Wiseman,—one of the five aldermen who were elected every two years to preserve the corporate franchise of the city, and who contrived to make up for the want of official duty by a redundancy of official importance; "Honest dealers, forsooth! That fellow Cocklescraft has ever been under the suspicion of the board. We have noted him, masters: but what could we do when his Lordship has always been personally present in the city, and has, I may say, encouraged the fellow as a trader,—because, forsooth, his custom helped to fill the exchequer of the province. Morals before money has always been my song; but it is preaching to a degenerate age—what have we to expect?"

"And the women," added Peregrine Cadger, "the women ran away with the man's wits. Why, mark you, sirs—what man, I would ask, but would grow bold and freakish,—ay, and wicked, —who has wife, maid, and widow, ever at his heels, singing and saying all manner of flateries, till, at last, one would think they had no other note."

"Oh, but it was horrible,—most aggravating and miserable, —this taking off!" groaned Willy, the fiddler. "Proudly and gladly would I have felt to be taken in her stead! I would suffer every misfortune—"

"And the worst of it is, Master Willy," interrupted Wise Watkin, "they have taken Mistress Bridget Coldcale—that's a loss to the province :—I should not lie if I said to the whole town."

"Why stand prating and grieving like gossips at a funeral," said John Firebrace, the smith, "whilst all the time the rascal thieves are putting more land and water between them and us. I think their worships of the council are somewhat tedious over the matter ; they talk longer than is necessary,—or else that old crop-limbed, vinegar-face, Rob of the Bowl, hath more to tell, than commonly it is his habit. It is special matter that has brought him to the port this morning. He knows more devil's-dealing than it pleases him, at all times, to let his neighbor hear. Yonder rides Master Verheyden, the Secretary," he added, as Albert now appeared at a distance directing his course towards the mansion of the Proprietary ; " he may hasten matters. I would that they would put us in the way of doing something to save our poor young lady from the jaws of these sharks !"

The smith had scarcely ceased speaking when Captain Daun-trees was seen coming towards the group. Whilst he was yet some paces off, he called out to the Lieutenant,—

"Master Verbrack,—quickly get thee to the fort, and march me instantly twenty men down to the quay. See that they be provided, Lieutenant, with all things necessary for service. Lose no time ; but away."

The Lieutenant instantly departed, and the Captain approaching the assemblage, continued,—

"John Firebrace, get thy horse, man, and thy weapon. Colonel Talbot rides down the opposite bank of the river, with a score of men at his heels. He counts upon you and your friends. Meet him quickly on the common behind the Town House."

These orders, hastily given, separated the company; and every one now hied towards the places appointed for these gatherings.

Already Colonel Talbot was on horseback collecting some of the more active young men of the town : and in a brief space—for in truth most of them were expecting the summons—a troop of some twenty were assembled, ready to follow wherever he should command. Amongst these were Arnold de la Grange and old Pamesack, both equipped and mounted after their accustomed fashion, in a manner that might have provoked a smile from the furred, and laced, and feathered cavalry of more orderly armies, but which, we may venture to believe, was quite as effective as a more gaudy furniture. Last in this marshalled array, came Albert Verheyden, pale, breathless, and almost frenzied with the narrative he had just heard of the disasters of the night. He staid at the mansion but long enough to substitute a more active horse for the clumsy animal on which he had made his journey to the town ; and then hastened to join the party who were about to be ferried across the river, and to scour the country along the opposite shore.

Meantime the musketeers arrived at the quay, where two barges being in readiness, the men were separated into equal divisions, and, very soon after sunrise, were embarked under the respective charge of Dauntrees and the Lieutenant, who, with all expedition, shaped their course towards the islands at the mouth of the river.

Talbot despatched a half dozen of the party to scour the shore of the Potomac below St. Inigoe's : the rest, under his own command, and attended by Albert, were transported to the opposite side of St. Mary's river, by every boat that could be mustered for such a service : and being now collected on the further bank, sprang forward, at the orders of their leader, on their career of duty, with an alacrity which showed how deeply they took to heart the outrage which it was now their purpose to chastise.

CHAPTER XXXII.

She turned her right and round about,
And she swore by the mold,
" I would not be your love," said she,
" For that church full of gold."

He turned him right and round about,
And he swore by the mass,
Says—" Lady. ye my love shall be,
And gold ye shall have less."

OLD BALLAD.

WHEN Cocklescraft and his crew had again doubled the point of St. Inigoe's, on their retreat, the sail of the yawl was spread be· fore the breeze, and she skimmed the waves like a bird of the sea. Blanche had yet scarcely shown signs of animation, except in the low and smothered moan that escaped from beneath the folds of the cloak which, with an officious care, the leader of the pirate gang had disposed for the protection of her person from the cold. Beside her crouched the housekeeper, sobbing and sighing and uttering ejaculations of alarm—one moment for her own fate—at the next, for the lot of her young lady,—and at intervals shrieking with a causeless terror, as the little bark, bending to the wind, dipped the end of her sail into the wave.

The seamen, now released from the oars, were called to the care of their bleeding comrades. Roche del Carmine, the mate, was already dead, and the other writhed in the torments of an unstaunched wound. The band were too familiar with the acci dents of war to be much moved by the fate of their companions,

17*

and accordingly, after applying a bandage to the hurt of the living man, and merely disposing the body of the dead one in a position least inconvenient to themselves, they assumed that indifference to the hazards of their condition, which has ever been a characteristic trait of the reckless temper engendered by the discipline of the buccaneer's life.

The beams of the sun had begun to bicker on the face of the waters when the fugitives reached the island of St. George's, the first of those few scattered islands in the Potomac which passed under the general name of the Heron Islands. During this brief voyage, Cocklescraft had in vain endeavored to soothe the maiden with kind words and protestations that no harm should befall her. He took her cold hand and it quivered in his grasp ; and when he released it, it fell lifeless back upon her bosom : he laid his palm upon her brow, and a clammy moisture bespoke the agony that wrung it.

"Dame," he said, addressing Mistress Coldcale ; "you are better skilled than I, in these woman qualms,—look to your lady, and tell me of what she may stand in need. You shall take her presently on board of the brigantine, and the whole vessel, if she require it, shall be given up to her comfort."

"She stands in need of her father's house," replied the dame, with more spirit than she might have been thought, from her previous fright, to possess. "She stands in need of friendly faces and kind hearts :—her soul is bowed down by misery. She will never open her eyes again, never, never—unless it be to look upon the friends from whom you have stole her. Oh, Master Cocklescraft—you have broken bread under her father's roof, and have sat in the warmth of his fireside—his old eyes have looked kindly upon you, and he has spoken words of welcome that have gone to your heart with a blessing in the very sound of them :—how can you heap torments on the head of his child ?

In sorrow and wailing have you borne her away, and she will quickly wither in your hand ;—you have stolen a flower that dies in the cropping. And oh, her gray-haired father !—with a broken heart, you have cast him down to the tomb."

"By St. Mary, woman, but I honor, love, and cherish the maid !" returned Cocklescraft. "Have I not loved her long, as never father loved her;—thought of her on the wide waters of the ocean, under every sun ;—dreamed of her night after night, in many a weary voyage ;—borne her image before me in storm and battle, in the chase and in the flight, beneath the stars in the dead hour of midnight, and at the feast at high noon ? Have I not made honorable petition for her, from her father— and been refused with scorn and foul insult ? And have I not now, at last, entrapped her as gently as she doth the winter bird that seeks a crumb upon her window sill ? By my faith, fairly have I won her, and proudly will I wear her, dame ! Her father! —I owe him nothing for his kindly greeting and warm fireside, and breaking of bread : he hath paid himself by his disdain and mockery of my suit. Have I not there," he added, speaking with an angry vehemence and pointing towards the bow of the boat—"given the life-blood of two of my best and bravest comrades to the old man's wrath,—and yet did I not myself turn aside the blow that would have laid him upon the floor of his own hall ?"

"Better that he had so fallen," replied the dame, "than live to witness what his old eyes saw last night. Better that he died outright, than live to lose his child."

"Be silent, woman," exclaimed the skipper, "if thou canst not give me fairer speech. When this anger is gone, and the maiden is more resigned, I will speak to you—not now. To your oars, good fellows," he said in a calmer tone to the seamen, as with the rising sun the breeze had fallen away and the sail flapped loosely against the mast. " We must pass through this narrow strait to the opposite side of the islands :—we shall find the brigantine there at anchor."

A confined channel, scarce above a pistol shot wide from shore to shore, divided the two islands immediately across the mouth of St. Mary's river, and afforded a passage for a light boat between. These islands, thickly timbered to the water's edge, effectually prevented, by their forest screen, the voyager along the inner shore from discerning the largest vessel which might be in the river beyond. It was, therefore, with undoubting confidence in the certainty of finding the Escalfador at her appointed ground, that the leader of these rude Argonauts commanded his men to labor at the oar whilst they shot through the strait I have described.

When they emerged upon the open river, on the outer side of the islands, the sun, looming through the thick autumnal haze, shot his fiery beam over the broad sheet of water, without disclosing to the anxiously-searching eye of Cocklescraft trace of brig or boat or sail of any kind. His vision, however, was circumscribed within a narrow horizon ;—for the mist which, at this season, broods over the landscape—the forerunner of a genial day—scarce brought within the compass of his observation the nearer points of the mainland, and effectually shut out all more distant objects ;—a circumstance which, however embarrassing to his present inspection, had so far been favorable to his escape from the prying eye of the sentinel on the look-out station of the Fort of St. Mary's.

" Ha !—twice have I been fooled by that old dotard of St. Jerome's," he peevishly murmured, when, after straining his sight in every direction, he became aware that the brigantine was no where to be seen ; " he has overslept himself, or given way to some freak of his devilish temper. Why did I trust a laggard with this enterprise? But that I spoke somewhat hastily to him last night, and would not have his displeasure, I would have seen him gibbeted e'er I would have given the brigantine into his charge. Yet he is trusty,—and has a devil's spice in him that fits him for such an outcome, too. He will be here anon;—the wind has left him,—and what he had, was in his teeth: the Escalfador does not keep pace with my longings. Patience for a season,—and meantime we will land on the island, comrades, and wait for our crippled admiral."

With this intimation he steered directly upon the beach. "John of Brazil," he continued, "use your time to scoop a grave for our comrade Roche, and see him bestowed as suits a Brother of the Coast. Joseph, you and a messmate will kindle a fire under yonder oak—these women are frozen into a dead silence Harry Skelton, get to the lower end of the island, and there keep watch upon the river, and report every thing that comes in sight. Now, Mistress Bridget, you and our lady Blanche shall have sway over the whole island;—the lady shall be an empress, and you her maid of honor. See, how quickly preferment comes! You have your liberty, pretty Rose of St. Mary's—so cheer up, and make a fair use of it."

To this ill-timed jocularity the maiden yielded no reply; and the skipper believing that, upon being left alone with Mistress Coldcale, she would perhaps relent into a more tractable tone of feeling, quitted the boat with the seamen who had gone to execute his several orders, and thus abandoned the two females to themselves.

"Alack, alack!" sobbed Blanche, as she raised her head and then dropped it on the lap of the housekeeper; "dear Bridget, what will become of us? I shall die, I shall die!—my poor father!"

"Poor indeed, mistress," replied the dame. "If we are not

rescued, he will never hold up his head after the loss of his child Oh, if our townspeople would but follow,—as I trust they will !"

" Is there a chance of it," exclaimed Blanche, " good Bridget, is there a chance of it ?"

" Ay, truly, my dear young lady,—good and reasonable hope that these villains have been watched and will be followed. Be of good cheer, and trust in Heaven. This bloodhound thought to find his vessel at the island, but the saints have befriended us, and the vessel has not yet come. All will go well, mistress,— such wicked men shall not prevail against the shield of innocence."

" The fire blazes cheerily, Mistress Coldcale—I pray you intreat our lady to come ashore," called out Cocklescraft from a distance.

" Arouse thee, child, I shall be at thy side," said the dame ; " it may be discreet not to provoke the skipper—he is a harsh man and may be rude, if we be stubborn."

" Mother of Grace, sustain me !" said Blanche, as her frame shook from head to foot, and she grasped the arm of her friendly attendant. " Even as you shall advise, I walk, Bridget—I pray you hold me," she added, as, raising herself on her feet, her loose and disordered tresses fell over her wan cheek and covered her breast and shoulders. " Oh, God, this trial will craze my brain !"

" Do not sink, dear child—you need fire, and this barbarous Captain has provided it—pray you, be of stout heart, and trust in coming help."

Encouraged by the support of her companion, Blanche feebly tottered towards the bow of the boat, and thence landed on the beach. Whilst she leaned upon Mistress Coldcale's arm and advanced towards the fire, Cocklescraft came forward to meet her ; and as he was about to address her in that tone of light saluta-

tion in which he had heretofore spoken, he was arrested in his
first words, by the maiden flinging herself upon her knees, immediately at his feet, and looking up in his face with her eyes be-
dimmed with tears, as she cried out for mercy—

"Spare me!" she exclaimed—"Oh, spare a wretched girl,
who has never imagined thought, nor spoken word of harm
against you. Save me from a broken heart and bewildered
brain—from misery, ruin, and disgrace! If I, or any friend of
mine, have ever given you offence, on my knees and in the dust I
entreat forgiveness:—pardon,—pardon a fault whereof I have ever
been unconscious. If one touch of pity dwell in your bosom, oh
think of the miserable being at your feet and send her back to her
home. Land me but on yonder shore, and I will, morning and
evening, remember you in prayers and invoke blessings on your
head!"

"This posture doth not become our queen," said Cocklescraft,
stooping to raise the maiden to her feet, who shrinking from his
touch crouched still lower to the earth. "This is but a foolish
sorrow. Do I not love you, Blanche? Ay, by the Virgin! and
mean to do well by you. I have stuffs of price on board the
Escalfador, which shall trick you out as gloriously as a queen indeed:—our dame here shall ply her skill at the needle to set you
forth quickly. And then that pretty robe of crimson and minever which unthinkingly you did refuse, you shall wear it yet, girl.
I have chains of gold and jewels rare, to make you gay as
gaudiest flower of the field. I will bear you to an enchanted
island, where slaves shall bend before you to do your bidding,
and where you shall have store of wealth to scatter with such
profusion as in dreams you have never even fancied. We will
abide in a sea-girt tower upon a sunny cliff, and through your
window shall the breeze from the beautiful, blue Atlantic fan you
to evening slumbers. My gay bark shall be your servant, and

ride, at your command, upon the wave ; whilst our merry men shall take tribute from all the world, that you may go braver and more daintily.   Cheer up, weeping mistress ; your mishap is not so absolute as at first you feared.   Your hand, lass !"

Blanche sprang to her feet with a sudden energy, and retreating a pace from her persecutor, cast upon him a look of resolute and indignant pride :

"Base wretch," she said, "I dare to spurn your suit.   Defenceless as I stand here, a weak and captive girl,—if it be the last word I have to utter,—I abhor you and your loathsome offer."   Then relapsing into that tone of grief from which this momentary impulse had drawn her, she added, "Did you think— did you think, Master Cocklescraft, when you stole me from my father's house, that fair speech from you, or promise of gold, could win me to be your wife ?   Oh, sir, if, in that error, you have heaped the sin of this deed upon your soul, quickly learn that not all the gold of all the mines, nor longest wooing, nor promise of a kingdom, if that were yours to give, might persuade me,—though the speaking of the word should lift me from abject misery or the pangs of death,—to give a favorable word to your suit.   With holy faith and saddest reverence, I call my guardian, the ever-blessed virgin Therese, to hear my vow ;—I never will be thine."

"A boat, a boat !" cried out the voice of the man at the lower point of the island,—and instantly this painful interview was at an end.   The seamen had since their landing been busy in depositing the body of the mate in a shallow grave, and had just set up a wooden cross, of fallen timber, chance-found in the forest of the island, to mark the spot, when the alarm from the look-out reached them.   Cocklescraft repaired with all haste to the beach, and was soon aware, not only of the boat to which the seaman alluded, but also of a second of the same description,

dimly seen in the haze, at no great distance behind the first.
They were both holding their course towards the mouth of St.
Mary's river, close on the eastern margin, as if their purpose were
to proceed down the Potomac. St. George's Island lay abreast
the opposite or western shore, and it was therefore necessary
for these boats, if they were destined for the island, to take a
course nearly across the entire breadth of the river, at its mouth.
As, at the moment when first descried, they gave no indication
of such a purpose, Cocklescraft (who did not doubt that these
were parties in pursuit of him) began to assure himself that his
retreat to the island was not discovered, and that his pursuers
were most probably bound to St. Jerome's. Again he cast a
troubled eye over the waters, in the hope to perceive the brigantine, for which, at this moment, he looked with increased solicitude, as he had reason to apprehend that, on her voyage up the
Potomac, she must pass the boats that were apparently on their
voyage downward. For some time, he gazed keenly abroad in
silence, or muttering only inaudible curses on the delay of Rob
with the Escalfador, and on his own folly in committing the
vessel to The Cripple's guidance. It was not long before the boats
had reached the Potomac. Here, instead of shaping their further voyage, as the skipper had been led to expect, towards the
Chesapeake, they took the opposite course and stood directly for
the island. They were near enough to make it apparent to Cocklescraft that each was filled with armed men, and if any doubts
of their hostile purpose had existed before, it now became altogether unquestionable. Hastening towards the spot where the
yawl was drawn up on the strand, the buccaneer ordered his
crew immediately to their posts. Blanche and Mistress Bridget
were forced to take their former seats, and the boat being shoved
off, was directed towards the point of land opposite the western
extremity of the upper island,—then only known as a nameless

sandy flat, thinly covered with pines, but of late rendered somewhat more familiar to public repute, by the comfortable accommodation with which it has been provided as a place of refuge
against the heats of summer, and for the luxury of its bathing.

"By St. Iago, we are hotly followed !" said the retreating
and anxious rover, as he now measured the size of the barges
with his eye, whilst they shot out from behind the cover of the
extreme eastern point of the islands and disclosed themselves in
full pursuit ; "and with swift craft, well manned. The devil
hath sent us a dead calm,—otherwise, with this rag of canvass, I
would show these lurchers the trick of a sea-fight : as it is, we
must show them our heels. Oh, that my good brigantine were
here ! I would defy twenty barges, and sweep through them all.
Lustily, good fellows ! slacken not :—halter and harquebuss are
on our track ; we die by hemp or leaden bullet if we are overtaken—so pull amain. You have been in as great straits before
and found a lucky ending. We shall see Rob anon, when this
mist shall lift its curtain : and, once in sight of our good bark,
we shall fight our way to her side. Courage, friends !"

In this strain of exhortation, Cocklescraft spoke at intervals
to his men, whilst anxiously looking to the rear he watched the
progress of his pursuers and seemed to count every wave that
broke against their bows. Not even his experienced eye could
tell which of the struggling rivals in this race had the swiftest
keel. So intense became the competition that soon all other
cares were absorbed in the engrossing thought of the escape.
The boat's crew fell into silence, and when the necessary orders
were delivered they were spoken in the low tone of familiar conversation, as if the speakers were afraid they might be overheard
by the enemy in their wake. If the concern of the leader and
his crew in their present condition was eager, still more did it
awaken the feelings of Blanche Warden and Mistress Bridget.

The maiden seemed to have forgotten her tears ; occupied with a more absorbing emotion than her grief, she found herself renovated in strength, and by degrees assuming an upright posture in the boat, whence, with an ardent and unblenching gaze, she kept her eye fixed upon the barges that swept along as messengers of hope to her deliverance.

Some three or four miles yet lay between the parties in the chase. Cocklescraft steered towards the upper headland of Piney Point—to use its modern designation—and reaching this, found a long sweep of the river ahead of him, bounded by a smooth strand unmarked by creek or inlet. At one moment he thought of running for the Virginia shore, and there, by doubling back upon his pursuers, aim to win the Capes of Potomac, in the hope of meeting the Escalfador ; but he could not count sufficiently on the speed of his boat to risk so dangerous a hazard.—

"If I can but keep my way till night, I shall baffle these hounds upon my track," he said, in pondering over the emergency. "A weary day it is before me, and a long run till night. Perchance, I may meet some stouter craft upon the water, some up-river trader, whom I may easily master,—and once on a broader deck, I will fight these landsmen with all their odds against me. Or, at the worst, I shall run ashore, if I am pressed, and take to the thicket, where at least, till day be done, I may lie concealed, and then find my way to the Chapel."

In this perplexity of doubt he still pursued his voyage. The point which he had passed momentarily screened him from the view of his pursuers ; but in due time the barges were again seen across the white sandy flat, looming to twice their natural size, and seemingly suspended in the air, by that refraction which, in certain conditions of the atmosphere, is often observed upon a low shore.

"They come, they come—Heaven be praised, they gain upon

us !" involuntarily ejaculated Blanche, as she rose from her seat, and gazed across the extremity of the point.

"Not so fast, my merry queen," said Cocklescraft, for the moment attracted by the lively utterance of the maiden ; "they do not gain upon us, mistress : you will learn presently that they must weather the point by that same circuit which you may see traced by our wake. Thou wilt be a better sailor anon. Steadily, good lads ! do not overwork yourselves ; we shall make a long run of it."

" Now, for some miles, the chase continued with little diminution of the space between the parties. At length it began to be perceptible that the barges drew nearer to the object of their pursuit : the shortened stroke of the oar denoted the flagging strength of the laboring buccaneers, whilst the unabated vigor of the pursuers showed that the chase was urged by men enured to the toil of rowing. Still, there was the energy of desperate men in the force with which the flying band held on their way, and Cocklescraft did not yet abandon the hope of wearying down the strength of those from whom he fled. Another hour, and the barges still crept up nearer to their chase. A death-like stillness prevailed on board the latter, broken only by the monotonous dipping of the oar and its dull jar upon the boat, as the seaman, with unvarying time, turned it in the row-lock and repeated his stroke. Still nearer came the barges and nearer, with fearful certainty.

"They come within musket shot !" exclaimed Cocklescraft. "To the land, boys ! we must even fight them on the land."

" Back your oars !" cried out Dauntrees, from the leading barge : " back, and lay to !" At the same moment he discharged a musket, of which the bullet was seen touching the water, in short leaps, immediately across the bow of the pursued boat.

A scream from Bridget Coldcale was, for a moment, the only answer that reached the ears of the Captain.

"To your feet, mistress!" said Cocklescraft, as seizing Blanche by the arm he placed her erect in the boat. "Fire at your peril!" was the reply he now gave to the accost of his enemy; "my crew sail under the protection of the Rose of St. Mary's. Have your weapons at hand!" he added, addressing his men; "we must e'en leave our boat, and this precious freight to these land-rats, and take to the wood. You cannot call me cruel, pretty maiden,—for I give you up, in pure courtesy, to your friends. You will remember the Master of the Escalfador as a gallant who would have made you mistress of as pretty a dowry as ever won maiden's good will. We have had a merry morning of it, girl,—I would it had been longer—but these churls behind forbid it : so, without more ceremony in the leave-taking—for I must needs be in haste—fare thee well, girl! Even without asking this favor, I kiss your cheek. To the shore, lads!"

As he spoke, and made good his word by stooping over the maiden and enforcing her submissiont o this parting token of his gallantry, the boat struck the sand, and, in an instant, leader and crew had sprung into the shallow water, and bounded to the shore, leaving but their wounded comrade and the maiden with her faithful companion on board of the boat. A volley was discharged from the nearest barge at the fugitives, but as the buccaneer; apprehending this, had given such a direction to his retreat as to keep the women in a line between him and his enemy, the balls were thrown wide of their mark, and the escaping crew were soon out of sight in the forest that covered the shore.

Upon the land side an enterprise was afoot of almost equal excitement to that upon the water. The party of horsemen that had crossed with Colonel Talbot to the opposite shore of St. Mary's river, submitting to the guidance of Arnold de la Grange and his old Indian comrade, were conducted along a path which threaded the thickets lying around the head of an inlet, that now bears the name of St. George's, and thence took a course down the peninsula towards Piney Point. Whilst galloping upon the further margin of the inlet by which the eastern side of the peninsula was formed, and yet two miles from the point, they perceived the yawl of Cocklescraft stretching across from the islands towards the main. A halt was immediately called by the commander of the party, and they were ordered to screen themselves and their horses from observation amongst the wild shrubbery of the spot.

"It is even as The Cripple of St. Jerome's told us," said Talbot. "This is the boat of the Olive Branch with her thieving knaves. You may know the skipper, Master Verheyden, by his flat bonnet and scarlet jacket. See, he looks sternward and waves his hand to his rowers as if he would hasten their speed."

"And I see the forms of cowering females at his feet," added Albert. "The boat makes for the point. A blessing on the day!—these marauders design to land. Oh, happy chance that we are here! let us not delay to set upon them."

"Hold, Master Secretary! be not too eager," replied the leader. "Think you they will land, if they see us lying at lurch to attack them? No, no! our honest friend of the Bowl hath stolen away their brigantine, and the cheated felons, all agaze at their mishap, are now seeking a hiding place where they may abide till night, and then, perchance, repair their misfortune by some other villainy. We should mar our best hope if they but catch a glimpse of us. So, quiet, gentlemen; your impatience shall find action soon enough e'er we get home again. Ah, good luck, friends! see how bravely sets the wind of our fortune;

yonder comes old Jasper Dauntrees, like a trusty comrade, hot in chase, with his barge trimmed to the nicety of an arrow's feathering. He follows close in the wake of the freebooter—and at his heels, by my faith, there opens now, from behind the point of the island, his second party. Push for it, old friend! The good powers cheer thee in thy race!"

"Master Cocklescraft," said Arnold, "will not be so fool-hardy as to land on that deep sand with two helpless women to take care of, whilst he has a soldier like Captain Dauntrees to track his march."

"You are right, Arnold," returned Talbot, after watching the leading boat for a space; the skipper steers wide of the beach, and means to make a run of it up the river : he is already passing by the point. Gentlemen, to horse again! we will get back towards the highland and there keep even speed with the chase, and, like well trained hawks, stoop upon our quarry in the nick of time. Beware the open ground, that the skipper may not see us on the heights."

In obedience to this command, the party set out quickly, by a retrograde movement, towards the upland, which, although somewhat remote from the river, gave them, at frequent inter-vals, where the cleared forest allowed, an extensive range of river view. Having gained this height, they traversed it in a line parallel to the course of the shore, ever directing their anxious eyes to the fierce contention between the boats for mastery in the race. Occasionally, in this progress, ravines were to be passed, a piece of marshy land to be avoided, or an open field, which might expose the party to the view of the boatmen, to be shunned. In all such passages of the journey, the services of Pamesack and of Arnold de la Grange contributed greatly to the speed with which this scouting company were enabled to keep pace with the rapid flight of the boats. With deep and

intense speculation did the horsemen watch the progress of the
chase, and measure the distance between the fugitives and their
pursuers.   Albert Verheyden, almost counting the strokes of the
skipper's oars as their wet blades flashed the sunbeams upon his
sight, rode for some time in despairing silence.

   " He loses not an inch !" he breathed to himself, as his
thought ran upon the freebooter's chance of evading his enemies ;
"he has men at the oar used to the sleight, and he will tire down
his pursuers."   Again he gazed, and with no better hope.   But
when, after losing sight of the river for some mile or two whilst
the party galloped over a piece of wooded low ground, he came
again in view of the boats, joy beamed from every feature of his
face as he exclaimed to his companions, "We advance upon his
flight and shorten the space between !   The skipper grows weary
of his labor : thanks to the Captain and his noble comrades, the
day begins to brighten on our enterprise."

   " We will halt here," said Talbot, reining up his steed upon a
summit which commanded a near view of that region, recognized
at the present day as Medley's Neck ; " the game is nearly run
down—and presently will come our time to speak a word of comfort to this renegade spoiler.   He strains for yonder point, as if
there he meant to land.   By Saint Ignatius ! it is a wise choice
he has made.   We have him, if his folly be so bold as to touch
that strand—we have him in a trap.   He comes—he comes,
driving headlong into our hands.   Follow !"

   Without waiting to marshal his troop, and even without
looking behind, Talbot spurred his horse to a gallop, and plunged
into the forest which covered the lowland even down to the river
brink.

   As Cocklescraft and his band deserted their boat and fled
into the wood, Dauntrees with the barges drove rapidly in upon
the shore.   A loud huzza from his men announced the recapture

of the maiden and Mistress Bridget. The Captain himself, by the aid of a boat-hook, made a spring from his barge with an agility that would not have passed unapplauded even at an earlier period of his life, and was the first to board the skipper's abandoned yawl.

"God bless thee, gentle damsel !" he exclaimed as he eagerly seized Blanche by both hands and almost lifted her into his arms, whilst the maiden, with scarce less alacrity,—her eyes laughing through the big drops that rolled down her cheeks,—threw her head upon his breast, and sobbed with convulsive joy—" God bless thee, dear Mistress Blanche ! we will make your father a happy man again. And you, old sweetheart, Bridget, they would have stolen *you* away ! By my troth, that Trojan war and rape of Helen the poets tell of, was but a scurvy adventure compared with this !—Lieutenant," he added, almost in the same breath, leave six files with our oarsmen to guard the boats ; and see that they draw off from the shore into a fathom water, there to await our signal when we return. The rest of the men will push forward on the track of the runaways. Follow, comrades ; we have no time to lose."

As the Captain spoke, he was already pushing his way into the wood, on the footsteps of the retreating pirates, at the head of some dozen files of musketeers. In another moment, the two females were left alone with the boats and their appointed guard.

"Spread yourselves across the neck," said Arnold de la Grange, as with a small division of the horsemen he had now reached a position not more than half a mile from the Point. "Pamesack, creep down on the shore, and report whatever comes in sight. The first man who finds the enemy will discharge his firelock. Scatter, gentlemen, scatter."

This little party of scouts were at the next moment extending their line across the extremity of Medley's Neck, and cautiously

18

drawing towards the Point. Some distance in the rear was to be
seen Talbot and the rest of the horsemen moving at a walk, in a
compact body, upon the trail of the ranger's advance, and silently
awaiting the signal by which they were to be guided to the
quarter where their attack was to be made. After a short period
of suspense, the report of a carbine, from the direction taken by
Pamesack, arrested the general attention, and, on the instant,
Albert, with three or four companions, set off at high speed
towards the spot. On reaching the margin of the little bay
which formed one confine of the neck of land, he discovered,
advancing at a quick pace, though yet some distance off, the
handful of men whom the wild adventure of the skipper had
brought into these desperate circumstances. They were in close
array, armed with pikes, and led forward by their reckless captain. The confidence with which they hurried upon their march
seemed to indicate an unconsciousness of any foe except the party
in their rear. This conviction was now instantly changed, as
they became aware of the presence of Verheyden and his friends.
Staggered by this unexpected disclosure, they were observed to
halt for a moment, as if to receive some counsel from their chief,
and then to advance with a steadiness that indicated prompt and
desperate resolve. Their ranks were formed with more precision ;
their pace gradually quickened, and they came nearer to their
enemy ; and having approached so near as to enable either side
to hear the command of the other, Albert could distinctly recog-
nize the voice of Cocklescraft exhorting them to the onset. In
another moment, they set up the war-cry which they had learned
from the Spaniards of the Gulf, and which had grown to be their
own, from the recollections of the bloody frays with which it was
associated—" A la savanna, perros !—to the field, dogs !"—and
thus shouting, anticipated the attack of their enemies by themselves striking the first blow.

Talbot had delayed to follow Verheyden, only until he could assure himself that the signal shot truly announced the presence of Cocklescraft's party. This was rendered certain by a messenger who rode back to report the fact, and, without loss of time, the commander of the troop repaired to the scene of the assault. The pirates had already forced the little party of horsemen to give ground, when Talbot reached the spot.

"Upon them, gentlemen," he cried aloud, without halting to form his men ; and, in an instant, was seen opening his way through the pikes of the buccaneers with his sword. Albert Verheyden, leading on the little band of untrained cavalry, followed with impetuous haste in the track of his commander. The compact array of the pirates being broken, a confused pell-mell fight ensued, with sword, pike and pistol, which was marked by various success. Two or three of the horsemen were thrown to the ground, and as many of the seamen slain. Albert's horse was killed by a pistol shot, and the rider for a moment was brought into imminent peril. Cocklescraft, animated as much by revenge, as by a determination to sell his life at a dear price, no sooner perceived the prostrate Secretary than he sprang upon him, and would have done the work of death, if Arnold de la Grange, who had followed Albert's footsteps through the fray, had not thrown himself from his horse and rushed to his comrade's rescue. He arrived in time to avert the stroke of the skipper's sword, by interposing his carbine, and, at the same moment, seized Cocklescraft by the shoulder and dragged him backward to the earth. The active seaman was, in an instant, again upon his feet, but before he could renew the fight with effect, he found himself overwhelmed by the musketeers, whose unobserved approach now put an end to the struggle.

"Hands off !" exclaimed Cocklescraft, shaking from him some two or three assailants, who had now crowded upon him, as the

blood of a recent wound over the eye trickled down his cheek ;
"hemmed in and overnumbered, I surrender :—you may do with
me as you will—I ask no favors at your hands." And saying
this, he flung his sword, with a moody and sullen anger, upon the
ground. "A fairer field on land or water, and by St. Iago ! we
would have disputed it with you till set of sun. We came not
prepared for this fight—we have neither arms nor ammunition to
cope with an equal force much less with the swarm that you have
brought on horse and foot against this little boat's crew. Take
your victory and make the best of it !"

"Silence !" said Dauntrees with the habitual calmness of an
old soldier : "Call your men to the foot of yonder tree, or I may
prick them thither with a halbert."

Under a chestnut hard by, the remnant of the buccaneers,
amounting to not more than seven men beside their leader, were
assembled. Some of them bore the marks of the severity of the
conflict in wounds upon their persons. Three of the skipper's
men were found dead upon the field. Their opponents had
escaped with better fortune. Two only were found severely,
though, it was believed, not mortally wounded ;—a few others
slightly. A guard was detailed to conduct the prisoners to
the boat ; the dead were hastily buried in the wood, and the
wounded borne on the shoulders of their comrades to the point
of embarcation.

It was already afternoon when victors and vanquished were
bestowed in due order in the boats. The horsemen had by this
time set forward on their homeward journey, eager to report the
good tidings of the day. The captured yawl, manned with a
proper complement of rowers, was consigned to the maiden and
her faithful Bridget, attended by the Secretary and Captain
Dauntrees—the former of whom, we may imagine, had many
things to say to the maiden, which, however agreeable to the

narrator, would make but dull entertainment on our pages.

All matters being now disposed for sailing, the squadron of boats, led by the yawl, put off in order from the shore, and, with moderate speed, bent their course towards the anxious little city.

Before sundown the maiden was placed in her father's longing arms on the little wharf of the Rose Croft, and, in due time, the prisoners were marched through a crowd of gaping townspeople into the fort of St. Mary's.

CHAPTER XXXIII.

No more the slave of human pride,
  Vain hope and sordid care,
I meekly vowed to spend my life
  In penitence and prayer.
                THE HERMIT OF WARKWORTH.

Oh were I free, as I have been,
  And my ship swimming once more on the sea,
I'd turn my face to fair England,
  And sail no more to a strange country.
                OLD BALLAD.

DURING the day occupied by the events narrated in the last
chapter, The Cripple of St. Jerome's remained in the dwelling
of Father Pierre. His misanthropy had relaxed into a kinder
tone, and contrition had spread a sadness over his mind. In
this temper he had made his shrift, and abjured the lawless life
and evil fellowship into which his passions had plunged him, and
now offered up a sincere and needful vow of penitence, to which
he was resolved to devote the scant remainder of his days. The
good priest did not fail to encourage the convertite in his wholesome purpose, nor to aid him with such ghostly counsel as was
likely to strengthen his resolution. At the period of life to
which The Cripple had attained, it is no difficult task to impress
upon the mind the value of such a resolution. When age and
satiety have destroyed the sense of worldly pleasure, the soul
finds a nourishment in the consolations of religion, to which it

flies with but slight persuasion ; and however volatile and self-dependent youth may deride it, the aged are faithful witnesses to the truth, that in the Christian faith there is a spell to restore the green to the withered vegetation of the heart, even as the latter rain renovates the pastures of autumn.

The Proprietary had directed the brigantine to be brought from Mattapany to St. Mary's, and she had, in consequence, been anchored in the harbor, a short distance from the quay, before Dauntrees had returned from his late expedition : the men left by Cocklescraft to navigate her were held on board as prisoners, under a small guard from the Mattapany Fort. The provincial court, the chief judicial authority of the government, had assembled on the same day, with the intention to continue its sessions until the cases of the conspirators were disposed of. The sitting of this court had attracted, from all quarters of the province, an unusually large crowd of attendants ; and the town was accordingly filled with farmers, planters and craftsmen from the interior, who, in character of suitors, witnesses, men of business, or mere seekers of news, occupied every place of public accommodation.

Such was the state of things at the close of the day to which we have referred. The faction adverse to the Proprietary, notwithstanding the vigilance with which they were watched, still found means for private conference. A few of the principal men who had not yet fallen under the suspicion of the public authorities, assembled in familiar guise under the roof of Chiseldine, and there consulted upon their affairs. The hope of rescuing Fendall and his companions by force, although somewhat depressed by recent events, was not abandoned. There were some sufficiently bold still to encourage this enterprise, and they spoke confidently of the assistance of friends, now in the port, who were anxious to bring about an immediate conflict with the Proprietary. It was deemed essential to the success of this attempt that the Olive Branch should be got into the possession of the conspirators : without the aid of the brigantine, neither the escape of the prisoners, nor the assistance of their confederates on the opposite shore of the Potomac could be relied on, even if all the other chances turned up favorably to the design.

These topics were duly debated in conclave, and the result was a determination to leave the enterprise in the hands of those who had projected it, either to be pursued or abandoned as the means at their command might counsel. With this conclusion the restless spirits, who had met at Chiseldine's, retired to organize their plans amongst their kindred malcontents throughout the town.

On the following morning when the hour for commencing business drew nigh, an unwonted throng of customers frequented the tap-room of the Crow and Archer. There was but little of that cheerfulness which usually characterizes such a resort : the occupants of the place seemed to be chiefly engaged with matters that rendered them thoughtful, and their conferences were held in under tones ; many loitered through the room in silence ; and it was manifest that the aspect of public affairs had impressed all with a sense of the weightiness of the issues which were pending. The concourse was no less conspicuous upon the quay. Here little knots of burghers and inland inhabitants, sorted according to the complexion of their political sentiments, whether of hostility or attachment to the Proprietary, were scattered about in quiet communings, and exchanging distrustful and hostile glances as they came within the sphere of each other's observation. The yawl of the skipper lay secured to the wharf, and the Escalfador, scarce a cable's length out in the stream, was near enough to present to the view of the townspeople the sentinels that paced her deck, and kept guard over the remnant of the pirate band, who were yet detained on board until their presence might be required by the authorities.

The arrival of Lord Baltimore at the Town House, attended by Albert Verheyden and the greater number of the members of the council, as it indicated his Lordship's intention to examine the prisoners in person, served to increase the public interest in the events of the day, and to draw a considerable portion of the crowd into the immediate neighborhood of the Hall of Justice. The Proprietary, with his friends, took possession of a chamber opposite to that occupied by the court, where they were soon joined by the sturdy old Collector, who, with an erect and vigorous carriage, and a face flushed with mingled resentment and pride of manhood aroused by the recent events, rode up to the door and alighted amidst the salutations of his townsmen and the clamorous expressions of their joy at the good fortune which had restored him his daughter. A brief interval brought Father Pierre, conducting Rob of the Bowl, to the same spot, and by order of the Proprietary they were both admitted into the chamber.

The prisoners had not yet arrived. In the mean time the council were occupied with such inquiries as the presence of Albert Verheyden suggested. The appearance and demeanor of The Cripple of St. Jerome's, engrossed the chief interest of the assembly. His age, his deformity, his singularly harsh and shrewd features, the extraordinary mystery of his life, his connection with the ruffians of the Chapel, his apparent contrition, amounting to melancholy,—above all, his presence in this conclave, amongst persons with whom he had never before exchanged a word, were circumstances of a nature to throw around him the eager regard of the bystanders. There was a peculiarly subdued and sorrowful expression in his countenance, as he gazed with silent intensity upon the features of Albert Verheyden and

18*

listened to his story of the disasters of that night of horrors in which Rob had first become acquainted with him. The old man's lip quivered and his eye glistened with a tear, as he dwelt upon the tones of the Secretary's voice, and watched the changes of his countenance.   At length, whilst the Secretary still continued his eventful narrative, unable longer to control his feelings or restrain his eagerness to catch every word that fell from Albert's lips, he heaved an involuntary but deep sigh, and muttered, loud enough to be heard by every one in the apartment—"Oh, God, I have been reserved for this deed !—in mercy have I been spared to save his life."   After a pause, he added in a voice of loud and fervent entreaty—"I pray you, gentlemen, raise me to the table that I may look him nearer in the face :—my eyes are old and dim" he continued, wiping away the tear with his hand,— "this seared and maimed trunk holds me too near the earth ;— it hath placed me below my fellow-man and taught my spirit to grovel—to grovel," he repeated with a bitter emphasis—"in the very mire of the basest fellowship.—Lift me on the table, I beseech you.—I have saved his life !—the saints be thanked, I have saved his life !" he uttered with a wild gesticulation. "Albert, I had made up my mind to save it with loss of my own !—I had, boy !"

The strange frenzy that for the time seemed to possess the deformed old man, the wild glance of his eye and the nervous tone, almost of raving laughter, with which he ejaculated these last words, gave rise to an instant doubt of the sanity of his mind ; but in a moment he subsided into a calmer state, and resumed his original self-command.

Upon a sign from the Proprietary his request was complied with, and he was lifted upon the table that occupied the middle of the room.

"Go on, boy," he continued, as soon as he was adjusted in

this position ; then suddenly checking himself for the familiarity of the address, "I crave pardon—I forget—Master Verhey-den," he added, choking with the utterance of the name, as now within a few feet of the Secretary he still more narrowly gazed upon his face—"I pray thee, go on !"

When the Secretary had concluded his narrative, a deep silence prevailed throughout the room, and all eyes were bent upon The Cripple, in expectation that he had something to dis-close which all were anxious to hear. He, however, remained mute, still fixing his gaze upon Albert ; and when the Secretary casually turned his back upon him, he reached forth his hand and caught the skirt of the young man's cloak, with an evidently unconscious motion, as if he sought by this constraint to prevent the Secretary from leaving him.

The Proprietary at length, as much struck with the deport-ment of The Cripple as the rest who witnessed it, and hoping to draw from him some history of himself, addressed him in a tone in which the severity of rebuke seemed to have been softened by the anxious interest he took in the endeavor to learn more of the singular person to whom he spoke. It was therefore with a grave, though scarcely stern manner that Lord Baltimore ac-costed him :

"Master Robert Swale," he said, "the Secretary's narrative which we have just heard has a dreadful import ; nor is it colored by a distempered fancy. We are all witnesses to facts connected with this fearful tale, that leave no room to doubt the scrupulous truth of all that has been told——"

"True—in every syllable, true !" interrupted Rob, with quick assent. "As God shall judge us, it is all true."

"It is a tale," continued the Proprietary, "fraught with crimes of ruthless men, who, we find, have lived in near com-panionship with you. Long has the province been frightened

with stories of wicked rites celebrated in the Black Chapel,—as
our people have been taught to call that accursed house. The
common terror could solve the mystery only by referring it to the
acts of the Fiend, and it has ascribed to *you* some fearful inter·
course with evil spirits."

"It hath—it hath, and with reason ! mea culpa, mea culpa,
mea maxima culpa !" muttered Rob, as he vehemently struck his
bosom with his open palm.

" More sober eyes have seen in your sequestered life and rare
communion with your fellow-men, but the evidences of a mind
soured by adversity—a mind, it would seem, not so humbly cast
as your condition might infer, but stricken, as the common belief
has signified, by some heavy blow of fortune."

A stifled groan spoke the listener's apprehension of the Pro·
prietary's words.

" All have been deceived : you have not lived that secluded
life which in charity many have imputed to you. No sorcery nor
witchcraft hath wrought these terrors, but the trickery of lawless
ruffians ; and what was deemed your solitude, it is now confessed,
was active and commanding fellowship in this den of robbers.
Thou art too far journeyed in the vale of years to be reproved,
even if time, which seldom fails to do his office, had not already
been the avenger of the past. Your interposition in behalf of
the Secretary's life, your removal of the brigantine and prompt
repairing hither, as well as rumors, which I trust are true, of
clear shrift and penitential vow, announce an honest though a
late purpose of amendment. We think you owe it now to the
consummation of this good purpose, that you divulge all it concerns us to know of that wicked haunt, the Wizard's Chapel, the
scene of so much grief and crime, and of its inmates. . Speak
freely, old man."

" My Lord," answered Rob, with a calm though somewhat

tremulous voice, "the story of my life I have confided to this holy man. Until my sand is run—would that its stream were spent !—that story lies in his bosom under the seal of the confessional. I dare not again rehearse it :—when I am gone he will tell it. It will be heard with curses by many—I deserve them ; —but if a life clouded by disgrace and stung with misery may atone for a deed of passion, I pray, with an humble spirit, that my story may raise one voice of pity.—But it doth not concern us to speak of this," he said, as in deep emotion he paused for some moments with his hand closely pressed across his eyes— "these are unaccustomed tears, my Lord,—I have not wept before to-day this many a long year.

"What concerns my coming to the province, the life I have led here, and the history of the Black House," he resumed after an interval in which he had regained his composure—"of these, I have no scruple to speak. Sixteen years ago, my Lord, I sailed from a port on the other side of the Atlantic, with some little store of wealth, consisting chiefly of jewels. My destination was the islands : my name was hidden from the world, and I had hoped to hide myself. Disasters at sea drove us upon this coast, where, in a winter's storm, such as I have never known but that, our ship was wrecked. I know not who survived—I only know that it pleased Heaven, for my sins, to prolong a life that I could have better parted with than any who found their grave beneath the waters. I chanced to save the larger portion of my valuables, and, on a raft of floating spars, was drifted into the Chesapeake, where a fisherman took me up almost lifeless, famished and starved with cold. He put me down at St. Jerome's—I had no wish to face my fellow-men,—and, for such hire as I gave him, provided me with comforts, the scant comforts my condition needed in that forsaken house, which then was terrible, as it hath been since—the house where Paul Kelpy murdered his own family. There, my Lord, I lived a solitary lodger, with no attendant near me except an aged woman, who afterwards abandoned me and took up her habitation at Warrington on the Cliffs :—she hath of late again returned. That winter passed away in suffering—ay, to the full measure of my deserts—and when spring came, my frosted limbs had rotted off, and I lay on my pallet that wretched, deformed, and unsightly thing thou seest me now. There, for many weary years, I dwelt, a man of sin and misery. Use made my state familiar, and I began to think that my penance would, at last, restore my peace of mind. In this lone spot, from which all the world turned away with shuddering, I did not dream that worldly passions could again be awakened. But it so fell out that, four years ago, a band of buccaneers in a trim brigantine, led by this ravening wolf Cocklescraft, tempted their fortune in these waters. They came in the disguise of traders, pitched upon the Chapel as their lurking place, won me to their purpose of unlawful commerce, and drove their craft with such success as you, my Lord, have seen. I consorted with them, first because they were outlawed men, and in that thought I took pleasure ;—there was sympathy, the food for which my heart was hungered. They built me a lodge, and came and went as my familiar guests—and I made money by them. Can you wonder, my Lord, that I became their comrade ? they made me their chief—I had their secret,—they gave me friendship,—and they brought me that devil's lure, gold—gold more than I had ever known before. Can you wonder, my Lord, that I became their companion ? The treasures of the Chapel needed guarding from curious eyes. I made the spot to be doubly desecrated—we had visors, masks, and strange disguises. I had the skill to compound chemical fires : we had sentinels on the watch, and plied our game of witchcraft seasonably, till the whole country was filled with alarm——"

At this moment, some tumult from without attracted the attention of the inmates of the chamber, and interrupted the further narrative of The Cripple.

At a distance, in the direction of the fort, was seen a guard of some ten or twelve musketeers advancing along the principal street of the city, led by Captain Dauntrees in person, and forming an escort to Cocklescraft and the prisoners who had been captured with him. Their progress was impeded by the crowd that thronged upon their path, amongst whom were some who scarcely attempted to conceal their sympathy with the prisoners, and who, by signs, if not by words, cheered them with the hope of deliverance from their present durance. Nods of recognition were exchanged with Cocklescraft, and significant gestures made which he was at no loss to comprehend. The press increased as they drew near the door of the Town House, and in the disorder incident to the introduction of the prisoners into the building, more than one of the movers in the late sedition found an occasion to assure the master of the Escalfador, by a brief hint, of their readiness to co-operate in seizing the brigantine.

Cocklescraft and his crew were conducted into the presence of the Proprietary by Dauntrees, who, leaving the guard in the hall or passage-way that separated the court room from that occupied by the council, ranged the prisoners within the apartment on either side of the door, which, being left open, exposed to view the musketeers, who were thus in a position to do their duty in case any difficulty should render their interference necessary; whilst the crowd, at the same time, intruded itself into the hall with such importunity as to leave but little space for the occupation of the guard.

Cocklescraft had lost none of the moodiness that characterized his demeanor after his surrender on the day previous. He was somewhat paler, owing to the wound upon his brow, which was now bound up with a bandage of black silk that, in some degree, enhanced the sickly aspect of his complexion. Still the fire of his spirit sparkled in his unquenched eye, and a sullen scowl, as he looked Albert Verheyden in the face, rested on his features. A slight but guarded expression of surprise flashed across his countenance when his glance encountered Rob of the Bowl. He was unaware of the presence of The Cripple in the port; nor had he, up to this moment, ever entertained a suspicion that Rob had deserted him. The escape of the Secretary he imputed alone to the carelessness of the seamen; the failure of the brigantine to meet him at the rendezvous, he set down to accident and unskilfulness, and her presence now in the harbor to a cause altogether disconnected with any conjecture of treachery in The Cripple. Even the old man's presence before the Council, he attributed to force, and believed him to be, like himself, a prisoner. In this conviction he now found himself before the chief authorities of the province. He was, of course, weaponless; and as all eyes were turned upon him, he stood with folded arms, his cloth cap dangling from his hand, gazing in silent defiance upon the assembly. He meditated no purpose of defence to the charges which he expected to hear : the facts of his late outrage admitted none, and the presence of the Secretary assured him that the crime he had attempted to perpetrate on All Soul's Eve had been divulged in all its enormity, and with such full identification of the actors in it as to render useless all attempt even at palliation.

The unabashed gesture of the buccaneer, his confident port and look, even of scorn, provoked an instant emotion of resentment in the Proprietary, as well as of the greater number of those who surrounded him.

" Viper !" he said, " dost thou approach us with this shameless front to brave our authority in the province ! Does no sense

of crime abash thy brow, that here, in the presence of those whom
thou hast most foully wronged, thou showest thy dastardly face
without a blush !   Richard Cocklescraft, you came hither, as all
men thought, a peaceful trader, and found the friendship of the
port accorded to you, without stint or. question.   Again and
again you left us, and returned ; and the townspeople ever gave
you hearty welcome to their homes.   How brief a span is it,
since we saw you breaking bread and sharing the wine-cup with
this aged father, whose daughter, execrable villain, thou soughtest
to carry off by force, in the dead hour of the night ?   Hast thou
not plotted against the life of the Secretary ?   Didst thou not
murder the fisherman, bloody and remorseless man ?   Didst thou
not, like a coward, strike at the gray hairs of this venerable
man, when thou stol'st upon him in his sleep ?"

"No !" replied the pirate leader, in a voice loud and angry,
undaunted by the presence of the chief functionaries of the province, and untamed by his captivity.   "He lies who says I struck
at the Collector ! though, by St. Iago, Anthony Warden may
claim no favor at my hands,—"

"Favor at thy hands !" exclaimed the Collector, who could
not sit quiet whilst the skipper spoke—" A boy, who undertakes
to play at man's game, with men !—A boy, to prate me thus !"

"I pray you, Master Warden," interposed the Proprietary,
mildly, "do not interfere."

"I struck not at the Collector," repeated Cocklescraft ; "I
look to match my sword with men not spent with age.   When
others would have beaten this old man to the ground, I saved
him.   I plotted not against the Secretary's life," he continued,
answering the accusations which the Proprietary had at random
heaped upon him.   "I slew the fisherman, as a hound that had
been set to track my path.   I carried away this old man's daughter because I loved her.   Are you answered, Lord Baltimore ?"

"Impudent outlaw!" returned the Proprietary, with an excitement of speech altogether unaccustomed, "dost thou beard us with the confession of thy crimes? Have the laws of the province no terrors for thee?"

"I never acknowledged your Lordship's laws," retorted the seaman, scornfully. "I have lived above them—coming when I would, and going when it pleased me. By St. Anthony, your Lordship hath but a sorry set of lieges! You might do well to teach the better half of the freemen to remember that Charles Calvert claims to be lord and master of this province—they seem to have forgotten it. You think I am saucy, my Lord; I have but one master here—Old Rob of the Trencher, my fellow prisoner:—we will die in company."

"Peace, knave!" ejaculated Rob, in his former peevish voice of command. "I know thee and thy villainies of old. Never again call me comrade of thine. Thou shalt not depart in ignorance of the favor you owe me, Dickon Cocklescraft. Know that I saved the Secretary's life—that I gave back the daughter to her father's bosom——"

"Thou?" exclaimed Cocklescraft, with a deeper storm thickening on his brow. "Thou! didst thou betray me?"

"I foiled thee," replied Rob, as a vengeful smile played on his features, "in thy horrid plot;—I saved the boy's life—ha, ha! I saved his life!—and left thee on the island without a refuge—thy villainy deserved it."

"Betrayed,—betrayed by thee!" vociferated the pirate, as with the swift spring of the tiger he threw himself upon The Cripple, and seized the long knife from the old man's girdle, and plunged it deep into his bosom, shouting as he struck the blow, "By St. Iago, I have paid thee for it!"

The suddenness of the deed took all by surprise, and scarce a step was made nor a hand raised to arrest the murderer, who, with a quickness that defied orderly resistance, turned towards the door, with the bloody weapon in his hand, and pronouncing aloud the watchword that seemed to electrify his men—"A la savanna!" rushed, at the head of his crew, into the hall. The guards at the door were no less unprepared for resistance than the persons within, whilst the crowd in the hall gave ground, with that sudden panic which belongs to all unorganized masses of men, and fled tumultuously before the buccaneer and his band —thus increasing the confusion and rendering it impossible for the weak guard of the hall either to follow the fugitives with the necessary expedition to overtake them, or to fire upon them, without risk of greater injury to friend than foe.

As soon as Cocklescraft was seen on the open ground in front of the Town House, driving with headlong haste towards the quay, the partisans of Coode and Fendall, constituting a considerable number of those who frequented the spot, increased the disorder by a clamor which, under the show of pursuit, in truth retarded the movement of those who endeavored to intercept the flying band. The momentary consternation in the chamber being over, the Proprietary and those around him, sprang from their seats and ran to the great door, whence they could witness the struggle of pursuit. Dauntrees, at the first moment, had repaired to his men, and was immediately busy in attempting to open a way through the crowd, in which he was greatly impeded by the tumultuous interference of the malcontents. Albert Verheyden, in the act of moving to leave the apartment, was recalled by the voice of the wounded man, and instantly returned to his side, where, with Father Pierre, he awaited in anxious suspense, the recapture of the prisoners.

Meantime Cocklescraft furiously urged his onward course. He had snatched a sword in the crowd, with which he became a formidable enemy to all who crossed his path, and soon discovered, from their shouts, that his nearest pursuers were in fact aiding his escape. The only exception to this was Talbot and our old friend Arnold, who, foremost in the melee, had at one moment, as they sped down the bank, come in actual contact with the fugitives, and Talbot had exchanged more than one pass with Cocklescraft. The crowd thickened on the quay; shouts rent the air, and cries of encouragement and strife resounded from all sides.

The passage over the quay was opened—the boat gained, the rope severed, the oars in place,—and in another instant the buccaneers were in full flight upon their accustomed element. The musketeers hasten to the wharf,—their small band jostled, pressed, and swayed by the incumbering crowd—an ineffectual volley is fired—Cocklescraft waves his hand in triumph—the Escalfador is won from the feeble resistance of her light guard, and the pirates are again upon their own deck. The cable is slipped, sail after sail drops from the yard or runs up along the mast—the brigantine swings round to a fair and stiff breeze under a cloudless heaven, and cleaves her way mid-stream towards the mouth of the river. A few harmless shot were fired from the fort, as she bounded past; and almost before the bewildered burghers were aware, she had swept beyond the limit of the harbor—her daring master standing at the helm and looking back at the town, scarce able to realize the truth of his own escape, as he waved his bonnet in derision of the gaping crowd. Many eyes still lingered upon this fleeting vision, until the white sails of the Escalfador disappeared behind the projecting headland which opened to her prow the broad current of the Potomac.

Not all could note this stirring strife of flight. A melancholy attraction drew back the Proprietary and his council to the chamber. When Albert was recalled to the side of the wounded man, it was but to hear his own name pronounced in a whispered accent, and then to see the sufferer faint away. For some minutes, Father Pierre and the Secretary, the only persons in the room, thought life was fled ; but whilst they still watched, the light of the eye flickered upon them, and, by degrees, a sickly animation returned to the body. When Lord Baltimore and the others had gathered around, Rob was able to speak. His voice was faint, and his gaze was upon the secretary.

"My web is wove," he said, in that figurative language which had grown to be his habitual form of expression. "Albert Verheyden, thou look'st upon—upon thy father— William Weatherby—a man of crime—and misery. Thy hand, boy—thy lips upon my brow—there—there," he whispered, as his son, pale as a spectre and trembling with emotion, bent down over his prostrate trunk and kissed his forehead. "Pity me, my son, and forgive me for thy mother's sake. Poor Louise—Louise—" and with this name again and again breathed from his lips, when no other sound could be heard, his spirit was gradually wafted from its mutilated and weary tenement of clay.

"I forgive thee—I forgive and pity !" breathed Albert, with sobs that shook his whole frame, as he threw himself upon the lifeless body of his father.

"My dear Albert, leave this place," said Father Pierre ; "let us go to the Chapel, and there thou may'st temper thy grief with prayer. His lordship will take order for the disposal of the body. I have a paper which I was charged, when this event should take place—and in his reckoning it was not far off—to deliver into thy hands. Come, and when we have done our duty at the altar, I will give it thee."

With silent step and slow, Albert leaning on the arm of the priest, they left the Town House, and walked towards the little Chapel of St. Mary's.

CHAPTER XXXIV.

HERE ends my tale. We have no longer an interest to follow the fortunes of the personages who have been brought to view in this motleyed narrative of trivial and tragic events. A brief memorandum will tell all that remains to gratify the inquiries of my readers.

After the crossings of fortune which we have read in the history of Albert and Blanche, we may presume the time, at last, came for the current of true love to run smooth as a glassy lake. The next festival at the Rose Croft found Father Pierre in a prominent official position, and the maiden a blooming bride upon the arm of the happy Secretary.

The worldly wise will be pleased, perhaps, to learn that, after some most liberal appropriations to charitable uses, by way of purification of the more than doubtful uncleanness of the Cripple's wealth, Albert fell heir to no small hoard ; and this gear, as it was generously distributed in acts of hospitality and bounty to the poor, we would fain hope the straitest casuist will allow, was not unjustly taken by the Secretary,—his title to it resting upon the will of William Weatherby, which was produced in due time by Father Pierre.

As to the conspirators, they were losers in every way. First, the buccaneer and his brigantine came not to their rescue ; and secondly, the trials proceeded without interruption.

Josias Fendall was fined in a very heavy sum, and imprisoned at the pleasure of the Proprietary. His brother and John Coode, from some apprehension of rousing too keenly the popular grudge, were more mildly dealt with. George Godfrey was sentenced to death, but finding favor upon the petition of his wife, had his punishment commuted into a rigorous confinement in the jail of St. Mary's.

What became of the other confederates of Coode and Fendall, the records do not inform us; but we may infer that the dominant party in the province felt their authority too slender to prosecute them with much severity—

> "They fear to punish, therefore do they pardon."

Touching our unfortunate friend of "the gentle craft," the warlike corporal, history happens to have embalmed his memory with the unction of a favorite, and to have consigned him to the notice of posterity with a distinctness of fame that would, if he could have contemplated it. have almost made him, in spite of his miseries, in love with rebellion. I find in the proceedings of the council, in the month of March following these events, "the humble petition" of Edward Abbott, a "poor, distressed, and sorrowful penitent," who most dolorously complains of his insufferable confinement, meekly confessing his sins, and affirming, by way of extenuation, that, in the commission of them, "he was so much in drink that he did not remember any thing either what was done or spoken at the time." And to this petition is appended the following entry,—

"The petitioner making his submission in open court, upon his knees begging pardon for his offence, the Justices are ordered to wave sentence passing against him, his lordship having granted his pardon."

And so, gentle reader, good night! We part, I would even indulge the hope, but for a short period; after which we may find motive to look again into the little city and renew our acquaintance.

THE END.

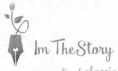